St Joseph's/DUNDALK.   JUN. 12. 2003.

THE CLONARD REDEMPTORISTS

To Tom!

I hope this book evokes some happy memories of times past! Enjoy!

God Bless!

+ Oliver of Dundalk

*To the two communities of Clonard monastery and church,
the Redemptorist priests and brothers and 'the people of
Clonard' who have served and worshipped there since 1896;*

*agus i ndíl chuimhne ar mo thuismitheoirí Tomás agus Annabella,
a's go h-áirithe ar mhuintir mo mháthar,
muintir Uí Bhrádaí, Sráid Getty, paróiste Pheadair Naomtha.
Bhí mór-chion aca ar 'Chluan Árd'
agus thug siad an cion sin damhsa, a's mé i mo leanbh.*

James Grant

One Hundred Years with the Clonard Redemptorists

the columba press

First published in 2003 by
the columba press
55A Spruce Avenue, Stillorgan Industrial Park, Blackrock, Co Dublin

Cover by Bill Bolger
Cover photograph by Paul Kavanagh
Origination by The Columba Press
Printed in Ireland by Colour Books Ltd, Dublin.

ISBN 1 85607 398 X

ACKNOWLEDGEMENTS

I wish to thank a number of people without whom this history would not have been written. It was Fr Kevin Browne who first suggested the idea while he was rector of Clonard. He has had to be patient for much longer than either of us thought at the time. Fr Patrick O'Donnell, for many years archivist of Clonard Monastery and extensive writer on its history, welcomed me and facilitated my work in every way. Fr Brendan McConvery, Irish provincial archivist, not only supplied me with numerous documents but has been a supportive and constructive critic throughout. He has also given generously of his time in undertaking the final editing of the text. I have drawn on the works of several historians, particularly in chapter 1; they are acknowledged in footnotes and bibliography. I am especially grateful to Tom McGrogan, now of Dublin, for allowing me to use his excellent research on Sevastopol Street, 1901-1911, which illustrates concretely several aspects of life in the Clonard area shortly after the Redemptorists' arrival. Like his brother, mentioned below, Tom was a Clonard altar boy in his youth.

A number of people helped with useful information at various times. Their assistance is acknowledged in the references.

Several relatives and friends gave much needed encouragement and read early drafts: Mary Patricia Grant, Barney McGrogan of Calgary, Canada, Christopher Napier, and Lorraine McGinniss of Perth, W. Australia.

Finally, this work has had two mentors, one Redemptorist, the other domestic, without whom it would never have seen the light of day. Fr Peter Burns has been a constant support from the very beginning; he has also read and commented on every draft. It seems very appropriate that he is, at the time of publication, rector of Clonard monastery. My wife Stella has word processed every syllable, provided space, endless cups of coffee and a determination to see the job through. She has also given substantial help in compiling the index.

To them all I am deeply indebted.

Contents

Notes for the Reader

On sources

This history is based largely on the Clonard Redemptorists' own Domestic Archives, with additional material from their provincial archives in Dublin, officially, Dublin Provincial Archives.

The principal source in the Clonard Domestic Archives is the monastery's Domestic Chronicle which has been maintained continuously, with only slight gaps, from the foundation in 1896. It must be said that this source is of variable value. Since it was kept over the century by ever-changing scribes (officially, the scribe was called the *chronista* or chronicler), it reflects their individual judgments as to what were the important matters in the life of the community, or the wider world, that should be recorded.

Occasional chroniclers limited their entries to quite trivial matters such as who went out for a walk and at what time or who came to visit and when they left. Fortunately, most were more informative and several gave detailed and interesting reports on monastic, diocesan and political matters and on the concerns of the church and the world at large.

The chronicle is at its most reliable when reporting facts which can often be corroborated from other sources. It is least reliable as a record of the views and opinions of the monastic community, particularly when reporting on controversial issues. In such situations, it can be difficult to decide whether the views expressed are the views of the chronicler himself or of like-minded confrères or of the generality of the community.

On rectors of Clonard Monastery

Some readers may find the frequent name changes of rectors of Clonard very confusing. Holders of this office were appointed or (later) elected, usually for a period of three years (*triennium*), which might be extended for a further three years. For convenience, a list of rectors who served during the century is included in Appendix 4, together with directors of the Men's Holy Family and bishops of the diocese of Down and Connor.

Introduction

The Redemptorist presence at Clonard, in the heart of the Falls Road, has been a spiritual beacon for four generations of Belfast Catholics. With the completion of their impressive monastery in 1900, followed by their splendid church less than a decade later, the Clonard Redemptorists have provided the city with a physical, architectural landmark of considerable beauty.

The name of Clonard monastery and church – Most Holy Redeemer – echoes the title of the Redemptorist Congregation, formally *Congregatio Sanctissimi Redemptoris*. But familiarly and locally, it has always been known simply as 'Clonard' or 'the monastery'.

Invitation from Bishop Henry

The Redemptorists were invited to Belfast in 1896 by Dr Henry Henry, the bishop of Down and Connor diocese. He wanted them to assist the local parishes cope with the spiritual needs of the vast numbers of migrant workers and their families crowding into the Falls area. This they have done with distinct success over the past hundred years. Clonard church has always been a 'missionary' church. That is, it has never had care of a parish, but has been rather a centre of worship from which its members travelled throughout Ireland (and at times beyond) preaching missions, retreats and other spiritual exercises; in fact, doing the principal work for which their congregation was founded.

Devotional practices

The church, from the earliest days of the original 'tin' church of 1897, has always provided the basic spiritual requirements of Eucharist and Reconciliation – daily and Sunday Masses and frequent stations of confessions. But it has also provided and developed, with episcopal approval, a range of devotional exercises for all those faithful, near and far, who wished to come. Clonard was founded at a time when Catholic Ireland was in thrall to devotional practices borrowed from continental European, particularly Italian, religiosity. Given the Redemptorists' Italian origins – they were founded in 1732 by the Neapolitan priest Alphonsus de Liguori – they were ideally suited to provide appropriate devotions: to the Blessed Sacrament, to the Sacred Heart of Jesus, to Mary the Mother of God and to the saints. They also brought to the great occasions of the church pomp, celebration, colour and music.

Confraternities, Novena, 'Mission to Non-Catholics'
Urged by Bishop Henry from the beginning, they established and developed confraternities for men, women and boys, which were claimed in 1957, on the occasion of their diamond jubilee, to be the second largest in the world, second only to the Redemptorists' parallel confraternities in Limerick. During the Second World War a visiting American Redemptorist established another Clonard institution, the perpetual novena in honour of Our Lady of Perpetual Succour, which grew so rapidly that, within a very short time, 'novena Thursday' or 'Clonard Thursday' became part of the fabric of Belfast Catholicism. The shared danger of the same war years dulled the edge of religious sectarianism to such an extent that the Clonard Redemptorists ventured to offer a 'Mission to non-Catholics' which flourished for several years from the late 1940s. It can be argued that this mission, by eroding barriers and opening the monastery to a wider Christian constituency, laid the foundation of later contacts which flourished in the reconciliation and ecumenical work of the late 1970s and 1980s.

Sacred music
Sacred music has been treated from the beginning of Clonard with the seriousness which it deserves in Divine Worship. The Redemptorists were fortunate in securing in 1898 the services of a brilliant Belgian organist, choirmaster and composer, the young Arthur de Meulemeester, who presided over music in the church until his death in 1942. Difficulties of the war years threw the Redemptorists back on their own resources. By coincidence, their own talented musician of this period, Fr John Torney, was not only Belfast born, but from the Falls Road, within the ambit of Clonard. Under his direction, the boys' section of the church choir was developed to an extraordinary pitch of perfection and, for a decade and more, was regarded as one of the best, if not the best, choirs of its type in Ireland. With the return of normality in the post-war years, the Redemptorists were able to enlist the services of another outstanding Belgian musician in Léon Rittweger, a product of the same Lemmens Institute as de Meulemeester. Since Rittweger's resignation from Clonard in 1968, a series of gifted local musicians has maintained the highest musical standards in Clonard church.

1969 and Aftermath
Clonard's geographical position on the frontier between nationalist/republican Falls and unionist/loyalist Shankill ensured that it would become uniquely embroiled, following the explosion of sectarian hatred in 1969. In one direction, the 'troubles' devastated attendances at Clonard church, particularly at

its confraternities and novena. In another, the Redemptorists had to resist fierce pressure to take sides politically and insist that Clonard church and its ministry were open and available to people of all political persuasions.

Change

The period from the Second Vatican Council (1962-5) witnessed dramatic change in the Catholic Church, with a series of reforms of the church, the liturgy, sacred scripture, religious freedom, priestly training, adaptation and renewal of religious life, the laity, to name but a few. It is fair to say that the Redemptorist congregation as a whole responded generously, indeed enthusiastically, to the promptings of the council as they affected their religious lifestyle and the numerous apostolates in their churches. Clonard was no exception. Its domestic records reflect in great detail its community's responses to reform from the early 1960s through to the late 1980s.

Clonard and its neighbours

The Clonard Redemptorist community seems to have enjoyed excellent relations with its neighbours from the earliest days, particularly 'the people of Clonard' (though there were misunderstandings from time to time), certainly with adjacent communities of religious sisters and brothers and, generally, with the priests of the diocese of Down and Connor. Relations with the Protestant inhabitants of the Shankill were frankly hostile in the early decades, until the shared danger of the Second World War years enabled a more generous spirit to prevail. With the development in the past three decades of ecumenical contacts and genuine efforts at reconciliation among clergy and their parishes and congregations on both sides of the sectarian frontier, a more understanding, truly Christian spirit has emerged, not just in spite of, but because of, the troubles.

The 'People of Clonard'

A consistent theme which runs through a century of the monastery chronicles is the high regard in which the 'people of Clonard' were held by the Redemptorists in their midst, for their generosity, the solidity of their faith and their loyalty to monastery and church. The closing decades of the century brought much pain to both Clonard communities, with the physical scars of redevelopment, the psychological damage of conflict and the rapid rise in non-practice of the faith, due in part to a widespread alienation between republicans and Catholic Church leaders. The Redemptorists recognise that non-practice does not necessarily mean abandonment of faith and church. For their part, they have shown by their recent refurbishment of their monastery that they are staying in Clonard, ready for the joys and travails of another century – at least.

CHAPTER 1

Before Clonard

In order to provide the reader with a context in which to set the history of Clonard monastery and its community, this introductory chapter will briefly explore the origins of the Congregation of the Most Holy Redeemer, the formal title of the Redemptorists. It will then trace the circumstances by which an eighteenth-century Italian religious order found its way to Ireland more than a hundred years after its foundation. Ireland in the nineteenth century had a Catholic ethos which requires some clarification for the modern reader. Perhaps less explanation is needed – for a northern Irish readership – of the economic, social and religious chacteristics of the Belfast to which the Redemptorists came in 1896. But since they touched, intimately at times, on the Clonard religious community in the course of the century just ended, they require some comment.

I WHO ARE THE REDEMPTORISTS?

The Redemptorists are a congregation or society of missionary priests and brothers living in monastic community. They were founded in Scala in the Kingdom of Naples in 1732 by the priest Alphonsus Maria de Liguori (1696-1787). Their specific mission is the preaching of the word of God, especially to the most abandoned souls.

Alphonsus de Ligouri
Alphonsus Liguori lived a long and intensely busy life. No brief summary can do justice to the exertions of a man who was, in turn, successful lawyer, missionary priest, founder of a religious congregation, bishop for thirteen years and ceaseless writer of devotional and theological works.

Alphonsus was a Neapolitan. That southern part of Italy had been a melting pot of civilisations for thousands of years. The dominant cultural tone of Naples during Alphonsus' life was Spanish, for Spain had ruled for 200 years until 1707, and Spanish was the everyday language of the nobility. As the Irish Redemptorist Fr F. M. Jones says in his recent biography of his founding father, the Spanish brought an 'intense religious spirit … a new love of pomp and ceremonial', and a new and haughty sense of proper form and self-esteem. This explains the social and religious ethos by which the Liguori family was marked. On a personal level, it explains Alphonsus's deep interest in the lives and writings of the great sixteenth-century Spanish mystics, Saints Teresa of Avila and John of the Cross.[1]

Family life and education

Alphonsus was the eldest of eight children, four boys and four girls. His father, Don Guiseppe, was a member of the lesser nobility, a captain in the Spanish royal naval service. Proud, authoritarian and obsessively ambitious for his family's social advancement, he decided that his son should be a lawyer, for such a career would be a reliable entrée to public life. Alphonsus was tutored at home in a broad curriculum. It included art, architecture and music, cultural requirements for a young nobleman. He displayed consider-able skill in all three, but especially music, in which his tutor was a pupil of Alessandro Scarlatti. Alphonsus became a skilled harpsichordist and composer, mostly of hymns, which he used later in his missionary work. His *Tu scende alle stelle* remains a favourite Italian Christmas carol to this day. Indeed, musical ability was a great asset to any missionary since, as Jones puts it, singing was an indispensable element of a mission. Without it, 'no true Neapolitan of whatever class would consider he had been in touch with God.'[2]

Alphonsus was precociously intelligent. He entered university just after his twelfth birthday and graduated as a Doctor of Civil and Canon Laws at the age of sixteen years and four months, requiring a legal dispensation since the normal graduation age was twenty-one. Then he practised in the courts as a junior advocate until he was nineteen or twenty. Meantime, his religious development was presided over by his mother, Donna Anna Caterina who, in contrast to her husband, was gentle, refined and cultured. Her personal religious life was more that of a cloistered nun than of a woman of the world. Everyday she supervised her children's religious training with great care. Indeed, she suffered much from scrupulosity, a trait which her eldest son inherited. Alphonsus was later to say that whatever good was in him he owed to his mother and, as an old man in his eighties, he still had the notebook in which, as a child, he had written prayers taught him by his mother.[3]

Priest and missionary

Alphonsus's distinguished legal career came to an abrupt end in July 1723 when he lost a high-profile action between two of the great Italian families, the Orsini (for whom he was acting) and the Medici. Shocked and disgusted at what he believed was political interference in the outcome, he turned his back on the law and on the 'world'.[4] In any event, he had been for several months convinced that he should become a priest. He was finally ordained in November 1726. It took his father many years to be reconciled to his son's decision.

Preparation for the priesthood in Naples at that time was informal by modern standards. In fact, the main source of formation was through membership of a 'clerical corporation' of which there were three. The group Alphonsus joined was the 'Apostolic Missions' whose main task was the preaching of parish missions in the kingdom of Naples. According to Jones, Alphonsus,

> owed everything in the way of his priestly formation to the Apostolic Missions – his spirituality, theological initiation and practical induction into the theory and practice of preaching, especially popular mission preaching.

Jones further attributes to the Apostolic Missions,

> a major role in the evolution of popular missionary preaching, technique and organisation; they devised and institutionalised a missionary method which Alphonsus was to perfect and which, with local adaptations, was to spread throughout Europe and North America in the following century.[5]

There is a final element in Alphonsus Liguori's religious development which few moderns could match. The 'intense religious spirit' of the Spanish influence provided for those who, like Alphonsus, responded to it, abundant opportunities for serious practice of the corporal works of mercy. So, for instance, as a member of one of the numerous sodalities for young noblemen, Alphonsus would have taken his turn at the Incurabili, the Naples hospital for the poor, making beds, changing linen, washing the sick and feeding the disabled. Membership of another sodality obliged him to help bury the poor. As a young priest he undertook in his spare time the difficult task of providing religious instruction for the street urchins of Naples, 'the children of the sun'. He also shared in providing religious support for criminals and their families. This included, on several recorded occasions prior to 1729, attendance at executions, from the condemned cell to the gallows. He later wrote a pamphlet on the subject for the guidance of priests which displays, in Jones's words, 'a gentle spirit and great trust in the mercy of God ... It comes clearly from the heart of a priest who has experienced what he writes about; no one could simulate such authenticity.'[6]

Founder

A short holiday in the early summer of 1730, after months of intense work, brought Alphonsus into contact for the first time with the poor herdsmen and their families of the Amalfi coastal area. This was in the mountain region behind the old episcopal city of Scala. Alphonsus was shocked by their ignorance and neglect, yet impressed by their desire for spiritual ministration.

Exchange of courtesies with the local bishop introduced Alphonsus to a community of Visitation nuns among whom was an extraordinarily intelligent and gifted woman, a visionary and mystic, Julia Crostarosa. (In the exotic style of the period, she was known in religion as Sister Maria Celeste of the Holy Desert.) A tortuous two years of seemingly endless consultations with one spiritual guide after another led Alphonsus to accept Julia and her visions as authentic. In these visions, Christ instructed her that two new religious orders were to be established in Scala. They emerged in 1731 and 1732 respectively as the Order of the Most Holy Saviour, a contemplative order for women, and the Congregation of the Most Holy Saviour for men, to be led by Alphonsus Liguori. The principal function of the latter group was to be the preaching of the gospel to the most abandoned. Their spirituality, like the nuns', was to be based on the imitation of Christ and, in particular, their attitude to poverty was to be modelled on the practice of St Francis of Assisi. The Congregation of men was formally initiated on 9 November 1732.[7]

Within a matter of weeks this inaugural foundation at Scala nearly collapsed. All four of Alphonsus's first companions abandoned him. But he persevered and within months a few men of quality joined him. Thereafter, progress was steady but never easy. By the time papal recognition was sought in 1749, there were four houses of the new congregation in the kingdom of Naples and two in the Papal States to the north. Pope Benedict XIV solemnly approved the new institute with its Rules and Constitutions on 25 February 1749. In the process, the name had to be changed to the Congregation of the Most Holy Redeemer, in order to avoid confusion in Rome where the canons of the Lateran Basilica had, as their formal title, Canons Regular of the Most Holy Saviour.[8] In accordance with usual practice in the Catholic Church, the formal title of the institute was in Latin: *Congregatio Sanctissimi Redemptoris*, abbreviated to C.Ss.R. In the English-speaking world they have always been popularly known as Redemptorists or, more familiarly, as 'The Reds'.

Crisis and expulsion
Recognition of the new congregation in the kingdom of Naples was a matter of enormous difficulty. For a start, the papal approval was never accepted by a government paranoid about its own authority. All it would concede was recognition, by a royal decree in 1752, of the existence of the Redemptorists, but not of their Rule and Constitutions. Various abortive attempts were made over the next three decades, driven by Alphonsus' probably excessive anxiety for full approval, though, in fairness to him, it must be said that suppression was threatened from time to time.

Finally, in 1779 a favourable opportunity seemed to present itself during a thaw in relations between the Kingdom of Naples and the papacy. The existence of the Congregation was reaffirmed by a new royal decree, but the Neapolitan government insisted that recognition of the Rule and Constitutions must be a matter for detailed negotiation. The outcome was a disaster for the new congregation and for Alphonsus personally. By this time he was in his eighties, recently retired after thirteen strenuous years as Bishop of St Agatha of the Goths, and crippled by ill-health. To save time for his two negotiators, he provided them with blank sheets of paper bearing his signature, so confident was he that they would only accept a worthy outcome. He had also insisted that they take an oath of secrecy, to protect the negotiations from possibly dangerous speculation. The outcome, when it was revealed in March 1780, showed that the negotiators had agreed to changes to the Rule (as recognised by Benedict XIV in 1749) which Alphonsus would never have accepted. Yet the negotiators' acceptance bore Alphonsus' signature, for they had used the blank paper he had given them. So Alphonsus was widely regarded as responsible. Whatever about the changes to the Rule – and they were serious – the preamble to the agreement was deliberately offensive to the papacy. It claimed that the new congregation owed its existence and continuing presence in the Kingdom of Naples to the royal decrees of 1752 and 1779, thereby refusing to admit its existence as a religious congregation in the church, approved by papal authority.[9]

Papal reaction was swift. The four Redemptorist communities in the Kingdom of Naples, since they no longer lived under the 1749 rule, were effectively expelled from the Congregation. Since Alphonsus was included in the expulsion, he ceased to be Rector Major. In his place, a Fr de Paola was appointed president (later Rector Major) of the two communities in the Papal States, at Beneventum and Scifelli. While the papacy allowed concessions in response to pleas from numerous bishops, the Neapolitans remained excluded until 1793, by which time Alphonsus was dead.[10]

Expansion over the Alps

Tragic though it was for all the Redemptorists, but especially for Alphonsus, the split of 1780 brought one great benefit. It broke the Neapolitan stranglehold on the new institute and opened the way for expansion. Rome, with its endless comings and goings of clerics from all over the church, held out great possiblities. A new foundation, including a novitiate, was made in the city in 1783. One of its earliest recruits was Clement Hofbauer, whom Jones describes as 'that restless hermit from Moravia'. He was to spread the Congregation north of the Alps, successively to Poland, Switzerland, Austria, Germany and Romania over a period of more than thirty years. Yet, largely on account of the widespread hostility to religion which accompanied and followed the French Revolution, he made but one permanent Redemptorist foundation. That was in Vienna in the year of his death, 1820.[11]

Clement Hofbauer had been appointed by its Roman administration as 'Vicar General of the Transalpine Province' of the Redemptorist Congregation. This 'province' was never formally declared but developed a life of its own in the early nineteenth century. Following Clement's death his role as Transalpine Vicar General passed to the first Frenchman to join the

Redemptorists, Joseph Passerat. A deserter from the French revolutionary army, he had made his way to Warsaw where Clement Hofbauer had sustained a mission for twenty years at St Benno's church. There he became a novice and Hofbauer's principal lieutenant.

It fell to Joseph Passerat to take the institution westwards across the Rhine. In August 1820, he made his first foundation at Bischenberg in Alsace. Others followed in France and Belgium, the latter being one of the few countries in Europe where there was complete freedom of religious organisation. The first foundation there was at Tournai in 1833. Several others quickly followed, including a novitiate and house of studies, both, of course, essential to secure future development. The vigour of the Congregation in Belgium was such that, over the next hundred years, it established eighty-eight houses in Holland, England, Ireland, Canada and North and South America.[12]

Canonisation

Alphonsus de Liguori was canonised as a saint of the Catholic Church in 1839. He was declared a Doctor of the Church in 1871, in recognition of the outstanding spiritual quality of his writings, particularly of his *Moral Theology* of 1748, which was so influential in countering the rigours of Jansenism throughout the church. In 1950, Pope Pius XII declared him patron of confessors and moral theologians, thereby acknowledging his life-long priestly work in reconciling sinners to God 'by gentle and direct appeal to the gospel'.

2 HOW THE REDEMPTORISTS CAME TO IRELAND

First contacts with Belgium

The Redemptorists came to Ireland by way of England, following contacts between English bishops and Belgian Redemptorists. In 1837, the English Bishop Baines visited the thriving Redemptorist Belgian province. He met the provincial superior, Fr de Held, and was so impressed that he invited him there and then to make a foundation in Wales. It was 1843 before the Belgian Redemptorists established a small community, not in Wales, but at Falmouth in Cornwall. A further small foundation followed at Hanley Castle, Worcestershire in 1844.[13]

Clapham

Neither of these foundations really suited the Redemptorists. They wanted a large establishment where the full monastic and missionary life would be possible. The first opportunity for this came in 1848, at Clapham in London, supported by Bishop (later Cardinal) Wiseman and by Fr de Held who was now the Redemptorists' 'Visitor of England'. Clapham quickly attracted new recruits of quality. In 1850, for example, there were seven novices of whom three were 'Oxford' converts from Anglicanism. One of these, Robert Aston Coffin, was a mature thirty-one year old who was to have a long career as superior of the Redemptorists in England. Another was the twenty-six-year-old William Plunkett, the first Irishman to become a Redemptorist; he was a former army officer and the third son of the Earl of Fingall.[14]

Bishop Eton, Liverpool

It was through their second major foundation in England, made at Bishop Eton, near Liverpool, in 1851 that the Redemptorists first extended their apostolic work to Ireland. The large Irish population in Liverpool made it inevitable that missions would be undertaken in Ireland itself. The first of these was in October 1851, at St John's Cathedral, Limerick, where over five thousand people attended the planting of the mission cross at the close. At Omagh shortly afterwards, twelve thousand people kept the priests busy in the confessionals from five in the morning until late at night during the course of the mission. At Enniskillen in 1852, the crowds were so great that the clergy had wondered where they came from. The following year, at Randalstown, ten thousand people assisted the raising of the mission cross out of a supposed population of five thousand. Such Irish experiences convinced some of the priests, notably the Austrian Fr Prost, who was superior of the missions from Bishop Eton, that Ireland promised a vast outlet for missionary work in keeping with the ideals of St Alphonsus. Prost was also convinced that a foundation in Ireland was essential. With the support of Archbishop Cullen of Dublin and Bishop Ryan of Limerick, an initial community was established in Limerick in 1853. Its first superior was the Belgian, Fr Buggenoms. This Limerick foundation, coupled with an awareness of the vast missionary potential in Ireland, encouraged the Redemptorists' general administration in 1855 to divide off an Anglo-Dutch province from Belgium, with three houses in Holland, two in England and one in Ireland. Just five years later, the English and Irish houses were grouped into a new Anglo-Irish vice-province, which in 1865 became a separate province.[15]

Irish-English tensions

Increasing contact with Ireland led quite rapidly to a serious imbalance between the English and much larger Irish membership of the Anglo-Irish province. Precise figures for the early years are hard to come by, but by 1880, of fifty-nine priests in the province, thirty were Irish, twelve were English; there were three Scots and the remaining fourteen were continental Europeans. This imbalance, accompanied as it was by the fact that Irish members rarely held positions of authority, generated tension between the Irish and English groups. This was in part a reflection of national antipathies, but social factors contributed as well. The English priests were virtually all from the professional classes and so 'regarded themselves as natural governors,' whereas the Irish were from a wider social mix and resented the superior attitude of some of their English confrères.[16]

Long administration of Robert Aston Coffin

Robert Coffin was appointed first superior of the new vice-province upon its establishment in 1859. He continued as superior after the province was declared in 1865, a position he retained until his appointment as bishop in 1882. His long administration never seriously addressed the problem of Anglo-Irish tensions. By and large, he urged all to follow the unrealistic official Redemptorist policy, which was that politics and nationality should have no part in religious life, while ignoring it – perhaps largely unconsciously – in his own administration. Coffin was a very able man, intelligent and ambitious. His long rule gave continuity and stability to the young Anglo-Irish province. Furthermore, he was highly regarded by the hierarchies of England, Scotland and Ireland as a spiritual director of both priests and bishops, which was good for Redemptorists generally. But he ruled autocratically, ignored advice and seems to have had an antipathy to non-English confrères. There is evidence that he was unsympathetic to a second Irish foundation, giving preference to the first Redemptorist house in Scotland, at Kinnoul, near Perth (1867-8) and a new house of studies at Teignmouth in Devon (1875). John Sharp, the historian of the early Redemptorists in Britain and Ireland, concludes: ' ... it seemed incredible that only one house had been founded in Ireland where the majority of the novices were recruited and where much work was still being performed.'[17]

Second Irish foundation – Dundalk

There was considerable support among the Redemptorists themselves for Belfast as the next Irish foundation but the bishop of Down and Connor, Patrick Dorrian, included 'the care of a parish' as an unacceptable condition. Dublin was considered to be over-supplied with religious. Archbishop McGettigan of Armagh expressed an interest in introducing Redemptorists to his archdiocese. A site was examined in Armagh city itself in 1873, but, eventually, it was Dundalk that emerged as the chosen location. In 1876 a temporary house was opened there.[18]

A separate Irish Province

It was only when Coffin left office to become Bishop of Southwark that what Sharp calls the 'suppressed sense of outrage' of the Irish members welled to the surface: 'Once articulated, it grew into a movement for Irish separation within the Province, implying a strong criticism of the previous direction of the Congregation.' The separation finally took place in 1898, with the inauguration of an independent Irish province on 1 April, to which Australia was added as a vice-province. Coffin had sent a group of six Redemptorists there in 1882. The first superior of the new province was Fr Andrew Boylan. When news of the decision was broken to the new Clonard community in the course of a general visitation in November 1897, it was welcomed as 'a much desired event'.[19]

3 CATHOLIC IRELAND IN THE NINETEENTH CENTURY

A time of change

Between the foundation of Limerick in 1853 and Clonard in 1896, Ireland had undergone dramatic changes, in politics, in the land and, perhaps most markedly, in the position and practice of Catholicism in everyday life.

Limerick was founded while the country was still traumatised by the repercussions of the Great Famine. Nationalist Ireland was politically prostrate following the death in 1847 of Daniel O'Connell and the ignominious failure of the Young Ireland rising in the following year. In the countryside, the Famine had taken its greatest toll among the cottiers and small farmers and their families. They constituted a substantial proportion of the two millions lost by death and emigration. This heavy loss facilitated the consolidation of farms. Larger farms became the norm, as did the fear of splitting them up. The Catholic Church in Ireland, as seen from the Rome of Pope Pius IX (1846-78), was in such need of reform that the man, Paul Cullen, chosen in 1849 to succeed Archbishop Crolly of Armagh, was sent – from Rome – with the additional powers of a papal legate and with instructions to call the first national synod of Irish bishops since the twelfth century. This was held at Thurles in 1850.[20]

By the time of the Redemptorists' second Irish foundation at Dundalk in 1876, politics had been jolted by the abortive Fenian rising of 1867, which kept alive the tradition of armed insurrection. However, the political interest of the 1870s was the revival of constitutional nationalism in the predominantly Protestant Home Government Association founded in 1870 by Isaac Butt. On the land, the tenant farmers were beginning to challenge the traditional assumptions about landlord rights, particularly in the west of Ireland where, following a localised famine, Michael Davitt and others in 1879 founded the Land League to press for tenant rights. Meanwhile, the changes in Catholic piety and church organisation were everywhere visible.

When Clonard was founded in 1896, Irish politics had come through nearly two decades of high excitement. In 1880, the young Charles Stewart Parnell had seized the leadership of Butt's Home Rule party (as it was now called); under his dictatorial management it became highly effective. In 1885, the great Liberal leader W. E. Gladstone became 'converted' to the idea of Home Rule for Ireland. But his attempt to make it a reality in the following year was thwarted by a patriotic outcry from the British Conservatives and Irish Unionists. This was echoed in the Liberal party itself, which split on the issue so that, despite the support of the by now large Irish party (controlling about 86 out of the 105 Irish seats at Westminster), Home Rule was narrowly defeated in the British parliament. Parnell's fall from grace in 1891 over the O'Shea divorce scandal split the Irish party into factions for and against him; they spent the rest of the decade in internal warfare of the bitterest kind. While the tenant farmers in 1896 were well on their way (through a series of land purchase acts) to becoming proprietors of their holdings and while the Catholic Church was determinedly self-confident, life, particularly in the north, was poisoned by unbridled sectarianism, brought to the surface by the fear of Home Rule on the one hand and disappointment at its loss on the other. In the early accounts of the foundation of Clonard, this sectarian bitterness is almost tangible.

Changes in Catholic outlook and practice

Changes in Catholic religious practice between the beginning and the end of the nineteenth century were seen, until quite recently, as so dramatic that they warranted the label 'devotional revolution'. The term was first used in 1972 by Professor Emmett Larkin in an important article in the *American Historical Review,* 'The Devotional Revolution in Ireland, 1850-75,' important because Larkin was the first historian of stature to draw attention to the changes in Catholic religious practice in the nineteenth century. Those readers who had reached, say, their twenties before the Second Vatican Council (1962-5), might recognise that what Professor Larkin was talking about was the formation of Catholic religious practice in Ireland into a mould which was not broken until that council. Most, if not all, of the Catholic practices on which several generations of Irish Catholics have been nourished – confraternities, sodalities, devotion to the Blessed Sacrament, the Sacred Heart, the Precious Blood, the Nine Fridays, the Way of the Cross, the Rosary, May Devotions, October Devotions, novenas to Our Lady, St Joseph, the saints, the Christmas Crib – were not there from time immemorial, as most of us thought when we fervently sang 'Faith of Our Fathers,' but were nineteenth-century introductions from continental, especially Italian, Catholicism.

Professor Larkin's choice of dates for this 'devotional revolution,' 1850-75, reflect the importance he attributed to the man most closely associated with changes in Irish Catholic religious practice, Cardinal Paul Cullen (1803-1878). There is no denying Cullen's importance, but much recent research, stimulated by Larkin's work, plays down the cardinal's indispensability and, at the same time, regards the idea of a 'revolution' in devotion as misleadingly dramatic. Changes in practice and attitude were already happening early in the century, largely under the influence of Maynooth College (established in

1795) and developments in the Catholic Church at large. As Mgr Patrick Corish puts it:

> These developments ... had been so all-pervasive that they would certainly have had a marked influence in Ireland had Paul Cullen never been Archbishop of Armagh (1849), of Dublin (1852) and Ireland's first cardinal (1866).

But he acknowledges Cullen's role:

> 'Nevertheless, his long years as bishop in Ireland (1849-78) ... ensured that what was new in discipline and devotion in the wider world would be firmly stamped on the Irish Catholic mind.'[21]

A turning point for the church at large was the long pontificate of Pope Pius IX (1846-78). In Corish's words, this long pontificate 'saw the Catholic Church settle into a mould that has only been broken in recent years' – broken by the impact of the Second Vatican Council. This mould became so important for the Ireland in which Clonard was founded that its main characteristics should be looked at.

The centrality of the Pope

The first, and by far the most important of these characteristics was 'a new sense of the centrality of the Pope,' or in the words of Mgr Ambrose Macaulay, an attitude which supported 'the enhancement of papal authority and Roman traditions in the church'. The enhancement of papal authority derived from a number of factors: first, the collapse of the old monarchies of Europe which had tended to interfere between the popes and their Catholic subjects; secondly, the political difficulties which Pius IX experienced with the rising tide of Italian nationalism caused him to emphasise the universality of his spiritual jurisdiction. It is no accident that the First Vatican Council (1869-70), the first ecumenical council in 300 years, defined the doctrine of papal infallibility. On a more mundane level, the centrality of the papacy was assisted by the nineteenth-century growth in communications, especially of sea, rail and postal services. Improved travel by sea and rail brought people to Rome in unprecedented numbers and the new post enabled Rome to supervise local churches more closely (and, incidentally, enabled bishops likewise to superintend their clergy) than ever before.[22]

This enhancement of papal authority was accompanied by an increase in clergy everywhere in the church. And the clergy were more disciplined and more professional, both in their attitude to their vocation and in their preparation for it.

Roman traditions of practice and devotion

Increasingly, then, during the long pontificate of Pius IX, Roman traditions of practice and devotion became the norm. Directed by the clergy (and the phrase is important), the laity all over the Catholic world devoloped a more personal religious devotion, 'more markedly Italian in general tone, genuinely more human, but not without some danger of sentimentality'. Hence, the synod of Thurles, summoned by Cullen in 1850, agreed several important pastoral decisions which were of great consequence for Irish Catholics. These decisions covered three important areas, namely, baptism, penance and marriage, the sacramental celebration of which was to be moved from the home to the parish church. The increasing focus on the parish church became one of the main features of religious practice in the later nineteenth century, cutting across the traditional Irish practice of 'stations' at private houses in rural areas. Wakes and funerals were badly in need of reform. Wakes in particular had become riotous affairs in many rural areas with drnking, dancing and games which included thinly disguised pagan survivals. The growing practice of removing the remains to the church for requiem Mass, instead of having Mass in the house, shortened the wake. However, the traditional wake, shorn of its old excesses, survived into the twentieth century as an acceptable ritual of mourning.[23]

A worldwide empire of the (Irish) Catholic faith

Already in the 1850s and 60s, outside observers like the English Cardinal Wiseman (in 1858) and the Irish Presbyterian James Godkin (in 1867) had noted that the Catholic Church in Ireland seemed full of confidence in its progress. Everywhere new churches and religious institutions were appearing. In the diocese of Down and Connor, for example, no less than thirty-five churches were blessed and opened between 1835 and 1865 under Bishop Cornelius Denvir. (Sadly, Denvir is remembered rather for his neglect of the growing needs of Belfast Catholics, attributed to his fear of Orangeism.) Irish Catholics came increasingly to see that their faith and their church gave them an unmistakable identity. Through emigration, particularly during and after the Great Famine, they effectively established a worldwide empire of the Catholic faith, parallel to the British Empire. There is no doubt that the Catholic Church in England and Scotland was transformed by Irish numbers. Similarly, Irish emigrants built up the Catholic Church in the United States and Australia. And to all these churches Ireland sent a supply of priests – a trickle at first, but more of a flood by the end of the century. It is truly remarkable that, at the First Vatican Council (1869-70), seventy-three of the bishops attending, or ten per cent of the total, were of Irish birth and 150 in all, or twenty per cent, were of Irish descent.[24]

Relations with other Christian churches

While the Catholic Church in Ireland was asserting itself, the Established Church was losing ground. It had already lost ground earlier in the century, with the entry of Catholics into public life after emancipation in 1829; it had lost ground over the payment of tithes in the 1830s; then came its disestablishment in 1869. If one adds the sectarian tensions generated, especially in the north, by the Home Rule issue, the last quarter of the nineteenth century was not a good time for relations between the churches. Indeed, Patrick Dorrian of Down and Connor (1865-85), was, in Corish's view, an aggressively Catholic bishop whose policy was 'to meet confrontation with confrontation'. A measure of his vigour is the change he wrought in the life of Catholic Belfast. When he succeeded the timid Denvir in 1865,

> there were three churches, one religious community and a very inadequate diocesan seminary in the town; twenty years later there were six fine spacious churches (a temporary one at Ardoyne and an eighth being built), two male religious orders, five orders of nuns, a flourishing seminary, handsome convents, homes for orphans and a hospital. The number of priests in the diocese had trebled.[25]

'Mixed' marriages – the decree 'Ne Temere'

Nowhere were the tensions generated by Catholic and Protestant differences greater than in the whole area of 'mixed' marriages. At the synod of Thurles, Archbishop Cullen tried to insist that a papal dispensation be required for each 'mixed' marriage. While he failed, the procedure in Ireland was still that the local bishop gave the dispensation, whereas in England, the provincial synod of Westminster in 1852 authorised a parish priest to give the dispensation. In Ireland, 'mixed' marriages passed more and more under the control of the Catholic Church, culminating in the papal decree *Ne Temere* (Pius X, 1908), which bound Catholics in such marriages to the Catholic form and also required that the children of such marriages should be raised as Catholics. Such an overwhelming assertion of Catholic control was readily seized upon by Protestant apologists in the north, like the Church of Ireland Bishop of Down, Dr C. F. D'Arcy and the leading Presbyterian layman, Thomas Sinclair, who saw little hope for their fellow religionists in a Home Rule Ireland.[26] *Ne Temere* continued to be a major stumbling block in interchurch relations until recent times.

Conclusion

So, by the mid-1890s when the Redemptorists established Clonard monastery, the Catholic faith and church in Ireland were vigorous and confident. The 'Faith of Our Fathers living still, in spite of dungeon, fire and sword' was strong in its call to martyrdom, if necessary, in its defence – 'we will be true to thee till death.' But it was strong in its practice, nourished as it now was by a wide range of liturgical and personal devotions, many of the latter given a quasi-liturgical status by being moved from the home to the

church. For example, the family rosary became an integral part of the May
devotions in honour of Our Lady and of the October devotions in honour
of St Joseph. The sacraments, of course, remained central: the Eucharist (but
extended, devotionally, by confraternities of the Blessed Sacrament and visits
to the Blessed Sacrament in which the direct influence of St Alphonsus
Liguori is acknowledged), and Penance – with what we now see as an
unhealthy emphasis on frequent confession, especially when linked, in practice, as a necessary precondition for each reception of holy communion.

4 THE BELFAST TO WHICH THE REDEMPTORISTS CAME

The Belfast to which the Redemptorists came in 1896 was, by any standards
of economic and demographic development, a truly remarkable place.
During the previous century, its population had increased from 90,000 to
349,000, thus making it the fastest-growing centre of population in the
United Kingdom. Its growth from town to city status was formally recognised by a royal charter in 1888, the year in which Robinson and Cleaver's
palatial department store was opened, and a further charter of 1892 entitled
the mayor to be called lord mayor.

Most of this growth had taken place in the second half of the nineteenth
century and was the result of the rapid expansion of the linen, shipbuilding
and engineering industries which became major employers of labour and
gave the city an international reputation. The supply of labour, mainly from
the counties immediately adjacent to Belfast, was encouraged by the destruc-
tive effects of the Great Famine (1845-51) on the local agricultural economies.

While linen was not only the oldest but also the most important industry, shipbuilding and engineering developed spectacularly alongside it.

Shipbuilding and engineering
Shipbuilding was driven by the engineering genius of the young Edward
Harland and the finance (and orders for new ships) provided through his
partner Gustav Wolff. From the early 1860s until the First World War,
Harland and Wolff built a series of ocean-going steamers full of new design
features. As a measure of their rapid progress, the workforce of 500 in 1861
grew to 6,000 in 1880. When steel replaced iron in construction in the 1880s,
ships got bigger and faster and were better equipped, culminating in the
Olympic (1911) and the ill-fated *Titanic* (1912), of 46,000 and 47,000 tons
respectively, the largest ships ever launched.[27]

The development of linen and shipbuilding enabled the growth of an
engineering industry in Belfast. There were twenty foundries in the city in
the 1870s, many of them in the Falls area, making every kind of machine for
the linen business except looms, which were made in England. In the 1850s,
Combe's Falls Foundry and Horner's Clonard Foundry were making hack-

ling machines. A Scot, James Scrimgeour, began making textile machinery in Albert Street. When he went bankrupt his manager, another Scot called James Mackie, took over. Mackie went from strength to strength, making an increasing range of textile machinery. By 1900 he and Combe Barbour were the largest engineering companies outside the shipyards. Other world-leading engineering firms were Musgrave's (patent house and stable fittings), Davidson's (tea-drying machinery and, later, as the 'Sirocco' works, the world leader in ventilation and fan manufacture) and by 1891 Thomas Gallaher had forty-six tobacco spinning machines at work in his York Street premises.

Finally, new methods of mass production were applied to whiskey distilling. There were three major distilleries in Belfast, one at Avoniel, another at Connswater and the largest, the Royal Irish Distillery, established by William Dunville and James Craig on Grosvenor Street (later renamed Grosvenor Road) in 1870. The last-named produced 2.5 million gallons of whiskey in 1890. Small wonder that in 1900 Belfast was responsible for sixty per cent of all Irish whiskey exports.[28]

There were numerous other smaller engineering works offering good wages to skilled workers. However, like the major employers, they were of little relevance to the Catholic workers of Belfast. While the census of 1901 showed that twenty-four per cent of the population of the city were Catholics, only a very small proportion of them were skilled workers.

The linen industry
Linen was the biggest employer and remained so into the twentieth century. By the time the Redemptorists came to Clonard in 1896, Belfast accounted for eighty per cent of the linen spinning capacity in Ireland and for a similar proportion of the estimated 69,000 employed in the industry.[29]

Wages
However, while linen provided extensive employment, wages in linen mills were notoriously the lowest in the textile industry throughout Britain and Ireland. There were several reasons for this: first, compared to the predominant cotton industry, linen was extremely labour intensive, requiring four workers to cotton's one; secondly, the workforce was predominantly female, women outnumbering men by three to one; thirdly, a large proportion of the employees, perhaps as much as a quarter, were under eighteen years of age, virtually all girls and many of them juveniles or 'half-timers'. The minimum age for mill-workers was slowly raised by legislation from ten years in 1874 to eleven in 1891 to twelve in 1901. These children attended school in the mornings and worked in the afternoons or vice versa; or they worked and went to school on alternate days. The latter was the experience of the old lady in the Clonard area who recalled to Fr Patrick O'Donnell that, as a half-timer

between 1904 and 1907, she earned 3s.4½d. 'the long week' and 2s.11½d. 'the short week'. St Gall's National School (as it was then), located beside Clonard monastery in Waterville Street, had 139 half-timers on roll between 1902 and 1905. Only fifteen of them went as far as fifth standard The contribution of such children to a family budget was often indispensable. Half-timing survived until the 1930s.[30]

Working conditions

Working conditions in the linen industry posed a serious health risk to practically every worker. After retting in a 'lint hole' or dam and drying in the sun, the flax had to pass through various stages in order to separate the woody stem and core from the valuable fibres. The first, breaking and scutching, were carried out in scutch mills. There followed hackling, sorting, preparing, carding and roving. In this last named stage, the flax passed through a frame onto bobbins and was then ready to be taken to the spinning room. All of these processes, from hackling to roving, took place in a dust-charged atmosphere which wreaked havoc on the lungs of the workers. Some employers, from the 1870s, piped steam into hackling, preparing and carding rooms to 'lay' the dust, but the real answer was the powered extractor fan which, however, was not made compulsory until 1906.

The spinning room was notorious for its hot and steamy atmosphere. Hot wet-spinning had been developed as the quickest and most efficient method of spinning. The women and girls who worked there as 'doffers', responsible for replenishing the supply of bobbins on the machines, usually went barefoot to save their shoes from the stinking water in which they had to stand. With so much heat and moisture, small wonder that chest complaints and 'mill fever' were common, together with hacked skin, swollen legs and ankles and, when older, varicose veins. In the weaving sheds, the atmosphere was also wet and damp with similar, if not quite so extreme, health risks. Generally, with better pay and working conditions, weavers were the envy of the other employees.[31]

Housing

An unhealthy working environment for linen workers was not helped by overcrowded living conditions. The main problem here was low wages coupled with high rents which forced mill workers to sublet rooms to other families or individuals who were often relatives or former neighbours from the countryside. Serious overcrowding was a common problem.

During much of the nineteenth century, the building of houses for mill workers was usually undertaken by the mill owners themselves because local contractors could not build quickly enough. In addition, because of very early starting and late finishing, workers had to live close to the mills. So, like other owners, Charters of Falls Mills, Malcolmson of the Blackstaff Works and Ross of Clonard built large numbers of small 'kitchen' houses, usually of four rooms, which they rented to their workers. However, there was a building boom in the last quarter of the century, with a peak in the 1890s, when house building was taken over by building societies, estate agents and land and investment companies. As Jonathan Bardon, the historian of Belfast, points out, among the most prolific developers were the estate agents R. J. McConnell & Company, 'probably the largest firm of its kind in Ireland ... [who] built all over the city and for every class'. They purchased Clonard House and its surrounding park land from the Kennedy brothers, James and Victor and, in the mid-1890s, had begun laying out the network of streets ranging from Dunmore Street to Cupar Street and from Springfield Road to Clonard Gardens. Bardon notes that McConnells in the 1880s were selling kitchen houses in the Shankill in lots of five for £345 and villas in Rosetta Park for £700 each. The highest paid bricklayers at the time were earning 35s.4d. a week – 7½d an hour for 56½ hours. Maximum rent for a kitchen house between 1901 and 1911 was 4s.6d., which was considered low, but when set against a woman's linen mill wage of 9s. to 11s., or an unskilled man's wage of 18s. to 20s. a week, it was a great burden.[32]

Diet
A final damaging by-product of low wages in linen was the poor diet of mill workers. For most of the last quarter of the nineteenth century, their diet was tea and white bread ('baps') three times a day. Butter, meat, even potatoes were a rarity. The poor standards of nutrition of young mothers was frequently compounded by their return to work – an economic necessity – just a few days after giving birth, which led to complications and, often, persistent ill-health. In addition, the care of their babies when these young mothers returned to work was a constant source of anxiety to medical men in Belfast. Babies and young children were 'minded' by old women or older children. They were often ill-fed and dosed with tea-and-whiskey or the cheaper laudanum to keep them quiet. Thirty per cent of 'mill children' died under the age of two and a half years.[33]

Employment opportunities for Catholics
While these appalling working and living conditions in and around the linen mills applied to all workers, irrespective of creed, it has to be said that their impact was more severe, proportionately, among the Catholic community of Belfast. The reason is that, while generally Catholics were slightly over-represented in linen employment, they were seriously under-represented in the more skilful, higher-paid sectors: for men this meant they rarely became weavers or foremen, overseers or clerks, but were more likely to be found as

roughers or hacklers. Catholic women employed in linen were predominantly doffers and spinners rather than weavers.

In his analysis of employment opportunities for men in Belfast in the period 1871-1911, Professor A. C. Hepburn concludes:

> It is clear that the high-wage industries were predominantly Protestant, and that the small Catholic presence tended if anything to become even smaller during the period, notwithstanding the enormous expansion of employment.

Catholics, in proportion to their numbers in the population at large, were seriously under-represented in shipbuilding, engineering, the building trade (where most were labourers) and printing. But they were over-represented as dockers, factory labourers, tailors, shoemakers, hairdressers, general dealers and above all, as publicans and wine merchants. The marked drop in the proportion of both Presbyterians and members of the Church of Ireland owning licensed premises is presumed to be the result of the temperance movement in the late nineteenth century. However, the manufacture of alcohol remained substantially in Protestant hands.[34]

Women had very limited job opportunities in the closing decades of the nineteenth century. Linen, as already noted, was their main employment, though they tended to be spinners rather than weavers. In general, Protestant women, especially Presbyterians, were over-represented in more 'comfortable' and better paid occupations as milliners, dressmakers, seamstresses and machine workers (as in textile finishing processes), while Catholic women were over-represented in less attractive, less 'respectable' work as washer-women, factory labourers, general dealers and domestic servants. Domestic service became an increasingly Catholic preserve up to the First World War; it never attracted city girls, hence country girls came in large numbers.[35]

Catholics explained the disparity of opportunity in employment as a sectarian conspiracy between Protestants, Unionists and Orangemen. As early as 1864, Bernard Hughes, the baker and first substantial Catholic employer in Belfast, had explained in evidence to a Commission of Inquiry:

> There are few Catholic employers in the town and the others will not take Catholic apprentices, for the workers will not work with them as either apprentices or journeymen. Every trade union has an Orange Lodge and their people know each other for they have signs and passwords, so that the Catholic population has no chance at all.

Bardon points out that the exclusion of Catholics was so complete that Bernard Hughes' explanation for it is understandable. But the role he gave Orange Lodges was as exaggerated as it was unnecessary. The reality was that Belfast was a predominantly Protestant city; all the major industries were owned by Protestants; the bulk of the skilled workers were Protestant and –

in the tradition of craftworkers in England and Scotland – it was they them-selves, not the employers, who selected the apprentices to their trade. The influence of the Orange Order was marginal and limited to unskilled trades.[36]

It should be remembered that, while Catholics were undoubtedly excluded from the better-paid occupations, the population of the city was so over-whelmingly Protestant that there were as many or more lowly-paid and unemployed Protestants as there were lowly-paid and unemployed Catholics.

A deeply sectarian city
While Belfast in 1896 could justly boast of its outstanding economic achieve-ments, the same could not be said of its religious and political record. Belfast became, during the course of the nineteenth century, a deeply sectarian city. The liberalism of the late eighteenth and early nineteenth centuries, when Protestants helped pay for – and attended the opening of – St Mary's, Chapel Lane (1783) and St Patrick's, Donegall Street (1815), quickly evaporated. The reason was the agitation for Catholic Emancipation in the 1820s and for the repeal of the Act of Union in the 1830s, both led by the arch-Catholic Daniel O'Connell, the first successfully, the second unsuccessfully. Both these move-ments alarmed the Protestants of Ulster in particular and determined them that Catholics would have no part in the public life of the province. If this was true of Ulster, it became even more true of Belfast from the Great Famine onwards, as the steady immigration to the town from rural Ulster brought with it many local tensions.

However, the most obvious manifestation of sectarianism, rioting, was not just a post-Famine phenomenon. There were serious sectarian riots in Belfast in 1812, 1835 and 1843. Further major outbreaks occurred in 1857, 1864, 1872, 1884, 1886, 1893, 1898 and 1912. While some of the worst riots happened at times of imminent political change, such as in 1886, 1893 and 1912, the years of Home Rule Bills, religious factors were also – one might say always – important. The experience of Fr John Tohill in 1886 provides a good illus-tration of official Catholic attitudes and reactions to the riots of those years.

He was then on the staff of St Malachy' College. He was also one of the honorary secretaries of a Catholic committee formed to look after Catholic interests and to collect evidence to lay before the government. When Fr Tohill was called before the Belfast Riot Commissioners of 1886-7, he attrib-uted the violence to, 'the incitements from the local Orange and Protestant press, pulpit and platform, in producing religious hatred of Catholics in our midst'. Similar sentiments were recorded privately in the Clonard Domestic Chronicle by the first rector, Fr Patrick Griffith, when he noted 'the hatred of Catholics with which Belfast Protestants are born ...' Fr Tohill also com-plained that the existence of Catholics was 'ignored in every department of public life in Belfast' and that they were 'treated as if they were an inferior and conquered race'.37

In general, the Catholic bishops and clergy tended to urge their flocks to refrain from rioting or provocation, by attempting to keep the peace – with clergy often appearing on the streets and urging people to go home, establishing vigilance committees and so on.

An important social result of persistent sectarian tension in late nineteenth-century Belfast was the rigid segregation of the population, particularly of working class people in the west and north of the city. Of the nine most segregated electoral divisions within the city, seven were in the west, in the Falls and Shankill areas, one in the nearby north-west (Ardoyne) and one in the east (Short Strand). Six of the nine divisions were predominantly Catholic. In general, Catholic districts were more or less exclusively Catholic, whereas most Protestant districts – outside West Belfast – contained Catholic minorities of varying size.38

Politics
Political representation for Catholics in nineteenth-century Belfast was minimal. In the fifty years before 1896 there had been only three Catholics elected to the city council – two Liberals, Bernard Hughes in 1855 and William Ross, mill owner, both of whose establishments were close to the Clonard monastery site, and a Conservative, the landowner John Hamill of Trench House. Bishop Henry was determined to change this. He saw Catholic representation on the corporation as essential since it was the largest employer in the city. Taking advantage of newly drawn municipal constituencies of which two were to have Catholic majorities (a concession won by Irish Party pressure at Westminster), the bishop established a Belfast Catholic Association to put forward Catholic candidates. While happy to support nationalist candidates at parliamentary elections, the bishop's supporters were determined to keep nationalism out of municipal politics. Their principal strategy was to insist on 'Catholic Rights'. This view was vigorously opposed by local nationalists, led by the young Joseph Devlin (1871-1934), who believed that Catholic interests were best served by linkage to the wider nationalist movement. However, in the first elections held under the new municipal arrangements in 1897, the bishop's candidates won all eight seats, in Smithfield and Falls wards. Devlin's paper the *Northern Star* denounced the Association candidates as, 'gentlemen who came from other wards ... to represent the working men of Falls and Smithfield ... When will they be seen in the the slums again?' Only one of the eight councillors lived in the Falls area; two lived in 'Malone Road mansions' – Dr Peter O'Connell, a surgeon at the Mater Hospital (Bernard Hughes's son-in-law, later High Sheriff of Belfast, 1907; knighted in 1908) and the estate agent William McCormick –

while most of the defeated nationalists lived in the wards they contested. In the eyes of the Devlinites, the Catholic Association leaders were not only 'bishop's men', they were socially removed from the people they claimed to represent.

The local nationalists of the Falls, lower middle-class publicans, grocers and schoolteachers and 'the betting men' eventually had their day when Devlin, in 1906, won the West Belfast Westminster seat back from the unionists, after a lapse of fourteen years. Until his death in 1934, 'Wee Joe' Devlin was the dominant political force in West Belfast.[39]

A city of migrants

Another important characteristic of late nineteenth-century Belfast – a characteristic it shared with industrialised cities in various parts of the world – was that its population consisted mainly of migrants. The earliest reasonably secure figures are those derived from the detailed returns of the census of 1901: estimates from the census show only 39 per cent of Belfast's population to have been city born. This figure increased steadily throughout the twentieth century – to 64 per cent in 1926, 74 per cent in 1951 and 76 per cent in 1961. The migrants did not travel very far – most came from counties Antrim, Down, Armagh and Tyrone. But migration made for a certain instability in cities like Belfast, which must have contributed to politico-religious tensions.

The social geographers and historians, in analysing migration into nineteenth-century cities, use the terms 'transience' and 'persistence'. Parts of cities became areas of 'transience' within and beyond which newly-arrived migrant families moved – often frequently – before finally settling down to city life, that is, before 'persisting' in the city. There is abundant evidence to show that migrant families in Belfast moved house frequently in the early years after coming to the city. For example, Hepburn and Collins show that, of the families recorded in the 1901 census returns, less than twelve per cent had lived in the same house in 1896 and were still living in it in 1906. This applied to both communities. It often took several fairly rapid moves – to another street within the same district, for example – before a family finally settled or 'persisted.'[40]

The Clonard district of Belfast into which the Redemptorists came in 1896 was a district dominated by the linen trade. Most of its inhabitants, therefore, were employed in the lesser-paid, less healthy sectors of linen, because the district was exclusively Catholic, abutting the exclusively Protestant Shankill. The housing in the district was predominantly – though not exclusively – mill housing, or at least of the two-up-two-down 'kitchen house' type. Most of these houses were overcrowded with large numbers of 'lodgers' – migrants, just like the tenants of the houses – who were taken in for the extra shillings they contributed to the rent.

A case study: Sevastopol Street

Recent research into one of the streets very close to Clonard monastery – Sevastopol Street – brings out clearly most of the characteristics of industrial cities identified by the social geographers and historians.[41]

For those unfamiliar with Clonard, Sevastopol Street is two streets removed on the Falls Road citywards from Clonard Street, to which it runs parallel and with which it is connected by Odessa Street. The intervening street, also parallel to Clonard and Sevastopol Streets, is Dunlewey Street. Sevastopol and Dunlewey are a reminder that the local mill owner, William Ross, made his fortune in providing linen shirts for the British Army in the Crimean War (1854-6); Dunlewey Street commemorates Ross's investment of some of his profits in property at Dunlewey in county Donegal.

Sevastopol Street ran from the Falls Road northwards to the main entrance to William Ross's mill. Just over a hundred metres long, it had forty terraced houses in two rows facing each other across a narrow thoroughfare. The detailed census returns for 1901 show that the street had 192 inhabitants of whom 126 were over the age of fourteen and 109 in employment. 108 or 56.25 per cent were returned as born outside Belfast; furthermore, only 40 per cent of families still lived in the same houses in 1903, only 10 per cent in 1909 and 7.5 per cent in 1911, clear evidence of the 'transience' referred to earlier.

Only one Protestant lived in the street in 1901. She was a Presbyterian lady married to a Catholic.

Given its closeness to Ross's mill – and to others in the area – it is not surprising that 59 per cent of the employed adults worked in the linen industry in 1901, rising to 64 per cent in 1911. Nor is it surprising, on account of the predominance of women in linen mills that, of the sixty-four residents employed there in 1901, forty-seven, or 73 per cent, were women; this reflects exactly the ratio of women to men in the industry as a whole. Another important fact to be corroborated from Sevastopol Street is that, both in 1901 and 1911, more than one-third of the women working in linen were married – 35 per cent in 1901 and 41 per cent in 1911. This emphasises the great importance of the economic role of women as breadwinners alongside their social role as mothers and homemakers – under the most difficult conditions.

The only other substantial employment for Sevastopol Street residents, especially in 1901, was in local iron foundries where only men were employed. In 1901, 17 men were so employed – 16 per cent of the street workforce, which was well above the average (9 per cent) for Catholic men in Belfast. But by 1911, due to the closure of the two local iron foundries, only four men still had jobs in the trade, a mere three per cent.

A final aspect of the census returns for Sevastopol Street which reflects the known pattern of Belfast as a whole was the large number of 'lodgers' recorded, most of them probably relatives. So, in a total of forty homes, there were twenty-four extended families in 1901 and twenty-seven in 1911. As a variation on this theme, several houses were each occupied by two families whose heads were born in the same locality outside Belfast. While it is uncertain, there is a strong likelihood that they were related. So, in 1901, the Rooneys and Monaghans from county Monaghan lived in number 2; at number 8 were the Masons and Duffins from county Armagh, while the Maguires and McGarrys from county Down lived in number 16.

The Clonard area

While much detailed research has still to be done into the social and economic history of the Falls district around the turn of the nineteenth-twentieth centuries, Sevastopol Street can confidently be taken as a microcosm of the Clonard area into which the Redemptorists came in 1896. An area which depended heavily on work in linen mills and on a high proportion of women in those mills, was by definition a poor area, women employed in linen being so notoriously badly paid. However, badly paid or not, their economic role in family life was vital and, since more than a third of the women working in mills were married, they had to be strong, physically and mentally, to sustain long hours of work in extremely unhealthy conditions, yet continue to bear children and run a home.

The social historians, in examining new migrants to cities like Belfast, explore the various factors which contribute to their 'persistence' and their formation, ultimately, into a settled community. Such helpful factors are kinship, the camaraderie of working together, sharing hardship together, the development of sporting and cultural activities (provided, in the case of the wider Falls community, by the Gaelic Athletic Association and, to a lesser extent, the Gaelic League), involvement in political activity (though opportunities were limited, given the divisions in nationalism in the 1890s) and the attachment to a local church as the focus of religious practice and fulfilment of spiritual needs. St Peter's parish was, by the late 1890s, overwhelmed by the sheer weight of the numbers of Catholic migrants to Belfast, which was the primary reason Bishop Henry invited the Redemptorists to come there. The new, poorly paid, hard-worked migrants must have seen in a religious order noted for its stern discipline and practice of poverty, a particularly attractive model of religious life. The fact that the members of the Redemptorist community of Clonard had, like themselves in the recent past, left family and native place, provided another common bond which may explain, to some extent, the fierce loyalty of the Clonard people to the Redemptorist congregation in their midst.

CHAPTER 2

The Foundation of Clonard

On 31 May 1895, Fr Edward Vaughan, the English (Anglo-Irish) provincial of the Redemptorists, wrote to Fr Patrick Griffith, rector of their house in Limerick. He said he had just received a letter from the Superior General, Mathias Raus, charging him and Fr Somers, second in command in Dundalk, 'to look out for a good site for a foundation in Ireland'.[1]

Bishop Henry

In his letter, Fr Vaughan had mentioned possible sites in Dublin or Derry. But the appointment of a new bishop of Down and Connor ensured that the new foundation would be in Belfast. This was Bishop Henry Henry, a native of Loughguile in north Antrim, who had a reputation of being well-disposed towards religious. Indeed it was widely believed in Down and Connor that the intervention of religious in Rome had brought about his appointment as bishop. Mgr Macaulay suggests that Henry's principal rival for the see, Fr Dan McCashin, was identified to Cardinal Vanutelli, Prefect of Propaganda, as 'the constant counsellor' to Bishop Dorrian and his successor, Patrick McAlister, in their long-running dispute with the Passionists at Ardoyne, in which the Passionists had been badly treated. The cardinal drew his colleagues' attention to this dispute. As Macaulay concludes, 'this may well have been the deciding factor in Henry's appointment'. Whatever the circumstances of his appointment, Bishop Henry was credited by a leading Irish Redemptorist of the time with a fine sensitivity towards religious. Fr John Magnier was a consultor to Superior General Mathias Raus. Writing to Fr Griffith in November 1896, he paid this compliment to Bishop Henry: 'I have not yet met anyone, not a religious, whose views about religious were more correct than those of Dr Henry.'[2]

The bishop-elect made his ordination retreat in the Redemptorist monastery of St Joseph in Dundalk. On 20 September 1895, he was ordained in St Patrick's, Belfast, by Cardinal Logue. Then, as the Clonard Domestic Chronicle recorded:

> ... shortly after his consecration, the bishop declared his intention of establishing a house of Redemptorists in Belfast. He determined to have us some place near the Falls Road where there is a vast Catholic population, some 30,000, without sufficient church accommodation or priests enough to hear their confessions.[3]

The existing churches of St Peter's and St Paul's simply could not cope with the rapidly increasing population of West Belfast.

A suitable site

Three sites were considered for the new foundation. One, at Cullingtree Road, was too small and confined. Another adjoined the Bon Secours convent on the Falls Road. It was a more attractive proposition, as the location was better and the site was the bishop's property. The nuns had been resident there since 1879 and paid the bishop a yearly rent of £58. The site would not have been large enough if the nuns remained, so the bishop proposed removing them and giving them a new convent. To this the nuns objected strongly and, according to a Clonard source, 'even tried to stir up feeling by saying the bishop was going to evict them from their convent'. The bishop admitted that the nuns regarded his proposal as 'tyrannical and unjustified'. In his turn, he regarded their reaction as 'cranky' and acknowledged that he would like to compel them to move. The nuns' 'refusal,' in the view of the Redemptorists, was,

> ... providential, for it was the cause of our getting a much more suitable site close by, though of course at greater expense ... The bishop looked further and finally came on our present site which was part of a park formerly belonging to a Mr Kennedy, mill owner, but which had been bought from him by Messrs R.J. McConnell & Co, Estate Agents, Mr Kennedy retaining a certain head rent.[4]

Clonard House

On 6 January 1896, the bishop, accompanied by Frs Griffith and Somers, inspected the house; all agreed it would be suitable. The Clonard record of the transaction conveys the strong impression that McConnells held the whip hand once they saw that the bishop was keen on the house and the adjoining site: '... they laid out the land ... in streets to suit their own purpose' and the deflection of the street to the right (the present Clonard Gardens) to avoid Clonard House curtailed the site considerably. There was already a mill dam in the middle of the plot which had the effect of ' ... narrowing it very much and increasing the difficulties of finding a suitable site for buildings upon it'. Since it was clear from the outset that the dam presented difficulties concerning right of way, not to mention a foul smell, another adjoining site was briefly considered. This was nearer Cupar Street, 'in the midst of McConnell's building site, further from the Falls Road, smaller and dearer ... and, as afterward appeared, intended to be surrounded by narrow back streets'. It was not proceeded with.

Negotiations for the purchase of Clonard House and three acres, two roods and twenty perches around the mill dam progressed slowly. Fr Griffith, in his own subsequent account of the foundation of Clonard, attributed this to the fact that Dr Henry kept the negotiations 'altogether in his own hands; no one could interfere,' although he acknowledged that, 'The bishop was at first nervous about letting McConnell know that he wanted the place for a religious order, fearing Orange bigotry might prevent us from getting it at any price.' Still, Griffith believed the bishop had other reasons for taking his time:

> ... he was building his new infirmary (the Mater Hospital) and his friend Fr Crickard was collecting for his proposed new church in Ballynafeigh (Holy Rosary) and Fr McDonnell PP, Ligoniel, was collecting for his. It would be inconvenient having us come on the scene before they had got their turn out of the people.

But, fearful that the continuing delay might finally jeopardise the Belfast foundation, Griffith urged the bishop 'to take the place as it was, with its risks and inconveniences'. This was in the last week of October 1896, the concluding week of the Belfast General Mission which was being preached by fourteen Redemptorists and fourteen Passionists, Fr Griffith working in St Patrick's parish, Donegall St. According to Griffith,

> The bishop replied rather testily, 'Well, will you undertake the risk of the mill dam?' I answered, 'I will, my Lord.' 'Very well', said he, 'I will sign the papers tomorrow.' And so he did.[5]

The mill dam was to be at the centre of years of legal wrangling which tried Fr Griffith sorely. 'I may begin,' he wrote in a lengthy memoir of the site transaction, 'by saying I doubt if a more troublesome piece of property was ever acquired ...' There were disputes about the precise boundary of the property, walls were built and torn down overnight, a gate was erected at the Cupar Street boundary and broken down on several occasions, there were stand-offs over these matters between Protestant and Catholic crowds, with police in between. But the boundary disputes were as nothing compared to the saga of the dam.

At the time of the purchase, the dam was virtually unused; it was even polluted and a health hazard in hot summer weather. Unfortunately, its owner, Fulton of the Clonard Print Works, was uninterested in the business, died prematurely and his family left the fate of the business entirely in the hands of their solicitor, a Mr McDowell. He led Griffith a merry dance for years, blowing hot and cold, first over alleged rights of way to the dam and, later, whether and for how much it could be bought. It was August 1904 before the Redemptorists finally bought it for £800. Griffith's stubbornness and his tendency to see Orange conspiracies everywhere possibly contributed more than a little to the delay. The final settlement appears to have occurred at the beginning of Patrick Murray's rectorship.[6]

To return to October 1896, the purchase price of the site was £2,360, together with a head rent to Mr Kennedy of £100 per annum. The bishop gave the Redemptorists possession of Clonard House as a temporary residence at £50 a year and, on 31 October 1896, accompanied by Fr Griffith, he took formal possession of it. On the following morning, Sunday 1 November, the feast of All Saints, Fr Griffith and his confrère Fr Walter Lambert left St Patrick's Presbytery, Donegall Street and crossed the city to say Mass for the first time in their new abode.[7]

Fr Griffith later recalled quite graphically those first Masses in what came to be known as the Oratory of the Most Holy Redeemer:

We prepared the altar, placed our coats on the floor and I commenced Holy Mass ... When I had vested and Mass commenced, we heard footsteps hurrying over the gravel walk outside, and by the time Mass was over and Fr Lambert commenced his, the room in which he said Mass was almost full with panting and wonder-struck people. The news had spread that priests were saying Mass in Kennedy's house. The remark of an old woman was eloquent. With hands raised toward heaven she cried, 'Glory be to God. Mass in Kennedy's house and in old times a Catholic crow daren't fly over it!'

When Fr Lambert's Mass was over, seeing the crowd of people present, I felt inspired to say a word of welcome to them and tell them that Our Lady of Perpetual Succour had come to establish a new sanctuary among them. This was, I suppose, the first sermon ever preached in Clonard.

From the very beginning the good people of Clonard showed their piety and good will. It was the depth of winter and at great inconvenience, as there was no available road to the house and no gas near, the people used to walk along a plank laid by the wall of the factory and grope their way with the help of a couple of stable lamps laid on the ground. ... This was a veritable stable of Bethlehem. The room was roughly fitted up. Mass was said every morning, our pulpit being a soap box covered with canvas.[8]

Fr Patrick O'Donnell has provided some concrete details of the first morning: the altar was a common deal table, the property of a Mr Morrison, a tailor, whose house at Odessa St corner was later known as Montfort House. Morrison carried the table himself to Clonard House, where the Masses were said in the large room to the left inside the front door. The only ornament there was a picture of Our Lady of Perpetual Succour donated by John Carvill, the sacristan of St Patrick's. John Hayes of Odessa St, a lame man of seventy years, boasted that he was the first person to hear Mass in Clonard House. An early purchase was a safe, 'to serve as a tabernacle', where the Blessed Sacrament was reserved for the first time on Sunday 15 November. The people were invited to visit the oratory at any time during the day.

The John Hayes mentioned above was a general helper in the first days and was known locally as 'Brother Hayes'. Reading between the lines of the early domestic chronicle, it seems that he was a bit of a nuisance. He was actually employed by Fr Griffith for a week and then 'sent away'. His place, for the remainder of November, was taken by 'a lad named John Hodgson' who was 'most useful'.

A serious problem for the small community was lack of lighting – it was the month of November. They relied on candles (when supplies ran out on one occasion, John Hodgson was 'sent off to buy a pennyworth ... at the nearest shop') until a Mr Reed 'the engineer at Ross's Mill ... got everything right'. On several evenings he came to Clonard House after his day's work and 'skilfully set up gas jets throughout the house'.

The early records of the foundation abound in tributes to the generosity of the local people in offering practical help, goods in kind and money. One morning during the first week, 'some women, without having been asked, generously undertook to wash the whole house and they spent the day scrub-bing the floors ... and the stairs and making everything clean and tidy'. A Mr McConville gave an armchair, a Mr McAllister gave a prie-dieu and a ciborium was given by a Miss Hodgson, who was to be a substantial benefactor of Clonard. From the very beginning,

> ... the inhabitants of Falls Road and its neighbourhood gave money every day to the fathers out of their scanty earnings and constant offerings flowed in for the support of the house and towards building the new church. ... The moneybox for [church building] was always well supplied with coppers ...

The Redemptorists were particularly impressed by the efforts of the mill women and girls who, on their own initiative, formed the 'Pious Union of the Most Holy Redeemer'. Members 'bound themselves to give 6d. or 3d. a week' towards the upkeep of the community, providing 'a constant though moderate source of income'. An early account book shows that during 1897 the 'Pious Union' contributions varied from almost £11 to over £17 a month, reflecting remarkable generosity in the giving and energy in the collecting. Another source of income was from 'a considerable inflow of intentions for Masses,' a high proportion of them for the 'Holy Souls in Purgatory'.[9]

Fr Griffith might well recall the gathering in the empty Clonard House as reminiscent of the stable at Bethlehem. That state was a far cry from the house in its prime. The architectural historian, Dr Paul Larmour, gives this account of the building:

> A fine stuccoed villa of regency type, symmetrical with two-storey bows to each end. Essentially neo-classical with coupled pilasters across the front and a tetrastyle Ionic portico, but with a Georgian Gothic fanlight.

> Built for the Kennedys, flax spinners. Architect's name not recorded, but
> must surely be Thomas Jackson. It is his style of house and he did build
> the Kennedys' weaving factory at Millvale, Falls Road, 1843-4, (now
> gone). (*Belfast: An Illustrated Architectural Guide,* 1987, p. 11.)[10]

The location of the house was equally impressive, set as it was in a beautiful
fourteen-acre park of trees, shrubs and green fields. The driveway was entered
by large iron gates situated near the present Odessa St-O'Neill St intersection
with Clonard St. A tradesmen's entrance gave access to the property from
Cupar St.

The tearing-up of the park in the interests of development was not lost
on the keeper of the early domestic chronicle:

> The greater part of Clonard park was in the possession of builders and
> during the second week of November [1896] the work of destruction
> began. The splendid trees and beautiful shrubs were cut down ruthlessly
> and the green sward was dug up.

In a curious way, converse sentiments were to be echoed almost one hundred
years later by the then chronicler of Clonard as he reflected on the end of the
era which had begun with the 1890s housing development. In 1990, the plaint
was the passing of the little houses and the good people who had lived in them,
driven out by 'bloody civil war' and the demands of housing redevelopment.

The sentiments just quoted about the ruthless cutting down of 'splendid
trees and beautiful shrubs' is part of a longer entry in the domestic chronicle,
which continued:

> ... The part of the park which belonged to the Fathers was then enclosed
> by a lofty wooden paling which was erected along the new Clonard Street
> by Mr Fagan [the builder of the temporary church]. ... Policemen in uni-
> form and plain clothes patrolled the grounds both day and night as a pro-
> tection to the Fathers. Reports were spread that the House had been
> attacked by Orangemen, but perfect peace reigned, notwithstanding the
> nearness of the Shankill Road.[11]

The necessity for police protection and rumours of alleged Orange activity
were ominous for the beginnings of the new foundation. Fr Griffith's early
years as superior were to be difficult in the extreme. But before that, the formal
arrangements between the bishop and the Redemptorist congregation were
made in Rome within weeks of possession being taken of Clonard House.

Formal contract of foundation

On 21 November 1896, a foundation contract was signed in Rome between
Dr Henry and the Redemptorist superior general Mathias Raus. It was witnessed by Fr Michael Kelly of the Irish College and the Irish Redemptorist
John Magnier, one of Fr Raus' consultors. Two days later, Fr Magnier sent
copies of the contract to the provincial, Edward Vaughan and the rector of

Clonard, Patrick Griffith, each copy being accompanied by a short letter of explanation of aspects of the contract. Magnier suggested that his letter be kept with the contract, 'for,' as he wrote, 'having been the interpreter between the Bishop and Fr General and Consultors, I write from perfect knowledge of the whole transaction.'

The contract, written of course in Latin, was very short. It had four clauses, two of which required no explanation; these were the first and third clauses. In the first, Dr Henry accepted that the Redemptorists might live and exercise their sacred ministry according to their rules and constitutions and whatever privileges the Holy See should allow them. In practice, as specified in clause 2, they were free from the routine burdens of parish work and at liberty to follow their vocation as missioners. The third clause accepted that the diocese of Down and Connor should have the first call (*primarium jus*) on the Clonard Redemptorists for missions and spiritual exercises.

What required explanation in the second and fourth clauses related to finance. In the second, the Redemptorists were obliged to take up the collections prescribed in the diocese, especially that on the first Sunday of the month, for the support of the bishop and clergy. The letter of explanation pointed out that this arrangement was necessary, but Dr Henry acknowledged that, 'in all collections, the fathers will never be deprived of their ordinary collection'; whatever that should be was always to be deducted from any diocesan collection. The fourth clause placed on the Redemptorists the entire financial responsibility for the foundation, thereby making them the 'possessors and proprietors' (*possessores et proprietarii*). As Fr Magnier explained:

> ... if [the fourth clause] puts on the fathers the whole expense, it also leaves them free: if the bishop were to pay for even a part of the property, he should of necessity be a co-proprietor. It was considered quite inadvisable to ask the bishop to oblige himself to any *speciale subsidium*; but his Lordship told us that the fathers can count on his helping them directly and indirectly to the utmost of his power.

The exchange of formalities included the 'aggregation' by superior general Raus of Dr Henry to the Redemptorist congregation, 'giving to his Lordship the most full participation in all our good works, and for this he is infinitely grateful'.

Fr Magnier's letter of explanation to the rector of Clonard continued beyond the formal requirements of the contract. It informed Fr Griffith of some of the bishop's observations and views. In the first of these, Dr Henry is shown as an astute clerical economist:

> The bishop was much pleased to hear that you had 500 at Mass on Sunday and guessed to within 2s. what you had received. This was to him a proof that you could, when fully established, count on £10 a Sunday.

Evidently the structure of a temporary church had been discussed, Dr Henry expressing a preference for brick: if it were 'anything near the price of iron it would be better,' but Fr Magnier had not mentioned brick to Fr General, 'nor shall I until I hear from Fr Provincial'. Another interest of the bishop was the establishment of confraternities in Clonard. He evidently pressed the subject, for, while Magnier parried as best he could – 'I did not go much into the matter as it is better to settle it with you' – he was clearly quoting the bishop's sentiments when he continued, 'The Boys' is a certainty. There is no doubt the men's will come. I don't suppose there will be any difficulty about the women,' since they would meet only monthly.

Finally, Dr Henry assured Magnier 'again and again' that Fr Griffith, in Clonard, 'must not fear. Funds will not be wanting.' Magnier focused on another anxiety which he knew Griffith entertained: 'I don't think you need fear in any way that the bishop will interfere with you except to help you,' which may have been cold enough comfort for Griffith, who had already experienced a year of dealing with Henry. As an (unfortunately anonymous) Redemptorist wrote retrospectively in 1922: 'Although Dr Henry professed great friendship for us, he was a difficult man to get on with.'[12]

Temporary (or 'tin') church
It is evident from Magnier's observations to Griffith that a temporary church was under active consideration as a matter of necessity. In fact, the letter from Fr Raus appointing Griffith superior of Clonard had instructed him to see to the erection of 'a temporary church according to the wise counsel of the bishop of the diocese'. The oratory in Clonard House soon became utterly inadequate, even when, with the addition of two more priests, Frs Michael Magnier and Vincent Bourke, the number of Sunday Masses was increased to four, at 9, 10 and 11 a.m. and 12 noon. A reminiscence of Fr Griffith's provides an idea of the cramped conditions at Sunday Masses: 'The fathers preached on a box covered with canvas and placed inside the simple altar rail opposite the door so that the preacher might be seen and heard by those in the hall and second parlour.' Nor were there any seats. The people stood or knelt on the floor and, at the 12 o'clock Mass, 'there was always an overflow congregation.'[13]

Fr Griffith invited the architect J. J. McDonnell, MRIA, to draw up plans for a temporary church and in December 1896 the contract was signed for a plain structure, opening on Clonard Street at the south-western corner of the Redemptorist property (approximately on the lower part of the present car park adjoining Clonard Street). The builder was John Fagan of Cosgrove Street, Belfast. For an outlay of £900, he provided a simple rectangular structure with brick walls and a corrugated iron roof, which later gave it the name by which it was affectionately known, the 'tin' church. Its floor dimensions were 125 feet from sanctuary rail to door and 40 feet from side to side; it seated 740 people comfortably in fifteen-feet long pews (each seating ten people, each costing 19s. 6d.).

The temporary church was completed in a little over three months. It was opened on Easter Sunday, 18 April 1897, but without ceremony. In a letter of 9 April from his Chichester Park residence, Bishop Henry, having expressed his pleasure at the building of the temporary church, explained to Fr Griffith:

> ... I would most willingly have given you permission for a formal opening and a collection ... on the third Sunday after Easter, as you desire, but for the fact that the Catholics of the city are engaged, as you know, in making a great united effort to pay off, by means of the coming bazaar, the accumulating debt on the Mater Infirmorum Hospital.
>
> As the great majority of our people belong to the working classes, we cannot expect them to contribute to many objects of charity within a short time. I have to ask you, then, to postpone the formal opening of the church until next year ...[14]

Once the temporary church was in use, it was found that, at a crush, it could seat 880 people. Indeed, on one Sunday in April, 'at the ordinary evening service,' the congregation was so large that the Superior, 'to test its capacity,' arranged a count as the people left the church. There were nearly 1,400 present! A few weeks later, admittedly without a count, this number was regarded as having been exceeded. As an indication that the figure was not an exaggeration, by early 1903 the church was catering for over 1,100 communicants at the close of each of the men's and women's confraternity retreats. By 1904, communicants of each confraternity exceeded 1,400.[15]

In accordance with usual Redemptorist practice of following diocesan custom as closely as possible, the decision was made that Sunday Masses in the temporary church should be at the same times as those in the city churches, that is, at 7, 8, 9, 10 and 11 o'clock a.m. and 12 noon. The best attended Masses were the 10, 11 and 12, because, as the chronicler noted, 'The people of Belfast, being for the most part working all the week, like a long sleep in on Sunday morning ...' He also recorded that the first 'May devotions' in the new church were extremely well attended and that, in the course of the month,

> a list was put up at the end of the church of things wanted for the altar service – a ciborium, a set of brass candlesticks to bear ten candles, a set of same to bear fourteen candles, six brass torches for altar boys, a candelabrum for Blessed Virgin's altar – all of which things were soon given us.[16]

Subsequently, the furnishing of the church continued piecemeal. In June, the Stations of the Cross were erected, a gift of the rector of St Joseph's, Dundalk,

Fr O'Laverty. The following month, 'two most beautiful pictures of Our Lady of Perpetual Succour arrived from Rome ... painted on mahogany', each authenticated by the Redemptorists' superior general as a copy of the original in the generalate and each blessed by Pope Leo XIII. One of these pictures was placed on the side altar of Our Lady of Perpetual Succour, the other in the community oratory in Clonard House. In addition to the high altar, there were three side altars or 'chapels', Our Lady's, St Joseph's and a third in honour of the Redemptorists' own Blessed Gerard Majella (he would be canonised by Pope Pius X in December 1904). A matter of days before the formal opening of the church, Mr Thomas Caffrey of Glen Road presented to the Redemptorists for the chapel of Blessed Gerard 'a beautifully carved' altar in oak. A new organ for the church was used for the first time on the feast of Our Lady of Perpetual Succour, 19 June 1898.[17]

While the postponement of a formal opening must have been a great disappointment to the Redemptorists, it did not damage their underlying cordial relationship with the bishop. He accepted an invitation to preside at a High Mass on Sunday 4 August, when the celebration of the titular feast of the church – Most Holy Redeemer – was held. (It seems that the title 'Most Holy Redeemer' had been expressly requested by the bishop himself.) Dr Henry, on the occasion,

> spoke very fulsomely from the altar, thanking God for the foundation of the order in Belfast and wishing, in his own name and that of the people, the fathers of the community a hearty welcome and every choice grace and blessing in the fututre.

Afterwards, with 'twenty of the city priests,' he was entertained by the Redemptorists to an excellent dinner provided by the Dominican nuns, Falls Road. It was 'a happy, genial occasion'.[18]

The solemn dedication of the temporary church by Bishop Henry finally took place on Sunday, 20 March 1898. As he had promised, he allowed a special collection in all the churches of the city to mark the occasion. The considerable total of £1,200 was raised in Clonard itself and 'large sums' in the other city churches. Fr Griffith estimated the Redemptorist debt on the site purchase and church building at £5,000.[19]

Monastery

The next building phase for the Clonard foundation was a substantial monastery. As the *Irish Catholic* (4 June 1898) expressed it: 'Fr Griffith, having provided accommodation for the faithful in his new church, has now set his hand to provide his community with a permanent residence within their own grounds ...' Plans had been drawn up by the architect of the church, J. J. McDonnell, during the previous year and submitted, as required, to the Redemptorists' general administration in Rome. From there they were returned to Clonard in February 1898 with a cautionary stipulation that the outlay should not exceed £11,000.

No less than eight local builders competed for the contract. Their quotations varied from £13,100 (Messrs A. & D. MacNaughton of Randalstown) to the cheapest, £10,500, tendered by Messrs Wm. J. Campbell of Ravenhill Road, Belfast, which was accepted. Campbell's tender matched exactly the architect's estimate. The contract was signed on 27 May, the first sod was cut on 9 June, the feast of Corpus Christi, and the foundation stone laid by Bishop Henry after Solemn High Mass on Sunday 15 August, the feast of the Assumption of the Blessed Virgin.

Of the sod-cutting ceremony, performed by Fr Griffith 'in the presence of the community and our poor people who assisted with evening devotions', the chronicler observed: 'The sod was soon broken up into many pieces by the people and taken away by them as so many relics.' According to custom, prior to his laying the foundation stone on 15 August, Bishop Henry was presented with 'a handsome silver trowel' by the builder. Enclosed with the stone were various coins, a copy of the *Irish News* of 14 August and a bottle containing formal details of the event. The *Irish News* of 16 August had this to say of the new structure:

> The new buildings will consist of confraternity room, parlours, refectories, community room, bishop's room, infirmary. There will be fifty-four bedrooms; it will be four storeys in height and executed in Belfast brick and giffnoch stone dressing.[20]

The large number of bedrooms was explained by the necessity to provide accommodation beyond the needs of the Clonard community, 'for the clergy and lay gentlemen wishing to make retreats, this being a special point of the Redemptorist rule'.[21] Fr O'Donnell recalls that the size of the monastery provoked cynical observers to dub it 'Griffith's folly', but they were unaware that the bulk of the accommodation was intended for retreatants, whereas the number of the resident community was intended ultimately to be eighteen or twenty Redemptorists. (In fact, retreats for 'lay gentlemen' never materialised in Clonard, except for a short time in the 1920s, although the clergy of Down and Connor diocese made their annual retreats there from 1900 to 1960.)

Building proceeded rapidly and smoothly, with but one recorded dispute between architect and builder. This was about the quality of the facing brick. The architect condemned it as inferior and insisted that, where it had already been used, it should be replaced. The builder objected. Fr Griffith intervened and a compromise was agreed: existing facing brick should remain but new work should use better quality material. Fr Patrick O'Donnell points out that time has vindicated the architect, for the brick on the upper strata of the monastery has worn much better than the rest.

The monastery building represents two sides of a rectangle, the longer facing south. Corridors and rooms of the first three floors are wide and spacious, while the rooms on the fourth are small, being under the roof and lighted by dormer windows. The original fifty-four bedooms were reduced to fifty when, in 1908, four rooms were merged to provide a library.[22] Fr O'Donnell provides the following architectural details:

> Surmounting the entrance doorway is a canopied niche surrounding a beautifully sculptured figure of the Redeemer and flanked by single windows having sculptured panels below and showing the arms of Pope Leo XIII as well of those of the Congregation of the Most Holy Redeemer. The windows lighting the corridors are of cut stone, running through the full height of the three floors and terminating with a Gothic stone arch and corbel mould. Over each ground floor window is a sunk tympanum, with carving in relief of natural foliage surrounding an emblem of the Passion.[23]

From the cutting of the first sod to occupation, the building of the monastery took just under two years which, as the chronicler noted, 'is a remarkably short time considering the dimensions, solidity and beauty of the building'. His account of the move to the new monastery on 2 May 1900 echoes the relief and delight of the small community of four or five priests and three brothers at having, at last, their own ample space – corridors to walk in when the weather was bad and the freedom of a large garden without having to cross a public street to get to it. The account also records the continuing generosity of local people: the transfer of furniture from Clonard House was quick 'for the people most readily offered their services in the work'. However, once the move was made, it became clear that the existing furniture was quite inadequate for the new building; but, the account concluded, 'we were not left long without substantial aid; both confraternities contributed generously towards supplying the want.'

The furnishing of the monastery must have proceeded rapidly, for the first test of its capacity came just ten weeks after the community took possession. In mid-July, thirty-eight Down and Connor priests made a four-day retreat and expressed themselves pleased with the new house.[24]

As had happened in the funding of the temporary church, the Clonard Redemptorists had to wait patiently before they were given episcopal sanction for a public collection to help defray the costs of the new monastery. It was late January 1903 before Dr Henry authorised Fr Griffith 'to solicit subscriptions from the people of Belfast' towards the new monastery 'and the balance still due on your temporary church'. During the month of February, Fr Griffith, still rector of Clonard since 1896, led a team of seven other Redemptorists in a door-to-door collection around the city. It realised a total of £1,567.8s.4d., which the rector, in issuing a public statement of thanks afterwards, described as 'a generous response'. As always with Fr Griffith, there was 'a special debt of thanks' to 'the working people who, out of very straitened means, gave generously and with a good heart'.[25]

House of Studies

The availability of such a large house as Clonard proved providential for the newly independent Irish province of the Redemptorists. After the 1898 separation from Britain, the house of studies of the larger province, at Teignmouth in Devon, was retained as an interim measure. But in 1900, realising that the expense of maintenance was too great for the reduced English province, Fr John Bennett, the provincial superior, decided to sell it. Students of the English province were sent, some to Mautern in Austria, others to Beauplateau in Belgium, to continue their studies, while the Irish students were transferred, as a temporary measure, to Clonard.

In mid-August 1900, the students travelled to Clonard in small groups. Within a week all twenty-eight of them were assembled with their prefect, Fr Patrick Murray. Once their summer vacation concluded on 2 September, they made a five-day retreat in preparation for the year's studies. Eight of them (including five already ordained to the priesthood) were studying Moral Theology with Fr Murray as lecturer. Nine others were studying Dogmatic Theology (under Fr Patrick Kilbride). The senior students also studied Sacred Scripture under Fr Richard Murphy, while the remaining eleven 'Philosophers' were tutored by Fr Eugene O'Donnell.[26]

The presence of the students added a considerable dimension to church services in Clonard, particularly their involvement in the choir and solemn liturgies. From September 1902, there were annual ordinations to sub-diaconate, diaconate and priesthood, spread over three days, which, with the first Masses of the newly ordained, were a great attraction for the regular worshippers. Three students were ordained in 1902, four in 1903 and six in 1904. Bishop Henry was the ordaining prelate on all three occasions. Domestic life for the Clonard community was also greatly enhanced by the students' presence, particularly on festive occasions. One of the highlights of the year was their dramatic presentation to the community, to which Bishop Henry was invited. The domestic chronicle entry for 29 December 1901 reads: 'Dr Henry dines with the community and afterwards the students present the play *Julius Caesar* before the bishop and community. Bishop expresses himself "very pleased".' While there is no mention of a similar performance the following year, it is very likely that there was one, for in December 1903, *The Merchant of Venice* was presented before the bishop, and in 1904, *Scenes from Macbeth*. One other domestic presentation is recorded, rather stiffly, by the chronicler on New Year's Day 1904: 'Students render in the Irish tongue an Irish play, *The Banishment of St Columba to Iona*, by one of this community.'[27]

However, as far as the Belfast public was concerned, the greatest impact of the Redmptorist students was their physical appearance on the streets of the city as, in a body, they took their recreational walks. The chronicler even made the claim, on the basis that it was 'commonly remarked' that,

> ... [the students] rendered the clerical appearance familiar in the city. Before their time, clergy, whether going to or coming from public functions, tried to avoid observation by never travelling in any large company. But the students reversed all that. The sight of a large group of ecclesiastics marching together was at first a strange sight in Belfast, but even the eyes of the Orange folk gradually adjusted to the 'Clonard monks'. It used to be a subject of notice and comment how briskly they walked and probably their athletic style of movement sometimes saved them ... from the running commentaries of such bigots as would have insulted them when passing, if they had dared!

The account says much about the low expectations of Protestant or Orange behaviour toward Catholic ecclesiastics entertained by the writer, particularly his speculation about the effect of the students 'athletic style of movement'. Acknowledging that whatever 'misconduct' was experienced came mostly from 'ignorant and vulgar children,' he concluded:

> ... we were agreeably surprised, everything considered, how inoffensively the Protestant element of the population behaved; especially as we never expected any manners from them.

The use of Clonard monastery as a house of studies had always been intended as a temporary measure. Its location in a large city was not regarded as conducive to the formation of young religious priests. In 1901, the Irish provincial administration made a new foundation which was, ultimately, to provide appropriate facilities for a house of studies. This was in the quiet retreat of Esker, county Galway, near the town of Athenry. Thither the Redemptorist students were dispatched from Clonard on 14 July 1905. The chronicler noted with some sadness: 'A general feeling of regret prevailed ... not merely among ... the community but, to a certain extent, among the citizens at large.'[28]

CHAPTER 3

From 'Catholic Dissension'
to Redemptorist Rejoicing 1904-1909

The Clonard Domestic Chronicle in the early years of the new century provides several glimpses of the political friction within Catholicism in the city
of Belfast. In July 1904, the Redemptorists' provincial superior, V Rev Fr
Boylan (a Maynooth man and later to be Bishop of Kilmore), at the conclusion of the Down and Connor priests' annual retreat at St Malachy's College,
'... endeavoured but in vain to heal the local clerical factionist split'. Nearly
four years later, in a reflection on Bishop Henry's death, the chronicler used
even stronger language, when he referred to 'the scandal of the Catholic dissension, which discredited the whole diocese,' though he was inclined to
blame, not the bishop, but the 'selfish intriguers' both lay and clerical by
whom he was surrounded.[1]

Political differences: Bishop or 'Less of the Bishop'?
The divisions between Bishop Henry's Catholic Association and Devlin's
supporters were deep. When the bishop founded the Central Catholic Club
in 1896 to provide for Catholic businessmen the kind of services their
Protestant opposite numbers enjoyed, Devlin founded the United National
Club in Berry Street where, unlike the bishop's, Irish culture was given a
prominent place and public discussion of politics was encouraged. Both sides
also realised the value of the press. The bishop had virtual control of the *Irish
News*, thanks to the influence of his predecessor, Bishop McAlister. Devlin
was forced to establish his own paper, the *Northern Star*, in 1897 to wage his
own propaganda war. The bishop's party tried to label Devlin and his associates as anti-clericals and secularists, despite the fact that they were, virtually
to a man, devout, practising Catholics. Devlin's image was probably not
helped, in the bishop's eyes, by his election, in 1905, to the national presidency of the Board of Erin, the umbrella title of the Ancient Order of
Hibernians. Outside its membership – it was particularly strong in Ulster,
especially in Belfast and county Tyrone – all kinds of extreme opinions were
held about the organisation. Suffice to say that the Irish bishops had banned
it as a secret society and Cardinal Logue remained an avowed enemy even
after the ban was removed in 1904. Interestingly, the man mainly responsible
for bringing about the removal of the ban, Bishop Patrick O'Donnell of
Raphoe, was 'a close personal friend' of Devlin's. It was also to his diocese
that the rector of Clonard from 1904-7, Fr Patrick Murray, had belonged.

By 1905, the Devlinites had substantially ousted the bishop's men from Belfast corporation; in June of that year they also won control of the *Irish News* and, in January 1906, Devlin won the West Belfast seat at Westminster from the unionists. Thereafter, the Catholic Association was in retreat. But the political activities of the bishop had seriously split the clergy of Down and Connor; certainly the city priests were deeply divided between the two political camps, as reflected in the Clonard record. Perhaps the most vivid illustration of the political conflict is provided by an election poster published by 'a fanatical rump' of the bishop's party for the 1907 Belfast municipal elections, at a time when Devlin was in the ascendant as a senior figure in the re-united Irish Party.

The poster is dominated by a central photograph of the bishop, surmounted by the slogan, *'The Only Issue!'* To the left of the portrait, it reads, 'Catholics of Belfast, rally round your revered bishop ...', followed by his claim to their support: 'Emancipated Belfast Catholics 1896. Persecuted by irreconcilable factionists and denied the right to direct and guide Catholic Organisation.' To the right of the bishop's portrait, four questions are put to the Catholics of Falls and Smithfield wards asking them if they approved of:

> organised rebellion against Ecclesiastical authority? ... the alleged 'true democracy' – politics divorced from religion?. ... yielding to the forces of secularism? ... the Berry Street War Cry – 'Less of the Bishop'?

The message concluded, *'If you do not, and we know that you do not ...'* (approve of these attitudes), then the electors were urged to vote for the bishop's candidates in both Smithfield and Falls wards.[2]

It was strong stuff and it was a grave embarrassment to many priests of the city and diocese. As far as the Clonard community was concerned, they seem to have been constantly anxious in the early years of the new century about the attitude of local priests to them. Despite the fact that the Redemptorists were the principal directors of retreats for the Down and Connor clergy, the chronicle carefully monitored the number of priests who accepted their invitation to dine in the monastery on its titular feast, the Most Holy Redeemer. It was an annual occasion on which the bishop presided at High Mass and then joined the community and diocesan priests for dinner. Thus, for example, in 1906, when the feast fell on 15 July, right in the middle of the clergy's annual retreat, the chronicler noted with evident relief: '... 34 priests dined with the community, a significant mark of growing friendliness and of successful diplomacy in mitigating their estrangement.' (The retreat was given, incidentally, by Fr O'Laverty, C.Ss.R., a former priest of Down and Connor and then vice-provincial, who 'created a most favourable impression' on the retreatants.)[3]

Clonard and the general election of 1906

1906 was a year of particular sensitivity for the Clonard community, because it had incurred the bishop's disapproval of its direct involvement in the general election in January on behalf of Joe Devlin. The long entry in the chronicle under the date of 16 January is very specific, if somewhat disingen-uous, about the extent of the community's involvement (... 'we did not directly interfere in politics ...'). In the following extract, 'United Irish League' was the new title of the Irish Party as re-united in 1900 under John Redmond, following the decade of the Parnell split:

> In view of the approaching general election, the directors of our local con-fraternities said a few words at the ordinary meetings, by special request, on the subject of mutual charity and the need of Catholic unity with the object of securing a nationalist Catholic and of excluding a Protestant unionist from the representation of West Belfast: for great bitterness existed at the time between [the] local branch of [the] United Irish League and [the] Catholic Association, which had divided clergy and laity, bishop and priests, into opposite factions.
>
> V Rev Rector (Patrick Murray) and four fathers who had suffrages voted in Argyle Hall for the nationalist Mr Devlin who was subsequently elect-ed by the narrow majority of 13; and who afterwards motored to the monastery to thank Fr Rector and Fr Cussen for using their influence in his favour. Thirteen associationists at the last moment refused to vote except at the personal instance of Bishop Henry or their H[oly] F[amily] Director, Fr Cussen. The latter induced them, as well as many others, to come to the hall and thus contributed largely to the tremendous victory over Orangemen.
>
> The election agents, too, were allowed the use of our telephone and these, with other circumstances indicative of our sympathy, even [though] we did not directly interfere in politics, served to establish the community high in the popular favour and affection. The local branch of the UIL passed, by request, a public vote of thanks to the fathers for their peace-making influence which had saved the situation.

This entry in the chronicle is followed by what is clearly a later addition, not-ing that 'towards the end of the year, all except the Rector were disfranchised in the monastery ...' The intriguingly suspicious and certainly incomplete explanation for this loss of the vote was: ' ... the other fathers, for reasons of obvious difficulty ... refused to present an appearance in the representation courts to answer objections lodged against their right.' Do we have a whiff here of the darker side of Devlin's 'machine' politics and possible Redemptorist complicity in it? At any rate, the Clonard community certainly had good rea-son for relief in the excellent clerical response to their festive banquet in July.[4]

'An odious subject'

Apart from the serious political divisions within Down and Connor, there were other considerations which might well have conspired against the Clonard Redemptorists around this time. The first, and perhaps the more important, was what the chronicle described as 'an odious subject', a series of slanderous attacks on their membership. The second was the outcome of apparently simmering disagreement between the bishop and some of his priests over parish 'supplies', which came to a head in July 1906.

The slanderous attacks on the Redemptorists began during the general mission they were preaching in twelve Belfast parishes in the first three weeks of October 1905. The attacks were not confined to members of the Clonard community, but were also directed at priests from their other Irish houses and from England, whom they had brought in to help. Scurrilous letters, some handwritten, but mostly typewritten, were sent to various Redemptorists accusing them of some form of immoral conduct. Others were 'addressed to Catholics in the city, particularly to female teachers and women resident in various parts of the city and suburbs'.

Typical of the content of these letters were the following: 'Beware, Christian parents, of the precincts of Clonard and keep your innocent daughters from the approaches to Clonard monastery,' or words to that effect, signed, 'A sorrowing parent.' Another ran somewhat thus: 'Beware of the eunuch, Fr N., the impure N., the rogue N., and the fool N.' One Redemptorist who was, in fact, in the Philippine Islands, was allegedly seen 'coming out of a bad house in the Shankill – a very peculiar instance of bi-location,' observed the chronicler. Another was accused of 'frequenting, for evil purposes, a certain house in Ballymacarrett'. The Clonard community was rather chagrined at the bishop's response to this last accusation. While protesting that he did not, of course, believe it, 'he instructed the monastery superiors to make enquiries ... with the comical result that the house was found not occupied at all at the time.'

The bishop himself was the next target, when the letter-writer, '... informed a female correspondent that His Lordship "kept two companions of ill-fame in Chichester Park and was suddenly surprised in complications"!'

At first the feeling in Clonard was that the letters were the work of Orange bigots, 'provoked by the grand public manifestation of Catholic faith and piety' during the general mission, but as word filtered back 'from the city and suburbs,' it became evident that they emanated from a disgraced priest who had previously victimised 'some of the most prominent priests of Down and Connor' in the same way. The unhappy man had, apparently, 'held for a long time a very prominent and public position' from which he was forced to withdraw because it became an open secret that he was 'addicted to drink and suspected of embezzlement'.

There was general agreement that it would be very difficult to prove the offender's guilt in court, but the Clonard Redemptorists were anxious to pressurise him into stopping his attacks. So they handed the matter over to their solicitor, Mr Frank Kerr. He employed 'a Protestant detective' whose success or otherwise is not clear. He did, however, submit one report which provided considerable merriment in clerical circles, Redemptorists included. As the chronicle recorded:

> ... [the detective] casually entering a room happened to overhear one priest saying to another ..., 'Did you know that Paddy Murray has found out the forger?' or words to that effect, both clergymen no doubt imagining that, in calling our esteemed superior by the familiar Maynooth name, their conversation would be Greek to the listeners present.

The episode, however, gave the Redemptorists little to laugh about, since the slanders continued against them 'individually and collectively for several subsequent months'. Eventually they stopped. Word filtered back through the clerical grapevine that the unfortunate man died shortly afterwards, having been, with great difficulty, reconciled at the last.[5]

Dispute over clerical 'supplies'

Such prolonged pressures cannot have helped relations between the religious priests and the diocesan priests of Down and Connor, relations which are subject to stress at the best of times. The second matter contributing to friction was the problem of parish 'supplies'. The 'simmering discontent' between the bishop and some of his priests seems to have come to a head in the middle of the priests' retreat referred to above – at Clonard – on 15 July 1906. On that occasion, the bishop limited the priestly faculties of the Redemptorists to Clonard church and of the Ardoyne Passionists and all diocesan priests to their own parishes. The Clonard chronicler explained:

> ... this regulation was aimed at those of the clergy who, without [the bishop's] approval, absented themselves from their churches on Sundays after having requisitioned supplies from the College (St Malachy's) priests or Clonard or Ardoyne to hear confessions on Saturday and say Mass for them on Sunday.

In future, express permission had to be sought from the bishop for each supply. To the great regret of the Redemptorists, the bishop's ruling applied also to the faculty of hearing the confessions of the sick, except in cases of extreme necessity – 'an ordinance,' they felt, 'both uncanonical and obviously full of very awkward difficulty for Superior and subjects alike'.[6]

Perhaps it is reading too much into the 'supplies' issue to link it to the factional divisions within the diocesan clergy. It may well have been a fairly routine disciplinary adjustment by the bishop in order to counteract excessive calls for supplies from his priests. However, the timing of the bishop's action and the prominence given to it in the Clonard record might suggest otherwise. Indeed, it was on this very same occasion that Dr Henry conveyed to the Redemptorists his approval of a considerably smaller church than they had wanted. Was the proposed new church a victim of tensions within the diocese? Idle speculation, perhaps, but the clerical history of the period remains unexplored. It has to be said that, to all outward appearances at least, the bishop's relationship with Clonard church and community remained unaffected. His annual visits for the titular feast of the monastery continued as usual and, as noted earlier, he was the ordaining prelate in each of the years 1902 to 1904 and visited the monastery during the Christmas season, when he enjoyed the students' dramatic productions.

Death of Dr Henry

Bishop Henry died suddenly on 8 March 1908 as he entered St Mary's Hall, 'to patronise a concert of sacred music'. A heart condition had troubled him for a considerable time and he was not helped, according to the Clonard chronicler, by the 'many cares which preoccupied him in founding [sic] the Mater Hospital and St Mary's Training College, added to the political differences which agitated the whole diocese ...' The chronicler continued:

> He was a great and good man, with combative qualities, who had the double disadvantage of being taken inexperienced from college life into the arena of active politics, and of being surrounded in his prominent position with advisers both lay and clerical who impressed few outside their own clique with a sense either of their discretion or disinterestedness. Had he been allowed to exercise his own [just qualities?], uninfluenced by selfish intriguers ... ,

the Redemptorists would have been 'spared the chagrin of building a church shortened by twenty feet ... and the country would have escaped the scandal of the Catholic dissension which discredited the whole diocese.' However, those who differed with him in religious principles 'admired his courageous independence'.

The funeral was of 'unparalleled magnitude', a display by Catholics of 'their loyalty to ecclesiastical authority, no matter how fearlessly they ventured to disagree with particular personages in [certain?] matters of policy and tactics ...', while 'leading Protestants respectfully closed their shops while the cortege passed'.[7]

On 11 March, the parish priests of the diocese met under the presidency

of Cardinal Logue to elect a vicar capitular who would administer the diocese until a successor should be appointed. There was no clear decision, so
the Cardinal nominated, as receiving most votes, V Rev Dr Laverty, PP of St
Matthew's, Ballymacarrett, who had been 'an influential adviser of the late
bishop'. Fr Dan McCashin was the other candidate 'run in opposition'.[8]

Election of Bishop Tohill - Redemptorist interest
Following the late bishop's 'month's mind' on 8 April, the parish priests of
Down and Connor met once again under the Cardinal's chairmanship, this
time to indicate by their votes whom they thought the next bishop should
be. The outcome was a tie, at twenty-five votes each, between Dr Laverty of
St Matthew's and Fr Patrick Murray, since 1907 provincial superior of the
Irish Redemptorists. A third candidate, Fr John Tohill, PP of Cushendall,
received five votes.

The Clonard scribe, who clearly relished the clerical politics of the
process, hardly concealed his pleasure at the outcome, though, in his view,
the 'news was more startling than surprising to people acquainted with the
trend of local opinion'. Fr Murray's qualities had been known to many priests
of the diocese since his arrival in Clonard in 1900 as lecturer in Moral
Theology and then as rector of the house from 1904-7. He had given the
Down and Connor priests' retreat, when he had,

favourably impressed [them] ... by his very obliging attitude on all occasions and ... by that spirit of thoughtful kindness, unobtrusive piety,
joined to a rare combination of personal humility, strict regularity and
capacity for affairs [so] that some of the priests had mentioned his name
in connection with the bishopric.

It seems that Fr Dan McCashin, the leader of one party, and referred to as
the 'Down candidate' in opposition to the 'Antrim candidate', Dr Laverty, let
it be known that,

he waived his own prospects in favour of V Rev Fr Murray and acquiesed
in the suggestion ... that, even if our provincial disliked the proffered dig-
nity, by concentrating their votes on him, they might effectively balance
the strong weight of suffrage on the opposing side.

As a result, a number of priests voted for Fr Murray who had never spoken
to him in their lives. But, as the chronicler claimed, 'the suffragists had been
so carefully organised and canvassed that already before the election took
place the exact result was anticipated ...' – except for one parish priest who
would have voted for Murray, thereby giving him a majority of one, but who
'got suddenly indisposed and did not attend'.

However, Fr Murray was not interested in a bishopric. Having at once
'with his usual quick perspicacity' grasped the full situation, he had avoided
both the bishop's funeral and his month's mind, liturgies which, as provincial

superior and former Clonard rector, he would normally have been expected to attend. His residence, as provincial, in the Redemptorists' Limerick house was no excuse. He was actually giving a retreat in Wicklow when the news of the Down and Connor vote was 'telegraphed' to him. Appealing to Cardinal Logue ('a friend or relative of his own'), he argued that there were several religious in the episcopate already and another one would carry the risk of 'developing friction as between the regular and secular elements'. He apparently also pleaded 'some insanity among relatives, however distant', which nobody believed and which only enhanced his standing.[9]

In the event, Fr John Tohill was nominated by Rome as Dr Henry's successor, even though he had attracted so few votes. Numerous priests had withheld their votes from him because they felt he could not win a majority. However, his appointment was popular. And it was clear from the outset that one of his priorities was to heal the divisions in the diocese. The Clonard record noted on the occasion of his consecration, 20 September 1908:

> He characteristically refused any addresses ... an action which illustrates the successful line of policy he had determined to adopt, namely, to recognise no factions, friends or foes and fall into line with other nationalist bishops of the country. This, of course, meant the abandonment of the Catholic Association policy founded by the late prelate, but marred by the [?] officious interference of politicians in the sequel. The result was that the loud resounding internecine strife that had dishonoured the diocese gradually died out and normally peaceful conditions, after spasmodic outbreaks at some subsequent municipal and parliamentary elections, were happily restored in the course of a couple of years.[10]

Further Redemptorist interest – an Irish Rector Major

The happy restoration of 'normally peaceful conditions' to the diocese of Down and Connor was the forerunner of a major occasion of rejoicing for Irish Redemptorists in general and the Clonard community in particular. This was the election, on 1 May 1909, at the Redemptorists' General Chapter in Rome, of Fr Patrick Murray as Rector Major (or superior general) of the Congregation of the Most Holy Redeemer. Evidently many of his fellow Redemptorists there adopted the same high opinion of him as had substantial numbers of Down and Connor priests. His connection with Clonard has already been referred to. Then, in 1907, he was appointed Irish provincial superior to succeed Fr Andrew Boylan when the latter was named as bishop of Kilmore diocese. It was in his capacity as provincial superior that Fr Murray attended the General Chapter of 1909.

The Clonard chronicle is eloquent about Fr Murray's appointment, rejoicing that: 'A thrill of honest pride and joy stirred the heart of the Irish province when the tidings was [sic] telegraphed to members at home or on mission ...' The chronicle claimed, however, that 'the news did not come as a complete surprise,' for, in manoeuvrings prior to the chapter, inquiries had been made by French and Dutch confrères about Fr Murray's 'antecedents'. Moreover, some English Redemptorists had speculated ('quite correctly') that the choice would go beyond continental Europe (the previous two generals, Mauron and Raus, having been French and Swiss respectively) and that, 'in the kaleidoscope of international opinions, principles and politics, the election of an Irish rather than an English or American general would be likely to secure the required majority.'

In the event, the Clonard chronicler fairly gloated over the change that had overtaken 'our little province ... from the time of the last chapter (1894) when some continentals, whether instructed to that effect or not, had practically alleged against its claim to independence that it could hardly govern itself ...' He went on to assert that the Redemptorists' domestic rejoicing was more or less equally shared by the priests of the dioceses of Down and Connor and Raphoe. In the former,

> ... the clergy who had voted him bishop [sic] felt exceedingly gratified by the announcement of his election, regarding it as the effect of their own previous choice which, no doubt, brought him into public prominence ...

Meantime, with a degree of historical fancy, the scribe continued,

> The clergy of Raphoe, with their Bishop Most Rev Dr O'Donnell, always so friendly to us, regarded the election of their diocesan as almost a personal compliment, reflecting credit on themselves who were yet as proud of their monks of old and still kept sacred the memory of their monastic Four Masters ...

He was probably on surer ground when he noted that,

> it became an open secret that Cardinal Logue could not conceal the pleasure he derived from casual references to Fr Murray ... as the Superior General ... of the Redemptorists.

Finally and with justice he mused:

> ... no community of the province had more reasons for thanking God and congratulating one another than that of Clonard where all had reason to regard his long tenure of office locally with recollections of mingled affection and admiration.[11]

As if to round off the Murray celebration, the chronicle recorded an anecdote about him which was related by an American confrère, Fr Joseph Hild, who called at Clonard on his way home from a theological conference which the new rector major had called at Wittem in Holland. Fr Hild, 'was full of genuine admiration for the new General, said he was the veritable type of St Alphonsus and the only man among us in Rome who could handle an Italian jarvey!' On one occasion, on the way to the railway station, with a dilatory

jarvey and a lazy horse, Fr Murray, realising that they were in danger of missing the train, 'in laconic Italian, which was all he had, told the driver that if
he did not reach the terminus in due time, he would not get one solda – a
remark which infused new life into horse and car and jarvey!'[12]

Comment

The last years of Bishop Henry's episcopate were a period of considerable
stress for the Clonard Redemptorists in their relationship with him. On the
one hand their political espousal of 'organised rebellion against Ecclesiastical
authority,' in the person of Joe Devlin at the 1906 general election, was itself
a calculated rebellion against the bishop's views led by the rector Patrick
Murray. And the bishop made his disapproval known, hence the subsequent
Clonard anxiety about their standing with the priests of the diocese. Happily,
this was allayed by the excellent clerical attendance at the retreat banquet in
July of that year. Meanwhile, the deep embarrassment of the sordid,
unfounded allegations against Redemptorist personnel, beginning in
October 1905 and continuing well into the new year, added considerably to
their difficulties. The process of finding a new bishop, following Dr Henry's
death in March 1908, brought unlooked-for affirmation, when the same
Patrick Murray was shown to be held in high regard by the parish priests of
Down and Connor. Patrick Tohill, the new bishop, moved quickly to heal
the wounds of dissension in the diocese. His restoration of 'normally peaceful conditions' made the news of Murray's election to the highest office in the
Redemptorist congregation the following year all the sweeter, particularly for
the Clonard community.

CHAPTER 4

Building the Church

Early disappointment

Bishop Henry, with a fine sense of occasion, used the Clonard celebration of the Feast of the Most Holy Redeemer in July 1906 to give the Redemptorists his sanction for building a new church.[1] However, the Redemptorists were not at all pleased with the church the bishop approved, nor with what they saw as his regrettable behaviour in the whole matter. It is no exaggeration to say that the subject rankled deeply and bitterly with the Redemptorists for decades – virtually every subsequent reference to the planning of the church was accompanied by a recitation of the perfidy of those senior clerics in Down and Connor who had the bishop's ear. And the villain of the piece was Fr Pat Convery, the acting parish priest of St Paul's.

The Redemptorists wanted a large church in the Romanesque style, similar to their much admired church in Limerick. The bishop insisted on a Gothic church which would seat 1,000, 'less, therefore, than ... Limerick ...' Perhaps more irritating than his final decision was Dr Henry's vacillation. A long note at the end of the domestic chronicle for 1906 fairly seethes with frustration. Over a period of months,

> ... [the] rector (Patrick Murray) was compelled to endure endless worry and anxiety in the submission of different plans, Gothic and Romanesque ... The bishop, who was supposed to be unduly influenced and prejudiced by jealous clergy and particularly the acting PP of St Paul's, kept the plans waiting after submitting them to another architect than ours; and so vacillated in his approval and disapproval that the rector and counsel of the house were inclined to flinging [sic] the whole business in sheer disgust and await better times and fairer chances.

One of the arguments attributed to 'our clerical critics and invidious opponents' was that a church 'on the full lines of M[oun]t St Alphonsus, Limerick' would give Clonard 'the Cathedral or, as one blusterer said, the "basilica" of Belfast.' So it was, according to the chronicler, that 'the devil of envy and avarice' prevented the Redemptorists from building 'a noble church in the most Catholic quarter of a bitterly Protestant and Presbyterian city'.[2]

A later source – a rather racy account entitled 'Foundation of Redemptorist Monastery, Clonard, Belfast,' an anonymous fifteen-page manuscript, dated 1922 – claimed that when the second set of plans 'for a grand Gothic church' was submitted to the bishop, 'He took his pencil and cut off about thirty feet of its length, thus ruining its proportions.' However, mindful of St Alphonsus' advice never to quarrel with one's bishop, the Redemptorists 'submitted'.

The building contract - Falls Road riots 1907

It was 5 August 1907, before the contract for building the church was signed. The builders were to be the McNaughton Brothers of Randalstown. The work, valued at £20,600, was to be completed in two years, with a margin of two months, 'to allow for exigencies and contingencies which alas proved to be very real, though the brothers were perfectly honest fellows worthy of sympathy'. (The Redemptorists knew the work of the McNaughtons well; they had recently built the new foundation at Esker, county Galway.)

This note of the church contract was followed, in the monastery chronicle, by an intriguing admission, coyly introduced by the phrase, 'It should be mentioned that ...' The admission was that,

> ... certain tenders from Protestant contractors such as Courtney were £2,000 lower than those [sic] accepted, but influences from outside were brought to bear on the question, representing that, if we chose a Protestant firm, we should lose in prestige what was gained by finance among the persecuted Catholics of Belfast.[3]

There is no indication of the source of the 'influences from outside'. Had it been exclusively clerical, it is likely that the chronicler would have said so. Politically, the area was then dominated by the supporters of 'wee Joe' Devlin, who had wrested the West Belfast parliamentary seat from the Unionists in January 1906. There is no doubt that Devlin himself abhorred sectarianism. But feeling among his rank and file (which would have included many Clonard confraternity men) was running high in that summer. In the aftermath of the Belfast dockers' strike, there were serious riots in the city which climaxed on Sunday and Monday, 11 and 12 August. Indeed, the meeting of the men's Holy Family confraternity, due on Tuesday 13 August, was cancelled, 'for fear of embroiling the members in the Street Riots that prevailed as a result of the dockers' strike and the "peaceful" picketing that followed'. The chronicler's account of the August rioting is as unapologetically partisan as it is inaccurate in several respects:

> ... The Unionists and capitalists diverted trouble from themselves by posting the military on the Falls Road to provoke the Nationalists. Hired gangs of Orange rowdies added fuel to the flame, raising faction cries and songs at the opening of the side streets. To bring matters to a climax, cavalry were directed to charge up and down the Falls, the Riot Act was read without satisfactory warning by a blagard [sic] Orange magistrate, and two Catholics were killed, while many were wounded by the discharge of

musketry ... Needless to describe the frantic fury of the Nationalists who, at once, proceeded to purchase arms privately ...

The chronicler claimed that one of the dead was a Clonard confraternity man who 'was to have been married on the morrow'. There was no doubt in his mind who 'the real miscreants' were: '... the wealthy sweaters and members of the Orange corporation whose record is so notorious as to need no comment.'[4]

While the 'miscreants' named were delighted at the military incursion as a distraction, it was in fact the government which sent in the military, in astonishingly large numbers – two thousand, six hundred soldiers, eighty cavalry and five hundred police. The magistrate later admitted that his reading of the Riot Act had been inadequate, while the use of live ammunition was against 'King's regulations'. The Clonard chronicler is most accurate in his portrayal of the 'frantic fury' of Falls Road nationalists.[5]

The rector of Clonard, Fr O'Flynn, was one of the first to subscribe to a fund for victims' relatives. He forwarded his subscription 'in a short note expressive of righteous indignation and protest against the outrage perpetrated on Catholic citizens on the public street'.[6]

Given the high pitch of sectarian tension in Belfast that summer, it is perhaps understandable that a major contract was withheld from a Protestant firm, even though its tender was the most competitive. However, at the same time, a much smaller contract (worth less than £400) for building a new hall at the back of the monastery was given to Courtney, named as one of the competitors for the church. The purpose of the new hall was twofold. In the short term, it was to replace the main entrance to the monastery while the church building was proceeding. But it was actually designed as a reception area for the poor who came to the monastery seeking alms. Their 'congested numbers' usually blocked the main entrance and 'rendered it very unpleasant for the introduction of any respectable visitors who happened to call'. In fact, Courtney greatly disappointed the Redemptorists by his 'systematic delay' and 'exasperating dodgery and trickery employed to prolong the job'. Only the threat to refuse him a 'testimonial' finally induced him to finish.[7]

Laying the foundation stone - Bishop Tohill

The first sod of the new church was turned by the Clonard rector, Fr O'Flynn, on 20 August 1907, the feast of St Bernard of Clairvaux. But it was October of the following year before the foundation stone was laid. The Redemptorists had planned this event for Sunday 19 July 1908, appropriately the titular feast of their Belfast foundation, the Most Holy Redeemer. The organist, M. de Meulmeester, had composed a special Mass for the feast. While it was probably intended for the occasion of laying the foundation stone, the new composition was given its première – and was 'executed with great éclat'. The reason for the delay in the traditional formality was the sudden death of Dr Henry on 8 March 1908, followed by the lengthy process of appointing a successor, Fr John Tohill, whose episcopal consecration took place on 20 September. Just a fortnight later, he obliged the Redemptorists by solemnly blessing the foundation stone of the new Clonard church on Rosary Sunday, 4 October.

The chronicler's account of the celebratory banquet on this occasion strongly reflects the pleasure of the Clonard community at the reaction of their Down and Connor guests to the antics of Fr Convery, ' ... whose name the common people associated with the opposition to our church'. Fr Convery,

> who sat at the Bishop's right, collared and monopolised his conversation during the dinner to the intense amusement of the clerical guests present, for he was publicly connected with the clique who were supposed to have signed a petition at a secret meeting to protest against his nomination by Rome.[8]

One passage in the chronicler's account of the ceremony provides an interesting insight into the behaviour of some of the 'Clonard faifhful':

> Once the outdoor ceremony had concluded, Bishop Tohill was mobbed and clapped on the back by an enthusiastic throng ... The attempt to reform the solemn procession after the blessing had to be abandoned. As the proceedings cannot be described as dignified and rubrical ... nonetheless they were a magnificent display of faith and devotion.

And that was not the end. When the bishop left the monastery at six in the evening, the enthusiastic back-slapping was repeated.

Finally, there was a tribute to the behaviour of other 'Clonard faithful':

> ... the people who live in the environs of our monastery, notwithstanding their poverty and the hard times, had gone to the expense of procuring flags and banners which they proudly hung from their windows to show their welcome for the new bishop on this glad occasion.[9]

Bankruptcy of the contractor

The building of the new church was beset with difficulties. Early in 1909, certainly by March, the McNaughton brothers 'experienced great difficulty with the (unnamed) quarrying company which ultimately broke up'. In particular, the quarry was unable to supply the foundation blocks for the granite pillars in the nave. This caused considerable delay and 'demoralised the workers', until another company took over and substantial progress was made. Then a Newry company failed to supply the pillars, so that they had to be ordered from Aberdeen.[10]

Accumulated problems brought the contractors' finances to crisis point about May 1910. The chronicle, under the date of 21 May, noted the brothers as 'in great straits', explaining that an immediate cause of this was that the Mount Charles stone they were using proved harder to cut than expected and this 'swelled their expenses'. More broadly, the brothers appear to have risked an unspecified 'undertaking' without sufficient capital to provide against emergencies. It seems, indeed, according to the 1922 'Foundation' account, that for some time the Redemptorists had been forced 'to raise large loans ... and advance the money to the builders so that the work might go on,' though this cannot be corroborated from contemporary evidence. Inability to 'meet current acounts' forced the McNaughtons to lay off workers, 'with the result that the work dragged on interminably and constituted an endless drain on their resources'. Then, when the building was 'about three-quarters finished', Ambrose McNaughton ('the brains, the carrier of the two brothers') died towards the end of May and Daniel, bankrupt, withdrew from the contract.

Architect assumes control

The architect, J. J. McDonnell, assumed control. He sublet various contracts, 'a tedious and expensive affair', the most important of which was the completion of the stonework. This was arranged with the Amalgated Stonecutters Society, (otherwise referred to as 'the Amalgamated Unions of local masons and stonecutters').[11] By mid-July they were noted as giving 'great annoyance' to the Clonard community because they prolonged 'interminably' the job of finishing the turrets and the limestone wall along Clonard Gardens enclosing the church grounds. When the Redemptorists proposed speeding up the work 'by getting the stones cut at the quarries for cheapness', the craftsmen threatened to strike.[12]

On 7 October, the architect reported to the provincial superior on the overall position of the church building. He had obtained details of all the accounts due by the McNaughtons, which amounted to a few pounds under £700. The largest debts, each around £200, were due to J. P. Corry & Co. (for timber), to T. Murphy & Son (bricks) and to United Stone Firms (for 'Shamrock and Mount Charles Stone'); other local contractors owed smaller amounts were N. MacNaughton & Sons (cement), Joseph Milliken (lead), John Currie & Co. (nails, etc.), W. Macfarlane & Co. (spouting) and George Jones (metalwork). If these could be paid off, then the Redemptorists would be legally free of the MacNaughtons and, at the start of the following week, McDonnell and the clerk of works (who, incidentally, was a nephew of Fr Griffith, now provincial superior) would assume responsibility for all accounts.

McDonnell's summary of the financial state of the building, as of 7 October 1910, showed that the initial contract price for the church was £20,600. Extras agreed on came to £570.11.6, bringing the gross outlay to £21,170.11.6. On the credit side, £20,636 were accounted for by certificates. This left a debit of £534.11.6.[13]

The Rector Major, Fr Patrick Murray, was not happy with the funding of the debt. In an anxious letter from New York, where he had just completed a visitation of North American houses, he provided Fr Griffith with a financial refresher course:

> ... You seem to forget about the arrangements of paying for the Church in Belfast. They are the following:1) Your debt must never exceed £15,000. 2) Your bill in the bank must not exceed £10,000. The rest of the £15,000 or less, as required, is to be supplied by the province. [pencilled insertion: 'At 3½%']. In case the province or Limerick or Dundalk cannot supply it otherwise, they can do so by selling their stock and reinvesting it in Clonard at 3½%. You have all permissions for this sale. It [sic] was sent from Rome by Fr Magnier.

Fr Murray had hoped that, on account of the delay in the building, the Redemptorists might have managed without selling any stock, but he appreciated that, in 'the new arrangement with MacNaughton' (that is, his withdrawal from the contract), it might be necessary. In any case, he wanted to know what the overall financial position was, '... the amount of the debt up till now and the amount still required to make [the church] fit for service'. In particular, he presumed that the high altar would be finished for the opening.[14]

'On the subject of the high altar' – Mr Davis of Cork

On the very day Murray was writing to Griffith, so too was the architect – on the subject of the high altar and the man who had won the contract to build it, John F. Davis of College Road, Cork. J. J. McDonnell's letter led to a heated exchange of correspondence between Fr Griffith and Davis which might possibly have placed the altar project in jeopardy. The correspondence provides an insight into the minute problems of the design and building of a large church on the one hand, and the misunderstandings between those involved on the other, all of which weighed heavily on those bearing overall responsibility. Fr Griffith may well have looked back on his early troubles with the Clonard site as a minor irritation in comparison.[15]

The immediate cause of McDonnell's letter was his accidental discovery that a change had been made in the design of a central feature of the high altar. The feature in question was the elliptical 'throne niche' above the tabernacle, in which the monstrance would be displayed at times of solemn eucharistic exposition. A seriously complicating factor was the degree of involvement in the planning and design of the church of Fr Murray, first as rector of Clonard and then as provincial superior, until he left for the General Chapter in Rome which elected him Rector Major. His sudden departure left many details unresolved. Another complication was the extent to which Murray had involved Fr Henry Berghman, a Belgian member of Clonard community, in discussions and meetings, to such an extent that Berghman, in a series of long, minutely detailed (and minutely, but beautifully, scripted) letters to Fr Griffith, assumed the role of guardian of the artistic integrity of the enterprise. Of Berghman's artistic gifts there seems no doubt, but a busy provincial superior can only have been seriously irritated by the frequency, length and style of letters which are Heep-like in their protestations of humility and yet quote 'Fr General' in virtually every paragraph, thereby identifying the writer as the long-time confidant of the new boss in Rome.

The 'throne niche' was one of the design details left unresolved at Fr Murray's departure. The dispute about it was very much a storm in a teacup. Unfortunately, Davis took very personally McDonnell's just complaint that he (Davis) had been wrong not to have informed the architect of the design change. The situation was not helped by the fact that, in the course of the correspondence, Griffith showed himself strongly on McDonnell's side, keenly aware that the architect now carried full responsibility for completing the church. In particular, in portraying McDonnell as a man of fair play, Griffith nevertheless concluded: '[he] will not be dictated to by those working under him,' words which drew from Davis the bitter response: 'I thank you for pointing out to me that I am only to be considered a common workman.'

The most difficult phase of the dispute was when Davis, smarting under imagined insults, laid down his conditions for the actual assembling of the altar. Having informed Griffith that he had about two-thirds of the marble work packed into fourteen cases ready for shipment, he insisted: ' ... before I send this on I would like that you would make certain that the new church is ready for commencing the work.' And he continued:

> For if on my arrival there everything in the nature of scaffold, piles, etc., etc., are not cleared out of the church – and the builder's men quite finished with the interior – I could not begin work.

(Note: Fr Griffith had underlined this passage in red ink, concluding with a triple exclamation mark). Davis gave two reasons for his conditions. The first was to ensure that the marble was not damaged by workmen. The second was that he had had such a chaotic experience constructing the altar in Esker that he could not face a similar prospect in Clonard.

Griffith's reply was stern, though it is hard not to imagine a hint of tongue-in-cheek:

> If the Czar of Russia were giving orders for his reception some place he could not assume a more arrogant tone ... Let me settle the question at once. Everything in the nature of scaffold, etc., will not be cleared out and you will begin or someone else in your place. You say it will take four or

> five months to build the altar and yet you have everyone cleared out before you begin! When might we be expected to open the church?

The letter concluded with assurances that the marble for the high altar would be protected from damage and that Davis would be given plenty of room in which to work.

Peace was restored following a letter of apology from Davis to Griffith in which he also indicated that he had made up his differences with McDonnell. Griffith replied in conciliatory and complimentary terms:

> ... your letter, just received ... has quite disarmed me. I found fault with your manner of address, but I admire your manly way of apologising. The former may have arisen from you not adverting to the force of your words. The latter showed the courage of a man not afraid to say I have made a mistake. The trouble about the altar was a misunderstanding – no need for apportioning the blame. ... You being a 'workman' who has worked his way up to be an employer of labour I consider your greatest reason for pride. I wish we had more such in Ireland. Teach your children to follow your example in this, but teach them also to measure their words and be temperate in dispute.

On the practical matter of his working conditions in Clonard, the provincial assured Davis that he would have ample space: ' ... the sanctuary where you will be working is 70' x 35', a nice sized church in itself,' which he would instruct McDonnell to clear out as far as possible.

With peace restored, Davis's final letter addressed the immediate problems of getting a first consignment of twelve cases of the altar marble to Belfast. It would be shipped from Cork in a few days. His son would travel to Belfast, supervise the transfer of the cases to Clonard, unpack and store the contents. He would himself follow the second consignment with his men to start erecting the altar and promised that 'when we do get to work we will do our utmost to get it finished soon'.

Finally, the man so often quoted (or misquoted) in all the correspondence about the high altar, Fr General Patrick Murray, had this to say to the provincial: 'I am sorry I ever undertook that altar and did not reproduce Limerick altar. There has been so much friction, especially for Mr McDonnell. However, Davis should get a fair chance as it is not his fault.' Murray – and Clonard – were more committed to Davis than Griffith was possibly aware, for the contract with Davis for the high altar, with Our Lady's and Sacred Heart altars, had been signed nearly two years previously, around 25 January 1909. There had been no unanimity about the altar designs from the start, as the domestic chronicle records: 'The designs of these altars which occasioned heated discussions and protracted criticisms for and against their suitability, were mainly contributed by Rev Fr Berghman.'[16]

Murray was not the only one to have regrets about the high altar. The unidentified author of the 1922 'Foundation' account mentioned earlier was very blunt in his criticism of,

> a high altar designed by the late Rev Henry Berghmans [sic] C.Ss.R. It looks well from the end of the church but has been much criticised. It is immense and not in keeping with the architecture of the church.[17]

The high altar was reduced in height at a later date which, unfortunately, cannot be precisely identified.

Anxieties about funds

In response to Murray's continuing anxieties about funds, J. J. McDonnell drew up, in April 1911, an estimate of the cost of completing the church. He set out specific amounts, totalling £2,265.18.6, under various headings: drainage, masonry, brick work, cut stone work ('exclusive of pinnacles'), carpenter and joiner, slating, plumbing, ironmongery, plastering, glazing and painting, extras for lead lights, fibrous plaster, asphalt roofing, holy water stoups, completion of electric lighting, heating work, contract for tiling, 'contract Earley for communion rail (£287).' Four contracts with J. F. Davis of Cork are listed separately: High Altar £1,500, Side (Our Lady's) altar £450, Sacred Heart altar £200, Communion rail for Sacred Heart £35. These make a grand total of £2,185 due to Davis. Further additions to the estimates included contracts for sanctuary steps (£71) and for completing the pinnacles of the church (£900).

Fund raising

The rector of Clonard, Fr Edward O'Laverty, had, meantime, made his arrangements for a postal appeal for funds. He had had 3,000 copies of a short circular prepared. It read:

> The Redemptorist Fathers, Belfast, ask your aid towards their new Church which is to be opened on Rosary Sunday, 1st October. Since it was begun four years ago many things which they did not foresee and could not prevent have almost doubled the expected outlay. It is under these circumstances they ask for your help and promise a daily remembrance in the prayers of the community.
> Contributions may be sent to the Very Rev Fr Rector or any Redemptorist Father.
> *Clonard Monastery*
> *Belfast.*

His aim, he told the provincial, was to send the circulars 'wholesale over England, Ireland and Scotland wherever I could get a penny. Nearly 2,000 are ready ... The only [problem?] would be how best to get these to the Belfast folk from whom we may expect anything.' In order to solve the problem, he was having a meeting on the following Sunday 'of gentlemen friendly to the community', as the chronicler put it, 'to act as an advisory committee in the proposal to raise funds for the clearance of our debt: and make arrangements for collection on occasion of opening of new church'. He had met the bishop to make arrangements for the opening and Dr Tohill had given him 'a free hand to do anything I liked to get money'. The bishop also promised 'the usual collection' in the Belfast churches of the diocese to coincide with the opening.[18]

The advisory committee consisted of two solicitors, Frank Kerr of Belfast and Thomas Maguire of Holywood, Dr Patrick McStay, Mr. Devine of Hughes's Bakery on Springfield Road, J. J. McDonnell, the architect of the church and 'Mr. McDonnell of Leeson Street'. Mr. Caffrey, proprietor of the Glen Road Brewery, missed the meeting but called afterwards with a suggestion that a list of subscribers drawn up recently by Fr Hubert CP, of Ardoyne, could be used for the Clonard appeal. The chronicler was quite dismissive of the meeting. It,

> did not serve much purpose as no definite programme was prepared or submitted to them for discussion and would have proved a fiasco except for some practical suggestions ... by Mr Thomas Maguire who afterwards came with a list of subscribers he had ... [drawn] up of his own accord.

Such criticism seems to suggest that Fr O'Laverty was not a man of business – he had admitted to Fr Provincial that he was 'rather nervous' about the approaching meeting. However, the meeting agreed on a scale of 'entrance charges' to the church on opening day. They were: '5s. for the centre or nave and 2s.6d. for the sides or aisles' in the morning and, in the evening, 2s. and 1s. respectively.[19]

In any case, the circulars were posted to clerical and lay friends of the Redemptorists in Ireland, England and Scotland. O'Laverty looked to Griffith for advice about Armagh: 'What is the [situation] with the Cardinal (Logue)? I should like to know before sending any to Armagh.' The response must have been negative, for the archdiocese was not circularised, nor were Derry or Down and Connor, probably because of their current financial burdens.[20]

Preparations for opening

In the course of September, preparations for the opening of the church proceeded apace. The imminent visit of the new Rector Major (on 9 September) provided an incentive to get the site cleared – the temporary fence enclosing the church was taken down, the huts and site offices were removed, the concrete piers which had supported the large cranes were demolished and various items of equipment were sold off.[21] On 21 September, advertisements were placed for three consecutive days in the *Irish News* and *Derry Journal*,

with a view to invite the attendance of contributors and appeal for subscriptions ... Collection cards were also printed and, by the kind offices of
the St Vincent de Paul Society, distributed through the agency of local
booksellers.

Preparations for the new church were tinged with genuine regret at the forthcoming departure from the old 'tin' church. As early as April-May 1911, the
Clonard chronicler had been 'counting down' the 'last retreat' in the old
church for each of the confraternities, Our Lady's Sodality 23 April-1 May,
Holy Family Men 1-7 May and Holy Family Boys' 7-14 May. The chronicle
recorded what must have been a concession to the last retreatants to mark the
end of an era, despite the stated reason for it:

> The old church being rather congested, the Provincial on this occasion of
> General communion permitted the women as well as the [men] to enter
> the garden where they wandered about chatting with one another and
> prying into the mysteries of the place.[22]

In that last phrase, surely the chronicler caught something of that fascination
which the enclosed life of the monastery holds for devout lay people and
explains, in part, the great loyalty of the people of Clonard to the Redemptorist
community during the past hundred years.

Official opening of the new church

With Dr Tohill's permission, Fr Murray had blessed the new church on
Saturday 30 September. He then said the first Mass at the high altar, while
his secretary, Fr Howell, said the first Mass at the Sacred Heart altar. These
were private Masses. On opening day,

> the usual succession of Masses from 7 to 11 o'clock was celebrated in the
> old church and after the 11 o'clock Mass the old church was finally closed,
> to the sorrow of many devout people, especially among the poor.

'Providentially,' recorded the chronicle, 'the morning of 1 October was bright
and clear, the fitting harbinger of such an eventful day ...' Catching the
enthusiasm of the occasion, it continued:

> ... a great throng of people had been waiting in the avenues leading to the
> new church, the poor who had hoarded their slender offerings for this
> occasion, mingling with the wealthy who had come for the purpose of
> contributing to our debt fund. V. Rev. Fr. Provincial [Griffith], assisted by
> Bro. Bernard, rang the bell for the first public Mass in the new edifice ...
> The nave and aisles were comfortably filled, the upper tribune was occu-
> pied by Christian and de la Salle Brothers and by Bon Secours nuns and
> Sisters of Charity, while the lower tribune was sparsely occupied by the
> people. The sanctuary was full of attendant clergy; but the church was not
> overcrowded by reason of the exceptional entrance charge.

This account would suggest that the enthusiasm of the occasion was tempered by the necessity of using it to best economic advantage in order to make inroads on the heavy debts of the church. It seems from the narrative that only the lower tribune was reserved for the local people, 'the poor who had hoarded their slender offerings for the occasion,' and that few of them managed the 2s.6d. entrance charge; hence the tribune was 'sparsely occupied'.[23] There is a curious reference to the 'enforced charge' in the domestic chronicle of the following March which suggests either that entrance charges were continued for some time after the opening (although there is no clear evidence for this) or that the imposition of the charges on the opening day had been a source of lingering resentment among the people. At any rate, the chronicle for 12 March 1912 records that, partly because of acoustical problems with the church and 'partly because of the enforced charge and differentiation between the occupants of nave and aisles, [the people] began to drop away from us by degrees'.[24]

The church bell

However, the opening of the church was a joyous occasion symbolised by the ringing of the bell 'for the first public Mass'. The bell had been blessed the previous July by Bishop Tohill on the feast of the Most Holy Redeemer (Sunday 17 July 1910). After High Mass in the old church, a procession had been formed to the new church where the bell was blessed 'before being fixed in its place'. The fixing was completed on the following day and the bell was tested. In the chronicler's account, his joy and enthusiasm are rather spoilt by his Catholic triumphalism:

> The new bell ... for the first time flung out its deep, liquid tones over the
> wide circuit of the adjoining streets and houses, attracting great attention
> – to the joy of the Catholics and the chagrin of the Protestants ...

It is an ancient tradition that a church bell should carry a short history of its maker and of those who caused it to be made. The bell-founder was Matthew O'Byrne of Dublin who, if he is to be judged by his correspondence, was a great enthusiast for his art. In August 1909, he had offered Fr Griffith a choice between a 29 cwt and a 42½ cwt bell, each at £7 per cwt, with fittings extra. Griffith opted for the larger one, for a total of £356.10s.[25]. By October, the bell was ready for casting, a ceremony which O'Byrne thought the provincial might like to attend. Given a few days notice, he wrote,

> ... I will be glad to see you and your friends here when you will see all the
> material going into your bell ... You may rest assured that I will turn you
> out an A1 bell in every sense of the word as I am delighted to get an order
> for a big bell for Belfast. I will leave nothing undone to make the bell a
> great success and you will see the grand material going into it ... the very
> same class of material as I put into the Longford peal of bells.[26]

The inscription on the bell reads:

Matthew O'Byrne, Fountain Head Bell Foundry, James Street, Dublin, 1910 fieri me fecerunt ad laudandum Deum in ecclesia S.S. Redemptoris apud Clonard, Belfast. Reverendissimus Patritius Murray, Rector Major. Adm. Rev. Edward O'Laverty, C.Ss.R., Rector. Plur. Rev. Patritius Griffith, Prov. Hiberniae.[27]

The key phrase in the Latin is: *fieri me fecerunt ad laudandum Deum in ecclesia ... apud Clonard* – '[The following named superiors] caused me to be made to praise God in the church of the Most Holy Redeemer at Clonard, Belfast.'

The High Mass

The celebrant of the High Mass at noon was Fr Augustine O'Flynn, 'late rector and present minister [second in command]' of Clonard, chosen as celebrant for 'his usually beautiful tenor voice' which 'never was heard to better effect' than on this special occasion. Dr Tohill presided at the Mass 'in Cappa Magna', that is, wearing his long cloak, which was an abbreviated way of indicating that he was robed for a very solemn occasion.

Celebratory banquet: Speech of Most Rev Fr Murray

When the ceremonies had concluded, the bishop and invited clergy were given a banquet. The sole interest of the Clonard chronicler in his record of the occasion was in the speech of Fr Murray, the Rector Major and Superior General of the Redemptorists. Murray was presiding over a major event in his own house, as it were, the house where he had been prefect of students and lecturer in moral theology since 1900, then rector until 1907, before being appointed Irish Provincial superior and finally, in 1909, elected Rector Major of the whole Congregation.

The speech was, by turns, humorous and serious, tactful and direct. Quoting St Alphonsus as wishing to found an order of priests 'to work in harmony with the bishops and clergy of our dioceses,' he began by thanking the bishop and priests of Down and Connor, the bishop in particular for his 'princely gift' to the Clonard building fund and for his generous invitation to appeal to the diocese for further funds. This invitation Fr Murray declined, 'on the grounds that we should depend on Divine Providence for the necessary assistance'.

The speaker then employed great humour to make a serious reply to one of the most persistent opponents and critics of Clonard who was present on the occasion, the parish priest of the adjacent St Paul's, Fr Convery. Repeating that he would not be making any further financial appeals to the people, Fr Murray,

praised the priests for their seasonable aid. He particularly thanked 'good

Fr Convery' for his large subscription, a reference so diplomatic and humorous that it raised a roar of laughter; and thanked him for sending his people to our church. The priests enjoyed the joke of the situation because, first, Fr Convery, the PP of St Paul's neighbouring parish was known to have frequently interfered with the freedom of both children and adults to attend our church or join our confraternities; secondly, because he had spoilt his own church by enlarging it so as to absorb some of our congregations; and, thirdly, because he was credited by public opinion with the most active share in the influence with the late bishop (Dr Henry) which resulted in curtailing the size and spoiling the proportions of our new church – though he dissembled in this respect, it is of interest to add that one of our fathers who happened to walk with him in the opening procession, hearing his remark that it was a fine edifice and amply spacious – 'Yes,' replied the latter, 'quite large enough for our purpose; and we owe our acknowledgements to those who tried to have it cut down though they did not mean to confer a benefit.' The silence and open-eyed wonder with which this remark was received showed that it had shot the mark and gone home. However, on this particular day he had encouraged his parishioners to patronise our church; and, in announcing the collection for Clonard had said that he wished his parishioners to top the list of the city parishes, which, indeed they did, God bless them for it.

Possibly taking advantage of his new position as a major ecclesiastical figure, Murray concluded by meeting 'very straight the objections of our invidious critics in clerical ranks'. He told them 'the whole truth', that since the foundation of the monastery and as a direct result of its co-operation in their apostolic labours, 'both the attendances and the revenues of the other city churches had tended not to diminish but increase'.[28]

An accoustical embarrassment
Unfortunately, there was one difficulty that marred the opening day and, as the chronicler noted, 'greatly embarrassed both ourselves and the people'. This was the poor acoustics of the church: 'both in the morning and in the evening it was found difficult to follow the words of the preachers on account of the echo in the building.' Acoustics of large buildings were then, and still are to an extent, an imperfect science. Clonard seems to have been particularly unfortunate. The pulpit, the one from the old church, had been placed inside the altar rails, by the pillar on the gospel side. Over the following year, various experiments were tried: a small flat sounding board was placed over the pulpit; though some thought a shell shaped one would be better, it was not tried, but the sounding board did not work. For months, those members of the congregation sitting in the centre aisle 'understood none of the ser-

mons'. This was one factor in the dropping away of the people 'by degrees', noted in March 1912, while 'Anonymous letters on the subject reached the house, rather sarcastic in the nature of their comments.' After a year, it was decided to move the pulpit outside the altar rails but the problem remained. The arrival of a new pulpit, in April 1913, placed further down the nave beside the first pillar from the altar rails, was a great improvement. But acoustical niggles lingered on and were not resolved until 1937, when an 'amplifier or loudspeaker' was installed and used for the first time on Sunday 22 August.[29]

Removal of the old church

With the new church in use, the old one had to be removed. The chronicler records with evident sadness that, during November, it was broken up and sold for scrap. This process revealed that the wooden floor was 'in an advanced state of decay beneath and even dangerously so'. Opinions among the local faithful about the old and new churches varied; one old woman was heard to say 'All the comfort is gone out of Clonard.' Meanwhile, the 'clerical wags' enjoyed winding Fr Convery up about 'the new Clonard building' in order to hear him 'declare that it was not a church but a cathedral or basilica'.[30]

The final passages in the domestic chronicle relating to the new church end, sadly, on a very sour note. Quite frankly, they amount to a savage attack on the workmen who built the church. Taking as his point of departure the ruins of the old church which, by November, formed 'an immense mound inside the enclosure wall', the chronicler continued bitterly,

we had a valuable illustration of Ulster industry in the case of these men who were employed to clear [the rubble] away. They, like the masons and carpenters and the painters and the rest of the skilled artisans, seemed to lay themselves out to prolong their job in the most unscrupulous fashion. It was like a long-drawn agony to watch the whole crowd of them from day to day, month to month and year to year. To make objections meant to create a sympathetic strike: while to suffer them to continue in their wholesale fraud was to see the finances of the monastery bled to exhaustion. Only in the case of the labourers employed to level the garden and the painters engaged to do up the nave were we able to defend ourselves by giving the loiterers the sack. But if all who deserved dismissal for dilatory and fraudulent neglect to do an honest day's work were sent about their business, we should find our last state worse than the first. The only one who came out of this with credit was Mr Davis of Cork who had contracted for the altars. Whatever we may think of his work, he was at any rate up to time and perfectly faithful to his word.[31]

By any standards, this is strong condemnation – of all involved, from craftsmen to labourers over a period of years – with a single exception. Had the chronicler a brainstorm? Was it a 'political' attack by a non-Ulster Redemptorist against Ulster workers? (There was a reference in the monastery chronicle under January 1909: 'much petty rivalry [manifested] itself among the northern workers against the southern workmen to whom their part of the architecture was entrusted during the course of erection.') Or do we get a glimpse here of a dark world of labour relations where industrial chaos reigned, an unpleasant situation which could not be commented on openly but entrusted to the privacy of the monastery chronicle? The state of things described echoes remarkably accurately the contemporary words of the sympathetic Frenchman, Louis Paul-Dubois, when he attacked the 'mental and moral decadence of the [Irish] nation ... [the] general absence of energy and character, of method and discipline' among a people 'distracted by denominational struggles, sectarian fanaticism and the first phases of anti-clericalism'.[32]

An organ worthy of the new church
Since the project to furnish the new church with an appropriate organ was launched at a time when, as it appeared, the church building was in midcourse, it seems fitting to give some account here of its equally difficult history.

A gift from the Clonard Confraternities
Towards the end of 1909, it became apparent that representatives of the men's confraternity had offered to fund a new organ which would be worthy of the new church. The source of the men's inspiration is not clear, but by the time the offer came to light, the project was being actively supported by Fr James Cleere, director of the women's confraternity, and Arthur de Meulemeester, the church organist. The director of the men's confraternity, Patrick Crotty, also supported the idea, though more discreetly than his confrère.

'A thoroughly fine organ' from Evans and Barr
How far thinking about the organ had advanced can be seen in a letter of 31 December from Cleere to the provincial superior, Patrick Griffith. A fund of at least £1,500 had already been decided upon. So, too, had the likely builder of the organ, Evans and Barr of Belfast. Cleere presented a plan. Evans and Barr should be approached 'to prepare a specification in union with our organist,' on the strict understanding that it need not be accepted. The specification would then be submitted to 'a competent authority to see that we are getting real value for money'. If satisfied on this point, Evans and Barr should be given the contract without competition. Fr Cleere expressed the situation persuasively: 'It would sound well and swell the funds: a Belfast

organ, built by a Belfast firm with Belfast money for a Belfast church. Wouldn't that sound fine?' De Meulemeester was quoted as approving what work of Evans and Barr he had seen and was of the opinion that 'it is altogether unlikely that there is any better organ work done in the country!' Cleere offered his own conviction:

> I believe Evans and Barr will be willing to risk even being a little out of pocket in the job for this reason: they want a big show organ for advertisement. We tell them if they do well, we shall say a word for them wherever we go, but if they do not, we shall damn them N, S, E and West and that we go a good deal about the country.

Small wonder that he concluded his letter with the p.s: 'Personally I plump for Evans and Barr.'[33]

That Cleere – advised, and possibly even instructed by de Meulemeester – had assessed Evans and Barr accurately was borne out by Evans' letter of the following September (1910), accompanying the specification for the organ:

> We are extremely anxious to obtain this valuable order and are therefore prepared to offer exceptional value rather than allow it go elsewhere as it would offer us a splendid opportunity of building an instrument second to none in this district.[34]

Disagreement over the outlay

Superior General Murray was puzzled by the figure of £1,500 being assumed by de Meulemeester; his limit was £1,000. In a letter to the provincial superior, de Meulemeester either genuinely or tactically misinterpreted Murray's position:

> Your plan of building in time an organ of £1,500 and spending only £1,000 at the start is next to impossible ... If you decide to spend £1,000 you will get a decent organ but one that is too small for the church. On the other hand, if you ultimately want a big organ, you have to decide at the start that you want a big organ so that the builder can make his preparation for the addition of extra pipes and stops, etc., later on...[35]

Murray assured the provincial that his limit was related to the overall debt on the church: 'If you are able to pay £1,500 and keep your debt under £15,000, I do not see anything against it.' Of course, if the organ were to be funded by 'outsiders', he would make no difficulty about it.[36]

The organ fund – a source of discord

The Clonard Domestic Chronicle, late in 1909, reflected the extent of irritation generated within the community by 'this wretched organ fund'. It noted that, while the confraternity men collected quietly within their membership, 'the lady collectors ... proceeded, with the best will in the world, to traverse the city and beg subscriptions in all directions...'[37]

The ensuing public embarrassment to the Redemptorists was compounded by a split within the women's membership, a small minority preferring that the fund should be applied to a new marble altar rail for the church.

The St Mary's Hall 'Soirée with a Dance'

The division among the ladies reflected a strong difference of opinion among some members of the Clonard community. This came to a head when it emerged that 'a soirée with a dance' was to be organised by the organ fund committee in St Mary's Hall in mid-January 1910. One member of the community, Fr Berghman (the mentor of the minority group among the confraternity women), took grave exception to the idea of a dance as a means of raising funds for Clonard. His stated objection was a moral one: so dangerous was dancing to the morals of those participating and so threatening to the good name of the Redemptorists that the event should be cancelled forthwith. Called upon for their views, the confraternity directors, Patrick Crotty for the men and James Cleere for the women, defended both the event and its organisers, pointing out that such dances were regularly used for fundraising in Down and Connor. Cleere wrote bluntly to his provincial:

> I am not in favour of dancing, but ... Only a lunatic holds that dancing is immoral. To quash the dance which our people contemplate is to tacitly impeach their morality and to believe that they know not how to conduct themselves. This I for one refuse to do ...[38]

And he had no doubt about the source of the discord:

> I shall never be got to believe that the cause of Fr Berghman's intervention is horror of dancing. He may think it is – but it is not ... I believe that if the money was being raised for an altar or altar rail with the condition that Fr Berghman was the designer, there would be very little heard against the method now proposed to get the money.[39]

The final concern of both confraternity directors was that the fund organisers ('real friends') should be saved from the humiliation of having the event cancelled. As Fr Cleere put it: 'The feelings of men like Jimmie McGarry and Hanratty ought to be taken into account. McGarry feels intensely the difficulties...'[40]

Difficulties for the fund-raisers

The St Mary's Hall event was held, but 'the men at the head of the fund' – and the Redemptorists – had not seen the end of their troubles. Raising the money for the organ proved a hugely difficulty undertaking. Griffith was dismayed when he learned, for the first time, in May 1911, that the committee's undertaking to raise £1,500 was 'on the understanding that half the amount would be procured from the "Carnegie Grant for Organs".' While this

Carnegie fund had been mentioned before, it had never been suggested as a condition.[41] As a result, the Clonard community was forced to pay half the amount, 'in order to check the progress of further gossip regarding the collection, leaving the Confraternity committee to refund the balance'.[42]

As a measure of the difficulties experienced, it was January 1912, that is, more than two years since the fund was launched, before the committee was in a position to forward their first payment of £500 to the Redemptorists. This coincided with the beginning of the construction of the new organ (which was completed in May of the same year.) A further sum of £300 was paid over in June, when the committee appeared to be negotiating a loan of £700 from the Munster and Leinster Bank to defray the remainder.[43]

The public view: A triumphant occasion
The wider public would, of course, have been unaware of background tensions. As far as the local media were concerned (which, in practice, meant the *Irish News*), the completion and blessing of the new organ were nothing short of triumphant. The paper chose to emphasise the Irishness of the enterprise, with the sub-headline 'Irish Industrial Triumph'. It also highlighted the musical splendour of the new organ, as 'An instrumnent of musical and artistic perfection', and gave 'Professor Arthur de Meulemeester' an opportunity to describe the technicalities of the new instrument and to provide an historical sketch of the role of the organ in church music. 'The organ is indeed a monument to the patriotism of the Redemptorists and to the ability of Irish workmen and the enterprise and up-to-dateness of an Irish firm,' proclaimed the editorial. However, the Clonard chronicler took quite a different view. Never keen on the organ project, he questioned the Irishness – and Catholicity – of the undertaking, pointing out that much of the work was done by 'English employees' all of whom were, 'unfortunately, Protestants.'[44]

The nobility of the intentions of those behind the fund was never in doubt. Perhaps, given the general economic circumstances of the time and the fact that most of the membership of the confraternities were poor working men and women (as Fr Cleere had noted in January 1910, 'they were subscribing, not out of abundance, but out of their hard-won earnings'), the undertaking was over-ambitious or even injudicious. Certainly the enterprise caused the Redemptorist congregation much embarrassment within the diocese and put strains on their relationship with their own confraternity members. These members were, understandably, unable to appreciate the delicacy of financial relationships between the majority secular and minority regular clergy in a diocese where the vast majority of Catholics were poor and where demands for funding of churches, schools and the Mater Infirmorum Hospital in Belfast were great.

CHAPTER 5

Early 'External Apostolic Labours' from Clonard

The conduct of missions and retreats was one of the fundamental reasons for the existence of the Redemptorists. In 1877, the first edition of the *Directory of Missions for the English Province* (to which, it must be remembered, Ireland then belonged) was published. Its object was 'to secure uniformity, regularity and the true spirit of our holy Founder in the method of conducting our apostolic labours'. The 1877 *Directory* was fully discussed in 1899 at the first provincial consultation of the newly formed Irish province. It was considered highly successful in its object and adopted for Ireland with only minor changes, including the title, which became *Directory of the Apostolic Labours in the Irish Province of the Congregation of the Most Holy Redeemer*.

The *Directory* was a small pocket book of about forty pages which each missioner was recommended to take with him on every mission and to 'observe accurately' what it prescribed. It set out, in minute detail, the duties of each member of the mission team.

For the purposes of this chapter, it is the final section of the *Directory* which is important. That section required the superior of each mission, upon his return to the monastery, to make out a report on the mission on a 'printed form' supplied to him by the chronicler of the house. The chronicler then wrote up the reports in a special book called 'External Apostolate, Missionary Works'. The intention was to provide missioners working in the same parish at a future date with useful information about practical arrangements such as the number of churches, their distance from each other, any special work done in the parish, and so on.[1]

Scope of mission reports
Fortunately for the early history of Clonard, the chronicle of missions and retreats was written up in considerable detail, revealing just how comprehensive the original report forms were. First to be reported on was the number of Catholics in the parish; then the usual occupations of the parishioners; next, the 'spiritual state [of the parish] before [the] mission' was commented on, together with any particular 'abuses' which required attention. We must assume that the missioners (or 'missionaries' as they insisted on calling themselves in the early years) obtained this information from the priests of the

parish, but sometimes the condition of the parish was stated so frankly that the comments hardly came from any self-respecting parochial clergy. Previous missions and retreats were recorded, usually those given within the previous decade or so, but sometimes the record would go back much further. Special ceremonies of the mission, such as the 'Amende' (the ceremony of reparation in honour of the Blessed Sacrament), and the consecration of the parish to the Blessed Virgin were reported; less frequently the Way of the Cross and, rarely in the north, the planting of the mission cross. Statistics for the reception of the sacraments of Penance and Eucharist were invariably given, with a distinction made between confessions heard by the missioners (which was one of the most important benefits for the faithful, according to the tradition of missions) and those heard by other priests.

A particularly interesting feature of the reports is the attention they gave to the provisions made (or very often not made) for the children of the parish during a mission. This stems from the deliberate incorporation of the idea of 'the children's mission' into the Redemptorist strategy. The *Directory* gave very specific details on the subject. Mission superiors were urged to recommend to parish priests the holding of a separate mission for children before the mission for adults. Failing this, it should be held simultaneously. It should ordinarily last a week, but otherwise 'at least a few days'.

The penultimate section of the report considered the state of confraternities, sodalities and similar organisations in the parish. The extent of such groups was quite remarkable, in particular the confraternity of the Sacred Heart (introduced to Ireland in the first half of the nineteenth century) and the young women's sodality of the Children of Mary. Quite remarkable also was the frequency with which sodalities were found by the missioners to be in a poor state. To remedy this, they usually made a number of appeals for new or returned members. These appeals were almost invariably successful in the short term, but long-term success depended on a confraternity being 'worked well'.

The mission report concluded with an assessment of the effect of the mission, supported by evidence and, often, by observations about what was omitted or needed to be done in the future to bring a parish to full spiritual health.[2]

Analysis of mission reports, 1897-1903
This chapter analyses reports on thirty-four missions given by Clonard Redemptorists in northern dioceses between August 1897 and June 1903. Such analysis provides some clear impressions of the practices and problems of parishes one hundred years ago. Occasional reports from later missions are included in order to support earlier material or because they are of particular interest.[3]

Missionary activity by diocesan clergy

The earliest Clonard reports provide interesting evidence that some bishops at the turn of the nineteenth-twentieth centuries engaged some of their diocesan priests in retreat or 'quasi-mission' work. Of the few examples recorded, all but one refer to the diocese of Down and Connor. The odd one is for Raphoe diocese, where, in giving the background notes to their 1903 mission in Termon parish, the Redemptorists reported: 'They have a triduum yearly by seculars,' that is, a three-day retreat or series of spiritual exercises preached by priests of the diocese.

The Down and Connor examples refer to Culfeightrin, Ballygalget, Portglenone, Crossgar and Rasharkin. The Clonard report for the August 1897 Culfeightrin mission notes: 'About three years before, some secular priests preached to them for some days and heard their confessions.' Two months later the observation was made for Ballygalget: 'Various retreats given by secular priests, the last three years previous.' In Portglenone a retreat was given in 1894, 'by some secular priests of the diocese'. Also in 1894, Crossgar, 'Had a quasi-mission ... by secular priest Fr Dan McCashin.' The last reference, from the report of the Rasharkin mission in 1900, informs that '... the C.Ss.R. gave them a mission 11 years ago and since [then] secular priests gave retreats.' The recurrence of the date 1894 in these reports seems to suggest that a particular effort was made in Down and Connor in that year, but missionary activity by priests of the diocese was not confined to it.

'Abuses'

The 'abuse' most frequently commented on (in twenty-one out of thirty missions) was Mass missing (or Mass 'losing' as it was sometimes called), usually in association with 'neglect of sacraments' or 'neglect of frequentation of the sacraments'. Mass missing was a matter of note in Coleraine parish in 1897 and in Portrush ('All summer season, servants and lodging house keepers never hear Mass – all of the Catholics depending for their livelihood on summer visitors'), Portglenone ('Loss of Mass was very habitual'), Larne and Whitehouse in 1898. However, in regard to Whitehouse, a distinction was made between 'the stable inhabitants of the parish [who] are good practical Catholics' and 'a certain proportion [who] are migratory and ... careless about Mass and sacraments'. The Catholic population of Whitehouse was 3,000, 'made up almost entirely of millworkers'. Other parishes notable for neglect of Mass and/or sacraments between 1899 and 1903 were Ligoniel, Portaferry, Crossgar, Rasharkin, Downpatrick and Glenarm, together with Dungiven in Derry diocese and Newry in the diocese of Dromore. However, in a number of instances, great distance from the church was acknowledged as a contributory factor. For example, in Portglenone parish there was, 'only one church, which implies many families are 5 or 6 miles away from church

on Sundays,' similarly in Crossgar, where the parishioners were, 'small farmers and poultry dealers, very much in need of instruction, ... distance for
many was great'. The people of Rasharkin, whose mission in May 1900 and
renewal in June 1901 were both described as 'very successful', turned out 'in
large numbers. ... The good attendance was all the more remarkable considering that most of the people live three miles from the church ...'. In Beragh
(archdiocese of Armagh), 'many had to come 4 or 5 miles to church' and in
Glenarm, some parishioners were 'very far from the principal church and
there [were] bad roads'. The same problem of distance from the church
seemed to lie behind the bitter complaint from some parishioners of
Tullylish/Gilford (diocese of Dromore), 'of the insufficient number of priests
and Masses, as communicants had to fast till late Mass'.

'Mixed marriages,' non-Catholic environments
'Mixed marriages' were noted as a particular abuse in Carrickfergus and
Coleraine (both 1897), in Portrush/Bushmills and Larne (1898 and in subsequent missions in both parishes in 1901), in Glenarm (1903) and clearly
implied in Killyleagh (1899). Because of mixed marriages, there was 'a want
of faith in considerable numbers' in Carrickfergus. In Portrush/Bushmills, the
children of mixed marriages were 'brought up in heresy and freemasonry';
such marriages, combined with 'the evil influence of Protestantism', led to a
situation in the parish where, 'there is not much religious fervour among the
people in spite of the zeal of the parish priest,' Fr John Campbell. A contributory factor was the small Catholic presence in the district, a mere three-hun-
dred ('publicans, servants, coastguards, fishermen') in a population of nearly
3,500. In a later mission in the same parish in 1904, Fr M. Magnier wrote
vividly of 'the chilling Presbyterian atmosphere' which made it hard for the
few Catholics 'to maintain the warmth of their faith and its practice'. It was
a public fact that many had 'become cold and almost entirely neglect the
practice of their religion' and he regretted that there were 'several who did not
answer the invitation to the mission'. Larne was in similar circumstances,
with just 1,500 Catholics in a population of 7,000. (In 1904, the 'particular
abuses' were reported there as 'apostasy from the faith and public concubi-
nage'.) It is not entirely surprising that neither parish had a sodality or confraternity of any kind. The missioners' opinion was that, in Portrush a confraternity 'would not be attended to' and in Larne 'there seemed no prospect
of keeping it up'. In Killyleagh, there was a serious imbalance in the Catholic
population, with very few men and the women mostly unmarried. The lack
of men is explained by the absence of employment opportunities for Catholic
men in a predominantly Protestant area where linen was the principal source
of work, hence Catholic men had to migrate, whereas Catholic women were
always in demand in the lower paid spinning sector of linen. This imbalance

in an already small Catholic population (750 out of 3,000) produced a pastoral problem: 'The young women growing up, if they keep company, keep it with Protestants. Hence – .'

Missioners were always sensitive about the negative effects on Catholics of living in a predominantly Protestant environment. Given the widespread inter-denominational hostility in the late-nineteenth and early twentieth centuries, it is not surprising that their views of other denominations were sometimes expressed in blunt language which was intended, of course, for private consumption only. Ahoghill was 'the centre of a decidedly strong Presbyterian element'. A mission in the Catholic parish there in 1905 revealed the extent of the fall from faith and practice among the parishioners. This was due, however, not only to what the missioners regarded as a hostile religious environment, but also to 'the terribly neglected state of the parish during the last thirty or forty years'. While missionary priests tended to measure neglect in a parish by the absence of missionary work, the fact that the last mission in Ahoghill had been given by a Jesuit priest in 1865 was truly remarkable by Down and Connor standards. Results of neglect were, on the one hand, that 'many [had] lost the faith practically by never going to Mass, confession or communion' and, on the other, the parish school was on the verge of extinction – there were only eighteen pupils 'inclusive of infants ...; the others, being distant, frequent non-Catholic schools'. Uniquely, the missioners identified 'no marriages' as an 'abuse' in the parish. During the mission, 'A number of the children were taken from the Protestant schools and some grown children that had been neglected on account of mixed marriages were baptised.' The mission was considered a success for a most unusual reason, namely, 'the fact that the people came to the mission at all'. The forty or so Catholics in the Cullybackey end of the parish were always portrayed by the missioners (1905, 1906, and, later, in 1920) as in a very precarious position. Fr Griffith, the founder of Clonard, was a veteran of seventy-five years of age in 1920. He was still, as in the early days of Clonard, seeing all Protestants as Orangemen. So, he reported of Cullybackey and its Catholic faithful (grown to fifty in number by 1920): 'This is a very Orange district with very few Catholics who have to struggle for an existence among this Orange crowd.'

Intemperance

Excessive drinking was recorded as a particular abuse in seven of thirty-four parishes. These were Ligoniel, where the Catholic population of about 1,000 were 'millworkers'; Newry, Larne, Glenarm, St Paul's, Belfast ('The abuse of drink is all too prevalent' in a district of 10,000 Catholics' – 1899), Portglenone ('among some of the men' – 1898) and Downpatrick, where in 1901 the missioners noted 'inveterate habits of drinking among the men and women of the working class'. While such few reports of alcohol abuse as a special problem may surprise the modern reader, so too must the even sparser records of temperance societies or confraternities. Only five of the thirty-four parishes had any form of temperance society or confraternity, namely, Coleraine (1897) and Carnlough (1900), Beragh (1901), Glenarm (1903) and Tullylish/Gilford (1903), but only in the last named could it be said to have been flourishing. In Coleraine, the 'Saturday League was commenced' at the Redemptorist mission of November-December 1897: 'It is a new temperance movement introduced by the bishop Dr Henry into his diocese lately.' However, at the mission renewal a year later, an exhortation to the people to join both it and the other confraternities in the parish met 'with very little success'.

The 'Saturday League' was strongly promoted within the Clonard confraternities, particularly during the very first annual retreats to men and women, in March-April 1898. Many men and women joined the League and over 1,000 leaflets explaining it were distributed to the ladies. The 'Temperance Association' in the parish of Beragh was 'almost defunct' at the mission of June 1901; a year later it was noted as 'not well worked'. Similarly, the 'Temperance confraternity' in Glenarm in 1903 was 'in bad condition'. While 'about 150 men and as many women' joined the 'Total Abstinence Association' at the Carnlough mission of May 1900, its progress a year later is not recorded. However, in Tullylish/Gilford, the Anti-Treating League was 'in good condition'; it appears to have been started on the initiative of some of the parishioners. The temperance movement in nineteenth-century Ireland had a fitful history. The early work of the great Capuchin, Fr Theobald Mathew (1790-1856) did not endure. New attempts begun in the 1880s were to prove more permanent, culminating in the foundation of the Pioneer Total Abstinence Association in 1898.

'Company keeping'
'Company keeping' was mentioned but once – without definition – as a local 'abuse'. That was at the Portglenone mission of May-June 1898, where the practice was 'prevalent' but 'was put a stop to' as a result of the mission. Portglenone had the added problem of 'The "Society of Ribbon-men"' in the parish, a rare survival of one of the agrarian movements of the nineteenth century; but, like company keeping, it was 'given up' by the end of the mission. Portglenone, incidentally, was the only parish from which missioners' reports reflect any overt sectarian tension. It was noted during the 1898 mission (held in late May-early June) that, 'Owing to bad blood between the Catholics and Orangemen, the evening service had to be shortened somewhat so as not to keep the people out late.' Catholics made up just about one-third of the population of the locality. Nearby Toomebridge, its Catholic population

of 1,500 made up 'mostly [of] farmers and fishermen', suffered in 1905 from a 'prevalence of secret societies'; but, as a result of the mission, 'a number of Fenians retired from [the] secret society'.

'Tariffs' or admission charges

An occasional abuse, difficult for the late twentieth-century Catholic to comprehend, was the levying of admission charges to the various exercises of the mission. At the Loop church in Moneymore, county Derry (archdiocese of Armagh), 'heavy charges at the beginning' of the 1898 mission were regarded by the Redemptorists P. P. Murray and Patrick Leo as one of the obstacles to the success of the undertaking. The people were not prepared for the mission: 'They looked upon it as a scheme for making money' on the part of the parish priest. Similar views were expressed two years later at Dungiven (Derry diocese):

> The general impression was that the object of the mission was to get money. The charges at the door kept the people away. Charges [were] 4d. a.m. and p.m. on weekdays. On Sundays 6d., 1s., and 2s.

In Beragh, the charge was a more modest one penny at the morning exercises, but the missioners were convinced that it 'deterred' at least some parishioners from attending. A subsequent mission in Dungiven in 1905 showed no improvement in the matter of charges. 'The objectionable method of collecting tariff at the morning and evening services' was listed with the weather, the state of the crops, and the great distance many parishioners had to travel to the church as one of the difficulties in the way of the mission. The tariff had clearly soured the relationship between priests and people in several rural areas of the parish. It was a contributory factor in Mass-missing and neglect of the sacraments and was responsible for 'an utter absence of the usual enthusiasm' the Redemptorists experienced on missions. The one consolation was the excellent response at Drumsurn church, 'as the unpleasant relations between clergy and laity did not affect this locality to the same extent as other parts of the parish'.

Spiritual neglect of children

Finally, the keeping of children from school was noted as a particular abuse in two parishes, Bellaghy (Derry diocese) and Newcastle (Down and Connor). In Bellaghy (1901), the 'neglect in sending children to school and catechism' was countered by special attention to the children during the first week of the mission. They had 'daily Mass and instruction. Their confessions were heard and there was a general communion.' In Newcastle (1902), the only 'particular abuse' in the parish recorded by the missioners was 'the absence of children from school owing to golfing being played in the locality'. Young boys were frequently employed as caddies in the early part of this

century. Evidently the few pennies they earned were genuinely more important to some parents than attendance at school. As in Bellaghy, the Newcastle
children received special attention during the mission; they were 'given a few
instructions, their confessions heard and a general communion'.

Given the well-developed ideas of the Redemptorists about children's missions, it is not entirely surprising that their reports reflected a general awareness among the missioners that children were neglected during mission time.
'Nothing was done for children,' was noted several times. Since a mission was
usually planned in advance between parish priests and missioners, the omis-
sion of arrangements for children must have been a deliberate decision by the
former. However, we must assume that the main reason was lack of time. The
usual length of a mission, certainly in rural areas, was two weeks and within
that time there was a mountain of work to be done with the adults, among
whom were the slackers and the hardened sinners, whose conversion was one
of the main objects of a mission. However, special arrangements were made
for the children wherever possible, as in the example of the renewal in
Drumquin parish (Derry diocese) in June 1903. The renewal was,

> given to a great extent for the sake of the children for whom nothing
> could be done during the mission [twelve months previously]. The
> schools were closed during the week and the children attended with great
> punctuality and in great numbers.

Parish confraternities
Confraternities and sodalities had, for a long time, been seen in Ireland as a
great pastoral aid in support of the faith life of the parish. The Clonard
reports indicate the existence of a considerable variety of parish confraternities (or sodalities or associations, as they were variously called). By far the
most popular was the confraternity of the Sacred Heart, recorded in at least
eighteen out of thirty-one parishes. There followed the Children of Mary, for
women, in seven parishes; the Apostleship of Prayer was noted in five parishes;
the Holy Family confraternity seems to have been confined to men and boys
and is noted in these reports as found only in Belfast parishes: St Mary's, St
Patrick's and St Peter's, in each of which it was paralleled by the Children of
Mary Sodality for the women. It was found also in Clonard church, where
the Redemptorists had a promising Holy Family confraternity for men
alongside one for women under the patronage of Our Lady of Perpetual
Succour and Saint Alphonsus. The Redemptorists had a Holy Family branch
for boys, as had St Patrick's. The Society of St Vincent de Paul, established in
Ireland as early as 1845, was recorded by the missioners as a confraternity.
While they mention it specifically in only one parish, Coleraine, it was evidently strong in Belfast, for St Mary's, Chapel Lane, hosted a week-long
retreat for '500 men of St Vincent de Paul Society' in August 1898 which was

preached by the Redemptorists. The only other sodalities recorded were those of the Holy Rosary and the Brown Scapular, both in Clogher parish (1900) and neither 'in a good condition'. Finally, in Tullylish/Gilford (1903) the Living Rosary Sodality was 'in a poor condition ...[with] no meetings in connection with it'.

A particular objective of missionaries was to ensure that, as far as lay in their power – naturally in co-operation with the priests of a parish – they left confraternities and sodalities in as healthy a state as possible. Unfortunately, taken in the round, their reports give a disappointing account of the state of these associations in the parishes in which they worked.

So, for example, in the year 1897, the confraternities of the Children of Mary and the Sacred Heart in the parish of Coleraine 'existed, but it was hard to find any trace of them'. A renewal in the following year included an exhortation to the people to join, 'but with little success'. At the same period, in Culfeightrin, the Apostleship of Prayer 'had died out through the death and change of priests'; of the parish's Sacred Heart confraternity, the missioners reported, '[it] had existed, but had been given up for some time'. They had tried to revive it in a mission renewal in October 1898, evidently without success, because in December 1901 the parish priest asked for a retreat, one of whose objects was 'to establish a confraternity already twice established and fallen through'. Another revival of a Sacred Heart confraternity was attempted during the Carrickfergus mission of October 1897. The 'greater number' of the parishioners had given their names to it 'in the past', but the response this time was a meagre fifty names. One revival which was successful was in Ballygalget parish, also in October 1897. On that occasion, the people – 'of simple habits ... [and] attentive to their religious duties' – readily joined the restored Sacred Heart confraternity. As a result, in May 1899, the Redemptorists could report, 'Now there were very few in the parish who were not members,' and they recorded the spiritual state of the parish as 'excellent'. The following month, the Sacred Heart sodality in Portaferry was found 'in a very flourishing state' and that in Killyleagh (October-November 1899) 'had done great things among the people'. However, Glenravel's was 'not in a good state; the clergy did not take much interest in it'. (May 1900) At the same time, while the Apostleship of Prayer in Carnlough was 'in a good condition', the Sacred Heart sodality was 'not well worked'; similarly, in the Strabane renewal (Derry diocese, June 1900), the Sacred Heart confraternity 'had fallen away since the mission: an exhortation was made but there was no response'. Rasharkin (1900-1) had better results. The Sacred Heart confraternity was revived at the mission in 1900, when two hundred men and three hundred women joined (out of a Catholic population of 2,000); one year later, the five hundred were still in membership and '[had] done well'. Meanwhile, the Sacred Heart sodality in Beragh was 'almost defunct' and

Bellaghy's was 'in a bad condition and no prospect of improvement', while in Newry 'confraternities were not flourishing'. Only a handful of parishes were without confraternities – Portrush and Larne because there was no prospect of keeping them up; no explanations were offered for their absence from Dungiven and Drumquin, while in Glenties parish (diocese of Raphoe) the Redemptorists reported in 1902: 'There is practically no confraternity and the PP did not wish it otherwise.'

The maintenance of a vigorous confraternity, from the evidence given above, seems to have been a task beyond the resources of most parochial clergy. None were more conscious of the difficulties than the Redemptorists themselves. The reports for the years under discussion include details of their retreats to their own confraternities, the men's and boys' Holy Family and the women's confraternity of Our Lady of Perpetual Succour and St Alphonsus. Two quotations, referring to the men's Holy Family, leave no doubt about the problems. The first one relates to March-April 1898, when the confraternity was not yet a year in existence, but had increased in membership from the original sixty to seven hundred men:

The confraternity is young and not yet fully disciplined. Though promising, it will require continual care and visiting to make it what it ought to be. (28 March-3 April 1898)

Just two years later, (April 1900), the membership having increased to one thousand, a tactical change in the timing of the annual retreat was considered necessary in order to counteract a falling away in attendance: 'It was the first time the retreat was held after Easter. It acted as a great corrective. The men usually fell away after Easter time, so the retreat was given April 22nd to 29th.' The Redemptorists in Clonard had one great advantage over their fellow priests in the parishes. They could afford to designate one member of the community whose primary task it was to give their respective confraternities the 'continual care and visiting' that they realised were necessary. The constant efforts of successive directors of confraternities at Clonard are examined at length in another chapter.

Before leaving the subject of parochial sodalities and confraternities, it is worth recording that the Clonard mission reports note the extensive and, it seems, successful efforts of the two large Belfast parishes of St Patrick's and St Peter's with their confraternities a hundred years ago. The Redemptorists gave the annual retreats to the women (Children of Mary) and men (Holy Family) in each of these parishes in 1897 and 1901 and again in St Patrick's in 1902. The turnout for each parish in 1897 was identical: 2,000 women and 1,500 men. In 1901, attendance in St Patrick's had increased substantially over 1897, to 3,000 women and 2,500 men, while in St Peter's, numbers had slipped back to 1,800 for the women, the men remaining at 1,500. Strong numbers continued at St Patrick's in 1902, with 3,000 women and 2,700 men attending.

Of even greater interest is the efforts of these Belfast parishes to provide additional spiritual sustenance for 'working boys and girls'. In October 1897, St Patrick's, St Peter's and St Mary's each provided a week's retreat for young workers. The numbers attending at St Peter's were 1,000; at St Patrick's 850 and at St Mary's 700. In November the following year, St Peter's offered a five-day retreat, 'To the boys and girls of the society of the Apostleship of Prayer' – a somewhat younger group than 'working boys and girls'. The attendance was an impressive 3,000. However, Fr Lowham, C.Ss.R., complained that, 'The time was too short to stir up those who were absent for a considerable time,' – absent, we can assume, from their religious duties. He concluded: 'Many of those of the age of 18 or 19 require something of greater length.' In May 1902 St Patrick's parish provided a five-day retreat for the 'Junior branch of the Holy Family confraternity'. The attendance was a commendable 1,500, under the direction of the same Fr Lowham, who reported:

> The work is difficult from the fact that you had to speak so as to suit the capacity of children who have just made their First Communion and say, at the same time, something that will benefit those who are on the verge of manhood.

Conversions

Conversions, the bringing back to religious practice of 'hard cases', the stuff of which mission stories were made among Irish Catholics of a later generation, were reported relatively rarely. They were occasionally quoted as evidence for the success of a mission. Portaferry (1899) and Newry (1901), provide examples, missions regarded by the Redemptorists as 'very successful'. In Portaferry, 'Many came who had been long years away from sacraments.' Similar sentiments were expressed about Newry. The parish priests of Portglenone (1898) and Tullylish/Gilford (1903) appear to have known their parishioners intimately for the missioners were able to report a full return to religious practice of all who had been careless. 'All who had been for some time from sacraments (and for whom especially the PP declared he got the Redemptorists),' noted the report from Portglenone, 'turned up to sermons and went to sacraments'. In Tullylish/Gilford, 'Individuals who refused to go to confession either made confession the following morning or arranged to go to their duties afterwards,' which seems to suggest that special arrangements were made for some wayward parishioners immediately following the mission. At Crossgar mission in 1899, there were several remarkable conversions of people who had lapsed for so long ('hadn't entered a church for 20 or 30 years') that 'They [were] looked upon as Protestants.' In Glenravel (1900), when 'Many attended [the mission] and approached the sacraments who had not been near the church for years,' the parish priest insisted that they were 'outsiders'! Finally, the Redemptorists reported an uneven response to the 1902 mission for St Paul's district, held in their own church at Clonard. It was part of a city-wide mission for the Catholics of Belfast: 'Very many who were years from sacraments made their peace with God, but very many more refused to do so ...' However, the report concluded hopefully about those who refused, '... if spared, [they] will probably turn up at some future mission. Where there are some 90,000 Catholics to be dealt with [in Belfast], it must always be so.' In a similar mission, in 1899, it had been noted of the people of St Paul's: 'a certain number of them very good, others very bad.'

Evidence of a successful mission
For the Redemptorists, some of the signs of a successful mission were: large and consistent attendances at the exercises of the mission particularly in the mornings; the spiritual disposition of the people, which was revealed by their enthusiasm at services and, in particular, by their willingness to confess and their demeanour in the confessional; the return to religious practice of those who had fallen away; the settlement of public scandals, where such was needed, and, finally, in those parishes in which a 'renewal' (usually after twelve months) had been asked for, the state of a parish seen to be as spiritually healthy as when the mission ended.

In Downpatrick in 1901, where the mission was 'very successful and compared by priest and people to the first great mission given in the parish in 1866 by the Passionists', the missioners remarked: 'Success shown by constant attendance morning and evening and their eagerness to get to confession.' The faithful of Larne (1898), 'attended well from beginning to end and came well disposed to confession. Work in the confessional was continual.' At the cathedral in Newry (1901), attendance was 'unprecedently large' and the four missioners were 'kept constantly engaged in the confessional' during the three weeks of the mission. People at times went to extraordinary lengths to get to confession. In Tullylish/Gilford, the 1903 mission was 'most enthusiastic. Confessionals so thronged that many remained out from work for 3 days in order to secure a place.' The small Catholic community of Killyleagh had its first ever parish mission in October-November 1899. When one of the 'masters' at the mill made difficulties about letting workers out to go to confession,

> Several remained away on their own account and were told to stay at home until the mission was over. The manager, however, corrected this later, and ordered full wages to be paid.

For their part, the missioners left on record their advice that the people ought to be discouraged from leaving work 'as they risk being dismissed'. The mill workers were indeed fortunate in having such an enlightened manager.

Similar evidence of a willingness to benefit from the graces of a mission was noted for those 'many' parishioners of Rasharkin who, at their renewal in June 1901, 'left their house as early as 3 am every day to secure a place' in the church. 'Many' in Whitehouse (1898), 'had to come a great distance and could only be in time by setting out straight from the mill after their day's work yet all came and came in good time.' Unfortunately, the missioners only occasionally reported the specific times of services. Seven o'clock both morning and evening seem to have been the most typical times, with eight in the evening in winter time. The earliest recorded start was 5 am for the mill and factory workers of Tullylish/Gilford in June 1903, with another morning session at seven and the evening session at 7 pm. The missioners paid some high compliments in their reports. The Catholic people of Ballygalget (1897) 'had a good reputation and deserved it'. In Portaferry, the parishioners who came out to their mission in 1899 'in large numbers' and showed an 'excellent disposition' were still in favour in 1901: 'They are a very nice people.' As a final example, the faithful on the Ballyscullion side of Bellaghy parish ('separated by [the] Bann which has to be crossed by a ferry') were complimented for their attitude (October-November 1901): They 'corresponded heart and soul with the grace' of their own mission. 'Full attendance morning and evening.'

Co-operation of parish clergy
The level of co-operation between parochial clergy and missioners was evidently very high, for adverse reports from the missioners were rare. In fact, in the early missions under review, only two reports contain serious criticism of parish priests. Both parishes were, by coincidence, in county Tyrone. One was Clogher (diocese of Clogher), the other Beragh (archdiocese of Armagh).

The first problem in Beragh (mission of June 1901) was the PP's insistence that he and his curate hear confessions throughout the mission. Not only did they hear two thousand confessions as against the missioners' six hundred, but of that six hundred, 'Many were outsiders coming for their Easter duty.' Further, the parish priest did not approve of ceremonies at missions, 'including the mission cross,' though it has to be said that there is little evidence for the ceremony of erecting the mission cross elsewhere in the reports for northern parishes. He insisted on a penny charge at the morning exercises, which the missioners regarded as a deterrent to attendance; and he was also keen on annual parish retreats which, in the opinion of the missioners, 'may be called a particular abuse'.[4]

No surprise, then, that there were conflicting assessments of the mission. For priests and people it was 'a great success'. The missioners' view was that it was 'neither a great success nor a great failure'. The failures, as they saw them, were the arrangements for confessions and the 'bad' morning attendance. Their report concluded:

To have a really good mission in this parish, the annual retreats should be discontinued, there should be three missionaries engaged, local confessors should hear the confessions of outsiders and only towards the end of the mission.

Problems in Clogher parish (mission in May 1900) were more serious. As the missioners reported, with considerable understatement:

There are obstacles to the success of the mission. Parochial arrangements are defective in many points: no daily public Mass in either church, or the Blessed Sacrament. On Sunday, the Masses are late which discourages frequentation of the sacraments. No catechism for children on Sundays. No opportunity given them for confession.

Although the mission lasted two weeks, the out-church was allocated a sermon with Mass on Sundays only. Yet, in spite of all these difficulties, the mission was reckoned a success.

Time allocation for missions

The most common complaint from missioners was the lack of time and, occasionally, a shortage of manpower allocated to a mission or parish retreat. In Strabane parish in October 1899, the three weeks allocated to the mission were divided between one week to 'the country district' and two weeks to the town. The result – in the town with 2,500 parishioners – was that the 'course of sermons had to be abridged and a large number of the confessions were necessarily heard by secular priests. An additional missioner would have been a great advantage.' The week-long renewal in the following June was, 'Disappointing. Too short.' In Belfast, in 1899, the week-long parish retreat in Holy Family was considered by the Redemptorists 'too short to do more than skim the surface of the parish'. That in the nearby Sacred Heart parish in the following week was 'altogether too short'. Similarly, in Randalstown in 1900: 'Retreat turned practically into a mission and a week was altogether too short.' The comment about a Portaferry retreat in April 1901 was much the same: 'This week was, like so many of the kind, a short mission,' but with the help of neighbouring priests, 'all the sacrament-going parishioners got to confession: about 1,000.'

Responsibility for the brevity of missions or retreats and their manning levels cannot be allocated in any particular direction, because they were a result of the balance between what parish priests requested and what the Redemptorists, given other commitments, could offer. While there is evidence from the earlier years of the Redemptorists in Ireland – and from their Alphonsian tradition – that they regarded long, well-manned missions as the ideal, in practice by the end of the century the norm was two weeks for a parish mission and one week for a parish retreat. When, in 1920, a three-week mission was given in Buncrana (diocese of Raphoe) with a team of four

Redemptorists, it was acknowledged as a 'big' mission and 'a rare thing' because it lasted three full weeks.

The mission 'renewal'

There were three principal means used by the Redemptorists to consolidate the good work of a mission: the mission 'renewal,' the 'Mission Remembrance' leaflet and 'The Mission Book'. As indicated earlier, the first and most important was the mission 'renewal,' normally given within twelve months, lasting a week and employing a much less formal approach than the mission. The hope of the missioners was that they should find the parish to be at least as spiritually healthy as it had been when the mission ended.

The 'Mission Remembrance'

The 'Mission Remembrance' was a learflet issued to each parishioner at the beginning of the mission. Its content and format changed very little in the long period between the foundation of Clonard and the Second Vatican Council in the early 1960s.[5] It was usually a four-page leaflet, of a size which would fit comfortably into a prayer-book or missal. The front page always carried a picture of Christ crucified, accompanied by the legend: 'Behold! How He loved! He died for me!' Then followed the name of the parish and the date of the mission. The remaining pages contained a serious admonition to the Christian, a selection of prayers and a brief summary of doctrine entitled: 'What every Christian should know.' Some of the prayers, such as acts of contrition, faith, hope and charity, were required to be recited at the end of the morning instruction during a mission in order, no doubt, to help those faithful who needed it, to develop a habit of prayer. Using the prayers on the leaflet after the mission was intended to consolidate the habit.

It is of interest to note that the Clonard archive contains two examples of the 'Mission Remembrance' in Irish, published in 1917 and 1925 respectively.[6]

The Mission Book

A more substantial method of consolidating the benefits of a mission was the circulation of *The Mission Book*, the first English language edition of which was issued from Mount St Alphonsus, Limerick, on 1 May 1855. Its full title was:

> *The Mission Book: A manual of instruction and prayers*
> *adapted to preserve the fruits of the mission,*
> *drawn chiefly from the works of St Alphonsus Ligouri.*

The Mission Book derived from a *Manual of Instructions and Prayers* assembled by the companions of St Clement Hofbauer in Vienna and published there in 1826. It was intended principally to do the work of a mission where a mission could not take place and also to 'keep up the fruit of a mission already given ...' As comprehensive as it was substantial, it carried sections on General and Special Devotions, 'Plain Instructions,' the Sacraments, Prayer (including 'wholesome Reflections for daily or frequent Meditation'), Indulgences and Instructions and Prayers for the Sick and the Dying. The last section carried the epistle and gospel readings for the Masses of the Sundays and major feasts of the liturgical year. The manual became a household book among the Catholics of Austria. Germany, Belgium, France, Holland, the British Empire and North America.[7]

Perusal of *The Mission Book* is 'heavy going' for most modern readers. But it faithfully echoes the early Redemptorist mission – 'like a military offensive ... planned to the last detail' – which is the purpose for which it was assembled.[8]

Geographical spread of Clonard missions
Parish mission and retreat work was given from Clonard over a wide area. By far the greater part was in the diocese of Down and Connor which was always given priority, in acknowledgement of Bishop Henry's invitation to the Redemptorists to make their foundation in his diocese. Of the other northern dioceses, Derry and Raphoe – at some distance behind Down and Connor – favoured the Redemptorists. Work in Armagh and Dromore was limited and marginal in Kilmore, though this may indicate a division of labour with the Redemptorist house at Dundalk. The Clonard records are unhelpful on this matter, as they are on the fact that, of dioceses in other parts of Ireland, Kildare and Leighlin (centred on Carlow) called on Clonard constantly. There was hardly a parish there but had either a mission or retreat from Clonard fathers in the early years. Other dioceses in which Clonard mission 'bands' worked were: Dublin (mainly in city parishes), Meath, Limerick, Killaloe, Waterford, Ossory, Ferns and Cloyne.

Conclusion: Surprising aspects of early Clonard missions
There are three aspects of early mission work from Clonard which may surprise the modern reader. First is the practice of 'tariffs' or charges of admission to church, particularly, it seems, at time of mission. Secondly, there is the uncompromising hostility on the part of the missioners to 'mixed marriages' and the imputation of blame to other Christian churches for creating hostile faith environments for the Catholic partner and the children of such marriages. In an age of ecumenism, such attitudes are a striking reminder of our divided past. Finally, readers who grew up within the ambience of Clonard in the late 1940s and the 1950s, when Redemptorists appear to have become obsessed with the sixth and ninth commandments, may have been surprised that the subject of 'company keeping' as a 'local abuse' was men-

tioned but once – in Portglenone in 1898. The writer remembers being told by an old Redemptorist in the 1950s (he had been ordained in Clonard and was a pioneer in the Irish Redemptorist mission to the Philippine Islands in 1906), that, in his missionary work at home, the big sermons were not on the sixth and ninth commandments, but on the seventh – justice in society, fair dealing in business, and an honest day's work for a fair day's pay.

Postscript: Mission reports 1920-50

In the hope of providing a wider context for, and some development of, the subjects of interest reported on in the earliest missions from Clonard, the reports of missions for the years 1920, 1930, 1940 and 1950 were carefully examined. The choice of dates was not significant. Ten-yearly intervals were chosen in the hope that reports, over such periods, would reflect distinctly changing attitudes or preoccupations on the part of parishes or missioners. Unfortunately, no such striking changes were revealed, apart from the first recorded use of 'motor cars' by the missioners in Fintona in May 1920. The use of such transport enabled the two Redemptorists to visit 'about 200 sick and aged people during the fortnight', much to the edification of the parish.

In place of striking developments, all that can be offered from these later years is limited information on several of the earlier preoccupations, particularly the continuing difficulties with 'mixed marriages', in parishes where they had been noted before. Ballymena, Coleraine, Ballyclare and Carrickfergus are mentioned, though the number of references is small. Parish confraternities are occasionally reported on, with the overall impression that, by 1940, it could be taken for granted that the confraternity was at last a reliable element in parish life – or was this a reflection of anxiety about the war? There is evidence, too, that definite arrangements for children at mission time had become the norm, as if the Redemptorists' own principles on the subject had at last prevailed.

CHAPTER 6

1920s to 1940s

The Clonard Domestic Chronicle of the early 1920s, in its fragmentary way, reflects some of the depression of spirit, verging at times on despair, of the wider Catholic community at the treatment meted out to its members, especially in Belfast. It echoes, too, the corresponding free rein, not to say support, given to 'Orange murder gangs' and 'uniformed bigots' (a reference to the Ulster Special Constabulary) by police and government.[1]

Political background

The years 1920-22 mark one of the lowest points in the history of northern nationalists and Catholics. They had enjoyed a generation of confidence from 1885 under the leadership of the Irish Parliamentary Party, when an all-Ireland parliament was a distinct possibility. They had shared a strong sense of identity as part of the nationalist majority of Ireland as a whole, a sense which was particularly strong among the devotees of Clonard monastery whose community was drawn from the four provinces. But between 1916 and 1918 a major split developed in Irish nationalism. This was the result, on the one hand, of the willingness of the Irish Party, under John Redmond's leadership, to accept the 'temporary' exclusion of six counties from the jurisdiction of a Home Rule Parliament as the only means of achieving self-government for nationalist Ireland; on the other hand, in October 1917, Sinn Féin committed itself to the use of force if necessary in achieving its goal of an independent 32-county republic. The UK general election of December 1918 – the first, because of the First World War, since 1910 – confirmed Sinn Féin's ascendancy in nationalist Ireland. They all but obliterated the Irish Party whose total of eighty-three seats in 1910 slumped to six in 1918; Sinn Féin captured seventy-three.

While Joe Devlin retained his West Belfast seat against no less a figure than de Valera, his political situation was overtaken by events. Between 1919 and 1922, the initiative lay, on the one hand, with Sinn Féin and, on the other, with the British Government and its unionist allies. Since the priority of the Sinn Féin leaders was national independence and the partition question (i.e. the fate of the northern nationalists) only secondary, the party's abstention from Westminster enabled the Ulster Unionists and their Conservative allies to dictate the shape of the Government of Ireland Act (1920). This act was to make partition an 'unalterable fact' in advance of the political negotiations between the British government and the Dáil leaders in 1921. In its pursuit of national independence, Sinn Féin failed to take account of the effect of its policies and actions not only on northern nationalists but also on northern unionists. In particular, the establishment of Dáil Éireann and the beginning of the War of Independence in January 1919 were viewed with alarm by the unionists who made political capital out of Sinn Féin's acts of lawlessness. All nationalists and all Catholics in the north were lumped by the unionists into the one ideological basket – all were potential rebels against the crown and, as such, unworthy of either trust or consideration.[2]

Involvement of Catholic clergy
One of the ironies of the northern situation was that partition promoted the involvement of the Catholic Church in public and political life, an involvement which had greatly diminished while the Irish Party had dominated nationalist politics. Church leaders' public statements arose largely from pastoral concern for Catholic victims of violence. They regarded this violence as stemming from a deep-seated religious bigotry and from the inability or unwillingness of the Northern Ireland government (when it was established in 1921) to afford Catholics, and their property, protection from Protestant violence. The widespread view among Catholics was that the northern government was unwilling, at best, to challenge Protestant violence and, at worst, actually organised it. Both sentiments are reflected in the Clonard Domestic Chronicle, as is the widespread Catholic conviction that deep-seated, anti-Catholic bigotry was a fact of life, a theme evident in Clonard records from the very foundation of the house.

It suited unionist propaganda to rail against the (Catholic) priest in politics. Little was ever said about the (Protestant) clergyman in politics, but he was extensively involved. To cite just one example, Professor Joseph Lee notes that during the December 1910 general election, no less than eighty-three Irish Protestant clergymen spoke from election platforms on behalf of the Unionist Association of Ireland in their campaign to bring their anti-Home Rule arguments before the British electorate. To the Protestant-unionist mind, his clergyman merely represented the Protestant voter, but Catholic priests dominated their flocks, instructing, even commanding them on how to vote.[3]

1920 riots
Against the background of general tension about the distinct possibility of a northern parliament and the activities of the IRA in the south and west of Ireland, serious sectarian violence erupted in Belfast in late July 1920. The immediate cause of the rioting was the IRA murder, in Cork, of the RIC

commander for Munster, Col G. B. Smyth, a native of Banbridge. It was not publicly known that Smyth was directly involved in the murder in March 1920, of the Lord Mayor of Cork (and IRA commandant) Tomás MacCurtain. On 21 July, a mass meeting of loyalist workers was held in the Workman, Clark & Co shipyard under the auspices of the Belfast Protestant Association. After 'some very hot unionist speeches about not allowing Sinn Féin and Roman Catholics to work in the shipyards any longer,' groups of men, some wielding sticks and other weapons, made their way to the larger Harland and Wolff yard. As the police recorded, there followed 'a regular hunt of Roman Catholic workers' in the shipyard. A number were severely beaten, with some thrown into the water and compelled to swim for their lives. The immediate result was a mass expulsion of Catholic and socialist workers from the shipyards, engineering firms and mills. According to the Clonard Domestic Chronicle, 'Even the women and girls were assaulted, beaten and chased from places of business. The very Catholic newsboys were set upon by organised rowdies and their papers seized.' There were no fatalities. But 'blind rumours' spread that evening and in the next three days, eighteen people were killed in what the *Irish News* called 'a carnival of terrorism'.

One of the early victims in this 'carnival' was the Clonard lay brother, Michael Morgan. As the chronicler recorded:

There was an outbreak of Orange bigotry in the neighbourhood. It originated with the Orangemen in Mackay's [sic] Foundry at the top of Cashmere [sic] Road. Shots were fired and our poor dear Brother Michael who happened to look [out] of the window in the top corridor at the time, was shot dead! More might have been shot had the community not taken refuge in the underground cellar. It is stated that the soldiers stood by and never interfered with the Orangemen doing their deadly work ...

This statement reflects the widely held belief among Belfast Catholics that the authorities were unable or unwilling to control loyalist gunmen, a situation to be repeated around the monastery two generations later. The chronicle of Brother Michael's death concluded with the edifying prayer that his 'innocent blood ... call down, not vengeance, but mercy and pardon on his murderers'. In fact, the tradition in the Clonard community is that Brother Michael, as he appeared at the window, was mistaken for a sniper and picked off by a military marksman. The rector, Fr John Kelly, in a telegram to the Press Association, denied reports that sniping had taken place from the monastery tower. And, in a letter to the press, one Clonard resident claimed that the military had been told by 'Orange hooligans' that sniping was coming from the monastery and that stones, thrown by an Orange mob over housetops, appeared to the military to come from the monastery – a 'finely arranged Orange game', thought the writer.[4]

During July and August, there were attacks on Catholic-owned shops and houses in Banbridge, Dromore and Bangor. Lisburn convent was attacked, as were the parochial house in Dromore, the Sacred Heart presbytery in north Belfast and St Matthew's Church in Ballymacarrett (twice, once in July and again in August). On Sunday 22 August, the IRA murdered District Inspector Swanzy in Lisburn, whence he had been transferred after the murder of Tomás MacCurtain. A Cork inquest jury had named Swanzy as one of the RIC murder gang. The result of his death was a general 'crusade against all members of the Catholic faith in Lisburn'. On 24 September, the Clonard scribe noted: 'This morning another row of houses was burnt in Lisburn and the Catholics had to flee for their lives.' Renewed rioting in Belfast that month caused thirty deaths.

By the end of 1920, sectarian violence had left seventy-three people dead, 395 wounded and 9,631 'expelled workers' had registered for relief with the Expelled Workers Fund under the patronage and active support of Bishop MacRory of Down and Connor. Countless families, both Catholic and Protestant, had been expelled from their homes. It was widely held among northern Catholics – even among moderate Devlinites – that the events which began in 1920 and continued sporadically until 1922 constituted a carefully planned pogrom aimed at driving the minority out of the state. The creation by the northern government, in October 1920, of the aggressively sectarian Ulster Special Constabulary confirmed nationalist fears and enabled the IRA to establish itself as the protector of the Catholic population. Whether attacks on the minority were planned or spontaneous, there is no doubt that by early 1920 Ireland had become ungovernable. In the south, the war of independence had become a constant round of shootings, raids, burnings and lootings, a veritable reign of terror by both sides.[5]

Summer 1921: Weekend of 9-12 July
It was inevitable that, in such a situation, sectarian outbreaks should occur in the north, with predictable tit-for-tat outrages and killings. The Clonard chronicler, in 1921, reported several attacks in the vicinity of the monastery in May ('during the Orange ructions after declaration of general election' [for the Northern Ireland parliament, in accordance with the Government of Ireland Act 1920]). In June, he recorded, 'more Orange shootings in the streets around the monastery' with the bell tower and, possibly, the facade of the church being struck. But from 9-12 July,

> The Orange pogrom broke out with a violence unprecedented in our vicinity; the pretext being an ambush of 'special' ruffians in uniform at Raglan Street [a short distance away, citywards on the other side of the Falls Road]; just as the former outburst [in June] was occasioned by the shooting of a constable alleged to have been implicated in the midnight shooting of some Catholic nationalists in our immediate neighbourhood.

The 'immediate neighbourhood' referred to here, Clonard Gardens, was literally across the street from the monastery, where lived the highly respected Duffin family. At 10.35 pm (not midnight) on 23 April 1921, an assassination squad of at least six RIC men (all later identified) shot dead the two brothers Patrick and Daniel, using revolvers fitted with silencers. A third brother, John, a teacher in St Paul's school, was locally believed to have been the primary target, but he was not at home.[6]

Continuing the account of the violence from 9-12 July, the Clonard chronicle implies that there was a concerted effort on the part of the police and 'specials' to have a last fling before the truce agreed between Lloyd George and de Valera should come into force on 11 July:

... Rifle and revolver firing was kept up intermittently from 9th (or Saturday night) till 12th (Tuesday). Police accomplices of the Orange murder gangs who had returned from various parts of the country in view of the 'Truce' due to begin on Monday 11th July, took up positions at certain Catholic centres so as to prevent the Catholics from coming to the aid of their co-religionists whose lives were attacked and whose houses had been looted and burned. Several rows of Catholic houses were thus destroyed at Cupar Street in the environment of Falls Road: nor was there any doubt in the public mind that the pillage and arson and murder perpetrated by the Orange scoundrels was engineered by the lodges and encouraged by Dublin Castle and Scotland Yard. For instance, word was sent to some Belfast clergy to prepare for trouble as it was known at Camlough [Newry] that the 'specials' were being dispatched for some sinister purpose and were due to arrive in Belfast on [Sunday] 10 July ... .

The monthly meeting of Our Lady's Confraternity was due on 'that memorable Sunday evening' at 4 pm:

but no bell was rung and the members, with a few exceptions, took the hint and remained at home; for the streets were, at intervals, swept with bullets and to be out of doors at all was a grave risk.

Likewise, the usual Sunday evening devotions were abandoned, no bell being rung.

Bravery of Fr Michael McLaughlin, C.Ss.R.

The chronicle records the brave action of one of the community, Fr Michael McLaughlin, at some unspecified time over that dreadful weekend. Fr McLaughlin was 'suddenly summoned to administer the last rites' to a Catholic man who had been shot by 'Orange fanatics who rushed unexpectedly from the back streets and fired into a group of Catholic men'. To reach the unfortunate man, Fr McLaughlin had to cross the line of fire 'at four points'. His 'example of courage and sacrifice' was not lost on the 'grateful Catholic population of the district who admired his devotion to duty'. Nor was it lost on his confrères 'who were anxiously awaiting his safe return from the danger zone'. A deputation of local men came to the monastery to suggest that the fathers 'should afford urgent shelter to the hapless and helpless victims who were burned out of their homes'. However, accommodation was found for them elsewhere.[7]

Bishop MacRory at Clonard

The feast of the Most Holy Redeemer, the titular feast of the Redemptorists, fell on the following Sunday, 17 July. It was one of the annual occasions when the community invited the bishop of the diocese to preside at their liturgy and to dine with them afterwards. The chronicle records:

> Before the dinner the bishop [Dr MacRory] took Frs Rector [Kelly] and O'Donnell for a walk over the devastated area and gave great comfort to the poor victims of this wanton persecution whom he visited at the schools and local halls where they were temporarily housed.

In all, 148 houses had been burned 'by the loyalist upholders of Orange law and order' during the weekend of 9-12 July. The chronicle paid tribute to the generosity of local people in providing food for the displaced and to local teachers who 'deprived themselves of their holidays in order to cook and serve the meals of the poor sufferers'.[8]

The burning of the houses of Catholics in Cupar Street, at the rear of the monastery, left the building exposed to 'real danger from shooting or bombing'. Already some of the windows had been broken by stones thrown from beyond St Gall's school yard: '... attacks by the Orangemen on Bombay Street were considered a manoeuvre to give them access to our premises as well as to dislodge our Catholic neighbours who would give their lives for us.' The Clonard chronicle for July 1921 acknowledged the defensive assistance of 'the local Irish Volunteer Force' who 'gratuitously acted as sentinels and kept night watch over the church and monastery during the perilous times when the Orange gang were known to have meditated an attack on us'. Such protection was needed because, 'it was in vain to apply to the military or police ... since they were known to be abettors and accomplices of the incendiaries and murderers who had looted and destroyed Catholic property.' The new rector, appointed in August in the normal triennial distribution of offices was Very Rev Timothy O'Twomey, a Corkman of strong nationalist views who had worked as a secular priest in Middlesborough before joining the Redemptorists. He had no hesitation in seeing that the Volunteer 'sentinels and guards at night' should be provided with 'refreshments'.[9]

1922 sectarian disturbances

Unfortunately, the monastery chronicle for 1922, like that for 1920, was very badly kept. This is true, not only in regard to 'worldly' and political goings-on which, one accepts, were not intended to be recorded unless for purposes of spiritual edification; it is also true of the normal ebb and flow of missionary and church work which is given sparse treatment.

The only entry to reflect the sectarian disturbances of 1922 is under the date of 10 July, which records that the annual retreat for the priests of Down and Connor was 'indefinitely put off because of disturbances in the city,' for 'The Orange rowdies worked themselves into special fury at this period.' Then, looking back over the year, the chronicler recalled those occasions when the rowdies 'showed what they could do, for during the months of March and May they entertained themselves by firing shots and throwing bombs in the neighbourhood'. However, apart from 'one or two shots' through windows of the upper corridors, 'we were allowed to live with our lives'. As in the previous year, windows facing Cupar Street were broken with stones. When these windows were wired up, 'the savages took to burning the gate that leads from our garden out on to Cupar Street'. At the request of the fathers, 'the specials came to put out this fire ... and because, I suppose, we recognised them by calling their attention to the ruffianism of their brothers ... they now patrol Cupar Street in graciousness to the C.Ss.R.'[10]

While recording a specific episode on 4 July, when 'the Orange snipers attacked us', with the result that a toilet cistern off the top corridor was 'riddled with bullets', the chronicle has nothing to say about two earlier shootings in April. In the first, on 17 April, according to Mary Harris (pp 132-3) who draws on newspaper and police reports for the incident, 'a former student of Clonard was shot while walking in the monastery grounds'. One witness said that a number of men were firing at a statue when a Lancia car (used by police) came on the scene. But, in a subsequent damages case, taken on behalf of the student, a judge expressed the view that the police heard firing, believed it came from the monastery grounds, and fired towards the students who were running for safety. The matter seems to have been left unresolved. A week later, the rector, Fr John Kelly, told the RIC that a student in the monastery believed that he had been shot at by a policeman with a rifle in a passing police car. The rector himself and several other students heard the shot. A few minutes later, when a student entered his room, he found a hole like a bullet hole in the wall near the window and a piece of lead in his surplice. The notorious District Inspector Nixon came with two head-constables to investigate. They were not convinced that the hole had been made by a bullet but rather it was made by an iron bar they found in the room. The piece of lead they regarded as a poor imitation of a bullet. They also reported finding a part of a sporting cartridge in the room. Fr Kelly was evidently not satisfied with this investigation for a few days later two other policemen carried out a further inspection. They were prepared to accept that the hole in the wall was a bullet hole and the lead fragment a piece of a bullet. But neither report accepted that the shot could have been fired from the direction suggested by the rector.[11]

With its understandable limitations, the Clonard chronicle for the early 1920s conveys something of the fears and anxieties of the Catholic population of the Clonard area and of Belfast and its hinterland. Nevertheless, as a community with no parochial duties, the Clonard Redemptorists would have been the first to acknowledge that their fears, anxieties and sufferings were slight compared to those of the diocesan priests who had to deal first hand with the devastation and carnage suffered by their parishioners in various parts of Belfast and in Lisburn, Banbridge and Dromore. They were immune also from the often unpalatable encounters with the Northern Ireland authorities which nominees of the bishop had to undergo in attempts to get some kind of even-handed treatment for Catholics in Belfast generally.

The experiences of the early 1920s confirmed the belief of northern nationalists and Catholics that the Northern Ireland government was the extreme sectarian administration they feared it would be, a belief that remained substantially intact over fifty years. The early twenties also confirmed a strong inclination of the minority to have nothing or as little as possible to do with the northern government. As Phoenix concludes:

> The minority for its part – a full one-third of the state's population – equipped with its own social infrastructure of church, schools, hospitals, sporting activities, newspapers, businesses and sectarian Ancient Order of Hibernians ... virtually opted out of the state, forming a kind of 'state within a state'.[12]

It was a highly dangerous situation which was allowed to fester unattended. From time to time sectarian tensions erupted into violence, the most extreme example being the Belfast riots of July-August 1935. On account of their location – mainly in the York Street and East Belfast areas – they raised barely a ripple in the Clonard domestic record.[13]

The Second World War period
However, that same record reflected, in terse style, many of the tensions and preoccupations of the Second World War period. The entry on 29 August 1939 unwittingly captures a moment close to the very beginning of the war. On that evening, a Rev Brother Corbett arrived at Clonard. A student of the Toronto province, he had, with his confrère Fr Cryan, been staying in the studendate of the Polish Redemptorists. They had been 'compelled to flee, at short notice from the English consul, owing to imminence of war between Germany and Poland'. The first aggressive act of the Second World War was, of course, the German invasion of Poland on 1 September 1939, following the faked Polish 'attack' on a radio transmitter the previous evening in the German frontier town of Gleiwitz. So the Canadians' escape was timely.[14]

The chronicler's preoccupation in September was with the new idea of 'black-out'. Early in the month he noted: 'A complete "black-out" – just as in England – has been ordered in the six counties, thus posing not a little inconvenience to the community. From sunset to sunrise all "internal" light to be concealed owing to the danger of air raids.' The provincial superior wrote obliging all members of the community to conform 'strictly and immediately' to the civil authorities' regulations in the matter. The first recorded casualty of the war was a two-week mission in Ballymoney, 'cancelled on account of "black out".' However, the novelty of the black-out did not last very long and the supply of respirators (gas masks) to the community 'some weeks ago' was barely noticed, as Northern Ireland generally relaxed after the first frisson of war anxiety passed.[15]

There were some in Northern Ireland for whom the war was 'England's difficulty ... Ireland's opportunity,' namely, the IRA. While the six counties were not intended as a centre of action, the new seven-county IRA Northern Command was unwilling simply to mark time: there were sporadic bombs and, on occasion, nationalist crowds burned gas masks and violated black-out regulations to show their distaste for the unionist regime and the British war effort. Following an alleged IRA attack on British soldiers on the evening of 3 September, the men's confraternity retreat was 'postponed indefinitely on account of the disturbed state of the city'.[16]

The generally relaxed attitude to the war continued until the fall of France, in June 1940, after which it was just a matter of time before the Germans turned their attention to Britain. Pre-war thinking had been that Northern Ireland was unlikely to be attacked by air, so that, when the fall of France brought the possibility closer, local defences were depleted because of shortages of equipment.[17]

The return of war references to the Clonard chronicle, in September 1940, was in the shape of two military chaplains to the British forces who participated, with thirty Down and Connor priests, in a one-day retreat. The first sound of sirens was heard on 25 October 1940 at about 10.35 pm, when the community 'took cover in the cellar', but the 'all-clear' sounded after twenty minutes. 'We were again disturbed by the "siren" about midnight,' recorded the chronicler, 'however, the danger was not really in our own area. Somewhere down Belfast Lough some bombs were dropped. It is thought only one enemy plane came over.' On a handful of occasions between then and the week before Christmas, there were references to siren warnings, but with no apparent alarm. On 26 October, 'The warning sirens sounded tonight after Benediction when the fathers were about to go to the church for confessions. The people in the church were quite undisturbed and remained as if nothing untoward was happening. Confessions went on as usual.' And

on the 14 December, there were two warnings and 'some A(nti) A(ircraft) firing'.[18]

The 1941 blitz

The major raids of April and May 1941 are reflected in the monastery chronicle. The first one, on the night of 7-8 April, was objectively speaking a minor
one, with just six German bombers dropping a small load of incendiary, high
explosive and parachute bombs on the docks, some residential housing and
the fuselage factory at Harland and Wolff. Casualties were 13 civilians killed
and 23 seriously wounded. The local view, echoed in Clonard chronicles, was
that this was, 'A big raid ... lasting several hours' in which 'several German
aeroplanes' took part. 'The attack was on the Docks. We went to the cellar.
Great damage was done by the bombs and a great conflagration could be
observed from the monastery windows.' That was on the night of Monday of
Holy Week. Because of the high risk of further raids, the traditional Holy
Thursday night adoration by the confraternity men before the altar of repose
was cancelled.[19]

A week later came the raid which is most remembered in Belfast because
of the sheer scale of the attack and the huge number of 745 civilians killed
and nearly 1,500 injured, 420 of them seriously. That was on the night of
Easter Tuesday, 15-16 April. There were scattered light attacks on Bangor,
Newtownards and Derry, but a force of over 150 planes concentrated on
Belfast. Much of the attack, with incendiaries and high explosives, was mis-
directed on residential areas in the north of the city, which accounted for
most of the civilian casualties. Damage was indiscriminate – linen mills,
churches, hospitals, schools, the central library, York Road railway terminus,
telephone lines and a further section of Harland and Wolff. The chronicle
captures the proximity and fury of the raid:

> A big scale air raid on Belfast lasting several hours. Again we took to the
> cellars. The din of A[nti] A[ircraft] firing, of the bursting of heavy bombs
> was terrific and shook the house. This time the raid was general. Great
> damage was done by fire bombs to business and residential areas. Crumlin
> Road, Antrim Road, York Road seemed all on fire. An appalling sight.

The general destruction resulting from the raid can be gauged by the fact that
70,000 people required emergency feeding the following day, while the fear
it generated triggered a vast evacuation of perhaps 100,000 from the city. The
common suffering caused the widespread abandonment of religious and
political animosities. Appeals for outside help brought a quick and generous
response from south of the border. Thirteen fire engines from Dún
Laoghaire, Dublin, Drogheda and Dundalk came north to help; private
funds from the south were offered to the lord mayor's appeal fund; relief centres were set up to receive northern evacuees, while meetings quickly took

place between northern officials and representatives of the departments of finance and local government in Dublin to discuss ways of easing the plight of refugees.[20]

The reference in the domestic chronicle to the next major air raid, on the night of 4-5 May, shows how Clonard and its Shankill neighbours shared in the wider breakdown of sectarian animosities. The crypt under the sanctuary of the church and the cellar under the sacristy had been fitted out as an air raid shelter 'and is open to the public, women and children only ... This act of ours has been very much appreciated by all, Protestants included. Prayers are said and hymns sung by the occupants during the bombing.' The raid of 4-5 May dropped more bombs than any other and caused greater damage to property and disruption of the war effort, particularly in the harbour area and the city centre; it took Harland and Wolff, for example, six months to return to full production: 'Very heavy bombs destroyed much of the commercial business of the city in this raid.' Fortunately, on account of the heavy evacuation and the, by now, established habit of people from the city taking refuge from air raids in the surrounding countryside, civilian casualties were greatly reduced from the Easter Tuesday attack. Still 150 people were killed and 157 seriously injured. A smaller raid the following night claimed fourteen more lives through a direct hit on some shelters, but damage to property was slight. That was the end of the Belfast blitz, although for the following three nights, 7 to 9 May, sirens wailed out again, driving the Clonard community to the cellar, 'but there was no regular raid, only "observation" planes'. A final alarm was raised in the early hours of 23 July 1941, but nothing came of it.[21]

There are several echoes of the air-raids in the Clonard record of 'external apostolic labours', that is, of missions and retreats. At the end of April, the annual Redemptorist retreat to the boarders in the convent school of the sisters of the Sacred Heart of Mary in Lisburn was to a considerably smaller number of girls than usual (to fifty, as against eighty the previous year,) 'owing to air raids'. Some parents had evidently withdrawn their daughters from a school so dangerously close to Belfast. The May air raids affected several missions given by Clonard priests during the week from 4 to 11 of the month. In Whitehouse, on the northern outskirts of Belfast, the attendance was so poor, 'owing to air raids', that an intended mission was downgraded to the status of retreat: 'The people are taking to the hills to escape from the Huns.' At Ballymena, where the mission went ahead as planned, the missioners reported that, 'During this week four air raids spoilt the morning attendance.' The mission in Holywood, a parish as close to Belfast on the south as Whitehouse was on the north, was considered 'a decided success, even though many Catholics had left the district on account of air raids'.[22]

Effect on men's confraternity

The early years of the Second World War, with the exception of the immediate aftermath of the 1941 blitz, had only a marginal effect on confraternity membership and attendance. The anxiety generated by the declaration of war on 3 September 1939 and the enforcement of 'black out' led to the annual retreats, normally held in October, being postponed: 'Owing to [black out], fear of trouble in the city, men going home in absolute darkness and being searched by the Specials ...' When the retreats were eventually held in the first half of November, the morning Mass was at seven o'clock, an hour later than usual 'owing to the darkness of the mornings'. But the later time was not suitable for the men because of the early start to their working day and attendance was 'very bad ... not more than 600'. However, the evening attendance was as good as 1938, 'in spite of numbers called up for the war – many in England – and some "rounded up" ...,' the last-named because of suspected Republican connections. In 1940, the annual retreats were held in early September, the last of Fr James Murray's directorship. He recorded:

> Attendance was not as high as other years, but owing to the war there is much night work which makes it impossible for many to attend. 151 have left for England since January. Yet the combined turnout for the general communion was 4,224.[23]

The air raids of April and May had a distastrous effect on attendance at the confraternity. It was reduced 'to about a fourth'. As Fr Walsh recorded:

> The whole city has been disorganised, so the men cannot be blamed for non-attendance during this trying time. ... Nine-tenths of the people of the city go to the country for the night and spend the night on the roads and fields. ... Some men whose families have gone to live outside the city in districts considered safe from air raids travel by train or bus to their families every night and some spend the weekend with their families ...

For Fr Walsh, the greatest immediate difficulty in the aftermath of the blitz was getting prefects and sub-prefects to take the place of those who had to resign for reasons of work or travel to their families in the country: 'Some sections have had three or four prefects or sub-prefects in 4 or 6 months.' He called an emergency meeting of prefects and sub-prefects for each division on 30 June and 1 July respectively in order to encourage them 'to work hard to keep up the confraternity in the trying times'.

Despite the trauma of the blitz, the annual retreats in September 1941 showed some signs of a return to normality. Attendances were 'extremely good ... to the surprise of everybody' and after the retreats the attendance kept up well, despite the continuing wartime problems of night work, shift work, 'many [members] across the water' and the black out which prevented many of 'the old men, always faithful attenders' from coming to meetings.[24]

But there was another unhelpful factor operating at this time. Directors were being changed too frequently. Fr James Murray had been replaced in mid-September 1940 by Fr John Walsh. In early July 1941, Fr Walsh was moved to Esker and Fr Peter Byrne from Limerick succeeded him. In the middle of the following February, Fr Byrne returned to Limerick to take over the men's confraternity there and was replaced in Clonard by Fr John Ryan. It was he who complained on 16 February 1942: 'It was quite apparent that the too frequent changing of director had had bad results. Members were careless about attendance, so also were P[refect]s and S[ub] P[refect]s.' Fr Ryan's observation is borne out by general communion statistics. The last year in which the Monday division recorded over 2,000 at a general communion was 1939; it was 1944 before they passed that figure again. The Tuesday division fell below 2,000 only once, in 1940, but it was 1945 before they got back to their substantial figures of the late 1930s.[25]

There were a couple of echoes of wartime conditions before the great surge in confraternity growth in 1945. First, there were the effects of a curfew imposed between October 1942 and January 1943, due to IRA activity. The curfew affected 'a large portion of the people living in St Peter's parish', who were required to be in their houses by 8.30 pm. The result was that, for this period, confraternity meetings were 'begun at 7.30 and concluded at 8.10 pm.' The other reminder of war was on Holy Thursday 1944. Just as the men were going into the church for the Holy Hour, 'the sirens were sounded'. Some of the men returned home, 'but the majority went in. The "all clear" went during the rosary.'[26]

Fr John Ryan considered that the annual retreats of 1943 and 1944 were well attended, 1943 showing a 'substantial mprovement on previous years' and 1944 'a good improvement on previous years'. He had no doubt that the celebration, in August 1944, of the centenary of the founding of the Holy Family at Liège in Belgium, 'made a good impression on the city and brought many members to the confraternity'.

The centenary date was 27 May, but the celebrations were scheduled for August. They took the form of a triduum, preached on the 23-25 of that month (Wednesday to Friday) by three former directors, the three Jameses, Deeney, Murray and Reynolds. 'Each night the church and all the corridors were packed with men.' On Sunday 27 there was a Solemn High Mass at which Bishop Mageean presided, with 'Dr W. Conway, professor of Canon Law in Maynooth – a former member of the Holy Family' as preacher. In the evening, there was a procession from Beechmount grounds to the monastery garden where the Redemptorist provincial superior, Fr Hugo Kerr, preached a special sermon and Dr Mageean imparted solemn benediction. The procession was joined by some hundreds of men from Holy Family confraternities in city parishes, so that 'at least 10,000 men marched' and at least 50,000 onlookers lined both sides of the road from Beechmount to Clonard. Apart from the numbers involved, this centenary celebration was the first public celebration of its kind for ten years. No doubt it both benefited from and contributed to the new wave of devotion set off by the launch of the novena to Our Lady of Perpetual Succour in the previous December. The centenary celebration was appropriate, too, at a time when the end of the war was becoming a distinct possibility: the centenary week coincided with the relief of Florence from the south by the Eighth Army and, nearer home, the liberation of Paris by the Allies and the French resistance.[27]

A Service of Remembering, 1991
The wartime period of shared suffering and mutual help was commemorated fifty years afterwards in a special ecumenical service, organised 'In Loving Memory' by the Men's Confraternity. Its full title was: *A Service of Remembering in Clonard Church, Belfast, April 15/16 1991 of those killed, those bereaved and those who risked their lives in the blitz of 1941.*

A thoughtful and reflective occasion, the central section of the service, which gave its title to the whole, 'In Loving Memory', had three parts: (a) 'Claiming the Dead'; (b) 'The Shelter of Clonard Vaults – recollections of fear, welcome, prayer and laughter' followed by the hymn 'Lead Kindly Light'; (c) 'Our debt to the ARP [Air Raid Precaution volunteers] – a tribute to all who risked their lives,' followed by the hymn (psalm) ' The Lord's My Shepherd'. The final section, preceding the concluding hymn 'Be Thou My Vision', was entitled, 'Sign of Peace and Reunion of those who sheltered in Clonard Vaults'.

The text of the order of service concluded with a reflection on the futility of war, taken from a homily Pope John Paul II preached during his ecumenical visit to Coventry in 1982: '... War should belong to the tragic past, to history. It should find no place on humanity's agenda for the future.'[28]

Proposed extension to Clonard church
The reader will recall from an earlier chapter that Bishop Henry's decision in 1906 to reduce the size of Clonard church 'rankled deeply and bitterly with the Redemptorists for decades'. There was also a strong temptation at the time to throw up the whole business of the church and 'await better times and fairer chances'. Such better times appeared to have arrived with the benevolent episcopate of Dr Daniel Mageean, for it was during his years as bishop that, presumably with at least his tacit approval, the Irish Redemptorist provincial superior, Hugo Kerr, sought and received from his Rector Major, Patrick Murray, permission to pursue the 'enlargement' of Clonard church.

Patrick Murray had been the rector of Clonard in 1906 who bore the disappointment of Bishop Henry's action. In approving the 'enlargement' proposal, he laid down just one condition, namely, that the financial responsibility for it should be undertaken jointly by the Irish provincial administration and the rectors of the Irish houses. The principal reason for this condition was 'the Galway debt, though dwindling,' that is, the outlay on the huge house of studies in Galway, completed in 1939. This large debt had led to subsequent criticism from some rectors that it had deprived them of 'many conveniences'.[29]

The one surprise about the project was the timing of its launch. Murray gave his permission in a letter dated 20 January 1945. He even warned of the difficulty of getting materials during wartime, not to mention their price. It may be that Kerr envisaged a protracted period of fund-raising before the work got under way, by which time the war would be over.

At any rate, no time was lost in setting up a fund. At the end of March that year, the rector of Clonard, Fr T. J. Regan, addressed the confraternity men, 'made known to them the plan to extend the church' and announced that a collection was to be taken up monthly. The first such was in mid-April. From then until early 1949, this collection is mentioned occasionally in the Chronicle of the Holy Family Confraternity. The last reference is at the meetings of 31 January and 1 and 2 February in that year. Thereafter all is silence. The enlargement of Clonard church never materialised.[30]

A post-war development: enclosed retreats
Two important wartime developments in Clonard were the perpetual novena which began in 1943 and the simultaneous foundation of the Clonard Boys' Choir, following the much-lamented death, in June 1942, of Arthur de Meulemeester. These topics are treated extensively in other chapters. Shortly after war's end, the Clonard community played a substantial part in developing, first, the enclosed-retreat movement and, secondly, a mission to non-Catholics. The latter was of such significance that it is given a chapter to itself. Since Clonard's part in the retreat movement was of limited duration, it is, for conevnience, considered briefly here.

Mount St Clement's, Ardglass
The enclosed-retreat movement was first brought to public notice in the north by Bishop Mageean of Down and Connor, in a pastoral letter of 1945. Discussions on the subject began at Clonard in April 1946, early in the rectorate of Fr Gerard Reynolds. From then until the following December the matter was further explored by the rector and his consultors at each of their monthly meetings. In September, an important practical decision was taken to purchase premises suitable as a retreat house. This was King's Castle, Ardglass, county Down, built by the Beauclerk family about 1840 as a

'Victorian rendition' of a medieval stronghold. But even before the decision, Fr Reynolds was looking to buy 'such house furnishings as could be secured cheaply at forthcoming auctions of military camp equipment'. These purchases included a 'military hut for erection in grounds at Ardglass to serve as chapel, refectory and sitting room for retreatants,' at a possible cost of £400 to £600. (The hut was subsequently erected in the spring of 1947.)

In order that the premises should not remain unoccupied, possession was formally taken on 16 October. Fr Reynolds was assisted, among others, by the parish priest of Dunsford and Ardglass, Very Rev Fr McKee. There was a procession in the afternoon, in which Fr McKee carried the Blessed Sacrament from the nearby St Nicholas' Church to the retreat house oratory. He said he was delighted there would be another home for the Blessed Sacrament in his parish. The alternative was that the castle might have become a Barnardo home, which Fr McKee himself had forestalled by securing the property by private sale on the eve of auction.[31]

Detailed discussions continued at Clonard. Presumably it was the location of the castle which prompted a suggestion that it be closed during the winter months, an idea which was rejected. The question of whether or not the new establishment should be independent of Clonard was, predictably, left for decision to the provincial superior. It was May of the following year before 'the first round in the work of retreats to the laity ... took place'. On the 18th of the month, one hundred and sixty young men 'from Ardglass and surrounding district' made a one-day retreat. The oratory could not accommodate them all for Mass, so while ninety of them heard Mass there in three relays, the remainder did so in Dunsford chapel.[32]

In the summer of 1947, the new retreat house had a courtesy visit from the recently elected Rector Major, Most Rev Fr Leonard Buijs. He was on his way from Dublin to Clonard which was in the middle of its golden jubilee celebrations. On the final day of those celebrations Dr Mageean, Bishop of Down and Connor, in the course of an after dinner speech, had expressed his satisfaction about the establishment of the new retreat house. When Dr Mageean sat down, the guest of honour, Dr John D'Alton, Archbishop of Armagh,

> observed to the provincial [Fr Kerr] that Dr Mageean had given him a glowing account of the retreat house and then added significantly, 'I wonder could you do anything for my diocese? The Servites, recently established in Benburb Castle may open a retreat house, but I would prefer the Redemptorists to take the matter in hand.' Fr Provincial thereupon undertook to show him a site on his next visit to Dundalk. ... [33]

However, the matter was not pursued.

By October of 1947, Ardglass had been 'severed from Clonard' and established as an independent community of which the first rector was Fr Joseph Wright.[34]

As an indication of the growing importance of the enclosed-retreat movement, the monastery chronicle records the return from Holland, in late summer 1948, of Frs Gerard Reynolds and John Gorey. They had spent two weeks there visiting retreat houses run by Dutch Redemptorists and 'got many hints and ideas about running enclosed retreats'.[35]

A second retreat house

So successful was Ardglass that, as early as 1951, the idea of another retreat house, this time on the upper Antrim Road in Belfast, was being mooted. The local parish priest, Fr McSparran, was quoted as giving 'a wholehearted céad míle fáilte to the idea'. The intention behind the new foundation was 'to relieve the pressure on ... Ardglass.' On 29 September the then rector of Clonard, Fr Gerard McDonnell, took possession, accompanied by Brothers Cuthbert and Anthony. However, nearly a decade was to elapse before St Gerard's, as it was to be called, opened for retreats. Funding was a problem. A very successful appeal in its aid was launched in Clonard early in 1953.[36]

Meantime, Ardglass remained the only foundation for the Irish Redemptorists' apostolate of enclosed retreats. Thus, when in August 1954 Fr John Whyte, home on holiday from India, was appointed in charge of 'the new lay retreat house in Limerick', he immediately went to Ardglass where, as the Clonard chronicler noted playfully, 'he will sit at the feet of the father of the retreat movement to receive wise counsel for his new assignment'. The 'father of the retreat movement' was Fr John Gorey whose bespectacled, rugged appearance and avuncular style endeared him to a whole generation of retreatants.[37]

The retreat house at Ardglass held pride of place throughout the 1950s. But at the end of the decade, when an entirely new, purpose-built retreat house on the Antrim Road site was completed, with accommodation in single rooms for one hundred people, the decision was made to close Ardglass. The very first retreat in the new establishment (now named St Clement's, the title of St Gerard's being given to the accompanying church) was held during the last few days of 1960 for a group of Irish Christian Brothers. The first lay retreat in the new premises was held on Sunday 5 February 1961, given by Fr Gerard McDonnell who, as rector of Clonard in the early 1950s had overseen its beginnings. One hundred men were expected on 5 February but, owing principally to a 'flu' epidemic, only seventy-one turned up.[38]

The Clonard chronicler chose a cutting from the *Irish News* of 6 February 1961, to pay tribute to the work of Ardglass and to the highly organised committee of laymen whose efforts had played such an important role in its apostolate:

The Down and Connor lay retreat organisation yesterday bade farewell to Mount St Clement's, Ardglass – its home for the past fourteen years – on a high note of success. For 1960 saw an all-time record set up for the number making enclosed retreats in the Ardglass retreat house, described by Most Rev Dr Mageean as 'the power house of the lay retreat movement'. The total number of retreatants for the year was 4,750, although the house was closed during July.

Finally, the opening of the new premises brought to an end the long tradition of retreats in Clonard monastery for the priests of Down and Connor diocese. A pastoral letter of the bishop's, read at Clonard on 12 February, announced that the priests' retreat for 1961 would begin on 17 July at St Clement's, Antrim Road. The chronicler commented: 'This means that priests' retreats will be discontinued here in Clonard.'[39]

CHAPTER 7

Confraternities 1

Beginnings

The establishment of confraternities in the new foundation of Clonard was one of Bishop Henry's priorities. He raised the matter in Rome at the time the contract was made between himself and the Redemptorists on 21 November 1896. When, two days later, Fr John Magnier, a consultor general, sent a copy of the contract to the first rector of Clonard, Fr Patrick Griffith, he warned in an accompanying letter:

> The bishop spoke to me about new confraternities. I did not go much into the matter as it is better to settle it with you. The Boys' is a certainty. There is no doubt the men's will come. I don't suppose there will be any difficulty with the women ...

The lack of difficulty with the women was because they would be expected to meet only once a month, while the men would be expected to have a weekly meeting, a substantial commitment for a small community struggling to establish itself.[1]

Once the temporary church was ready for occupation on Easter Sunday, 18 April 1897, 'the bishop gave no rest to Fr Griffith ... until he erected three distinct Confraternities, one for men, one for women and one for boys'. Griffith, with demands for parish missions in Down and Connor already mounting, held out for as long as he could. But by June 1897 the women's confraternity (of Our Lady of Perpetual Succour and St Alphonsus) was launched, with Fr Griffith himself as director. The men's confraternity followed in July, with Fr Vincent Bourke as its first director. He had charge also of the boys', established the following day. The custom of men and boys having the same director was to continue until 1950, when Fr Harry McGowan became the first full-time director of the boys' confraternity.[2]

What confraternities offered

The Clonard confraternities offered the same essential spiritual assistance to their members as did most other confraternities or sodalities. (It is worthy of note that, at this time, the diocese of Down and Connor was one of the best endowed with confraternities in Ireland.) There was a weekly meeting, a monthly communion, two retreats annually and the various benefits that derived from formal organisation into sections under a prefect and sub-prefect, who could keep members up to scratch on attendance. Other benefits included friendly camaraderie, healthy rivalry in attendance at meetings and in acquisition of new members and smartness of turnout at confraternity, parish or diocesan functions such as processions, pilgrimages and so on.

Clonard's strengths

The Clonard confraternities had special strengths due, in the first place, to the fact that they were organised by a religious community which had more personnel to call on than had parishes. Secondly, the Clonard priests had no parochial responsibilities, which meant that they were able to focus their energies much more narrowly than diocesan priests. Thirdly, superiors were able to nominate an individual priest as director of a confraternity and this became his principal apostolic work. That the Redemptorists were mission-ary preachers meant that they had a special expertise in the organisation and spiritual management of large groups of people.

In practice, the spiritual services offered in the Clonard confraternities were exceptionally well organised and presented. Perhaps the best proof of this is the remarkable success of the confraternities in attracting ever-increasing memberships, a general truth for the period between 1897 and the 1960s. In addition, what we might call the support services in the Clonard confraternities were highly developed. The director was assisted by a small team of secretaries and by a larger number of prefects and sub-prefects, who were, in pairs, responsible for each section. When the men's confraternity split into two divisions in October 1924, there were four secretaries for each. At the beginning of 1925 an additional one for each division was appointed.[3]

The secretaries' tasks were to supervise the practical administration of the confraternity sections, in co-operation with prefects, and to attend to necessary documentation. The principal duties in regard to the latter were the registration of new members; the maintainence of records of membership, which were essential when members eventually claimed 'jubilees' – silver, golden and diamond; and the preparation, annually, of 'section books', which were essentially attendance records. Practical supervision meant a constant liaison with each section prefect in order to assemble information under such heads as: change of address, poor attendance, members ill at home or in hospital, members out of town, members deceased, etc. Some of this information might be required by the director promptly. For example, if a member were seriously ill, the director would want to visit him. If a member died, the director would want to call upon the family to offer sympathy, would want to arrange a requiem Mass, to announce the death to the division and ask for prayers and so on.

The prefect's duties were the maintenance of the section book, following up careless members, providing the range of information indicated above to the secretaries and keeping a weather eye out for forthcoming 'jubilees' in the section. Persistent absentees would be visited and/or written to by their prefect; if that failed, the director would intervene personally. The sub-prefect's function was to help the prefect with his tasks and, in his absence, to deputise for him. At the time of the 1924 split, each division had thirty-two sections; by 1931 each had forty sections.

The sermon

The weekly meeting consisted of recitation of five decades of the rosary, followed by a sermon and benediction of the Blessed Sacrament. Before the sermon, the director would make announcements about confraternity and church business – a weekly bulletin to keep members informed about matters affecting the confraternity. The sermon was particularly important. It was not always a sermon as such, on matters of doctrine and morals, though series on the sacraments and the commandments, prayer and devotional practices frequently recurred. Often, however, the 'sermon' was more in the nature of an informative lecture or talk on a wide range of subjects. Social topics were recurring favourites – communism, socialism, trade unionism, often linked to the church's teaching as expounded in the great social encyclicals of the popes. Historical subjects were always popular: the Jewish people, the great religious orders and their founders, the Protestant churches, freemasonry, the lives of the saints, aspects of the Redemptorists' own history. As one director noted in 1932, after a series to mark the Congregation's bi-centenary: 'The men took a deep interest as they always do with anything connected with C.Ss.R.' Not infrequently, the subject would be dictated by what was happening in the wider world. Hence the trial and sentence of Cardinal Mindzenty, the Hungarian primate, in March 1949, provoked a strong sermon from Fr Seán O'Loughlin. As he noted: 'The episode aroused the greatest indignation throughout the whole Catholic world ...' Further, he sent a telegram of sympathy to Pope Pius XII, by which '10,000 men, members of Holy Family, Confraternity, Redemptorists, Clonard, Belfast ... deplore recent outrages against the church in Hungary ...' The '8,000 women, members Our Lady of Perpetual Succour Confraternity', joined 'in sympathy and protest ...'4

STRATEGIES TO MAINTAIN INTEREST AND SUSTAIN MEMBERSHIP

Visiting preachers

As happened in other aspects of the Clonard church apostolate, confraternity directors were constantly on the lookout for visiting preachers to offer variety to members by way of a new face, a new voice and a new topic. Returning missionaries were a favourite, especially if they had been former directors of the confraternity. An early example was Fr Patrick Leo (director 1898-99). In

1909 he was rector of Opon on the Philippine Island of Cebu and visited Clonard on his way to the general chapter of that year in Rome. Naturally, his subject was the church and the work of the Redemptorists in the Philippines. Another was Fr Michael Hannigan, in July 1936, en route from Australia to another general chapter. He spoke to the confraternity 'on what the "Irish storm birds" had done to plant the faith in Australia'. He had been confraternity director for a few months in 1915 before leaving for Australia. The years immediately following the Second World War brought a rash of visitors, many of them chaplains in various services. The Belfast Redemptorist, Fr Dan Cummings, deputised for the director for two weeks in July 1947; 'his talks on his war experiences were very much appreciated'.[5]

Friendly rivalry
Directors employed numerous other strategies to provide variety and hold the attention – and loyalty – of members. The structure of the confraternity in divisions and sections within divisions facilitated a friendly rivalry based on weekly attendance at meetings, monthly turnout for the division's Communion Mass or for retreats and their accompanying General Communions. The ability of a division or a section to sustain or increase its membership was probably the greatest source of rivalry.

Liturgies and devotions
From time to time, directors took existing devotional or liturgical practices and adapted or developed them into an attractive format. For example, there seems to have been a long-standing practice of a procession in honour of Our Lady held within the church sometime in the month of October, the month of the Rosary. In 1925, Fr Patrick Carroll added similar processions in May and June, in honour of Our Lady and the Most Blessed Sacrament respectively, each section being pepresented by its prefect, sub-prefect and one of its jubilarians. Several subsequent directors acknowledged the great popularity of these processions with the men and, as one noted in 1949, '... they take a very poor view of it if they are omitted'.[6]

Solemn Benediction
The devotional ritual of benediction of the Most Blessed Sacrament, the usual end to weekly meetings or other evening services, was employed in its solemn form to mark special occasions such as the end of a retreat, the conclusion of a jubilee or large procession. Solemn Benediction was a colourful ritual, with ministers robed in cloth of gold or gold and white. Impeccably attired altar boys, usually in red cassocks under white surplices added formality and colour. There would be incense in abundance and soul-stirring music from organ and choir appropriate to the occasion. Finally, in the Clonard style, the high altar (or temporary altar on outdoor occasions) would

be swathed in a profusion of flowers and lighted by hundreds of candles, creating a stunning display. As if such a spectacle were not sufficient to celebrate the glory of the Lord and his house and bind its members to their confraternity, Fr James Murray, in September 1937, invited the local St Peter's Brass and Reed Band (Clonard was within St Peter's parish) to come to the close of the annual retreats. The band accompanied the hymn singing. Then, 'At the benediction, four scouts with trumpets sounded the "general salute". It was the first time and the men were very thrilled.' Thus began a long and fruitful involvement of St Peter's band within Clonard church – they had for some time been associated with outdoor functions.[7]

Gregorian chant
On other occasions, the liturgy of the church was employed to good effect in drawing the members more fully into the celebration of the eucharist. An outstanding example of this can be found in the decision of Fr James Reynolds in April 1933 to begin the teaching of Gregorian chant to the men of both divisions with the ultimate objective of enabling them, as a body, 'to take the part of the choir in a solemn high Mass which will be offered once or twice a year for the spiritual and temporal welfare of the Confraternity'. He saw the communal singing as 'bound to help much in attaching the men to the Confraternity'. Even though he chose the simplest of the Gregorian Masses, the *Missa de Angelis*, it took more than a year before he was satisfied that the two divisions combined were ready for a solemn high Mass. The first such Mass ('A big event in the history of the Confraternity ...') took place on Sunday 30 June 1935, with the rector of Clonard Fr John Brady (known for his fine voice) as celebrant. 'The singing of the Mass was splendidly rendered,' noted the confraternity chronicle, ' ... the singing ... by such a huge number of men produced a fine impression'.[8]

A repeat of this Mass was arranged for the following January, on a Sunday close to the feast of the Holy Family. The occasion had the added attraction that the bishop of the diocese, Dr Mageean, presided. As Fr Reynolds recorded: 'About 2,500 members took part in the singing of the Mass ... The effect was thrilling and uplifting, not only on the men themselves, but on all who were privileged to be present.' He went on to hope that 'this high Mass will be an outstanding annual event from this on', and his plan was that by next time, the men would have mastered the *Ecce Sacerdos Magnus* (Behold a Great Priest), the liturgical greeting for a presiding bishop. Sadly, Fr Reynolds was unable to realise this ambition. In June 1936 he was appointed rector of Mount St Alphonsus, Limerick. The solemn high Mass remained for many years a testament to his imagination, energy and sureness of touch in engaging the loyalty and religious emotions of the Holy Family men. Before 1936 was out his successor, Fr James Murray, had formed, 'Two new sections [one in each division] ... composed of choir men and singers to assist in the singing of the Gregorian Mass'. Sadly, by the early fifties the original intention of the annual solemn high Mass had been nearly forgotten. The last reference to it in the Clonard Holy Family chronicle was in January 1956.[9]

Pre-Vatican II: Dialogue Mass
In that same month, Fr Christopher McCarthy announced a new liturgical undertaking. This was that the monthly communion Masses should in future be sung. A year was spent in preparation, a member of the community rehearsing the men for five minutes before each confraternity meeting. The initiative did not survive for long in that period of liturgical change, for by the end of December 1958, Fr McCarthy was noting: 'A new venture was begun – the dialogue Mass at the monthly communions.' To this end, classes in the Latin of the Mass were offered to any interested members, so that they could lead the responses; a further help was the provision of a printed 'dialogue Mass card' which was distributed to all the men. In yet another attempt to engage the members more fully in the eucharistic liturgy, volunteer Mass servers were recruited, with an assurance of lessons in Latin. Unfortunately, there were few volunteers. In many respects, these initiatives were anticipating one of the early documents of the Second Vatican Council, the Constitution on the Sacred Liturgy of 4 December 1963, which decreed that 'full and active participation [in the liturgy] by the people is the aim to be considered before all else'.[10]

Catholic Action
A final area of Catholic life which was exploited by confraternity directors eager to add variety and interest to the weekly round of meetings was Catholic Action, encouraged particularly by Pope Pius XI (1922-1939) whether formal, that is, '... performed under the direction or mandate of a bishop', or informal.

The (formal) Catholic Action group, the Legion of Mary, was first called upon in 1949 by Fr Seán O'Loughlin. He needed help 'in the work of looking up careless [members] in the Boys' Confraternity'. Members of two legion *praesidia* assisted. Nearly ten years later, Fr Christopher McCarthy went a step further by forming a *praesidium* within the confraternity with the title 'Our Lady Co-Redemptrix'. That was in 1957. Its work was twofold: 'to visit permanent sick members' and 'go round all those whose names are on the lapsed file cards'. Yet another Catholic Action group to be recognised by Fr McCarthy was the Y(oung) C(hristian) W(orkers), who had a section of their own appropriately named 'Christ the Worker'. Meanwhile, in 1952, on the initiative of the rector, Fr Gerard McDonnell, a Clonard branch of the Pioneer Total Abstinence Association was established, exclusively for members of the confraternities.[11]

Savings Bank 1931

There are two outstanding examples of Catholic action in the informal sense which require mention for their intrinsic interest. Separated by three decades in time, their objectives were closely related. The first was the establishment of a savings bank in 1931. Three local businessmen, secretaries of the confraternity, Messrs McGowan, Smyth and Kennedy, called on the director, Fr Mangan, early in January to propose to him the setting up of a confraternity savings bank. According to Fr Mangan's record, he approved of the idea on four conditions: first, that the name 'confraternity' should not appear in the title – it should be called simply 'Savings Bank'. The second condition was that the Redemptorists should have no responsibility 'for the bank and its business'. Thirdly, the bank must be located 'outside of the grounds of the church and monastery'; and, lastly, that the men put their proposal to the bishop for his approval. Fr Mangan made another suggestion, 'not a condition', that the three should approach the Clonard branch of the Society of St Vincent de Paul and 'ask them to erect a bank'. This was done, but 'the Vincent de Paul people ... definitely rejected the proposal'.

The trio met the bishop, who asked for a few days to consider the matter, during which time he 'came to the director ... and asked him to put in writing his views'. Fr Mangan did so. He 'declared from his experience in Limerick he believed the bank could be an agent for much good, that it would encourage thrift, make the men better, help to stop gambling and excessive drinking,' and, of course, repeated his own four conditions. Dr Mageean thereupon 'not only gave his consent but ... wished the undertaking every success'.

The next step was to secure suitable premises. 'Felix Sheehan's house [in Clonard Street, opposite the monastery], vacated for nearly a year,' was purchased and necessary alterations made. The Munster and Leinster Bank agreed to act as trustees and to provide for the savings bank the same facilities as it had for the confraternity bank in Limerick. Dr Mageean performed the opening ceremony on a Monday evening (a confraternity evening) in August. As the *Irish News* reported the bishop's speech: ' ... Catholic Action takes many forms, but to my mind one of the most necessary forms of Catholic Action is to encourage thrift among our working classes.' In a lighter vein, having noted that popular suspicion of banking was not as it used to be, 'He added, amidst laughter, that the Clonard Savings Bank would be going strong when the Bank of England was down.' History has proved otherwise! But, since the savings bank was outside the responsibility of the Redemptorists, unfortunately for the historian no further mention is made of it in the Clonard records.[12]

Credit Union 1964

Fr Hugh McLaughlin's launch of Clonard Credit Union, in the second half of 1964, was not as fortunate as its savings bank predecessor had been, in the matter of episcopal support. Dr William Philbin, bishop of Down and Connor, had 'no objection' to the credit union, 'but did not wish to be publicly connected with the Credit Union movement'. His wish was, of course, respected. Dr Cahal Daly, then Professor of Scholastic Philosophy at Queen's University, Belfast, had no difficulties of 'public connection'. He agreed to preach to the Monday division of the men's confraternity on 25 January 1965 and then to bless and officially open Clonard Credit Union's temporary office in 'the old poor hall' attached to the back of the monastery, which had been 'extended by voluntary labour'. In a gesture of solidarity with the credit union, (which would not have been tolerated by superiors thirty years earlier), Fr McLaughlin agreed to become one of its fifteen directors, with the post of 'membership officer', as the common bond was membership of the confraternity. Among the founding members and stalwarts of the Clonard Credit Union over the years, mention must be made of John McConvery, J. Hill, T. H. Rice, Dan McGuigan, Joe McCann and Rose Fitzpatrick.[13] The Credit Union continues to flourish.

A moral tale: The Clonard Picture House 1931

Finally, there is an exemplary tale from the 1930s which, even if it fits rather loosely under the heading of Catholic Action, must be told as a period piece and for the memories it will evoke for older neighbours of Clonard. It concerns the old Clonard Picture House, located opposite the Falls Road public library. The director of the confraternity was always vigilant in matters of public morality. Fr Cornelius Mangan recorded in the confraternity chronicle in February 1931: 'Again and again complaints were made by the men [concerning] the Clonard Picture House. The pictures were at times very bad and the conduct most reprehensible.' Eventually, at a shareholders' meeting, a Mr James McSorley called on the management 'to clean up the house'. He told the meeting that clergy were constantly complaining to him. Indeed, on the day of the meeting he had had a letter of complaint from Archdeacon Convery of St Paul's. When management expressed resentment that complaints were made to a shareholder and not to them, McSorley challenged them to meet local clergy. They agreed. A meeting was set up at the cinema, to be held immediately after a Tuesday night Clonard confraternity meeting, the clerical side being represented by priests from St Paul's and St Mary's parishes and by Fr Mangan for Clonard Holy Family Confraternity. When only two directors turned up, 'McSorley kicked up a shindy and accused the committee of unfair play.' A second meeting was arranged, the outcome of which was that the directors undertook, in writing, to give every consideration to the deputation's concern 'in respect of the conduct in the house and the showing of pictures'. That they took the clerical concerns seriously is indicated by their appointment of a 'vigilance inspector' whose task was 'to patrol the house and prevent unseemly conduct'. A further concession to a 'special request' of Fr Mangan's was the agreed closure of the picture house on Good Friday. The 'Diamond' picture house, a short distance from the 'Clonard', and the 'Arcadian' in Albert Street 'were also made to close on Good Friday'.[14]

This review of the life of the Clonard confraternities, in showing the deployment of a wide range of devices, from friendly competition between sections and divisions to the adaptation of devotional and liturgical practices and the use of various forms of Catholic Action, brings out very clearly the conviction about confraternities expressed frequently by Redemptorists in their mission reports. This was that, for a confraternity to succeed, it must be 'well worked'. The advantages enjoyed by the Redemptorists over diocesan priests in their direction of confraternities have been acknowledged above. But none knew better than the Redemptorists that such advantages did not exempt them from the hard work required to sustain a successful confraternity.

Public celebrations at Clonard
There is a final example of the strategies employed by the Clonard Redemptorists in 'working' their confraternities which must be given its own space. This is the public celebration of important events in the history of the confraternities, or of the Catholic Church at large, which was a characteristic of the Clonard community especially after the political turbulence of the 1920s began to subside. Public celebration, often with great pomp and pageantry, involving large numbers of participants and onlookers, was a strategy the Redemptorists deployed extraordinarily well. Since the Clonard Redemptorists were exempt from the care of a parish, the only organised 'congregation' they had was the membership of their confraternities.

Major events in the life of the church so celebrated were the Holy Year Jubilees of 1901, 1926 and 1951, the 1932 International Eucharistic Congress which was held in Dublin and the universal Redemption Jubilee of 1934, by which was marked the 1900th anniversary of the completion of man's redemption through the death and resurrection of Our Lord. The centenary of Catholic Emancipation was a great cause of celebration for Irish Catholics in 1929. Another centenary affecting the church at large, in 1958, was the commemoration of the apparitions of Our Lady at Lourdes. The Redemptorists, with their strong Marian devotion, made a great occasion of it, as they had for the same reason celebrated the 1500th anniversary of the Council of Ephesus in 1931.

Commemorations of events in the life of the confraternity were the 1944 centenary of the founding of the Holy Family Confraternity in Liège, Belgium. In 1947 and 1957 there followed, respectively, the golden and diamond jubilees of all the Clonard confraternities. Events with a limited involvement of confraternity members, but with an intense degree of interest were, particularly, pilgrimages – to Rome in 1950 for the Holy Year, to Knock shrine in 1949, to the shrine of Blessed Oliver Plunkett in Drogheda from 1936 onwards and, in 1933, the unusual 'pilgrimage of the unemployed' to London, sponsored in July of that year by *The Universe*, the English Catholic newspaper, and promoted by the director of the men's confraternity, Fr James Reynolds.[15]

If these occasions are set down chronologically, it is clear that the years from 1926 to 1934 were particularly 'busy'; the decade from 1934 to 1944 was quiet, partly due to the Second World War; then between 1944 and 1958 there were major celebrations about every four years.

The following table gives some idea of the extent of such activities:

	MAJOR CELEBRATIONS	MINOR CELEBRATIONS
1926	Holy Year Jubilee	
1928		Delegation to Limerick diamond jubilee
1929	Centenary of Catholic Emancipation	
1931	15th Centenary of Council of Ephesus	
1932	Eucharistic Congress in Dublin	
1933		*Universe* pilgrimage of the unemployed
1934	June: Catholic Truth Congress October: Universal Redemption Jubilee	
1936		Diocesan pilgrimage to shrine of Bl. Oliver Plunkett, Drogheda
1944	Centenary of first Holy Family confraternity	
1947	Golden Jubilee of Clonard Confraternities	
1949		Pilgrimage to Knock Shrine
1950		Holy Year pilgrimage to Rome
1951	Holy Year Jubilee	
1957	Diamond Jubilee of Clonard Confraternities	
1958	Centenary of Lourdes Apparitions	
1966		Centenary of Redemptorists' care of miraculous picture of Our Lady of Perpetual Succour – Pilgrimage to Rome

Pressure of space allows only two examples to be illustrated in detail, to convey something of the extraordinary atmosphere of these occasions. These are the 1926 and 1951 Holy Year jubilees respectively. However, the involvement of the Holy Family Confraternity in the Eucharistic Congress of 1932 was so exceptional that it is considered in some detail in Appendix 2.

1926: Holy Year Jubilee

The Holy Year jubilee celebrations of 1926 were, by comparison with the first public procession of the confraternity women in 1901, a vast undertaking. When Fr Carroll announced to the men of the Holy Family, about three months in advance, that they would make the Holy Year jubilee 'in processional order through the streets of Belfast' the confraternity experienced, in the words of the domestic chronicler, 'a flutter of mild excitement'. According to the same source, the reason for the excitement was the prospect that,

> Belfast, the hotbed of heretical fanaticism, was to witness a Catholic Association parading its thoroughfares accompanied by bands playing Catholic hymns and led by their rev. director in his religious habit wearing the stole of office ...

There was no concealing the great anticipation that 'bigoted Belfast' should witness and, of necessity, be impressed by 'the peaceful, orderly and well-disciplined conduct of its Catholic fellow citizens ... which will contrast most favourably with the riotous, din-creating clamour of its own peculiar demonstrations'.

Each of the confraternities – men's, women's and boys' – had three Sunday afternoons allocated to it in the summer months, on which they made the visits required to obtain the jubilee indulgences. The men's confraternity began the series on Sunday 16 May with visits to St Mary's in Chapel Lane, St Peter's in Derby Street, St Paul's in Cavendish Street and, finally, Clonard church. They were joined by the men of the Sacred Heart confraternity in St Paul's, so that the procession divided neatly into three groups – the two Clonard divisions and St Paul's confraternity. Each division took it in turn to visit one of the churches to recite prayers for the Holy Father's intentions, while the other groups remained outside, 'the members kneeling on the streets outside the churches'. All three groups, finally, visited Clonard where, according to the *Irish News*, 'The vastness of the magnificent interior was sufficient to accommodate all ...' The newspaper recorded 'Deeply impressive scenes' in which,

> in beautiful weather over 5,000 men and boys wearing confraternity regalia and carrying flags and banners with religious inscriptions, marched between two lines of people extending from ... Clonard, down the Falls Road, Divis Street, Mill Street and into Smithfield as far as St Mary's Church.

They were escorted by bands, St Peter's Brass and Reed, St Malachy's Pipers and Clann Uladh Pipers, who led the procession playing 'Faith of Our Fathers', 'To Jesus Heart All Burning' and 'Full in the Panting Heart of Rome':

> ... the words of these beautiful hymns were rendered by the processionists with intense religious fervour ... while the refrains were taken part in, with
>
> due solemnity, by the assembled thousands along the line of the march.

At the conclusion, in Clonard, 'The congregation rose *en masse* and sang with whole-hearted devotion, the soul-stirring hymn, "Confraternity Men to the Fight".'

It is significant that, in his thanks to all participating in the procession, Fr Carroll 'also paid a tribute to the police who regulated the traffic all along the route ...' Such a public acknowledgement of the police was an indication that nationalist, Catholic Belfast was beginning to accept, if not approve, some aspects of the northern state.[16]

Street decorations

These 'deeply impressive scenes' were re-enacted by the men's confraternity on the following Sunday and, for a third time, on Sunday, 20 June, instead of the intended 30 May, when bad weather caused a postponement. It was during the second Sunday of the men's processions that there began to appear for the first time what was quickly to grow into one of the great characteristics of Clonard celebrations, namely, the decoration of local streets with altars, religious banners, pictures, flags and bunting in the papal colours of pale yellow and white. On the first Sunday, the Redemptorists had arranged their own modest decoration of the church front. It had consisted of two papal flags, a scroll with the words 'Praised be Jesus, Mary and Joseph' and 'a double line of bunting – limited to papal colours'. The community was evidently delighted by the subsequent response of the local people:

> During the week rumours floated in that great preparations were being made for the decoration of the route for the ensuing Sundays. During the course of the second procession, several of the streets displayed flags and scrolls, 'God Bless the Pope', 'God Bless Clonard Holy Family', being the wording on some. ... The preparations by the public at large for the third and last procession [of the men's confraternity] were still more elaborate than heretofore ...

The weather on the eve of this (postponed) third procession of the men, on Sunday 20 June, was threatening,

> Yet, in spite of this, ... up went the decorations, this time on a stupendous scale for on this day the route was practically ablaze with papal flags, with pictures of Our Lady or His Holiness thereon. Several of the side streets erected beautiful altars on that end abutting the Falls Road and the houses therein were decorated with green boughs.[17]

Procession of women

The women's confraternity followed the men's, 'in holy rivalry', as Fr Mangan put it, on the first, second and fourth Sundays of June. The boys' had three Sundays in July. Over three and a half thousand women and girls, 'marched, sang and prayed with a regularity, a piety and a faith that edified all, Protestants as well as Catholics, who, all along the route of the procession, thronged to see them'. The route chosen by the women and the order of churches visited, was different from the men's.

The chosen route was through Oranmore Street to Springfield Road, down Springfield Avenue and through Cavendish Street to St Paul's Church, where the first visit was made. From St Paul's, the procession headed city-wards on the Falls Road. With trams from Castle Junction to Springfield Road diverted between two and five pm, the participants were able to march four abreast on each side of the tramway line. At the end of every five sections a banner was borne, depicting variously the mysteries of the Rosary, the Sacred Heart, Our Lady of Perpetual Succour, one of St Joseph, and the 'Little Flower', St Thérèse of Lisieux. The rear of the procession was brought up by four altar boys,

> robed in red soutanes and white surplices, bearing on their shoulders a car beautifully decorated, on which rested a large statue of Our Lady Immaculate draped in white and blue, and surmounted by a crown of exquisite roses and lilies ...

While another division visited St Mary's, the bulk of the procession moved around Smithfield, returning by way of King Street to the Falls Road. From thence all proceeded to St Peter's, circling round via Albert Street while the third division made its visit. Finally, the whole procession returned to Clonard church which was 'beautifully and appropriately decorated, the papal arms and flags, interspersed with bunting, being a conspicuous feature in an artistic scheme'. For the first of the three processions of the boys' confraternity in early July, 'upwards of 1,600 members' assembled. They followed the same route as the men had done and visited the churches in the same order, 'singing hymns and reciting the Rosary'.[18]

The summer of 1926 seems to have been an extended religious festival for the people of the Falls Road from St Paul's Church down to St Mary's in the heart of the city. As an extension to the Falls parishes of the religious celebrations of the previous year in Rome, the processions with their colour, their music, their prayer and formality provided a reminder of the universality of the church and the loyalty of its humble, local members to its visible head in Rome. From the purely human point of view, at a time when the working people of the Falls could not afford holidays from home – even 'Bangor and back' was beyond the reach of most – and when the Dunville and Falls Parks were the only source of a few hours' respite from densely crowded living conditions, the weekly Jubilee processions of that summer were a welcome diversion.

1951: Holy Year Jubilee

The 1951 Holy Year Jubilee on Sunday 10 June, witnessed one of the most elaborately organised processions ever undertaken by the Clonard Redemptorists. It was also the largest because it was the first occasion on which the men's and the women's confraternities – and the boys' – joined together in public procession. At the request of the Redemptorists, the route of the procession broke new ground. The designated churches for the jubilee visits were the old-established St Peter's, St Mary's, St Patrick's (Donegall St) and St Malachy's (Alfred St); but the bishop was persuaded to substitute St Teresa's, St John's, St Paul's and Clonard – the inclusion of the first two churches being an acknowledgement of the extensive development of the upper reaches of the Falls area since the 1930s. The women's divisions assembled in the 'Norfolk' tributaries of the Glen Road, the boys' in Glen Parade and the men in the Arizona Street area.

Elaborate public address system

Another novel feature of the occasion was the use of an elaborate and highly successful public address system. It was originally intended to use a number of vans fitted with loudspeakers and placed at intervals along the route. But something more sophisticated was adopted, as Fr O'Loughlin recorded:

> Messrs Tannoy (the Sound System Firm) suggested that we cover the whole route of the procession from St Teresa's to Clonard with loudspeakers placed on poles along the route. This idea seemed a vast undertaking at first, but, as the cost would not be unreasonable, it was adopted first with hesitation and then with enthusiasm ... this system proved the secret of the success of the whole undertaking,

in that the prayers, hymns, etc., were relayed simultaneously to all points along the route. At first, some opposition threatened to develop in the process of approval of the scheme 'when it came up before the Improvement Committee of the Corporation'. But a 'non-Catholic' member of that committee intervened to support the Clonard application since the public address arrangements were to be used for a few hours only. Fr O'Loughlin was delighted not only at the approval, but at the fact that, ' ... the speakers were actually attached to corporation [sic] telephone posts and trolly-bus standards. Not a bad achievement in "black Belfast"!'

One problem remained. This was communication with 'base' in Clonard, so that the movement of the procession could be accurately monitored. Several possibilities were considered and rejected. 'Walkie-talkie sets' were proposed, 'but they couldn't be got'. Police radio cars were considered, since the police would be supervising the route anyway, 'but feeling on the Falls Road would not allow this – though it would have solved the problem ...' However, there is no indication either that the police were approached or that they would or could have helped if asked. Radio-equipped taxis, for unexplained reasons, were also rejected. So the final decision was that telephones should be used. Friends of Clonard living near each of the three churches agreed to allow Fr Michael Connolly to use their telephones as he moved, by car, from point to point ahead of the procession: Mrs. Kavanagh at St Teresa's (at the corner of the present Glenhill Park), Mr. Séamus Keating at St John's (his home is now part of O'Donovan Rossa GAC social club) and Dr McSparran at St Paul's (between Cavendish Square and Springfield Road).

'Base' in Clonard was the Catholic Truth Society kiosk outside the church, in which the rector (Fr G. McDonnell) was ensconced with a telephone extension from the monastery and a microphone. Alongside him was Fr Liam O'Carroll, 'who answered the prayers given out by the rector, thus setting the pace for the processionists'. At the appropriate times, signalled from Fr Connolly via the rector, two brass bands (assembled in front of microphones in the church grounds) provided music for the hymns. While several bands had offered their services for the procession, only two, St Peter's and the recently formed St Patrick's, Milltown, were chosen since no bands were to march with the procession.

The procession began to arrive at Clonard about 5 p.m. and it took fifty minutes for all 15,000 participants – in seven divisions – to take their allotted places for solemn benediction before the large altar platform erected in front of the monastery gates. Here Dr Mageean, bishop of the diocese, delivered 'a stirring address' in which he said that Catholic Belfast was on the march:

> ... and an inspiring sight it is. You, the members of the Clonard confraternities, drawn from every parish and district in this great city, made a colourful and impressive scene as you marched in well-ordered formation to the music of the bands. ... Our jubilee procession was no proud, vaunting display of our unity and strength, no challenge to any section of our fellow-citizens, but a special act of worship to our Creator and Redeemer. At its head was carried the processional cross, the symbol of our redemption.

It was a matter worthy of note to Fr O'Loughlin that the materials for the altar platform were supplied by McNeill (Engineering), Duncrue Street. 'Though a Protestant firm,' he observed , 'they made no charge,' – a gracious ecumenical gesture.[19]

CHAPTER 8

Confraternities 2: Growth and Decline

A problem of historical sources

The surviving sources for the history of the Clonard confraternities are very uneven. Both confraternities are mentioned regularly, but briefly, in the domestic chronicle of the house. The history of the first thirty years of the women's was written by their then director, Fr Cornelius Mangan, and published in 1927: *Clonard Confraternity of Our Lady of Perpetual Succour and St Alphonsus: A Short History of 30 Years 1897-1927.* While primarily a work of piety, it does provide some account of the development of the women's confraternity during those years. There is no similar record of the men's Holy Family Confraternity during the early years. At least, if there was one, it has not survived. However, beginning in 1924, the 'Chronicle of the Holy Family Confraternity, Clonard' provides an almost continuous and at times extremely detailed account of the men's confraternity up to the present day, compiled by successive directors. Like the domestic chronicle, its content and coverage depended very much on its various keepers, with a fuller record being made in the early decades of Clonard's existence than in the later ones. Unfortunately, no parallel record for the women's confraternity has survived,.

Growth of the women's confraternity, 1897-1927

There is no record of the number of women who attended the first confraternity meeting in June 1897, but according to their first (partisan) historian, Fr Cornelius Mangan (1927), 'judging by the large number that was present at the first General Communion, a few months later, it is evident that there must have been at least seven hundred.' This suggests, perhaps optimistically, that the women filled the temporary church at their very first meeting, in contrast to the men and boys who, a month later, could muster a mere sixty each. However, there is no doubt that the first retreat for the women's confraternity, in April 1898, was a remarkable success which established the sodality on firm foundations. In June of that year, the members were formally organised into sections, each of which was placed under the protection of a patron saint and under the administrative care of a prefect and sub-prefect.[1]

The first public act of the women's confraternity was a series of visits they made to city churches in the early spring of 1901 in order to avail of the indul-

St Alphonsus de Liguori (1696-1787) who founded the Redemptorists in 1732.

Patrick Griffith, C.Ss.R. (1844-1926), the founder of Clonard; born in Mountmellick, Co Laois. A priest of the diocese of Kildare and Leighlin, he entered the Redemptorists in 1881-2. Rector until 1904, he was also the first director of the women's confraternity.

Clonard House. From an early photograph. The Redemptorists took formal possession on 31 October 1896.

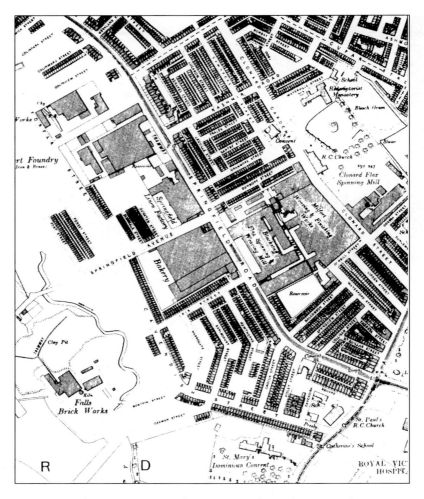

Ten years on – the monastery site as shown, upper right, in the 1907 Ordnance Survey.
The temporary church is shown as 'R. C. Church'. Note that, while the monastery is
surrounded by mills and the beginnings of dense housing, it is still on the edge
of the rapidly expanding city

Henry Henry, bishop of Down and Connor, 1895-1908, who invited the Redemptorists to make a religious foundation free from parochial obligations.

Mill girls. Women like these were among the first financial supporters of the Clonard foundation.

Tempoary ('Tin') church which sat side-on to Clonard Street at the lower end of the present car park from 1897-1911.

Interior of temporary church. Its nave, 125 ft by 40 ft, could seat 740 people but frequently held nearly twice that number.

The monastery was first occupied on 2 May 1900, having been built in less than two years. Cynics called it 'Griffith's Folly' because it contained fifty-four bedrooms, most of them intended for lay retreatants.

Redemptorist students, Clonard, 1903. From 1900 until 1905, the
monastery was the house of studies of the recently (1898) formed Irish Province.

Building the new church. Begun in August 1907, it was dogged by difficulties
and did not open for worship until 1 October 1911.

John Tohill, bishop of Down and Connor (1908-1914), who presided at the opening of Clonard church. The Redemptorists regarded him as having shown towards them, 'many signs of his affection and esteem.'
(Courtesy of Gerry McNamee, Archivist, St Malachy's College.)

Patrick Murray, C.Ss.R. (1865-1959). Lecturer in Moral Theology at Clonard from 1900; rector 1904-7; Irish provincial superior 1907-9; Redemptorist Rector Major 1909 until his retirement in 1947.

New Church of the Most Holy Redeemer,
CLONARD, BELFAST.

Solemn Dedication,

By Most Rev. Dr. TOHILL, Lord Bishop of Down and Connor,

On Rosary Sunday, 1st October, 1911.

Solemn High Mass (Coram Pontifice) at 12 o'clock.

SERMON BY THE LORD BISHOP.

Evening Devotions at 7 o'clock.

SERMON BY MOST REV. FR. MURRAY,

Superior General, San Alfonso, Rome.

COLLECTION AT BOTH SERVICES IN AID OF BUILDING FUND.

Admission (Evening), - - - Aisles—One Shilling.

IRISH NEWS, LTD.

Admission tickets for church opening 1911. The necessity of raising as much money as possible at the opening of the new church strained the hitherto excellent relations with the poor faithful of the Clonard area.

An early photograph of monastery and church.

The McDonnell family. The father, J.J., was architect of temporary church, monastery and 'new' church. Two sons became Redemptorists, Gerard, [standing left] (later rector of Clonard, 1950-3), and John ('Johnny'), [on his left] who was the last Redemptorist to be buried, in 1980, in the crypt of the church his father had designed.

Interior of the 'new' church, showing the original high altar, designed by the Belgian Redemptorist Henry Berghman, a member of the Clonard community. It was made and erected by John F. Davis of Cork.

A later photograph of the church interior showing the reduced high altar. The date of the reduction is uncertain, but it must have preceded the apse mosaic of Christ the Redeemer, installed in 1931-2 by Oppenheimer of Manchester.

Altar boys, Clonard, 1929, pictured with Jerry O'Shea, C.Ss.R.

THE ONLY ISSUE !!

Catholics
OF
Belfast!

RALLY ROUND YOUR REVERED BISHOP.

The Most Rev. H. HENRY, D.D.,
Bishop of Down and Connor,
Consecrated 22nd Sept., 1895,
Emancipated Belfast Catholics
1896.
Persecuted by irreconcilable
Factionists and
denied the right to direct and guide
Catholic Organization.

Catholics of Falls & Smithfield Wards,

ANSWER :—

Do you approve of organised rebellion against Ecclesiastical authority ?

Do you approve of the alleged true "democracy" — politics divorced . . from religion ?

Do you approve of yielding to the forces of secularism ?

Do you approve of the Berry Street War Cry - "Less of the Bishop" ?

IF YOU DO NOT,
AND WE KNOW YOU DO NOT,

VOTE FOR
O'Connell & Savage
IN SMITHFIELD WARD;

And VOTE FOR
Magee & M'Donnell
IN FALLS WARD.

⚜ God Save Ireland ⚜
FROM ANTI-CLERICALISM.

A Bishop Henry election poster, Belfast municipal elections, 1907. Dr Henry was combative in his involvement in local elections, which brought him into conflict with mainstream nationalists led by 'Wee Joe' Devlin.

REMEMBRANCE OF THE MISSION

Behold! How He Loved!

He Died for Me!

Preached by the Redemptorist Fathers
ST. MALACHY'S, COLERAINE,
NOVEMBER 2nd till NOVEMBER 16th, 1924.

DURING THE DAY.

When you begin your work, say : All for Thee, O Lord ! O my Jesus, all for Thee !

Ṡaċ níḋ aṛ ḋo ṡon-ṛa, o a íoṛa, ṡaċ níḋ aṛ ḋo ṡon-ṛa.

When you are tempted, say: Jesus and Mary, help me ! or a " Hail Mary."

íoṛa ⁊ a Ṁuiṛe cuiṛiġ liom.

When inclined to anger, say : O my Jesus, give me patience ! My Mother Mary, restrain my tongue.

O a íoṛa ṫabaiṛ ḟoiġṛo ḋam.

A Ṁuiṛe Ṁáṫaiṛ cuiṛ ṛṛian le mo ṫeanṡa.

When you have committed a fault, say :—O my God, I am very sorry that I have sinned against Thee, because Thou art so good ; I will never sin again.

O a Ḋhia tá ḋóláṛ móṛ oṛm, ṛá ṡuṛ ṗeaċtaiṡ mé aḋ' aġaiḋ-ṛe, ḋe ḃṛiġ ṡo ḃḟuil tú com maiṫ ṛin ; ní ṗeaccóċaiḋ mé níoṛ mó aṗíṛ ṡo ḃṛat.

Before and after meals bless yourself and say grace.

AT NIGHT.

Say your night prayers, examine your conscience, and make an Act of Contrition. Say also the three "Hail Marys" and the little prayer to Mary, as in the morning.

When in bed, fold your arms in the form of a cross, and say to yourself : I must die ; I do not know when—nor how—nor where ; but if I die in mortal sin, I am lost for ever. O Jesus, have mercy on me.

Caiṫṛiḋ mé báṛ ḟaġáil, níl ḟíoṛ aṡam, cia an t-am, cia a nóṛ, cia an áit : aċt má ḟáġaim báṛ i b-ṗéacaḋ maṛḃṫa, tá mé caillte ṡo ḋeo. A íoṛa, ḋean tṛócaiṛe oṛm.

A íoṛa, a Ṁuiṛe 'ṛ a tóṛeṛ, ḋeiṛim ḋiḋ mo ċṗoṛḋe aṡuṛ m'anam.

A íoṛa, a Ṁuiṛe 'ṛ a tóṛeṛ, ḃíḋíṛ taoḃ liom aṛ uaiṛ mo báiṛ.

A íoṛa, a Ṁuiṛe 'ṛ a tóṛeṛ, ṡo ḋteiġiḋ m'anam aṛ an ṛaoṡal ṛo i ṛíaċċain liḃ.
—(loṡa 300 lá.)

Bilingual mission 'Remembrance' 1925, recalling a Redemptorist mission in St Malachy's parish, Coleraine. That some of the prayers are given in both English and Irish reflects the considerable interest shown by the Clonard community in the Irish language, an interest which it retains.

Silver Jubilee celebrations of Our Lady's Confraternity, 1922. The ladies are shown in procession at the junction of Clonard Street and Falls Road and, later, assembled in the monastery garden for solemn benediction of the Blessed Sacrament.

The first prefects and sub-prefects of Clonard Holy Family Confraternity with Frs Lowham (Director), Griffith (Rector) and Creagh. Fr Lowham was director from 1899 to 1902

29. Golden Jubilee celebrations of all Clonard confraternities, 31 August 1947. Archbishop John D'Alton of Armagh (later Cardinal) at Beechmount grounds, accompanied by V Rev Gerard Reynolds, C.Ss.R (Rector) and J. J. McDonnell Jnr, C.Ss.R.

Dunmore Street decorated, August 1947.

The 'Big Yank',
Matthew Meighan, C.Ss.R.,
who brought to Clonard the
Perpetual Novena in honour of
Our Lady of Perpetual Succour
in 1943; seated is
Dr T. J. Regan, C.Ss.R., Rector.

gences attached to the universal jubilee proclaimed by Pope Leo XIII to mark the beginning of the new century. On four consecutive Sundays, Fr Griffith the first director, assisted by Fr Patrick Kilbride, led over one thousand women from Clonard to the designated churches of St Peter's, St Mary's, St Patrick's and St Malachy's. They prayed as they walked, but there was no singing, no banners were carried and, since the procession avoided the main thoroughfares, no special arrangements were made for diverting traffic. It was an undertaking that 'demanded much courage and daring in those days. But Fr Griffith was not a man to shrink from difficulties and danger.'[2]

After eight years as the first rector of Clonard, Fr Patrick Griffith left in 1904 to become Master of Novices in Dundalk. Fr Patrick Murray succeeded him as rector of the house and director of the women's confraternity. Shortly after his appointment he had to host the first ever visit to an Irish Redemptorist community by a Superior-General of the congregation. This was the Swiss Most Rev Mathias Raus, who chose Clonard as his first stop in his visitation of the new province. A special general communion was arranged for Sunday 10 July 1904; Fr Raus celebrated the mass, at which over one thousand women received. The confraternity made great strides under Fr Murray's direction. When he left Clonard in 1907 to become Irish provincial superior, the membership had increased to 1,600.[3]

Fr Murray's election, in May 1909, as Redemptorist Superior-General, was a source of particular joy to the women's confraternity. Only two years earlier he had been their spiritual director; and two years later, when he returned to Ireland for the opening of the new Clonard church, he preached to the women at their last meeting in the old church. That was on Sunday 10 September 1911.[4]

The new church, October 1911
The new church, opened on Rosary Sunday, 1 October 1911, made possible a great expansion – with comfort – of all attendances at Clonard. The women's confraternity was no exception. As a mark of the increase in membership, the attendance at their general communion following their first retreat in the new church in 1912 was a remarkable 1,928. It was remarkable also for the fact that it was the first time that the women's general communion numbers exceeded those of the men of the Holy Family confraternity, a superiority they were to enjoy for many years. Attendance at general communions may be taken as a rough guide to the active membership of the confraternity. On this basis, there were 2,392 active members in 1914; in 1917, there were 2,470; in 1925, 3,500 were recorded and, in 1926, the year preceding the separation of the confraternity into two divisions, there were 'over 3,600 members'.[5]

Women's second division

By the mid 1920s, growth in numbers indicated that a split in the confraternity was inevitable. Lack of space was particularly noticeable on the occasions of retreats and general communions – the times in the year when special efforts were made to renew the commitment of wayward members. On these occasions,

> hundreds, unable to get seating accommodation, were obliged to stand in the passages, up the nave and down the aisles. The sanctuary was packed to its utmost capacity, the organ loft and tribunes were likewise filled to overflowing. Such overcrowding was, from every point of view, most undesirable.

With the approval of his superiors, the director Fr Con Mangan got the necessary permission from Dr MacRory, bishop of Down and Connor, and the second Sunday of January 1927 was fixed for the division.

Appropriate ceremonial marked the occasion. The bishop agreed to preside at a special Mass and general communion. While not obligatory, the service attracted between 2,600 and 2,800 communicants, five priests requiring thirty-five minutes for the distribution. A final meeting of the united confraternity was held at seven in the evening. As Fr Mangan recalled: 'Long before half past six it was impossible to get a seat in the church.' The highlights of the occasion were the special sermon from former director (1921-1926) Fr Collier (he 'preached exactly three-quarters of an hour!') and the singing of the *Te Deum*, in alternate verses by two choirs of one hundred voices each, one located in the organ gallery, the other near the pulpit.

A third highlight, literally, was the magnificent visual display of the high altar, a reminder of the importance given to the sense of solemnity and occasion by the Redemptorists and of their ability to provide appropriate settings. As Fr Mangan recorded:

> The High Altar, arrayed in lines of brilliant light and decked with flowers, appeared at its best. The blaze of almost five hundred candles shone on it. Beautiful bouquets of chrysanthemums of amber, yellow and white, delightfully blending with tulips of scarlet and yellow, tastefully adorned it. Finally, the dazzling blaze of electric light from a dozen powerful lamps of two hundred candle power each, playing on the Altar and newly decorated dome, completed the most beautiful picture Clonard was ever known to present.[6]

Growth of the (men's) Holy Family confraternity

According to its chronicle, the silver jubilee of the Holy Family Confraternity in 1922 marked a 'steady and constant' growth in numbers 'year after year'. The opening of the new church in 1911 not only provided more accommodation, but brought 'a large influx of new members'. It soon became evident, as it had in the case of the women's, that the confraternity would have to be 'divided into two weekly meetings'. Such division was, apparently, about to be made when 'the outbreak of the Pogrom of 1920 with all its attendant sufferings and misery for the Catholics of the city' delayed the project. A decision was finally made at the beginning of 1924 to arrange the division.[7]

Second (Monday) division

It was decided that the general communion at the end of the annual retreat in October was a suitable time for the separation to take place. There was already an internal division within the confraternity for convenience of accommodation in the church and for attendance at monthly communion. One division occupied the gospel side of the church and made its communion on the third Sunday of each month; the other occupied the epistle side and made its communion on the fourth Sunday. Each division had thirty-two sections with a membership of 1,818 and 1,637 respectively, giving a grand total of 3,455. It was agreed that the larger first division should retain the traditional day of meeting, which was Tuesday. After consultation with their members, the prefects and sub-prefects of the second division voted for Monday as their day of meeting. So, the last general communion of the 'united confraternity' was held on Sunday 26 October 1924 at the 8.45 am Mass celebrated by Dr Mulhern, Bishop of Dromore. Dr Mulhern was invited because, according to the confraternity record, 'his interest in the Holy Family Confraternity in Newry is well known'. He also preached at a special meeting on that Sunday evening; during the Solemn Benediction, 'the *Te Deum* was sung by about fifty men from each division in alternate verses,' in thanksgiving for God's blessing on the confraternity to date.[8]

'Steady and constant' growth continued throughout the remainder of the 1920s and into the mid-1930s. By the end of 1931, each division had forty sections. The best indicators we have for numbers at this period are general communion figures. The 2,822 who received at the last 'united confraternity' general communion of 1924, had grown to 3,788 in 1930 and to 4,707 in 1933. It is possible that the figures for 1934 and 1935 surpassed these.[9]

'Forced emigration'

The first clear setback to growth in the confraternity was in the spring of 1936. While the total communion figure for the half-yearly retreat was 4,455, Fr James Reynolds noted:

> Numbers are down on the corresponding period last year. Between 200 and 300 members have gone to England for the past four months to seek for work and have got it.

His successor, Fr James Murray, in reviewing the statistics for 1936, remarked,

'Not a subject for congratulations' as attendance both at meetings and communions in both divisions was down by almost two hundred. While repeating the 'exodus to England for work' as an explanation, he thought other reasons might be given, 'especially the lethargy of the prefects and sub-prefects'. This decline in attendance continued through 1937, but there was a recovery in 1938, though not quite to the high point of the mid-1930s.[10]

An article in the *Irish News* noted the end of Fr Murray's three-and-a-half year term of office. The paper used the occasion to attack what it called an 'iniquitous system' of forced emigration of young Catholic men to take up employment in England and Scotland, quoting statistics from Clonard Holy Family as part of its argument. The article gave the loss of confraternity members as 384 in 1937, 220 in 1938, 547 in 1939 and 293 for the first six months of 1940. The implication was that all or most of these men were forced emigrants:

> The men concerned have no choice: they either abide by the instructions given them by officials at the Labour Exchange to take up work in England or Scotland or else they are struck off the Bureau. There is a strong belief in Belfast that Catholics are specially selected for this work ... as the figures for Clonard Confraternity would indicate.

There was the further point, 'argued', according to the article, 'in the Northern parliament', that the lot of these men's families had not been improved. It was alleged that the wages paid to the men were sometimes as low as £2 per week: 'When board is taken out of this there is very little left to send home,' so that, 'in a big percentage of cases' families were worse off than before.[11]

Third (Wednesday) division
The more immediate impact of the Second World War on the men's confraternity has been considered in the chapter on that period. There was certainly a significant increase in confraternity membership between 1944 and 1945 – over three hundred for the Monday division and over five hundred for the Tuesday division. The idea of a third division, first mooted as far back as 1928, was again brought forward and the newly appointed director, Fr Frank Russell, immediately announced 'an intensive recruiting campaign for new members for the third division'. This was in October 1945. On 14 February 1946, he noted in the confraternity chronicle: 'Our strength is such that I have sought the permissions necessary for the start of a third division.' February meetings averaged 1,824 for the Monday and 1,941 for the Tuesday division. During Lent, he approached Bishop Mageean, Mgr Hendley, the parish priest of St Paul's, and his own provincial superior, setting out two important reasons why there should be a third division. First, there was 'disrespectful overcrowding' at the weekly meetings and monthly communions and, secondly,

Hundreds were flocking back to the confraternity from the forces and war work in England and these men, who were badly in need of the spiritual helps of the confraternity, simply could not be accommodated with any degree of comfort.

Fr Russell noted that the bishop and the monsignor were 'very enthusiastic' but 'our own superiors had a certain amount of difficulty'. However, they were won over and Fr Russell planned to launch the new division on Wednesday 8 May, the feast of the Solemnity of St Joseph, since St Joseph was to be its patron.[12]

Fr Russell has left behind a detailed account of his planning of the new division. He first asked for volunteers from the existing two divisions to transfer to the new one. 'After repeated appeals,' he got 1,660 volunteers. Next, he invited five members to act as secretaries, Messrs James Gilmore, Malachy Murphy (both retired chief superintendents in the post office), Séamus O'Brien, a solicitor, and two well-known local businessmen, J. B. Kennedy, Jnr and Patrick Torney. It was decided to arrange sections 'on the basis of districts'. The city was divided into eight districts 'with so many sub-divisions', the idea being 'to place members from the same locality in the same section'. However, the method was not rigid. Men were given the option of going into a section with others not living in their locality, for example, 'relatives or a group of pals ... who would have a good influence on one another if placed in the same section'. Each of the existing divisions had forty-two sections. It was decided to reduce these to forty and to start the new division with the same number. Lastly, two sections of the boys' confraternity, which were made up of boys over fourteen years of age, were allowed to volunteer for the third division. Eighty boys did so.

Fr Russell's narrative concluded: 'Finally, all the spadework being done, it was decided to give the new division a hearty send-off and special celebrations were arranged for Monday and Tuesday, May 6th and 7th ...' Dr Mageean agreed to preside and Mgr Arthur H. Ryan, Professor of Scholastic Philosophy at Queen's University, to preach. Mgr Ryan complimented the confraternity as the second largest 'in the entire Catholic world', second only to Limerick. And he continued: 'Such an amazing development in a city not predominantly Catholic [was] surely a tangible proof that the blessings of God [had] been liberally poured out upon [the members].' There was solemn benediction each evening, at which 'the sacred music was beautifully rendered' by the full Clonard choir under Fr John Torney. The new division was inaugurated on Wednesday 8 May by a special meeting of all its officials – secretaries, prefects and sub-prefects, orderlies – and in the following week the confraternity met for the first time in three divisions.[13]

1947: Golden Jubilee of all confraternities

1947 was the golden jubilee year of all the Clonard confraternities, so large-scale celebrations were planned for the end of August, as was customary. Dr Mageean agreed to address each division of the men's confraternity on the Monday, Tuesday and Wednesday (25-27 August) of the jubilee week and Dr O'Neill, bishop of Limerick, accepted an invitation to speak to the three divisions of the women's confraternity. His Grace John Francis D'Alton, Archbishop of Armagh, agreed to preside and to preach at the final rally of both confraternities at Beechmount grounds on Sunday 31 August.

The local Catholic press did the occasion proud, both the daily *Irish News* and its weekly counterpart, the *Irish Weekly* and *Ulster Examiner*, with fulsome accounts and lavish photography. The *Irish News* reported:

> ... The procession from Clonard Church to Beechmount ... was one of the most imposing, colourful and edifying scenes ever witnessed in the city ... Twelve deep, it extended over a mile long, which [sic] was bedecked with papal flags, bunting, religious scrolls and arches erected at many points. Upwards of 400 stewards in addition to members of the police force marshalled the crowds.

At the conclusion of the ceremonies, telegrams were read from His Holiness Pope Pius XII (with Apostolic Benediction), from the Lord Mayor of Limerick and from Most Rev Fr Buijs, Superior General of the Redemptorists.

A private view of the procession, confided to the Chronicle of the Holy Family Confraternity by its new director, Fr David Harris, was less sanguine. Evidently there were tensions between himself and Fr James Cleary, director of the women's confraternity, about their respective roles in organising the jubilee. Fr Cleary was 'doing most of the organising ... He has experience of all these things before, having been director of the men's confraternity in Limerick when similar celebrations were held,' while Fr Harris was given the task 'of corresponding with bands and meeting officials of different departments in the city. The correspondence is pretty heavy.'

Fr Harris noted that things went wrong in the procession. For example, when the time came for various Redemptorists to recite the rosary along the route, 'in spite of the fact that Fr Cleary appeared to have made very precise arrangements, ... there did not appear to be many about.' Fr Harris complained, too, that, 'The procession ... was on the slow side,' though an accompanying cutting from the *Belfast Telegraph* attributed the slow pace to the press of people on the footpaths which delayed progress by half an hour. While asserting that 'everything at Beechmount went off well' – and he graciously complimented the Sisters of Mercy for their generous help, in particular for the altar which they 'beautified ... for us at their own expense' – he wrote at length about a problem with the public address system, supplied by Messrs Erskine Mayne. As a result of using ground rather than overhead cables at Beechmount, the sound was seriously distorted between muffles and booms in some parts of the grounds, as 'some of the people from time to time stood on the cable'. However, despite these reservations, 'things were carried out well'.[14]

Junior men's division 1951

Within a six-month period beginning in October 1950 there were two major developments in the Holy Family Confraternity. First, the director of the men's confraternity was relieved of responsibility for the boys' and a separate director allocated to it. The men's director, Fr Seán O'Loughlin, 'warmly welcomed' the decision and noted: 'The fact is that the three divisions of the men so occupies ... the director that he could not give the time to run the boys' efficiently.' Secondly, yet another confraternity division was established in March 1951. This was the Junior Men's, under the patronage of the Redemptorists' own St Clement Hofbauer. Fr O'Loughlin explained the rationale behind the new division:

> For a long time it has been felt that the gap between the Boys' Confraternity and the men is too wide. It was suggested that there should be something in between – by way of a senior division of the boys'. It was considered that after 13 years a boy needed something more than the talks to children usually given to the Boys' Holy Family – though he was not yet mature enough to profit by the lectures for men.

Or, as the community chronicler put it: 'its purpose is to secure ... special help for adolescents suitable for their age and the dangers surrounding modern youth.'

Since the ordinary age for members was to be over thirteen and under sixteen years 'or thereabouts', all boys over thirteen were transferred from the boys' to the new division and 'all youngsters in the three men's divisions who were under fifteen' were asked to leave and join the new division. Fr Harry McGowan, already in charge of the boys' since October, was appointed director of the new division, which was to meet weekly at 8 pm on Fridays. There was general satisfaction with recruitment for the new division; by June 1951, the numbers were 'getting on for 500'.[15]

However, the Junior Men's Division did not survive for long as a separate unit. In February 1960 it was 'amalgamated' with the three men's divisions, five sections being allocated to the Monday division, eleven to the Tuesday and one to the Wednesday division. Their sections were distinguished in each divison by the fact that they retained a static position in the church while, as customary, the men's sections rotated. 'By doing this,' noted the then director (Fr McCarthy), 'it is easy to keep a careful check on these youths who need, perhaps more than anyone else, all the graces that the confraternity bestows.' There is no explanation in the written records as to what became of the principles on which the Junior Men's was established just nine years earlier, particularly the assertion that, while needing 'something more than ... talks to children', the thirteen-to-sixteen year olds were 'not yet mature enough to profit by the lectures for men'. However, early in 1964, the division was reinstated under Fr Hugh McLaughlin, who had been Fr McCarthy's sub-director. He noted: 'About 184 attend [on Fridays at 8 p.m.] but we hope to build it up.'[16]

1957: Diamond Jubilee of men's confraternity

Unlike the Golden Jubilee celebrations in 1947, which were held in August, the Diamond Jubilee of the Confraternity was commemorated as close to the foundation date (20 June) as possible, in the 'confraternity' week beginning Monday 24 June and culminating on Sunday 30 June. Another contrast with 1947 was that there was no great public procession. Instead, the climax in 1957 was an open-air high Mass on Sunday in the monastery garden, without any presiding prelate. In the spirit of the changing emphases in liturgy at the time, the men as a body sang the 'People's Mass' by Dom Gregory Murray, OSB, conducted by Fr Francis O'Rourke, C.Ss.R., to the accompaniment of St Peter's Brass and Reed Band. The proper of the Mass was sung by Clonard Choir, under M Léon Rittweger. Soloist in Cesar Franck's *Panis Angelicus* was Seán Green, the 'Belfast tenor'. The special sermon for the occasion was preached by the Rector of Mount St Alphonsus, Limerick, V Rev Gerard McDonnell, a recent rector of Clonard. (His father had been the architect of Clonard monastery and church.)[17]

A commemorative booklet was published to mark the occasion, with a cover specially designed by 'the talented artist Gussie Hughes'. There was a foreword by the rector of Clonard, V Rev Charles McNiffe, a few short articles, one of them a reflective piece on the work and spirit of the confraternity and its officials; another was a brief 'History of the Confraternity'. There were two reminiscences, one by a 'Confraternity Man' who had become a member in 1918 and another in which, 'A Veteran Salutes the Prefects'. Finally, there were numerous photographs, including no less than six interior views of packed congregations, five of the men's divisions and one of the boys'. The commemorative booklet gives membership figures from several dates in the past to illustrate the growth of the Holy Family confraternities, as follows:

Progress of the Confraternity in Numbers

Year	Men's Divisions	Boys'
1897	60	60
1904	1218	545
1928	3765	1598
1931	4392	1621
1957	7172	2126

Grand total in 1957: 9298.[18]

Giving figures for years as close as 1928 and 1931 is not particularly meaning-ful, especially when two important growth periods, the early to mid-thirties and the postwar 1940s are omitted. In 1949, for example, a total of 5,863 men in three divisions was recorded at their annual general communion. Allowing for absences and sickness, numbers were probably higher. In fact, on 1 January 1950, Fr Seán O'Loughlin noted: 'After the end of year "purge", the numbers per division were as follows: Monday, 2,113, Tuesday 2,417, Wednesday 2,014. Total: 6,544.' Statistics for the commemorative booklet, it seems, were compiled hastily.[19]

THE CONFRATERNITIES IN DECLINE

Administrative lapses

The figure given above for 1957 – 7,172 – is the only available figure between 1952 and 1963 because, for reasons unknown, directors between these dates ceased to record statistics in the confraternity chronicle. When next the practice was resumed, by Fr Hugh McLaughlin in 1963, numbers had fallen considerably. Appointed director in January of that year, he discovered two serious adminis-trative lapses. First, the register books for consecration of new members in the Tuesday and Wednesday divisions were two years behind. Fr McLaughlin feared that missing records could create problems for future directors, 'when jubilees [were] claimed'. Secondly, and more seriously, he discovered that 'the [director's] private interview with prefects had not taken place for three years.' So he began the laborious round in mid-February. Fr Seán O'Loughlin had written about the chore in 1950:

> This is one of the bigger and most tedious tasks of the whole year, but it is vitally important that it is done well. If the prefects realise that they must give an account to the director about every member, it helps to sharpen their wits about doing the job.

At any rate, after Fr McLaughlin's interviews with prefects in 1963, 'nearly 800 names were removed from section books'. In the meantime, the card files for the Tuesday and Wednesday divisions had to be completely revised with the help of the legionary *praesidium* attached to the confraternity. The Tuesday files were in a particularly bad state, contradictions between cards and section books exceeding five hundred, largely because members did not report changes of address. By early 1964, the numbers on section books were, by division:

Monday 2,222; Tuesday 1,987; Wednesday 1,678; Total: 5,887.[20]

Problems with prefects

Problems, however, continued for Fr McLaughlin during 1964. He noticed that attendances dropped 'after the traditional break from meetings during Lent, when missions were going on in the city parishes'. Worse still, attendances 'never recovered and dropped considerably after the [summer] holiday period, even though the half-yearly [retreat in April and May] did arrest it for a time'. There were serious problems, too, with prefects. Part of the difficulty seems to have been the 'new code imposed [on the secretaries] according to the Limerick style', that is, based on methods used in the Redemptorists' confraternity in Limerick. The Clonard secretaries felt it had been 'imposed' on them and were not happy with it. Part of the code affected prefects: hitherto prefects had had responsibility for 'writing notices' to absent or careless members. Under the Limerick system, such notices were written by the divisional secretaries. As a result, 'prefects were losing interest.' This showed very markedly at the end of year interviews for 1964, when Fr McLaughlin discovered that 'many [prefects] regarded the chain [of office] as an honorary decoration'. As a result, he made no less than forty-two changes in his list of prefects and sub-prefects, 'but found it difficult to fill all vacancies'.

Fr McLaughlin's continuing anxieties led to the establishment of 'a special commission' early in 1966 to elicit suggestions for 'updating the confraternity.' It had two meetings. One suggestion, that evening Mass, now liturgically acceptable, should replace the weekly meeting, was rejected. Another was that there should be a confraternity membership card. This was acted upon. A practical outcome of the meetings was the realisation that sections were 'too widely scattered for any prefect and sub-prefect to manage'. However, it was late in 1968 before Fr Mullin, Fr McLaughlin's successor, pursued this matter. In October of that year he held a 'referendum' to explore 'the possibility of arranging sections according to districts', which would facilitate the work of the prefects. (There are echoes here of Fr Russell's aim, in 1945, of arranging sections in the new third division 'on the basis of districts', which, however, he did not apply rigidly.) But before Fr Mullin could take any action, he was replaced as director by Fr Paud Egan who assumed office in January 1969.[21]

1969 and its aftermath

Fr Egan's time as director was dominated by the troubles. He had but a few months to settle into his new post when the events of 15 August forced him into a leadership that he had not sought. The hour-by-hour account in the Clonard Domestic Chronicle of that fateful day contains the following entry:

> 4 pm. Fr Egan, watching from the windows upstairs, saw a young lad stagger and fall in Waterville St. He rushed down to the oratory, got the oils, ran out across the line of fire where young Gerard McAuley lay in a pool of blood. He had been shot in the back outside St Gall's school. Fr Egan anointed him. Gerard died almost immediately. The houses in Kashmir Road and on the other side of Bombay St were blazing ...

A few days later, Fr Egan escorted the Mayor of Limerick around the Clonard area. This was on 21 August. The mayor's visit was evidence of the anxieties felt in his city where, because of the Redemptorist connection, there had already been an offer made to house Belfast refugees. Indeed, on the day of the mayor's visit, Fr Patrick Cunning of the Clonard community was setting out for Limerick with a bus load of fifty-two refugees, who were to be housed in the Redemptorists' retreat house there. Six days later when James Callaghan, Home Secretary in Harold Wilson's Labour government, 'came to see the destruction around the back of the monastery', it was Fr Egan who 'handed him a letter concerning the troubles in this area'. In his capacity as director, he was, in the months following, frequently invited to meetings with British army officers and local 'republican' leaders 'to discuss local defence'.[22]

An immediate impact of the troubles was that any kind of major initiative in regard to the confraternity – such as, say, a proposed reorganisation of sections – was postponed indefinitely. The short-term priority was to maintain as great a degree of normality as possible. Perhaps there was an element of wishful thinking in the monastery record under the date of 29 August: 'In the church and Clonard community, everything is back to normal, except [that] the Men's Confraternity is a little earlier than usual.' For, before September was out, after noting the tension in the city and unrest caused by rumours, the same record notes: 'The effect of the riots can be seen in [that] the attendance at all church functions in Clonard is far below the normal.' However, as late as May 1970, Fr Egan was observing in the Chronicle of the Holy Family Confraternity:

> Although politics, soldiers and rioting dominate men's minds and form a common topic of conversation, the Confraternity has not, so far, been badly affected by the 'Troubles'.[23]

The first clear indication in the Clonard domestic record of the serious effect of the troubles on the confraternities – both men's Holy Family and women's Our Lady's – is found in the brief entries referring to the annual retreats for each in 1972. Of the women's retreat, customarily held in September, the record notes, without comment: 'About 900 attended from each of the first two divisions and about 400-500 from the third.' October was the traditional time for the three divisions of the men to make their retreat: '... attendance was encouraging in view of the political situation, although it was not as good as that of the ladies.'[24]

Boys' confraternity

Remarkably, in October 1972, at the very time when available figures were showing the great extent of the decline in attendance at the men's and women's confraternities, the boys' confraternity was 'started off again'. The boys' had collapsed in the autumn of 1969 because parents feared for the safety of their children. In early October 1972, the rector, Fr Michael Browne, aware that an indefinite closure might become permanent, announced that he would reconvene the boys' the following week, keeping the direction of the effort in his own hands until Christmas. Eighty boys turned up for the first meeting. But it rapidly became apparent that the new arrangement would not hold. In order to keep a boys' confraternity in being, the decision was made, with the agreement of the neighbouring schools, to restrict membership to the pupils of St Gall's and St Finnian's primary schools. The arrangement was that they should come to Clonard church immediately after school in alternate weeks.[25]

Adult confraternities in decline

Returning to the fortunes of the adult confraternities, in the summer of 1973, 'due to a steady decline in attendance,' the third division of the men's was abandoned; and, in October, the retreats of the surviving two divisions were 'not well attended'. By the end of 1977, the domestic chronicler reported as follows:

> Men's Holy Family Confraternity: 1,000 members in 2 divisions; weekly meetings. Ladies Confraternity: 2,500 members in 3 divisions; monthly meetings.

Thereafter, the heavy losses were openly acknowledged, as in this note following the close of the men's annual retreat in October 1978: 'We no longer think in terms of thousands, but an average attendance of 600-700 is something to thank God for, especially in Belfast as it is in these times.' On that basis, the men's 1978 retreat was regarded as successful. Similar words were applied in September 1979 to the women's annual retreat: ' ... where we spoke in terms of thousands 30 years ago, we speak now in terms of hundreds, but for what we have we are grateful.'[26]

The truth is that the troubles brought rapid devastation to the Clonard confraternities. The figures for 1972 are sufficient testimony to that fact. Thereafter the policy of the Redemptorists was one of containment and survival. It is easy to see in retrospect that, by the second half of the 1960s the glory days were over. There seems little doubt that the reaction against traditional devotions which came in the wake of Vatican II would have had a diminishing effect, however slow, but the location of Clonard monastery ensured that the troubles would have maximum effect in frightening away from the confraternities the majority membership which came from outside the immediate area.

'Clonard mission for men'

In 1981, an imaginative decision was taken to replace the men's confraternity annual retreat with a 'Clonard mission for men', to which all men were invited. Of the 800 or so who attended for the week of 5-11 October, about 150 were not confraternity members. On 21 March 1982, the third division of the women's confraternity met for the last time because the average attendance for some years had been as low as 200. It had begun in 1944. A sterling attempt by the men's director, Fr Seán Keeney, to mark in a special way the 85th anniversary of the Holy Family Confraternity mustered between 700 and 800 men on Sunday 16 May 1982. There was an impressive concelebrated Eucharist by former directors of the Holy Family, Frs David Harris, Seán O'Loughlin, Seán Mullin, Hugh McLaughlin, Aodh Bennett, Patrick O'Keefe and others, with Fr McLaughlin as the special preacher. Unfortunately, Cardinal Ó Fiaich and Bishop Philbin were unable to attend.[27]

Despite such attempts to inspire a return of members, despite dedicated work by director after director, despite the annual sermon or service conducted since 1985 by a visiting Protestant minister as part of Church Unity Week, the story of the men's confraternity through the 1980s and into the 90s, is a story of continuing decline. While the annual 'Clonard Mission for Men' could attract between 700 and 800 in 1982, by 1990 this number had fallen to 'over 400', which, nevertheless, could be described as a 'good' attendance. In 1994, the number recorded was 'just over 300'. Such annual mission figures were the result of a special effort. The true state of the men's confraternity is revealed by attendance at weekly meetings. In 1988 this averaged 195 for the Monday division and 210 for the Tuesday division; these statistics were accompanied by the bald statement: 'The Sunday monthly communion was dropped last year.'[28]

The women's confraternity, meeting only once monthly, fared somewhat better, but was also losing ground. In 1983, for example, the half-yearly retreats in late April-early May attracted attendances of about 700 each. Of the annual retreat in September that year, the chronicler wrote:

> The attendance was good, but not very good. It is a fact that the Confraternity is slowly but surely declining in numbers. ...The present director [Fr Wadding] has not spared himself.

In 1985, the chronicler produced comparative figures to show the decline, in overall numbers, of the women's confraternity 'general communion'. The 'general communion' at the final Mass on the closing day was traditionally regarded as the high point of an annual retreat. The figures were as follows:

Year 1927: 3,929; Year 1967: 5,224; Year 1985: 1,185.

By 1988, the annual retreat of the first division of the women's confraternity was regarded as 'well attended' when 560 members were present at its close.[29]

However depleted, Our Lady's confraternity continues to survive after a hundred years. Similarly, the men's Holy Family goes on into a new millennium. The precise state of the men's was set out in a commemorative booklet published in 1994 on the occasion of the one hundred and fiftieth anniversary of the founding of the Holy Family confraternity in the Belgian city of Liège. In 1994, there were two small divisions, Monday and Tuesday, consisting of twenty-six and twenty sections respectively. Each section had seven or eight members, giving a total membership of just over three hundred. Reflecting its title, *How We See Ourselves*, the pamphlet viewed the confraternity as 'a counter-culture group' operating 'against the tide' of the times, yet affirming itself as,

> a mature association. Members find help and support in it for the deeper spiritual needs a man becomes aware of as he moves into his middle years. The friendship and prayer of the confraternity is back-up for the long haul which has to be lived in faith, hope and love, one day at a time.[30]

This affirmation echoes precisely the fundamental reasons for the foundation of the Clonard confraternities in 1897.

CHAPTER 9

The Perpetual Novena
in honour of Our Lady of Perpetual Succour

One of the unquestioned successes of the Redemptorist apostolate in Clonard church has been the perpetual novena in honour of Our Lady of Perpetual Succour. Established in 1943, it continues to flourish at the beginning of the new millennium.

Images
Only the most cynical or uninformed opponents of the Catholic Church believe that it encourages or even tolerates the 'worship' or 'adoration' of images or that it advocates 'worship' of the Virgin Mary or the saints. Images or icons or 'holy pictures' are seen merely as visual aids to prayer, and prayer to the Mother of God or the saints is seen as appropriate intercession within the church viewed as the Communion of Saints.[1] Perhaps more puzzling to the well-disposed – and to many Catholics – is the large number of titles by which the Blessed Virgin is addressed. Cardinal Newman provided a useful answer to this problem when he suggested that, 'Each of the titles of Mary has its own special meaning and drift, and may be made the subject of a distinct meditation.'[2]

Brief history of the icon and the Redemptorist connection
The image or icon of Our Lady of Perpetual Succour is unusual in the Western church in that it is distinctly Eastern or Byzantine in style. Experts agree that the icon originated in Crete sometime in the fourteenth century, that it acquired a reputation for miracles, and that it found its way to Rome about 1499 where, as a result of visionary directions from 'Holy Mary of Perpetual Succour', as Mary of the icon called herself, it was given in charge to the Augustinian friars in their church of St Matthew in the Via Merulana. It was venerated there for three hundred years until 1798, when the church was destroyed by an invading French army. The icon was finally placed in the friars' own oratory at Santa Maria in Posterula. There it remained hidden until 'rediscovered' by a young Redemptorist in the early 1860s.[3]

In 1855 the Redemptorists had made their new headquarters (named Sant' Alfonso) in Via Merulana on a property that included the site of the old St Matthew's. They knew nothing of the picture of Our Lady which had been venerated there. However, on an occasion in the early 1860s it emerged that a young member of the community, Fr Marchi, not only knew the picture but knew where it was. He told how, as a boy, he had served Mass for the Augustinians in Santa Maria in Posterula. There he became acquainted with an old brother who had belonged to St Matthew's for a decade before it was destroyed. Fr Marchi remembered how the old man had frequently and insistently spoken to him of the picture, its miraculous reputation and its connection with St Matthew's.

The Redemptorists were naturally interested in the story. Eventually, the Rector Major, Nicholas Mauron, formally requested Pope Pius IX that the guardianship of the picture be given to the Redemptorists. The Pope readily acceded. The icon was then transferred to Sant' Alfonso and solemnly installed on 26 April 1866. It was on this occasion that the Pope gave the injunction to the Redemptorists to make the Mother of Perpetual Succour 'known to the world'.[4]

Crowning of the icon
So rapidly did the devotion spread in Rome that within a year there were requests to the diocesan chapter from several parish priests that the icon be crowned. Such crowning was a customary method of acknowledging the spiritual influence of a devotion, for which three principal conditions had to be met: the devotion had to have ecclesiastical approval, it had to be of long historical standing and many miracles had to be attributable to it. Approval was given and on 23 June 1867 the picture was solemnly crowned in Sant' Alfonso.[5]

Symbolism
The five inscriptions on the picture are in abbreviated Greek. They read, from left to right and from the top downwards: 'Mother – of God,' (this title is divided by Mary's crown); 'Archangel Michael'; 'Archangel Gabriel,' and, to the right of the infant Jesus' halo, the abbreviation means 'Jesus Christ'. Eastern convention dictates that the background should be, not a landscape, as in Western sacred art, but a single colour, gold, which signifies paradise to which Mother and Son belong. It dictates the colours of the various garments and the folds in them, the covering of the Archangels' hands as they touch the instruments of Christ's passion and, finally, the formal poses of Mother and Son. However, most experts also see a slight movement away from rigid Eastern formality in the softer contours of the faces of mother and child and in the slight inclination of Our Lady's head towards her Son, allowing a hint of Western feeling into an otherwise strictly conventional portrait representing spiritual subjects.

Content of the picture
The icon shows a somewhat startled divine child. He has, apparently, just

seen Archangel Michael holding the spear and the sponge on a hyssop stick, instruments of his forthcoming passion, from which he has turned so sharply that his left sandal is dislodged, only to see Gabriel on the other side holding the remaining instruments of the passion, namely, the Cross (in Byzantine style) and the nails. In his distress, the child seeks comfort by grasping his mother's right hand with both of his, while her left hand gives him added support and comfort. Finally, it is the mother's eyes, looking at us suppliant Christians, that draw us into contact with her and her son. To the Eastern Christians, this icon is unquestionably of Mary the Mother of God who comforts her infant as he foresees his suffering and death and who invites us Christians into a profound engagement with him. Indeed, in Russia such an icon was known as 'Strastnaia' or 'Our Lady of the Passion'. The Redemptorists, when they took over guardianship of the icon, were keenly aware of the instruments of Our Lord's passion as a common element with the insignia of their own congregation.[6]

Idea of a perpetual novena
The Redemptorists took their guardianship seriously and acted promptly on Pius IX's injunction. Soon copies of the original picture in Sant' Alfonso, authenticated by the Rector Major, found their way to Redemptorist houses and churches all over the world. Clonard, for example, received two authentic copies shortly after its foundation and weekly devotions in honour of the Mother of Perpetual Succour quickly followed. Redemptorists in the United States of America were particularly active in promoting the new devotion, eventually developing the concept of a 'perpetual novena'.

The Perpetual Novena comes to Clonard
Unlikely as it might seem, it was war – the Second World War – which brought to Clonard a new form of devotion to Our Lady of Perpetual Succour, for which the monastery was to be famous. On Friday 15 October 1943, two American Redemptorists, chaplains to the American forces then massing in Northern Ireland, paid a courtesy visit to their Irish confrères in Clonard. Their names were Fr Raymond Keenan and Fr Matthew Meighan.[7]

The visit of the two chaplains to Clonard coincided with an important devotional event in Clonard history which has since been forgotten in the excitement generated by the perpetual novena of Our Lady of Perpetual Succour. This was the first solemn novena in honour of the Redemptorists' own saint, Gerard Majella, the humble lay brother who had died in 1755 at the age of twenty-nine, a prodigious miracle worker in life and in death. The American visitors were highly impressed by the novena and it became a subject of conversation between Fr Meighan and his host, the rector, Fr T. J. Regan. Fr Meighan said the attendance was splendid; it reminded him of the perpetual novena they had back home in honour of Our Lady of Perpetual Help (as the Americans called her). Fr Regan, as he wrote later, was enthused by his guest's account of Our Lady's novena, of its 'wonderful success and results in confessions, attendance at Mass and Holy Communion'.

Fr Kerr, the Provincial, agreed to have the novena begun in Clonard and said he would get the Redemptorist communities in Dundalk and Limerick to follow suit.

Meantime, Fr Regan invited his guest to preach to the Clonard congregation. His subject was devotion to Our Lady of Perpetual Help and the remarkable success of the perpetual novena in American Redemptorist churches. As Fr Patrick O'Donnell C.Ss.R. writes: ' ... in the Belfast of 1943, ... a live American chaplain was a treat not to be missed. The attendance was so great that the doors were closed fifteen minutes before the devotion started.' Hundreds had to be turned away, including the occupants of a taxi which had been hired at the other end of Belfast. The strong accent of 'the big Yank', as he was remembered, his eloquent language and sweeping gestures held the people spellbound. He was, without doubt, a charismatic figure who, however, as Fr O'Donnell mischieviously observes, had another *persona*, a distinctly hard-nosed one, when facing his GIs. A young priest who heard him address American servicemen in St Patrick's Church, Donegall Street, reported that his language was unprintable.

However, Fr Meighan was uniquely qualified to inform his Irish listeners about the perpetual novena in American Redemptorist churches. Between 1932 and 1940 he had been national promoter of the novena in the United States and since 1934, until volunteering for war service, had broadcast it every Friday from radio station WNBX in New York. Whatever the effects of his eloquence on American servicemen, he certainly won over his Irish Redemptorist confrères and the people of Clonard. Towards the end of November 1943, Fr Regan obtained permission – as canonically required – from the Bishop of Down and Connor, Dr Mageean, to introduce the perpetual novena, to be held every Thursday, beginning on Thursday 9 December.[8]

It was decided to prepare for the occasion by a solemn novena, to begin on 29 November and conclude on 8 December, the feast of Mary's Immaculate Conception. The Clonard chronicler reflected the great stir of the occasion:

> This novena was truly a record, both as [to] the crowds attending it and the religious enthusiasm pervading it. From the first day to the close ... the people, young, old, men and women, flocked into the church to pay homage to Our Lady of Perpetual Succour. Never was there seen in Clonard such a concourse of people ...

Mass was said each morning at 6.30, 7, 7.30 and 9.30, while the prayers of the

novena were recited from the pulpit. At the 7.30 and 9.30 Masses, 'the people sang appropriate hymns in honour of Our Blessed Lady, the organ being
played by one of the fathers'. At the devotions each evening at half-past
seven, 'the church was crowded to overflowing'. The chronicler thought the
devotions,

> very impressive, the people listened each evening with rapt attention to a
> short discourse on Our Lady of Perpetual Succour. A special feature ...
> was the blessing of the people each evening with a large sized picture of
> Our Blessed Lady by the priest from the pulpit.

His record concluded with the hope that the novena 'will have far-reaching
results in the spiritual life and morals of the citizens of Belfast'.[9]

So, on Thursday 9 December 1943, the perpetual novena in honour of
Our Lady of Perpetual Succour began in Clonard church. 'This perpetual
novena,' it was noted, 'consists in the carrying out on Thursday weekly of the
same devotions performed during the solemn novena.' The Redemptorists
were at pains to explain the new idea of 'perpetual' novena carefully. Fr T. A.
Murphy set out their ideas on the subject in the prestigious clerical journal,
The Irish Ecclesiastical Record, in an article entitled, 'Mary's Perpetual Novena'.
The idea of a 'novena' or nine days of prayer was well understood, based as it
was on the 'continuous prayer' with which for nine days the apostles and
other early Christians 'including Mary the mother of Jesus' awaited the coming of the Holy Spirit at Pentecost (Acts 1:14). Perseverance in prayerful petition to God was expressly recommended by Our Saviour himself, in the
examples of the man in Luke 11:5, 8 whose late night request for bread was
answered by his friend because of his persistence and the Canaanite woman
in Matthew 15:22-28 whose doggedness was rewarded with the cure of her
daughter. As to the 'perpetual' aspect of prayer, Fr Murphy wrote:

> More closely defined, it is an act of devotion to the Mother of God which
> is repeated on one day of every week, so that the faithful may begin it any
> week of their choice and continue until they have a novena completed.[10]

On the first Thursday, there were four Masses in the morning at the shrine,
evening devotions at eight o'clock and an afternoon session at 4.15 for the
children, whose attendance was 'simply marvellous'. There was also, from the
beginning, a children's Mass at 9.30 on Saturday mornings. On 20 January
1944, a fifth Mass at the shrine was added; on 3 February, an additional session of devotions at 7 pm; on 20 April a third evening session at 9 pm was
commenced; on 4 May a fourth session at 6 pm and, finally, another afternoon session at 3 pm, 'to accommodate the old and feeble and women with
very young children'. By any standards, it was a remarkable expansion, from
four Masses and two devotions to five Masses and six devotions in the space
of five months. The Masses were extremely well attended and the sessions of

devotions to overflowing. As the chronicler wittily remarked, 'Were it not for the members of the Clonard fire brigade [his personal term for the voluntary church ushers], it would be impossible to control the vast concourse of people at each of the meetings.'

The evening devotions were short, designed to take no more than thirty minutes, consisting of 'the Little Rosary of the Immaculate Conception, Readings of Petitions and Thanksgivings, Novena Prayers, Sermonette, Blessing of the Sick and Benediction'.[11]

In the succeeding years, the novena continued to flourish. In October 1947, the normal Saturday evening devotions were 'transformed into a Novena service owing to the number who cannot attend on Thursday'. The huge Thursday attendances continued to the extent that 'Clonard Thursday' became a phenomenon in the life of Belfast among Catholics, certainly, who came from all over the city and beyond, but also to some extent among non-Catholics, a number of whom participated in the novena from the start.[12]

1948: Crowning of mother and child

The year 1948 was particularly eventful for the novena. Two important manifestations of public fervour provided evidence of the influence of the devotion and, at the same time, gave it further impetus. The first occasion was briefly recorded in the monastery chronicle under the date of 28 January:

> At the Perpetual Novena devotions today, the rector Fr G. Reynolds put on public view a beautiful new gold monstrance and chalice, the free voluntary gifts and tributes of the grateful clients of Our Lady of Perpetual Succour – rings, brooches, cuff-links, watches and watch chains, engagement and signet rings, earrings with all their precious stones were tastefully and artistically put into the beautiful gold monstrance to be used for the benediction at the Perpetual Novena devotions.

The second occasion was a much more formal one, the result of a very ambitious project. This was the crowning of the images of Mary and the Divine Infant in the enshrined picture of Our Lady of Perpetual Succour. It took place on her feast, Sunday 20 June 1948. The crowning, performed by the rector, was in conscious imitation of the crowning of the original miraculous picture in Sant' Alfonso, Rome, in 1867.

The crowns were exact replicas of the originals in Rome, made from gifts given by the people. Each crown, in beautifully worked gold, was inlaid with twenty-six precious stones, 'many of them ... taken from engagement rings and family jewellery'. There is no written record of the process which resulted in the crafting of the two sets of gold artefacts, the monstrance and chalice and the two crowns, but it seems safe to assume that the more modest project of monstrance and chalice, launched, presumably, at an early date in

1947, was met with such a large response that the materials were available for the working of the two crowns.[13]

The crowning was the culmination of the Solemn Novena for the feast of Our Lady of Perpetual Succour in 1948:

> During the nine days' preparatory novena, five thousand people thronged the church every night during the devotions, which had to be duplicated. On the day of the crowning, loudspeakers carried the devotions to the huge crowds outside the church unable to gain admission.

By the time the crowning took place, about 350,000 petitions to Our Lady of Perpetual Succour were being received at Clonard each year, while letters of thanksgiving, telling of favours received, were over 13,500 a year. The annual attendance at Our Lady's shrine was estimated at one million.[14]

1949: New shrine

During the months of August and September 1949, the refurbishment of the shrine was completed by the erection of ornamental gates to the front and side, so that it was for years afterwards referred to as the 'new shrine'. The rector, Fr Reynolds, pulled off a considerable coup for Clonard and the perpetual novena, by securing the Redemptorist Superior General to bless the improvements. Fr Leonard Buijs, a Dutchman (he had succeeded the Irishman Fr Patrick Murray who had retired in 1947), had just completed a virtual world tour in his first visitation of Redemptorist houses all over the globe. He agreed to bless the shrine at the final novena session, 9 pm, on Thursday 8 September. He surprised an 'immense congregation' by addressing them for fifteen minutes in perfect English – no notes, no fumbling for an appropriate word. He was highly complimentary about the novena and its reputation in the Redemptorist world, telling his hearers that 'almost everywhere Redemptorists asked [him], "Have you been in Ireland?" "Have you gone to Belfast?"' Not surprisingly, Fr Buijs was mobbed afterwards by an enthusiastic congregation. However, on the following day in a private address to the Clonard community, while acknowledging the unique position of the faith in Ireland, he warned that Ireland could not remain forever immune to the pressures from a secular world and urged his confrères to be ahead of and forestall new dangers.[15]

Visiting preachers

Fr Reynolds was very assiduous in bringing to Clonard foreign visitors whom he would invariably persuade to address either the confraternities or the novena congregations. He was keenly aware of the curiosity value of foreign accents in parochial Belfast (witness the effect of 'the big Yank' in 1943), but, more importantly, he realised the value of the affirmation of the faith of the universal church that such visitors could provide. At the end of August 1950,

Clonard had visits from no less than four overseas bishops, two of whom addressed all six Thursday sessions of the novena. Both were Redemptorists, both on their way to Rome for the proclamation, later in the year, of the dogma of the Assumption of Our Lady. The first was Dr Murray, coadjutor Archbishop of the Canadian diocese of Winnipeg; the second was the celebrated Bishop Edmund Gleeson, the Irish-born bishop of Maitland, New South Wales, who, though in his eighty-first year, was still a dynamic preacher. Bishop Gleeson, in fact, launched a special novena of nine Thursdays, timed to conclude with the proclamation of the dogma of the Assumption on 1 November 1950. On the occasion of that proclamation, the whole facade of Clonard Church was illuminated in celebration, as a large photograph in the *Irish News* of 2 November testified.[16]

Impetus to devotion: Marian Year 1954
Devotion to Our Lady received a great impetus in the early 1950s from the declaration by Pope Pius XII that a special Marian Year would be celebrated, beginning with the feast of the Immaculate Conception, 8 December 1953. Such a major celebration provided official confirmation, not that it was needed, that the perpetual novena to Mary under the title of Perpetual Succour was fully in line with the thinking of the church. Indeed, from a domestic point of view, the novena had grown so large and influential that fears were expressed in Clonard about the survival of other traditional devotions. For example, the Clonard chronicler recorded, in October 1954, with evident relief, of the solemn novena in honour of St Gerard Majella:

> ... attendance at Mass and devotions is splendid. St Gerard was more or less relegated to the background in recent years in Belfast, but this does indeed have all the appearance of a real revival of devotion to the good saint.

Similar anxieties had been expressed earlier, in 1947, about the traditional devotion of the nine Fridays in honour of the Sacred Heart, 'which has been somewhat obscured by the Thursday Perpetual Novena'. To rekindle the devotion, an improvement of the Sacred Heart shrine had been undertaken ('... picture recessed and illuminated') and a solemn votive Mass, with appropriate devotions, inaugurated.[17]

It is difficult to trace precisely the fortunes of the weekly perpetual novena from the mid-1950s onwards, because the references to it in the domestic record are few and far between, so much was it taken for granted as part of the monastery's apostolate. We know that, late in 1956, it still supported six sessions each Thursday afternoon and evening, at 3 pm, 4.15, 6.10, 7, 8 and 9 pm.[18]

Decline

Ironically, the first indication of a decline in the perpetual novena coincided with the return of its 'founding father', Fr Matthew Meighan, who came to preach the solemn novena in June 1965. His return, it seemed, guaranteed a remarkably large turnout (exaggerated by the local press as 10,000 per evening), but the reality was otherwise. According to the chronicle: 'In recent times the numbers have fallen off considerably here and in the other city churches,' that is, in Clonard and in those city parishes which had introduced the perpetual novena in the 1940s, following its success in Clonard.[19]

The general decline in attendance at devotional exercises in the wake of the Second Vatican Council was widely acknowledged by the 1970s. Thus, in December 1973, the Thursday novena sessions were reduced from six to three. Of the solemn novena of 1976 it was noted: 'There was general satisfaction with the people's response, allowing for the universal falling away in attendance at devotional exercises in church.' In October of the same year, the admission was made on the occasion of St Gerard's solemn novena, 'We have reconciled ourselves by now not to expect the large attendances which were a feature of other days.' Acceptance of smaller congregations is evident too in the record of the solemn novena in June 1977: 'Attendance was good and sustained right through; say a daily 2,500 to 3,000.' At the same time, the chronicler acknowledged that, at Clonard's sister church at Mount St Alphonsus, Limerick, the solemn novena was drawing 'an estimated 20,000 a day' (actually 29,000 in twelve sessions) and he complimented his Limerick confrères as only an Irishman could, with the salute, 'Up Garryowen!'[20]

Revival and development of solermn novena

This reference to Limerick is timely, as far as the history of the solemn novena in honour of Our Lady of Perpetual Help is concerned. The reader will notice the change of title; the ungainly word 'Succour' had been replaced by the more accessible 'Help' when the Limerick Redemptorists made a decision in 1971, 'to revive and, if possible, to develop the Novena'. This revival and development was at first modestly and then spectacularly successful under a small team of Redemptorists directed by Fr Vincent Kavanagh. Attendance in Limerick rose from 4,000 per day in two sessions in June 1971 to 23,000 per day in nine sessions in June 1976. By 1981, attendance at the Redemptorist church in Limerick, aided by a marquee in the grounds and sessions in two parish churches in the city, had risen to 50,000 per day in twenty-four sessions.

In 1977, the Solemn Novena 'moved out of Mount St Alphonsus' to the recently restored twelfth-century Holy Cross Abbey, county Tipperary. This was with the active encouragement of the Archbishop (of Cashel and Emly), Dr Thomas Morris. Other dioceses followed suit – and with similarly outstanding success – so that in 1980, when Fr Kavanagh petitioned the Holy Father to make a short video-recorded message for the 1981 solemn novena, no less than two archbishops and five bishops wrote to John Paul II in support. These were Archbishops Morris and Cunnane (Tuam) and Bishops Daly (Ardagh and Clonmacnoise, later Down and Connor, then Armagh), Lennon (Kildare and Leighlin), McCormack (Meath), Harty (Killaloe) and McNamara (Kerry). The petition was successful.

These bishops, like the Redemptorists themselves, were not concerned with mere numbers, though it must be said that the vast congregations everywhere were a welcome sign. They were interested in the new opportunities the solemn novena offered for individual spiritual renewal and conversion. As Bishop Daly said in his letter to the Pope, of 8 October 1980:

> The outstanding feature of the [Novena] exercise was the unprecedently large number of confessions, many of which were instances of return of the careless to the sacraments and of genuine conversion of heart ...

Father Kavanagh and his team saw the solemn novena as 'a new form of the Redemptorist Mission' which was particularly suitable for densely populated urban centres (but was equally successful in rural areas). While admitting that preaching during the novena was, unlike the traditional Redemptorist mission, 'directed to mass audiences with a view to influencing as many people as possible,' nevertheless, carefully chosen themes ('Handing on the Faith in the Home,' 'The Christian Family in the 1980s,' etc.) gave 'unity and devotion' to the preaching. The solemn novena was preceded by 'an intense publicity campaign' aimed at people within a twenty mile radius. It was presented to the people as a 'Festival of Faith'. As the 'advance publicity' leaflet for the 1979 Solemn Novena in Clonard explained:

> ...The Solemn Novena – nine days when people come to pray and sing in a very happy, joyful atmosphere. ... A time when many people make a comeback. A popular time for people who have been 'away' for years to come back to God in the sacrament of Confession ...

'Community Singing' was an important ingredient in the novena, particularly attractive to young people. Fr Kavanagh estimated that forty per cent of the novena congregations were under twenty-five years of age.[21]

If the solemn novena 'moved out' of Limerick to surrounding dioceses in the west and south of Ireland, it also influenced the devotion in other Redemptorist churches. It was, however, 1979 before a distinct improvement was recorded in Clonard. The domestic chronicler noted: ' ... what is outstanding is the success story of the solemn novena in honour of Our Lady of Perpetual Succour this year. Clonard, thank God, is no exception.' In 1979, there were four sessions of the novena daily with a fifth session on each Sunday, timed to end on Our Lady's feast on the third Sunday of June, and always begun on the Saturday week before. It should be said that the success of 1979 had nothing to do with the papal visit to Ireland that year, because the visit was not announced until late July, by which time the solemn novena was well over.[22]

1980: 'An ambitious leap forward'

In 1980, the novena organisers in Clonard, under the new leadership of Fr Willie McGettrick, decided to capitalise on the considerable success of 1979. As the chronicler put it, they took 'an ambitious leap forward, in upping the number of sessions from 5 [actually four] last year to 8 this year'. In regard to publicity, 'The word has been spread far and wide via posters, leaflets, pulpits.' The importance of forward planning was recognised: 'Careful planning from car park to organ gallery worked out superbly well,' so that the 1980 outcome surprised the Clonard community:

> ... the Lord smiled on our brashness and we ourselves were surprised at the response. Estimates vary, but a figure of 9-10,000 daily average attendance would seem reasonable. The 6.15 pm and 7.45 pm sessions in particular taxed our resources to the full – crowds spilled over into the tribunes, community chapel, back along the lower corridor as far as the refectory and some were perched on the stairs ...[23]

Numbers were encouraging; so was the evident 'fervour of the people'. The chronicler allowed himself a little nostalgia: ' ... it was touching to see the joy of so many of the old friends at seeing the old splendour of Clonard shine forth as in other days.' Such nostalgia was nowhere more in evidence and, perhaps, never more needed than on the occasion of the solemn novena of the following year, because it fell in the midst of the hunger strike deaths. Four hunger strikers, beginning with Bobby Sands from Twinbrook – a local man – died during the month of May and two more were to die in July. The solemn novena, wedged in between, was extremely well attended, offering some comfort:

> Against the drab background of the Falls Road and Clonard Street as we see it today, we can only repeat what many old timers are saying, 'We have seen wonderful things today.'[24]

Within the monastery and church, accommodation and hospitality had to be provided for the numerous helpers, clerical and lay, Redemptorist and non-Redemptorist, who provided essential services to the novena. In 1983, for example, twenty Redemptorists were involved; in 1988, 'helpers ... included most, if not all, of our professed students and other seminarians, Redemptorist priests, Bros Martin and Paschal, diocesan priests H. Rooney, P. McWilliams, Colin Kirk ...' Extra priests were required particularly to deal with the large number of confessions. Two other developments which facilitated the large numbers of people seeking confession were, first, the practice of offering penitential services, usually four in number, during the Saturday of the novena; secondly, caravans were provided in the monastery grounds as confessionals from 1986 onwards. While something of an entertaining novelty at first, the caravans, usually three in number, became very popular with novena-goers. It was also in 1986 that the organisers began the practice of offering counselling to people suffering from alcohol problems. Trained counsellors from Alcoholics Anonymous offered their services. At a later date, counselling for drug-related problems was also made available.[25]

1984: Consolidation and episcopal affirmation
If 1980 was the year of the 'ambitious leap' for the solemn novena, 1984 was the year which, by a further small step, consolidated it as a major and secure element in the Clonard apostolate of popular devotion. In 1984, novena sessions were increased from eight to ten per day. As noted earlier, a daily attendance of 9-10,000 was regarded as a reasonable estimate in 1980. In 1982, this had increased to 'about 15,000 daily'.[26]

Another important feature of the 1984 solemn novena was its formal endorsement by the recently appointed bishop of Down and Connor, Dr Cahal Daly. Dr Daly had succeeded Dr William Philbin when the latter retired in September 1982, having reached the age of seventy-five. Unlike his predecessor, who seemed always to have had an excuse not to visit Clonard, Dr Daly was ready and willing. Invited in 1983, he apologised for not being able to come and 'sent a message of greeting'. But in 1984, he joined the novena 'towards the end ... sat in the sanctuary for the 8 and 9.30 sessions. He did not preach, simply asked the congregation to pray for him that he 'say always the right words' – the last phrase a reflection of a bishop's difficulty in making public statements in the fraught conditions of the troubles. Thereafter, Bishop Daly rarely missed a visit to the solemn novena until he became Archbishop of Armagh in November 1990. His auxiliary, Bishop Farquhar, was also a regular visitor, as was Bishop Walsh after he had settled in to Down and Connor as Bishop Daly's successor. Bishop Michael Dallat, appointed auxiliary to Bishop Walsh in February 1994, paid his first visit to the novena in June 1996.[27]

This welcome display of episcopal support which began in 1984 was very much at the solemn, formal end of the novena spectrum. At the other end, the last session of the last day of the novena – beginning at 10.45 pm and ending considerably after 11.30 pm and that in high summer – gave the organisers an irresistible opportunity to indulge the 'popular' aspect of the devotions in a finale, Irish style. As the chronicler recorded:

> The last session ... (packed church) was entertained by [Fr] Clem MacManuis with 'The Mountains of Mourne' and by Seán Maguire [fiddle] with a beautiful Irish tune.
> Afterwards, '... It was an unusual sight to see the mighty crowd pouring

into the car park at the approach of midnight.' This popular finale, which would hardly receive episcopal approval, remains a feature of the last night of the solemn novena and is simply referred to in the Clonard Domestic Chronicle as 'the usual concert'. On occasion, it has lasted considerably beyond midnight.[28]

Invitation to women preachers

From the early 1990s, a new 'novena team' began the practice, which has continued in an expanded form, of inviting women to address sessions of the solemn novena. First to be invited, in 1993, was Carole McRoberts, a deaconess of the Presbyterian Church and a member of Cornerstone Community. In the following year, a Church of Ireland rector, Rev Kathleen Young, was joined by a Catholic, Sister Miriam Brady, a St Louis sister. Each addressed two sessions of the novena. This pattern was repeated in subsequent years: in 1995 the speakers were the Methodist theologian Gillian Kingston and Trish Rockett, a Catholic chaplain; in 1996, the centenary year, Professor Mary McAleese, professor of Law at Queen's University, accompanied the widely respected Presbyterian Rev Ruth Patterson who preached on 'Mary'.[29]

The invitation to women to preach at the novena, radical to some, long overdue to others, was simply a reflection of the increasing awareness of the importance of women in the life of the church, particularly since the novena celebrated the Mother of Jesus. Already, since 1990, the ecumenical practice had developed in Clonard's celebration of Church Unity Week each January, of inviting clergy of other Christian traditions to address each of the four sessions of the perpetual novena on the Thursday of that week.

The solemn novena as celebration

The Redemptorists never attempted to conceal the celebratory aspect of the solemn novena.

While the serious, prayerful import of the novena was never lost sight of, the human face of the nine days was a cheerful and uplifting experience: the bustle of large crowds coming and going on Clonard Street from early morning to late at night, always in daylight, for it was midsummer, with its added chance of sunshine and warmth; the great mix of social and age groups; the renewal of old friendships; the congregational singing accompanied as often as possible by the guitar (often played by Fr John Hanna); all these contributed to a carnival atmosphere. Meanwhile, the serious work of prayer (of petition and thanksgiving) and the abundant opportunities of making one's peace with God made the solemn novena a supremely happy time. An outward symbol of this happiness and celebration, in the Clonard tradition, was the decoration of streets in the area. Banished for years by the blight of the troubles, street decoration made a welcome return at the solemn novena of 1985. As the chronicler recorded on the day before the novena began:

... the people of Dunmore and Oranmore streets and others too have decorated the streets lavishly with bunting and flags. The Scala boys painted
out the ugly graffiti on the former girls' hostel and the wall of Ross's Mill
in Clonard Street.

A special effort was made for the celebration of the golden jubilee of the
novena in 1993. In addition to flags and bunting, several streets were decorated with 'flower boxes', there was 'a huge gable mural' painted at the
entrance to Dunville Street, the mural of Mary in the church car park was
'done up' and, within the monastery grounds, 'the garden wall was lined with
lovely flags'. A commemorative booklet was printed and sold and a special
video to mark the jubilee, entitled *Make Her Known*, was prepared by two
teachers at St Louise's Comprehensive College, Patrick Fleming and Brian
Kelly. Two thousand copies were made and put on sale during the solemn
novena at £10 each. Sales were noted as 'Doing well'.[30]

Generosity of novena-goers
The festive atmosphere loosened the purses and pockets of novena-goers. The
1989 solemn novena stands as a remarkable testimony to their generosity. On
that occasion, the Clonard community decided to make a special appeal for
funds for church renovation. The rector, Fr John O'Donnell, made the
appeal personally at each session, explaining the necessity of the work to be
done and the means by which it would be financed – two thirds to come
from provincial funds and one third, approximately £60,000, to be raised by
Clonard itself. The collection was taken up on the final day of the novena.
The sum raised was £60,000![31]

Present position
There is no doubt that, in the 1980s and 90s, the Clonard domestic scribes
focused on the success of the solemn novena, which is secure as a major event
in the life of Clonard every June. The weekly perpetual novena devotions
were not forgotten but they were not celebrated. They have, however, maintained a steady devotional presence over the past three decades when so many
other pious practices have suffered from post-Vatican II reaction, or the troubles, or both. As noted earlier, the number of Thursday sessions had, at the
end of 1973, been reduced from six to three; there was an additional session
on Saturday evenings, giving four in all. When this Saturday session was
removed in February 1984 to make way for arrangements for the new vigil
Mass of Sunday, it was added to the existing three Thursday sessions. These
four sessions, with a variable total attendance of between one and two thousand, continue into the new millennium.[32]

CHAPTER 10

Mission to Non-Catholics

The shared wartime experience, in helping to break down sectarian tensions particularly in Belfast, made possible an important post-war chapter in the history of Clonard, namely, the Mission to non-Catholics. It was the first mission to non-Catholics ever given in a church in Ireland and it began in Lent 1948.[1]

A number of events, outwardly unconnected, led to the decision to launch the mission. On the Sundays of Advent 1947 a series of sermons had been preached on the subject of non-Catholic churches and groups which were well-established in Belfast: the Church of Ireland, the Salvation Army, Spiritualism, Christian Science, Presbyterianism and Methodism. The sermons were not only well attended, but numerous Protestants came, brought along by Catholic friends from whom the word filtered back to the monastery that many of the non-Catholics had been impressed by what they had heard. For some of them the experience was disturbing and thought-provoking, for they heard Catholic priests speaking dispassionately and effectively about the history and beliefs of the various groups discussed in the sermons. The historian of the first and subsequent missions, Fr D. Cummings, C.Ss.R., was strongly convinced that the second important event leading to the initial mission was the recently begun perpetual novena in honour of Our Lady of Perpetual Succour and in particular the wealth of prayer it generated. There was also the fact that, from the beginning – and this still obtains nearly sixty years later – a number of non-Catholics attended the novena every Thursday, some of them sending in petitions and thanksgivings to be read out, just like the Catholic participants.

A specific incident was the immediate cause of the first mission. One evening, not long after the Advent series of sermons, two young Protestant men came to Clonard monastery and asked to speak with the Rector, Fr Gerard Reynolds. One of them explained that he had recently purchased a business in a very Protestant part of Belfast. He had found on the premises a history of the Catholic Church written by a professor of Maynooth. The book interested him, but in reading it he had encountered various points of Catholic doctrine and practice that he could not understand. Was there any way in which he – and others, for whom he was speaking, equally interested in the Catholic religion – could have the various points of difficulty explained?[2]

So the question arose. Would it be possible to arrange for non-Catholics a series of talks in the monastery church? Assuming ecclesiastical approval, would, first of all, the 'non-Catholic' press of Belfast accept for their advertisement columns notices of such a series of talks? If the advertisements were taken, would the invitation be accepted? If accepted, would there be any unpleasantness or even disturbance in the church – or, perhaps worse, might the talks even lead to sectarian incidents in the shipyards, factories, mills or business premises? The possible sources of trouble were numerous. On the Redemptorist side, there had to be faced the problems of a suitable content and format and the fitting of such a programme into the schedule of an extremely busy church.[3]

The first mission, Lent 1948

The decision was taken to provide a series of talks, one on each of the six Sundays of Lent, 1948. The time chosen was 8.30 pm, roughly half an hour after the last Sunday service, evening devotions, had ended. This would allow time for the church to clear. Catholics were asked not to come unless accompanying a non-Catholic friend. It was decided to call the talks 'A Mission to non-Catholics' and, under this heading, an 'Order of Time' was set out in notices submitted to the three 'non-Catholic' newspapers:

(1) Answers to Objections against the Catholic Church;
(2) Hymn: 'Lead Kindly Light';
(3) Reading from the Sacred Scriptures;
(4) Talk on Questions about the Catholic Church;
(5) Hymn: 'Nearer my God to Thee';
(6) 'Our Father';
(7) Final Hymn.

Not merely did the 'non-Catholic' press – the morning *Newsletter* and *Northern Whig* and the evening *Belfast Telegraph* – accept the notices and print them as submitted, but they placed them in prominent places in their columns. As Fr Cummings noted, 'All this was as inexplicable as it was encouraging.'[4]

It was reckoned that each session would last about thirty-five minutes, with ten minutes allocated to answering objections to the Catholic Church and about twenty minutes to the talk. However, apart from the first night, proceedings took nearly an hour and no one seemed to mind. On this opening night it was explained that only written objections would be answered, sent in either by hand or by post, or dropped in the Question Box which was placed prominently in the porch. The scripture readings were to harmonise with the subject matter of each talk; all were invited to join in the recital of the Lord's Prayer; all the verses of each hymn were sung, alternate verses being rendered by a soloist from among the choir-boys; and, at the end, those who wished were invited to remain to listen to further hymns from the choir.[5]

Much trouble was taken to draw up a suitable programme of talks, but finally six headings were agreed upon:

(1) Purpose of the talks. Necessity of Religion. Was Christ really God?
(2) The True Church.
(3) Does the Catholic Church interfere between the soul and God? What is the purpose of the Catholic Church? (This talk was prefaced by a brief commentary on 'What you see around you in this church.')
(4) Grace. Sin. Confession.
(5) The Real Presence. The Mass. Holy Communion.
(6) Our Lady. The Saints. Prayer.

Two Redemptorist priests were appointed to give the mission, Seán O'Loughlin and Daniel Cummings.

It is a measure of the newness of the venture and the desire to present the subject-matter appropriately for their non-Catholic audience that the priests consulted the only manual then available. *Catholic Evidence Training Outlines* had been compiled in 1925 by Maisie Ward and Frank Sheed for the Catholic Evidence Guild of Westminster.[6] The task of the Guild was to present Catholic doctrine to inquiring non-Catholics in an English environment which was substantially apathetic to religion. The main lessons of the manual were two-fold: first, that speakers should spend most of their energies in stating and explaining Catholic doctrine, not in proving it: 'If a man does not know – really solidly know – what you mean by God, what is the use of proving to him that there is one?' Secondly, the non-Catholic hearers should be spoken to as if they were 'totally uninstructed Catholics'. However, one important difference with England was that non-Catholics in Northern Ireland were anything but apathetic to religion. Hence the anxiety of the Redemptorists to be ready, particularly for the more extreme attitudes to the Catholic Church, as an object of hatred for example, because viewed as an enemy of God and as a teacher of false doctrines. They were also aware, of course, that some non-Catholics in Northern Ireland were deeply interested in and full of goodwill towards the church. Fr Cummings summarised this phase of the planning:

> On the basis of such ideas, a strategy for the talks was formulated. They were to be interesting, explanatory, and, where needful, supported by clear proofs from the scriptures. While on the one hand it was firmly resolved that the talks would be thoroughly Catholic and uncompromising, on the other it was equally resolved not to make them controversial, argumentative, much less provocative.[7]

The belief of the Redemptorists was that Catholic doctrine, as truth, when presented plainly and carefully, and received simply and without prejudice, 'has a force of its own to win acceptance'.

The final and most difficult phase of preparation was writing the talks. Fr Cummings admitted:

> To a priest who is accustomed to preparing sermons for Catholic congregations, there is singular difficulty in endeavouring to expound Catholic doctrine to a non-Catholic congregation ... practically every word has to be weighed carefully ... phrases sounding orthodox and forceful to Catholic ears may be unnecessarily harsh and discordant in the ears of non-Catholics; words and sentences rich in meaning for Catholics are often meaningless to [non-Catholics].[8]

On the first Sunday night the church was cleared, as planned, after the evening devotions. The empty church made some of the community wonder if they had been unduly optimistic; if fifty or a hundred non-Catholics came that would be a splendid beginning. The reality amazed everyone. By 8.25 pm the church was well filled and by half past there was scarcely a vacant seat. Since many people were still coming in, a few minutes grace was given. The preachers remembered the atmosphere in the church as highly unusual, 'an amalgam of strangeness, curiosity, tension and interest'. But from his first words in the pulpit, the preacher received the keenest attention from his listeners.

The service lasted about forty minutes. At the end, many of the visitors remained in the church. A great number walked around, looking at the altars, the sanctuary, the stations of the cross, the statues, confessionals and the Catholic Truth Society booklets. A few members of the Clonard community mingled with them, chatting and answering questions and difficulties. This was quickly recognised as a most valuable exercise and as the mission progressed the Redemptorists became more and more convinced that direct, personal contact was more valuable than any sermon or pamphlet.[9]

The Question Box

On the following morning, the Question Box was opened. Most questions were straightforward and courteous. Some were petulant in tone; some bigoted; some 'exhibited signs of religious insanity' (Fr Cummings' words). Roughly eighty per cent of the questions derived from the Protestant teaching that the Bible alone is the rule of faith. Many points of Catholic doctrine and practice were raised and proof of their validity from scripture was demanded. The doctrine most frequently questioned was purgatory. Then, in descending numbers of questions, came prayer to Our Lady and the saints, image-worship, the Pope and the church, why Catholics never go to

Protestant services, the meaning and purpose of holy water, the brethren of
Our Lord, transubstantiation, infant baptism and, lastly, the necessity of baptism.[10]

During the following days, letters began to arrive by post. Some writers
explained that they had to rush away for bus or train on the Sunday night
and had been unable to use the Question Box. These letters showed that non-
Catholics were coming to the mission from Armagh, North Antrim and
other parts of the north. (Later, some came from Dublin to attend.) Some
letters did not raise any questions but simply offered sincere thanks and congratulations. In sharp contrast, a few letters offered pity for the 'benighted
spiritual condition' of the missioners, who were acknowledged as sincere but
had gone astray. Prayers would be offered that they would abandon their
idolatry. One militant called on the priests to give up 'this humbug' and
threatened that 'on next Sunday night, if God will, I will be there and challenge you in the church'. God must have had other designs, for the challenge
did not materialise. Finally, a touching letter, unsigned, just initialled, ran as
follows: 'Priest! Could I be a secret Catholic? I do not want my friends to
know. I am willing to attend your services. I do not know what I am expected
to do.'[11]

Each written question was carefully considered and listed. Since the number of questions far exceeded what could be dealt with in the allotted time,
preference was given to those most frequently asked. It was decided, and
strictly adhered to, that in the spoken replies in church, there was to be

> no trace of disdain or rancour or righteous indignation, but each ques-
> tion, no matter how bitter or provocative, was to be read aloud distinctly
> and the answer given calmly and concisely. This was done and proved
> very effective.

So, the small minority who came to hear 'heated replies, indignant denials
and vehement denunciations' were disappointed. Likewise, reporters from
the 'non-Catholic' press who came 'to cover' the mission had no inflamma-
tory material to print.[12]

Because the time allocated in each service to answering questions was, of
necessity, so short, books and pamphlets were put on sale which would provide fuller replies and spread Catholic teaching. These were obtained from
the Catholic Truth Society in Dublin and London. Each Sunday evening,
after devotions, the two CTS boxes in the church were emptied of their normal contents and refilled with a special supply of booklets on doctrine,
apologetics and church history. Outside the church, a CTS stall displayed
more of the same and also a selection of larger Catholic books suitable for
non-Catholics. They proved attractive and a considerable quantity was
bought.

As a final gesture of help to those participating in the mission and to continue its work after the six Sunday services were finished, the questions submitted and answered during the six weeks were put into booklet form. Its title was *Souvenir of Mission in Clonard. Your Questions – Our Answers*. It had an introduction of almost five pages which dealt briefly with the existence of God, the necessity of religion, indifferentism, the marks and the identity of the true church, the infallibility of the church, and the two sources of divine truth, namely, scripture and tradition. Thirty-nine questions and answers were followed by a short selection of prayers including the Our Father, the Hail Mary and the Apostles' Creed. On the last Sunday of the mission, 2,000 of the booklets were placed near the rear of the church and the participants invited to take one – if they wished – as a souvenir. Not a single copy was left.[13]

Some results of that first mission were immediate and evident. Quite a number of non-Catholics, mostly young men, asked for instruction in the Catholic faith. Numerous requests were received from non-Catholics for another mission in the near future 'on distinctly Catholic lines'. Due to wider demand, the souvenir booklet was reprinted for sale; 16,000 copies at two pence each were sold within a very short time. The Redemptorists received considerable positive feedback about the impact of the mission in Protestant circles in Belfast, even including masonic lodges. As Fr Cummings reported:

> We had separate visits from two Freemasons who came, Nicodemus-wise, at night for a friendly chat. They informed us that the mission was the constant topic of conversation in the Freemason lodges of the city. This was surely peaceful penetration of a unique kind in Belfast.[14]

Finally, it was noted that the number of non-Catholics attending devotions and the novena to the Mother of Perpetual Succour had increased as a result of the mission.

The second mission, Advent 1948

It was decided to give a second mission on the Sundays of Advent in the same year 1948, conducted by Fr James Coogan, a former professor of sacred scripture and Rev Dr Seán O'Riordan, the current scripture professor in the Redemptorist house of studies, Cluain Mhuire, Galway. Responding to the non-Catholic request, 'What we want is a mission such as you give to Catholics,' the preachers agreed to deal with Catholic moral principles and some of the eternal truths.[15]

The order of service was essentially the same as on the first mission. Advertising was wider than before, particularly because of the distribution, through Belfast and the surrounding districts, of thousands of leaflets by members of both men's and women's confraternities. Once again, Catholics were urged not to come unless accompanying a non-Catholic friend.

Nevertheless, some came. But it was reckoned, 'by numbering those who on entering the church did not genuflect,' that the average attendance of non-Catholics was about seven hundred. While this was markedly down on the first mission, when the average attendance was calculated at 1,350 non-Catholics, the organisers were quite sure that the weather was an important factor in the depleted numbers.[16]

This second mission reinforced many of the lessons of the first: the statement of Catholic teaching uncompromisingly, but courteously; the value of the invitation, at the end of each service, to inspect the church and its furnishings, the sacristy and adjoining corridors; and the availability of several priests from the Clonard community to chat and answer questions. In the sacristy were displayed sacred vessels, vestments and missals. It was noted that the visitors 'seemed to pay particular attention to anything relating to the Mass'. When a priest was answering a question or explaining a point, he was invariably surrounded by a small group: 'They seemed anxious not to miss anything.' The tone and atmosphere of these personal meetings was generally free from vehement bickering and quite friendly, aided as they were from time to time by small incidents which generated humour. One of the episodes best remembered in Clonard occurred one Sunday during this mission. The lights in the sacristy fused, producing consternation in the darkness. Two of the visitors were electricians, Protestant men from the shipyards. They quickly repaired the fuses and one of them announced: 'We came here to give you the light,' which raised a laugh and promoted good feeling.[17]

Indeed, one of the outcomes of this second mission which was a matter of great satisfaction to the Redemptorists was 'a marked increase in friendliness and goodwill' towards them. This was supported by numerous compliments about the conduct of the mission and its impact on individual non-Catholics, like the Protestant who said to his friend: 'This mission has been a revelation to me. I expected to see hooded inquisitors!' With such warm approval, it was perhaps appropriate that this mission should conclude on St Stephen's Day, in the quiet, peaceful atmosphere of Christmastide.[18]

The talks and lectures of this mission were published as a booklet of some fifty pages, with a foreword by the distinguished parish priest of St Brigid's, Mgr Arthur H. Ryan, DD, DPh. A thousand copies of the booklet, at two shillings each, were sold at once.[19]

The third mission, Lent 1949
The third mission took place on the Sundays of Lent 1949, given by the Redemptorists J. J. W. Murphy and, once again, Seán O'Riordan. This time, lecture topics were included which faced some of the most difficult subjects for Christians in Northern Ireland, such as civil and religious liberty; the Pope and liberty. The order of service was adjusted slightly, so that it opened with

prayers from scripture and included a short period of silent prayer. And before each service, the Clonard organist gave a recital. The attendance was good, with an average of about six hundred each Sunday and a maximum of eight hundred.[20]

This mission ended on Good Friday night with a vivid sermon on 'Good Friday' by Fr Murphy, who had recently returned from Palestine, where he had served as a chaplain to the Brigade of Guards. He had also already established himself as a leading authority on the Holy Land.[21]

There were requests for the mission to continue, but, in closing it, the Rector of Clonard, Very Rev Gerard Reynolds, regretted that pressure of commitments to other parish missions made any extension impossible. However, he promised another mission for non-Catholics in the autumn.

The National Union of Protestants
It is of interest that during this third mission communication was opened between the Clonard Redemptorists and the National Union of Protestants (Ireland). This latter group, with its headquarters in Belfast, purported to be, 'The voice of the Protestant People,' though many Protestants, north and south, would have repudiated such a claim. The motto of the NUP was: 'Set for the Defence of the Gospel.' (Phil 1:16).

There had been an approach from the NUP a year earlier, during the first mission. A letter from the organising secretary, Mr Norman Porter, invited Fr Cummings and Fr O'Loughlin to a public meeting in the Ulster Hall. This meeting would give the priests the opportunity of giving 'a full reply' to questions Mr Porter had submitted during the mission. The priests were assured of 'every possible consideration and Christian tolerance'. However, since the letter was dated 18 March 1948 and received by registered post on the following day for a meeting on 23 March, the invitation was not taken seriously and no reply was sent.[22]

On 11 April 1949, in the course of the third mission, Mr Porter phoned Clonard monastery to ask for a private interview with Frs Murphy and O'Riordan. This was agreed to and, on the following evening, Mr Porter and three colleagues visited Clonard. They later described their reception as cordial. For over two hours they discussed matters of doctrine and practice with Frs Murphy and O'Riordan. But they renewed Mr Porter's earlier complaint that questions they had submitted had not been answered and this was happening again in the third mission. They were told that, in the limited time allocated at each session, it was impossible to answer the large number of questions which had poured in from different people. Five or six questions were as many as could be answered at any one session. The Redemptorists had also promised a verbal reply to any enquirer who called to see them and it was on this basis that they had agreed to meet the four NUP members.[23]

As a result of this meeting, Frs Murphy and O'Riordan decided to publish a full set of answers to the NUP questions. But before this could be done, the NUP published a booklet of their own on 21 April, just ten days after their visit to Clonard. The NUP publication was called *Questions to the Lecturers at Clonard Roman Catholic Church*. It covered their own questions which had been answered during both the first and third missions and those of their questions which remained unanswered at the time of publication on 21 April. Fr Cummings observed that the answers quoted by the NUP in relation to the first mission were 'mutilated and therefore misleading versions of the fathers' answers'. He also noted their unfair practice in relation to (as yet) unanswered questions: their pamphlet quoted each question and followed it with the remark: 'Clonard: No answer'.[24]

The NUP agreed to Fr Reynolds' request for a further meeting, but on 'neutral ground', which was, in fact, the Catholic-owned Royal Avenue Hotel in Belfast. The meeting, described in an agreed press statement as 'informal' and involving 'some clergy and laymen of the various Christian denominations' was held on the evening of Tuesday 16 August 1949. There was a numerous attendance of the executive council of the NUP, including its president, Rev Canon Henry O'Connor, MBE, its secretary, Rev Douglas Stranex, MA, its treasurer, Rev Ian Paisley and Mr Norman Porter, organising secretary. The Clonard representatives were the rector, Very Rev Gerard Reynolds, who chaired the proceedings, and the conducting missioners, Frs J. J. W. Murphy and Seán O'Riordan.

The subsequent press statement was brief but positive, particularly where it dealt with what actually happened at the meeting. It acknowledged the 'absolute sincerity' of either side in argument, the satisfactory clarification of several points by the Redemptorist missioners and expressed the hope that exchanges would continue. Canon O'Connor had had to leave the meeting early. He subsequently wrote to the newspapers claiming that the press statement had been 'drawn up by the priests' and, had he been there at the conclusion of the meeting, he would not have signed it. This accusation was met by a swift response from Fr Reynolds, published in the 'non-Catholic' dailies of 25 August 1949. Canon O'Connor's recollection was 'not correct'. If he were to consult his NUP colleagues, he would find that the statement was drawn up and agreed by both sides. 'It was then read aloud for the assembly and two members of the NUP copied the statement and with their own hands delivered it to the press.' There was neither acknowledgement nor apology from either Canon O'Connor or the NUP, but Fr Reynolds' letter was the last exchange between Clonard and the NUP.[25]

According to Fr Cummings' account, there was serious discord within the NUP. There were whispered accusations that their delegates had 'sold the pass', an accusation which some of them stoutly denied at a NUP meeting on 6 November 1949. In the September issue of their journal *The Protestant*, they had presented an account of their meeting with the Clonard priests which, in Fr Cummings' words, was 'utterly garbled and replete with inaccuracies'. Despite that, they acknowledged the friendliness and cordiality of the meetings and admitted that 'Dr O'Riordan, with much patience, dealt with all the questions that had been put to them, and clearly outlined the position of his church' – a compliment which vindicated the spirit and the approach which had actuated the Redemptorists from the start of the mission and from which they were never deflected.[26]

Thus ended direct contacts between the NUP and the Clonard priests. Frs Murphy and O'Riordan in due course dealt, as promised, with the NUP's thirty-six questions and with the contents of the NUP's booklet of 21 April 1949. This they did in three separate pamphlets published at the end of that year by the Catholic Truth Society, Dublin. In them every question was answered and every text from the scriptures, every quotation from the Fathers of the Church, ecclesiastical writers and historians was fully and accurately documented.[27]

Subsequent missions

The next two in the series of missions, in Advent 1949 and Lent 1950, were open to Catholics as well as non-Catholics. New approaches were tried in order to make the services attractive. For example, on the Sundays of Advent 1949, the common title of 'Question Time' was used, a promise was given that fifty of the more interesting questions would be answered and eight Redemptorist priests dealt with the questions. The answers to the questions were very fully reported in the Belfast 'Catholic' newspaper, the *Irish News*. The paper had been an important ally in the splendid publicity it gave each mission from the beginning in 1948. The number of people attending was so large that two sessions had to be held each Sunday at 7 and 8.30 pm. In Lent 1950, there was a return to the normal practice of entrusting the mission to just two priests. This time they were Fr Cummings and Dr Robert Culhane. Once again, numbers were so large that two sessions were required each Sunday.[28] At the end of this mission, another one was announced for the autumn, on the six Sundays of Advent. This was to be for non-Catholics only, Catholics, as in the first missions, being asked not to attend unless accompanying a non-Catholic friend.

With large numbers of Catholics excluded, the Advent missioners, Frs James Cleary and – once again – Daniel Cummings, were able to estimate an average attendance of between four and five hundred non-Catholics. This was in spite of bitterly cold weather on at least three Sundays, two of them with substantial falls of snow. The Redemptorists also noted a total absence of bitterness, and indeed, a great cordiality. This cordiality was not shared by two highly respected Presbyterian ministers who gave their personal impressions to the *Ulster Protestant*:

> Altogether it was very interesting, clear and subtle, by specially gifted and trained priests. Like poison gas, very insidious, and unfortunately likely to impress weakly instructed Protestants. The antidote would appear to be an intensive campaign in the Protestant churches to instruct Protestants in the fundamentals of their faith, and effort at union amongst the various sects.[29]

The National Union of Protestants was at work in the background of this Advent 1950 mission. They claimed to be defending the gospel and advancing Christianity by importing, from Australia no less, a 'converted Roman Catholic,' whose standard subject was an 'attack on Good Shepherd Convents and Laundries'. During the Clonard mission she held meetings in various parts of Belfast. Reports filtering back to Clonard suggested that this lady was not impressive. In the light of disclosures in recent years about the treatment of such girls by their families, their church and the institutions in which they were confined, the woman's history probably deserved a better hearing than it got. But in 1950, a voice such as hers would simply not have been heard in her mother church as, apparently, it was not particularly well listened to in a sensational, startling-revelations-by-converted-Roman-Catholic kind of meeting under NUP auspices, whose object was to vilify the Catholic Church and stir up sectarian bitterness.[30]

Bishop Daniel Mageean

The progress of the Clonard Mission to non-Catholics had been watched with intense interest by the Bishop of Down and Connor, Dr Daniel Mageean. He acknowledged its work, in his 1951 Lenten Pastoral, as the first attempt in Ireland at a type of mission which was known in Europe: 'It has at least served to dispel erroneous ideas of our religion, to soften prejudice and to smooth out asperities and misunderstandings. For that we must all be grateful ...' Any bishop would have been pleased that such missionary activity was going on in his diocese. But Dr Mageean had also a keen personal interest in the undertakings of the Redemptorist Congregation in Ireland – his brother and three of his nephews were among its members![31]

Mission reduced

The Clonard Mission to non-Catholics was continued twice-yearly, on the Sundays of Lent and Advent, from its beginning in 1948 certainly until the Advent of 1950. By 1952 it had been reduced to an annual undertaking confined to four Sundays in November, a practice which continued until 1967 when Clonard church was abandoned in favour of St Mary's Hall in the city centre. The move from Clonard seems to have been influenced by a serious decline in attendance, combined with a desire to concentrate the work of the non-Catholic mission in the new Catholic Information Centre which was formally opened in January 1968, in St Mary's Hall, Bank Street, 'in rooms formerly occupied by the Apostolic Workers'.[32]

It was natural enough that the numbers attending the Clonard mission to non-Catholics should decline over a period of time. The number of non-Catholics in greater Belfast (the principal catchment area) who were interested in Catholicism was finite, so that the large numbers of the early years could not be sustained. As we have seen, Fr Cummings' account of the first five missions, from Lent 1948 until Lent 1950, made a serious attempt to decipher the numbers of non-Catholics attending. This was always difficult, even on those occasions when Catholics were urged not to attend unless they were accompanying non-Catholic friends; numbers of curious Catholics came anyway. It was well-nigh impossible on those occasions when Catholics were free to come, as in Advent 1949 and Lent 1950. Following those early estimates, it can be said that, while numbers held up in the early 1950s (for example, between 600 and 700 attended in November 1952), they were in marked decline by the mid to late 50s. Average attendance in 1955 was between 200 and 300, but by 1957 it was 'notably less ... between 150 and 200', though some members of the Clonard community blamed this reduction on the IRA campaign of those years. The last specific figures in the Clonard record are for November 1959. They place the average attendance between 130 and 150. Among brief comments in the Clonard Domestic Chronicle in subsequent years, there is the blunt acknowledgement that the 1965 mission began 'with a very small attendance'.

November 1965 was really the end of the Clonard mission to non-Catholics as it had operated since 1948. It is easy to say in retrospect that it should have been ended sooner or, at least, given a new format. Perhaps it should. But it is arguable that it was wiser to hold to a well-tried formula in relating to non-Catholics (or 'separated brethren' as they were beginning to be called in 'Vatican II speak') at a period when Catholics themselves were in turmoil and needed time to digest what the Council had to say on the subject of relations with other Christian churches.

But in 1966, all was change. Members of all communions were invited to Clonard to a series of talks on the 'Constitution on the Church' of the Second Vatican Council, given by two of the Redemptorists' most distinguished theologians, Dr Gerard Crotty and Dr L. Hechanova, a Philippine Redemptorist temporarily based in Ireland.[33] It could be argued that this series was aimed more at the education of Catholics in the thinking of Vatican II than at other denominations, but elements of the non-Catholic mission were retained in the promise of 'Bible Services' and the well-established 'Question Box', both of which had been important points of contact with non-Catholics since 1948.

From Clonard to St Mary's Hall
In 1967, further changes accompanied the move to St Mary's Hall. The 'lectures' or 'talks' were once again for non-Catholics only; non-Redemptorist speakers were invited; a short film was shown after each lecture and a different choir was invited to lead the hymns at each meeting.[34]

Correspondence course: 'The Truth about the Catholic Church'
The dangerous situation in Belfast after August 1969 ensured the cessation of the overt mission to non-Catholics. Thereafter, reliance was placed on the quiet operation of the Catholic Information Centre in St Mary's Hall. This grew out of two strategies, based in Clonard, which had supported the in-church work of the non-Catholic mission from the earliest days. The first was a special weekly meeting for interested non-Catholics, held on Monday evenings in the Clonard Hall in Waterville Street.[35] The second was the establishment, in the early 1950s, of a correspondence course of twenty-one letters under the general title of *The Truth about the Catholic Church*. Each letter was about 2,500 words long and was presented in a clear, honest and simple style, permeated by an awareness of God our loving Father. Both style and spirit were, whether consciously or otherwise, a remarkable echo of the missionary qualities of St Alphonsus Liguori.

The final letter, headed 'What is your Decision?' was accompanied by a short message from the director. This began 'Dear Friend' and asked the correspondent, if he or she had found the course interesting, to tell their friends about it. Enclosed with the final letter was a small card entitled 'My Daily Prayer', containing four short statements of faith, together with a short prayer for faith, a prayer for hope and three short prayers of contrition, love of God and resolution never to offend God again. The card concluded with an appeal to the recipient to say the simple prayers earnestly and faithfully to God, 'the most understanding and the most forgiving of all fathers'.

The director was, in fact, Fr Daniel Cummings, the Belfast-born Redemptorist whose plain but sincere Belfast manner and his recent work as a wartime chaplain to the Irish Guards had made him so agreeable to many of the enquiring non-Catholics. He continued in charge of all aspects of the mission until September 1956 when he was transferred to Limerick to become superior of the retreat house there, a relief from 'a most difficult task which did not leave him much free time'.[36]

New management

Fr Cummings was succeeded as director by another northern Redemptorist, Fr Hugh Arthurs, a native of Keady in county Armagh, with Fr Alec Reid as his able assistant. Fr Arthurs was responsible for involving members of the Legion of Mary in the practical organisation of the non-Catholic mission. They were singled out for special congratulation, in the monastery record, for their help in the mission of 1961; they 'did excellent work during the mission, led hymns, etc.'

The availability of written material for interested non-Catholics had always been important, as Fr Cummings' account of the early missions clearly shows. There were, first, the Catholic Truth Society pamphlets which were displayed for sale; then the various booklets of questions and answers produced in the course of the missions by the Redemptorists; finally, there was the correspondence course devised by Fr Cummings to maintain continuity for those non-Catholics whose interest in Catholicism had been stirred by the missions and also to offer privacy for those who felt unable to attend Clonard in person. By the mid-1960s, stocks of the correspondence course had become depleted, so Fr Reid, in 1965, organised variety concerts in St Mary's Hall in April and November, 'to finance the work for non-Catholics, to buy correspondence courses, etc., issued by the Catholic Enquiry Centre'.[37] Around the same time, Fr Reid was organising 'a new movement called "Catholic Witness" – to help in making our Catholic faith known to those outside'. This was launched in June 1966 at a time when recent Paisleyite demonstrations against Irish Presbyterianism had embarrassed virtually everyone in Northern Ireland outside certain fundamentaalist groups – though the timing was entirely coincidental.[38]

1969: The Troubles

It was the widespread civil disturbances from August 1969 onwards, in which the Clonard area was deeply enmeshed, that put an end to the non-Catholic mission as it had operated for twenty years. The subject is not mentioned again in the Clonard Domestic Chronicle until the end of 1977. In a reflective passage, typical of the way in which year's end tended to be marked in the monastery chronicle, the writer took as his point of departure the splendid celebration of Christmas night – 'a magnificent and moving celebration ... like old times'. He continued:

> ... it is consoling to realise that our separated brethern have an interest in Clonard and are drawn to our church and services. How many – we cannot say, but there are indications that, if times were normal, they would be glad to come to us.

As an example, he quoted a conversation in which a man asked one of the community when they intended to restart lectures to non-Catholics. The priest replied that the time was not right 'owing to the troubled situation in the city'. When asked why he had raised the matter, the man related a recent experience in which he, the only Catholic in his workplace, had invited two Protestant colleagues to come to Clonard for the concelebrated Mass on the feast of the Immaculate Conception (8 December). The men were 'enthralled by the experience'. The chronicler insisted that this was not an isolated case and continued:

> May we hope that Clonard will have a 'second spring', another golden age when civil strife will have passed and the interdenominational dialogue of post-conciliar days will bear fruit in an uninhibited meeting of minds and hearts — with Clonard as a focal point for this area. It is pleasant to speculate about this, but the religious scene, both inside and outside the Catholic church, is too confused at present to encourage prophetic utterance.[39]

The chronicler reveals a vision which the zealous layman had not yet grasped. With the removal of civil strife, the scribe does not see the restoration of lectures to, or instruction of, non-Catholics, but the coming to fruition of 'the interdenominational dialogue of post-conciliar days'. So, it was not just the 'widespread civil disturbances from August 1969 onwards' which dealt the fatal blow to the Clonard non-Catholic mission as it had operated for twenty years. It was also, and more profoundly, the sea change in Catholic attitudes to the other Christian churches which had resulted from the deliberations of the Second Vatican Council. Such change was, in fact, explained to Clonard-going people of 'all religious communions' as early as November 1966 when they were invited to the annual series of talks given that year on the 'Constitution on the Church' (*Lumen Gentium*) which had been solemnly promulgated by Pope Paul VI on 21 November 1964. On the same day, a solemn decree on Ecumenism was issued, dealing with 'the restoration of unity among all Christians'. When next the subject is restored to regular comment in the Clonard domestic chronicle, the concept of 'Mission to Non-Catholics' will give way to 'ecumenical dialogue'.

CHAPTER 11

Ecumenism at Clonard

Monitoring of early ecumenical contacts

Practical ecumenical contacts at various levels between the churches had been monitored with great interest by the Clonard community since the eve of the Second Vatican Council. One of the earliest examples was the visit, in February 1961, of Archbishop Michael Ramsay, then Archbishop of York and Archbishop designate of Canterbury, to Archbishop John Charles McQuaid of Dublin. Dr Ramsay's assertion, 'Unity between us must come,' was noted enthusiastically. Early in May of the same year Pope John XXIII was visited by Queen Elizabeth II and the Duke of Edinburgh; the 'splendid' scenes of the reception at the Vatican were shown on the new – to Northern Ireland – medium of television, provoking predictable and contradictory responses.[1]

Nearer to home, the Clonard Redemptorists were delighted by the invitation extended, early in 1962, to one of their academic confrères, the scripture scholar Fr Seán Kelleher, to speak to a group of fourteen Presbyterian ministers 'in premises adjoining Crescent Presbyterian church'. Fr Kelleher had come to the notice of the clergymen – 'a group who meet for prayer and discussion every Tuesday' – through press reports of a sermon he had preached at the opening of the university year on the subject of the ecumenical movement. They invited him to speak further on the subject, but within a cautious framework of their own devising, which included 'examination of the positive, enduring elements of the Reformation and ... the necessity of a personal approach to God'. According to the Clonard record, the talk was 'well received and was followed by an hour of frank discussion. All agreed it was a definite sign of a change in the times when such a meeting took place in Belfast.'[2]

Hostility towards ecumenism

Sadly for ecumenism, the scope for change in Northern Ireland, difficult at any time, became more difficult in the middle 1960s, with the whipping up of political and religious hysteria against any sign of 'Lundyism' or 'betrayal' on the part of political or religious leaders. This state of affairs was the direct result of the exchange of 'friendly' visits between Captain Terence O'Neill, prime minister of Northern Ireland and Seán Lemass, his opposite number in the Republic of Ireland. To people of such views, the Irish Republic was the political enemy just as the Roman Church was the religious enemy. What was seen by some as a holding out of the hand of friendship was seen by others as the first step towards entrapment and absorption into an unacceptable political or religious control. So deep-seated were the suspicions and hatreds of history that the 'not-an-inch' and 'No Surrender' mentality carried the day. If one adds to this the outbreak of civil disorder in 1969, it is understandable that ecumenical contacts suffered. Indeed, ecumenical matters do not feature again in the Clonard Domestic Chronicle until the early 1980s.

1980: An Anglican in Clonard pulpit

As far as most Clonard-going people were concerned, ecumenism suddenly appeared in public early in 1980, with the announcement of a special ecumenical service on Thursday 24 January. This was part of Clonard's participation in Christian unity week, which had developed around the feast of the Conversion of St Paul, 25 January. The high point of the special service was an address by Canon John Austin Baker, the Anglican sub-dean of Westminster and chaplain to the speaker of the House of Commons. As the Clonard record noted:

> Several hundreds attended and among them a goodly proportion of our separated brethern. It was a homely and happy ceremony organised by Fr Christy McCarthy who is deeply involved in the ecumenical movement and, with Fr Scott and others, has many contacts with 'the other side'.[3]

The background to Canon Baker's visit

Fr Christopher McCarthy was, indeed, 'deeply involved in the ecumenical movement' and it was his deep involvement which brought about the appearance of the distinguished Anglican in the Clonard pulpit. Behind it all lies an interesting and edifying story which began with the establishment, in the autumn of 1978, of a Bible Study Group for Catholics. This was a result of a request to Fr McCarthy from the brothers Jim and Pat Lynn, who felt that many young Catholics, encountering evangelical and fundamentalist Protestants in their workplaces in Northern Ireland, were 'bombarded with bible quotations that are supposed to prove that there are errors in their beliefs and in the teaching of their church', and needed help 'to have a reason for the faith that is in them'. Shortly afterwards, Fr McCarthy introduced a few of his Protestant friends to the group. They came with diffidence and reluctance, which was matched on the Catholic side. But as weeks went by, the atmosphere grew easier and each 'side' became increasingly edified by the openness of the other.[4]

Early in 1979 one of the Protestant members of the group was visiting friends in London, in the Anglican parish of All Saints, Dulwich. When leaving the church after Sunday services, he saw two noticeboards side by side which advertised Anglican and Roman Catholic services respectively being held in the church. His remark, 'You wouldn't see that where I come from,' made a deep impression on the Vicar, Rev Desmond Parsons. Around the time of the 1979 United Kingdom general election, a discussion group was established at All Saints, to enable parishioners to address their lack of knowledge of Northern Ireland. The group was told about the Catholics and Protestants who met for bible study in Clonard, in the Catholic Falls Road area and who were, by their openness and honesty, learning something about the underlying causes of the troubles. A suggestion that All Saints might invite some of these Clonard people over was followed through and, on 14 November 1979, four members of the bible group, two Protestants and two Catholics, led by Fr McCarthy, arrived. They spoke on Ireland to both Anglican and Catholic congregations and the bible group held a question and answer session in the church crypt.

Just before the party had left for London, the Irish newspapers had given wide coverage to a sermon preached at Westminster Abbey on Sunday 14 October 1979 by Canon Baker, which showed great sensitivity about Ireland in its relationship with Britain. Through friends in Moral Rearmament, a meeting was arranged for the Clonard group with Canon Baker. They found in him a man of great honesty and spirituality who had been deeply impressed by Pope John Paul's recent visit to Ireland and his message on the situation there, which the canon saw as twofold: 'Correct injustice; reject violence.' Canon Baker was already planning a series of lunchtime lectures at Westminster with the aim of educating his fellow countrymen on Ireland past and present. (In the event, the attendance at each lecture was about one hundred and fifty, including members of the government, of parliament and of the upper echelons of the civil service.)[5]

Canon Baker accepted Fr McCarthy's invitation to preach in Clonard during Christian unity week, 1980. Bishop Philbin, reassured by a copy of Canon Baker's Westminster Abbey sermon, supplied to him by Fr George Wadding, rector of Clonard, gave his blessing to the enterprise. In his Clonard sermon, Canon Baker outlined ways in which the communities in Northern Ireland should endeavour to come together. Jim Lynn, in his 1981 memoir of these events, was not exaggerating when he recalled: 'The people took him to their hearts. The fact that a man whom they identified with the Establishment should show such concern for them won them over.' Small wonder that Canon Baker received several requests from families for help with cases of prisoners in Long Kesh.[6]

The visit of the Clonard bible group members was quickly reciprocated by the Vicar of Dulwich and two of his congregation who came to Belfast in April 1980. In three days they had sixteen appointments with Protestant church leaders, teachers from Protestant and Catholic schools and with families from the Catholic Turf Lodge area who included wives and mothers of men in the 'H-blocks'. The visitors learnt at first hand of the effects of violence, unemployment and discrimination, but they also witnessed great courage and great faith. On 22 April, the Vicar is noted in the Clonard record as having engaged in an 'ecumenical discussion' with the Clonard community. Later that day, Fr Wadding addressed a small but select audience at the (Presbyterian) Union Theological College, Belfast. His subject was, 'War, Violence and the Christian'.[7]

Canon Baker returned to Northern Ireland for Christian unity week in 1981. On that occasion he was invited by Cardinal Ó Fiaich to preach in Armagh Cathedral, the first non-Catholic ever to do so. He also preached in St Anne's Cathedral in Belfast, as well as Clonard, where the gathering of about 1,000 people was genuinely ecumenical. Not only were clergy of various denominations present in the sanctuary, led by Dr Arthur Butler, Church of Ireland Bishop of Connor, but a considerable number of them mingled with the general congregation in the body of the church. Following a relaxed social gathering in Clonard Hall, a three-hour vigil for peace with justice was held in Clonard church, directed by Fr McCarthy. Simultaneously, as a result of a suggestion made by Rev Parsons, a vigil was held in All Saints, Dulwich.[8]

1982: The quickening pace of ecumenism

The year 1982 witnessed a distinct quickening of pace in ecumenical initiatives in the diocese of Down and Connor. The new bishop, Dr Cahal Daly, appointed in September on the retirement of Bishop William Philbin, lost no time in establishing a diocesan commission for ecumenism. This was done in November, with Canon Robert Murphy (Holy Rosary) as chairman and Fr Hugh Crossin (PP, Whiteabbey) as secretary. About the same time, an announcement was made that a community of reconciliation under the patronage of St Columbanus would be established in Belfast within twelve months. (In fact, it was finally inaugurated on 23 November 1983 – the saint's feastday – at 683, Antrim Road). Coinciding with the Columbanus announcement, the Clonard chronicle noted under the date of 19 November 1982:

A Jesuit priest, Fr B. McPartlin, has arrived for a few weeks. He will work with Sr Mary Grant of the Little Sisters of the Assumption who, with some companions, is trying to establish the experimental Cornerstone Community of Reconciliation on the Upper Springfield Road.[9]

1983: A special year for ecumenism in Clonard

The Clonard arrangements for Christian unity week in January 1983 were a personal triumph for Fr Christopher McCarthy, the prime mover in the community's ecumenical contacts. For the first time, a bishop of Down and

Connor attended an ecumenical service in Clonard church. It was Dr Daly's first opportunity to do so since his appointment to the diocese the previous September. He 'led the worship', in the company of Dr William McCappin, the new Church of Ireland bishop of Connor, Rev Charles Eugene, Chairman of the Belfast District of the Methodist Church and Rev Dr Jack Weir, Secretary of the Presbyterian General Synod in Ireland. Dr Daly's attendance was the first public affirmation by the bishop of the diocese of the ecumenical work of Clonard. Fr McCarthy's personal triumph was completed by the presence, as distinguished visiting preacher, of his old friend Canon Baker, now elevated to the bishopric of Salisbury in the Church of England. Fr McCarthy had attended the bishop's consecration early in the previous February.

The presence of an already distinguished Anglican bishop in the pulpit of a Catholic church on the Falls Road in the deeply troubled early 1980s is a measure of how far churchmen in Northern Ireland were ahead of politicians in reconciliation. The Clonard Redemptorists had no difficulty inviting a member of the British establishment – admittedly a sympathetic one – to preach in their church. As the churches' correspondent of the *Belfast Telegraph* pointed out, Bishop Baker was a 'conventional product of prosperous, middle-class Anglicanism: Marlborough and Oxford, then the Army and fourteen years lecturing in theology'. While by no means perceived as a radical, he was yet on the minority wing of the Anglican General Synod in urging Britain's unilateral nuclear disarmament (a serious political issue of the day). More radically, he had engaged in a dialogue with one of the Maze hunger strikers in 1981. He had also had a two-hour conversation with IRA leaders in Dublin which, however, left him discouraged. He regarded it as a dialogue of the deaf.

Meanwhile, one of the more symbolic acts of that 1983 service of reconciliation was captured by the *Irish News* (16 August 1983):

> At this year's service, a Protestant elder from the Shankill Road carried the [open] bible up the aisle of Clonard and then read it to the congregation from the sanctuary. It was a simple but, in the circumstances, a deeply significant ceremony that caught the spirit and promise of this annual celebration. The text was from John 15:1-5 and 17:6-11: 'I am the vine, you are the branches ...'[10]

Death of Fr Christopher McCarthy

The passage just quoted from the *Irish News* was part of a tribute to Fr Christopher McCarthy, one of Clonard's great ecumenists, who died on 28 July 1983 of spinal collapse. For several years past he had suffered great physical distress which, in his last months, had necessitated the constant help of loyal Clonard men, 'from early morning till late at night', in attending to his physical and material needs. The monastery record identifies Seán O'Neill, Arthur Lynch and Frank McLaughlin as particularly helpful in these corporal works of mercy. Fr McCarthy had been born in Limerick city in 1910 and ordained priest in the Redemptorist House of Studies, Esker, county Galway in 1935. He served in India and Sri Lanka (Ceylon, as it then was) for eleven years, for four years in Australia and two in California. His varied missionary work gave him a breadth of vision and a great respect for other faiths and points of view. Typical of this was his friendship with members of Moral Rearmament, a movement founded in Oxford in 1921 by the American-born evangelist Frank Buchman. It was frowned upon by the Catholic establishment, but it made possible important Anglican contacts in London. These led, ultimately, to a series of distinguished Anglicans, beginning with Canon Baker, participating in the Clonard Church Unity programmes. Fr McCarthy acknowledged that, in his last years, his Moral Rearmament friends – who joined in his prayer and bible-study apostolates – were 'a tower of strength and comfort'.[11]

Bishop Daly: Ecumenism beyond 'Christian Unity Week'

Dr Cahal Daly took another positive ecumenical step when he strongly supported the arrangements made by his diocesan commission for a service of reconciliation on Pentecost Sunday, 22 May 1983, in St Malachy's Church, Alfred Street, Belfast. Dr Jack Weir, the widely respected Presbyterian minister, was invited to preach and the Corrymeela singers shared in the sacred music. In a circular urging attendance at the service, Bishop Daly noted: '... it will extend the concern for reconciliation between Christians to other times than the week for Christian Unity. The work of reconciliation is a great need in our situation.' In support of this latter conviction, it is interesting to note that, in another circular issued about the same time, in which he urged the Catholic faithful to avail of the spiritual benefits of the special Holy Year indulgences, one of the good works that he suggested was 'Attendance at an ecumenical service'. A Pentecost service of reconciliation became a feature of ecumenism in the diocese of Down and Connor.[12]

The pattern of 'Christian Unity Week' at Clonard

In October 1984, the Clonard Redemptorist community gave 'the task of looking after ecumenical matters' to two of its members, in succession to Fr McCarthy. They were Frs Gerry Reynolds and Gerry Cassidy. By this time the annual celebration of Christian Unity Week in Clonard had acquired a distinct pattern. The major ecumenical service took place on the Wednesday evening, with a distinguished guest preacher, the attendance of senior clergy from the Catholic and major reformed churches – Church of Ireland, Presbyterian and Methodist – and appropriate music performed by Clonard choir. Invitations were sent out in good time, usually at the beginning of the previous December, which assured Protestant guests that the service would be 'a service of prayers, hymns and scripture readings chosen by the Irish Council of Churches'. In November 1985 Rev Bill Jackson, the Presbyterian minister of Shankill Road Mission, preached on successive nights to the men's Holy Family Confraternity ('He got a warm welcome from the men,' noted the chronicler, 'and pleased them greatly by his sermon.') The practice of inviting Protestant clergy to speak to the confraternity men was integrated into the Christian Unity Week arrangements from January 1986. At the same time, a visiting speaker was invited to address all four sessions of the Thursday novena in honour of Our Lady of Perpetual Succour. Finally, from 1987 onwards, in collaboration with the Redemptorist community at St Clement's retreat house, Antrim Road, Belfast, a theological conference was held, usually on the Friday of Christian Unity Week, in which the principal speakers (normally two) represented the Catholic and reformed traditions respectively.[13]

(Note: The inclusion of the men's Holy Family Confraternity in Christian Unity Week services to the apparent exclusion of the women's should not be seen as discriminatory. In the Clonard tradition, the men's confraternity met weekly on week nights; the ladies' met only monthly and on Sundays. Since Sunday is the busiest church day for all denominations, it was rarely used then for ecumenical activities.)

Distinguished visiting preachers
In the early years, an attempt was made to invite the distinguished preacher to return for a second year, but this proved difficult to sustain. As noted earlier, Canon Baker preached in 1980 and again in 1981. He returned for a third time in 1983, but that was a special occasion to mark his elevation to the House of Bishops. In 1984 and 1985 the special guest was Canon A. L. Allchin of Canterbury Cathedral. Rev James Torrance, 'a leading theologian of the Church of Scotland' teaching in Aberdeen University, attracted an audience in 1986 of between six and seven hundred of whom 'the majority were Protestants'. He returned in 1987 and delivered 'a good sermon which spoke of the intransigence of the Catholic and Protestant churches as a partial cause of our troubles'. Rev Torrance was the last speaker to return for a second time. The guest speaker in 1988 was Dr James Mahaffy, Church of Ireland bishop of Derry and Raphoe. The choice in 1989 of Rev Kenneth Newell, minister of Fitzroy Presbyterian Church, Belfast, was an acknowledgement of the constructive ecumenical work being done in the Clonard-Fitzroy Fellowship, which had been formed in the early 1980s. Since 1984, the leader of the Clonard group in this fellowship had been Fr Gerry Reynolds. As an indication of the influence of the Clonard-Fitzroy fellowship, the chronicler noted that the church was '80% full' for the 1989 service.[14]

The Clonard-Fitzroy Fellowship

A further word should be said about the Clonard-Fitzroy Fellowship, which continues to thrive after twenty years. The fellowship began in 1981 as an inter-church Bible study group established by Fr Christopher McCarthy of Clonard and Rev Kenneth Newell of Fitzroy Presbyterian. Members belong to the congregations who worship in Clonard and Fitzroy churches. The number participating in the fellowship in any year has never been more than thirty from each congregation.

While retaining its initial focus on bible study and prayer, the fellowship has developed considerably. It sees itself variously:

as a school of Christian spirituality where each member can learn about the other tradition;

as a forum, first, for re-examining traditional doctrinal differences and, secondly, for genuine dialogue about the conflicting political loyalties in Northern Ireland society;

as an organiser of reconciliation services;

as a witness to other congregations of the value of such a local fellowship;

as an explorer searching for the Reconciled and Reconciling Church that is coming to be; and, finally,

as a gathering of friends who are able to socialise together and enjoy one another's culture.

In order to realise this vision of itself, the fellowship set out a series of objectives which included: the development of mutual understanding and friendship; the fostering of the spiritual growth of members and the sharing of their fellowship experience. A wide range of appropriate activities was designed to ensure that these objectives were achieved: regular meetings of the full group and smaller groups in which prayer and a deeper understanding of the scriptures would be paramount, but in which the shared doctrinal, moral and spiritual heritage of the two traditions would be affirmed and differences re-examined; an annual weekend together; occasional social gatherings; and, finally, dialogue with cultural and political groups involved in the life of Northern Ireland.

While the essential work of the fellowship lies in its own regular meetings, it has sponsored other important links with, on the one hand, the wider Clonard and Fitzroy congregations and, on the other, outside groups. Of the latter, the most important has been a series in which members of political parties, particularly those connected with the various paramilitary groups, have been invited to present and debate their points of view with clergy and laity from various churches. In this undertaking, the fellowship was assisted by Fr Alec Reid of Clonard who, in addition to his long record of mediation with and between paramilitary groups, was appointed by his community to

'ecumenical and peace' work in 1993. The fellowship has also organised theological conferences which catered for both clergy and laity in separate sessions, allowing each group to exchange views with distinguished speakers
from both reformed and Roman Catholic traditions.[15]

As already noted, Rev Kenneth Newell of Fitzroy had preached for the
first time in Clonard in unity week 1989. This was reciprocated in December
1990 when the then rector of Clonard, Fr John O'Donnell, C.Ss.R., became
the first Catholic priest to preach in Fitzroy Church. Later, in unity week
1996, Rev Newell was to become the first Presbyterian clergyman to preach
at a Perpetual Novena session in Clonard on the subject of Mary.

Members of the Fitzroy-Clonard Fellowship, together with the
Cornerstone community and a 'children's group' made ecumenical history of
another kind when, on 11 September 1992, they responded to an invitation
from President Mary Robinson to visit Áras an Uachtaráin. A group of fifty-
five was led by Fr Gerry Reynolds, accompanied by Rev Kenneth Newell and
Rev Sam Burch. The visit concluded with a recitation, in which President
Robinson joined, of the 'Prayer for the Reconciliation of the Churches'
which had been included in one of Clonard's ecumenical goals since 1984-5.[16]

New dynamism in Clonard: Frs Reynolds and Cassidy
The appointment of Frs Reynolds and Cassidy brought a renewed dynamism
to Clonard's ecumenical activities. They were helped, no doubt, by the
greater openness in Down and Connor diocese, thanks to the positive attitude to ecumenism of the new bishop. The two Redemptorists also made a
serious attempt to devise a plan of campaign for future ecumenical action. In
February 1985, they placed before their Clonard confrères a set of six goals, at
the same time appealing for 'more community participation' in their work.

These goals embraced the Clonard Redemptorist community itself and people who usually worshipped in Clonard church; they also committed the two
priests to specific courses of action, including the establishment of a reconciliation project 'with the churches of the Shankill and the parishes of the Falls'.

The Clonard community was asked to support the idea of 'home and
away' meetings with representatives of the various churches. Since 'away'
meetings depended on invitations, 'home' arrangements were easier to make
– typically informal invitations, especially to clergy of other denominations,
to lunch in Clonard, preceded or followed by a friendly, but honest, exchange
of views.

Worshippers in Clonard were, in the first place, to be urged to pray for
reconciliation among the churches. Ten thousand copies of a prayer for reconciliation were distributed. In addition. members of the Clonard congregation were invited to prayer services in Fitzroy Presbyterian Church and St
Michael's Church of Ireland on the Shankill Road. The two ecumenists were

also anxious to develop in the Clonard congregation 'an appreciation of the changes in the way the Catholic Church views other Christian communities since Vatican II'. They also wanted them to be able to explain Catholic doctrine, worship and moral teaching to members of other churches. Finally, they wanted them to be open to enrichment by the insights of their fellow Christians. Facilitated by confrères, Frs Reynolds and Cassidy addressed various Clonard groups – novena and Mass congregations and confraternities – on the ecumenical mission of the church.[17]

There were three specific courses of ecumenical action to which the two Redemptorists committed themselves. First, they participated in two well-established inter-church projects, Fr Cassidy in the Corrymeela community of reconciliation at Ballycastle, county Antrim and Fr Reynolds in the Prison Fellowship, whose offices were at University Street, Belfast. Secondly, and rather ambitiously, they each undertook 'to include an inter-church project in the missions and retreats we both do, either singly or together'. Thirdly, they set themselves to work for reconciliation with the churches of the Shankill and the parishes of the Falls.

Corrymeela Community
Fr Cassidy's association with Corrymeela ultimately lasted for six years, from 1984 to 1990. His attachment was mostly in a half-time capacity, but with a full-time spell for six months in 1985. His briefings at community meetings introduced his fellow Redemptorists to the breadth of activities undertaken in Corrymeela: assisting with the formation of volunteer groups, many of them from abroad ('helping them to understand the N. Ireland situation'); being available to the staff, particularly volunteers and their co-ordinators, to 'listen and share'; working with 'seed groups' of young people aged 18-23 years, who attended for six weekends, with sixth-form Christian education groups and with inter-chaplaincy groups (mostly from England); being a presence to adult groups like 'Cross' – widows of innocent people killed in the troubles, to Lagan College parents, other family groups and study groups. In all this activity, Fr Cassidy was seen as 'a Christian education worker ... a Catholic presence at the centre'. But as a member of the staff team of nine, he had staff meetings for two days each month, shared in staff study days twice in the year, participated in organising the annual theological conference and represented Corrymeela at conferences of 'lay centres' in Britain and Europe. Fr Cassidy was later succeeded at Corrymeela by fellow Redemptorist Fr Patrick O'Keefe.

Prison fellowship
In a similar way, Fr Reynolds brought new insights from the Prison Fellowship. The monthly meetings which he attended brought together people who were involved with the fellowship in different ways:

Volunteers, who write to or visit prisons, volunteers who give time to staff the rooms [of the Fellowship, at University Street], the three full-time staff of PF, board members, chaplains to prisons. Meetings are prayer of praise together, talk by invited speaker, intercession in small groups for prisoners.

In the course of his first year's membership of the Prison Fellowship and in conformity with its practice, Fr Reynolds formed three support groups in the Falls area which met in one another's homes. Their meetings combined reflection on an agreed scripture reading with intercession for prisoners and for the reconciliation of the churches.

Inter-church project on mission work

The ambitious goal of including an inter-church project on mission work proved extremely difficult to realise. Frs Cassidy and Reynolds applied the idea to a parish mission they gave in Dromore, county Down, in May 1985. As they reported: 'We tried to communicate a vision of the church in Dromore that was larger than the Catholic parish ... Our overall theme was the unity the Father wills for his people.' While they admitted that the scheme did not work, they believed that the idea ought to be explored further. That it was is brought out by the fact that, first, by the early 1990s, the Irish Redemptorist Province accepted 'Cross-community dialogue and ecumenism' as 'a dimension of all pastoral endeavour' by the three Redemptorist communities in Belfast. Secondly, by the same time, the Clonard mission team was declaring that they preached an instruction on ecumenism during each mission and that they were always on the lookout for possibilities of encouraging ecumenical development.[18]

Shankill-Falls reconciliation project

The 'Shankill-Falls Clergy and Church Workers Fellowship' as it was formally known (or Shankill-Falls Fellowship for short) first met 'in the manse house of the Woodvale Presbyterian Church' on 14 November 1984. To it were invited the clergy from the parishes or congregations which impinged on the Shankill-Falls 'peace line'. The meeting consisted of 'prayer and a shared reflection on the mystery of unity, based on Ephesians 4:1-7'. Similar meetings followed in December and in February 1985. In January 1985, the Fellowship had a conference in Clonard with Canon Allchin of Canterbury during Christian Unity Week. All stayed for lunch with the community where they were joined by three wives of members. Meetings in March and June 1985 were days of prayer and sharing in St Clement's Retreat House and the Columbanus Community respectively.

One of the earliest preoccupations of the fellowship was the involvement of local people – from the constituent parishes and congregations – in the ministry of ecumenical reconciliation. As a result, one of its first fruits was the Shankill-Falls inter-church prayer group which met for the first time in December 1986 and agreed to meet on the first Monday of every month thereafter.

Fellowship meetings involve prayer and reflection, talks by invited speakers with expertise in community problems and by members of the fellowship sharing aspects of their tradition. Current and recurring community issues, such as fear and intimidation, are kept under constant review.

As part of its contribution to 'practical' reconciliation, the fellowship organises from time to time summer youth programmes, sometimes with an international, but always with a strong ecumenical, dimension. In more general ways, it supports a range of ecumenical contacts by publicising and helping to organise inter-church events.[19]

Variations in Clonard arrangements
The 1989 Christian Unity Week ought to have been the last to be held in Clonard, had a decision of its church staff been acted upon. (The 'church staff' are those members of the community, chaired by the 'Prefect of the Church', who are responsible for the organisation of services in Clonard church.) This decision was made in October 1988. At the same meeting another decision with ecumenical implications was taken, namely, to end the Thursday night bible class, founded in the mid-1970s by Fr McCarthy. While this class, according to the chronicle, 'made a great initial impact which continued for many years ... enthusiasm for it has waned so much that it was ending its own life'. If there was any anxiety about enthusiasm for the Christian Unity Week services, it must have been dispelled by the excellent response to Rev Kenneth Newell in January 1989.[20]

The unity services of 1989 also reflected an earlier Clonard ecumenical initiative, sponsored by Fr Gerry Reynolds. This was the practice of inviting clergy from the reformed churches to live for a time in the Clonard community. For example, the visiting preacher to the Thursday novena sessions in 1989 was Rev John Caldicott, Anglican vicar of Christchurch, London. He had spent the four weeks of August 1986 in residence at Clonard. The 1989 arrangements also continued the practice, begun the previous year, of a 'covenant service' for the joint divisions of the men's Holy Family Confraternity conducted by a Protestant minister. Interestingly, from its beginning in 1988 until 1994, this facet of the annual unity services was the preserve of Methodist clergymen – Rev Samuel Burch of Cornerstone Community in 1988; Dr Norman Taggart in 1989 and, in the following years, Rev Donald Kerr, Rev Kenneth Wilson, Rev Arthur Parker, Rev Dennis Bambrick, Rev David Clements of Woodvale and, finally, Rev Kenneth Thompson of Donegall Square in 1994. Methodist 'domination' was broken in 1994 when one of the confraternity divisions was addressed by Mr David

Porter, a cross-community worker for Belfast YMCA, who had lived with the Clonard community for some time the previous year. In 1995, the last in the series of covenant services was held in St Matthew's Church of Ireland, Shankill Road.[21]

The balance of unity week invitations to preach at the Thursday novena sessions was somewhat in favour of members of the Anglican tradition. The theme of these sermons was, naturally, the Mother of Jesus, particularly her role in the church. In 1986 and 1987 the preacher was a Brother Damien, of the Anglican Society of St Francis. As noted earlier, Rev John Caldicott, vicar of Christchurch, London, preached in 1989. The Church of Ireland rectors of St George's, Belfast and Holy Trinity, Portrush, were the preachers in 1992, 1993 and 1995. The Methodist tradition supplied preachers in 1990, 1991 and 1997, Rev Sam Burch, a founder member of the nearby Cornerstone Community, being particularly prominent. The sole Presbyterian contributor was Rev Kenneth Newell of Fitzroy, in 1996.

Despite the decision of the Clonard church staff, in October 1988, 'to end the Church Unity Octave' in 1989, it was still celebrated in 1990. However, the chronicler's record for that year of the main function of unity week, the Wednesday evening ecumenical service, was uncharacteristically negative. This may hint at an underlying unease in the community about the value of continuing with the existing format. While the church was 'half full', in spite of 'wet, cold, snowy' weather, the chronicler regarded the attendance as 'poor' and he concluded: ' ... the novelty has gone ... more churches have a service of their own ...' Whether unease among the Clonard community had any bearing on events, it is a fact that the Wednesday ecumenical service for 1991 was not held in Clonard church. Instead, there was 'a day of fasting and prayer' from 11 am at the Methodist Church, Springfield Road. The objective of the fasting and prayer was 'that all the people of the Shankill and the Falls may discover their unity in Jesus' and everyone who wished was invited to join Protestant and Catholic members of Cornerstone at any time during the day. The day was concluded by 'an inter-church celebration of our "Oneness in Jesus",' at which the preacher was Rev Frank Topping, Methodist chaplain at the University of Kent.[22]

Springfield Road Methodist Church was again the venue in 1992 for the Wednesday inter-church service. Several members of Clonard community attended and were impressed with the sermon of Rev Timothy Kinahan, rector of St Dorothea's Church of Ireland parish, Gilnahirk. However, by 1993 Clonard church was restored as the venue for the Wednesday service, when Rev David Kerr, Methodist, preached on the theme 'Bearing the Fruit of the Spirit for Christian Unity' (Galatians 5:22-23). The Clonard service was now organised jointly by the Cornerstone community, the Clonard-Fitzroy

Fellowship and the recently formed Currach inter-church community. (Currach was formed in August 1992 at 2 Workman Avenue, Springfield Road.)

New approaches were explored, as in the 1994 joint presentation of the service by two women, Sister Geraldine Smyth, a Dominican, and Rev Lesley Carroll of the Church of Ireland. Their theme was 'The Joy of Unity in Friendship and Prayer'. The approach in 1996 was to invite 'some people [to] tell their stories' on the theme 'Blessed through each other like Jesus and John at the Jordan' (Matthew 3:13-17). A further initiative, in 1997, was the recital, by Protestant ecumenists, of the prayers of the faithful at each of the Masses in Clonard on the Sunday of unity week.

Too much should not be made of the October 1988 decision to end the Christian Unity Week in Clonard. Its only concrete effect was to remove from Clonard church to other venues the central ecumenical service, customarily held on the Wednesday of unity week. And this removal was only temporary and spasmodic – to Springfield Road Methodist Church in 1991 and 1992 and to the YMCA headquarters in Wellington Hall, Belfast, in 1997, when the format was a discussion on 'Inter-church marriages in a divided society'. Even at these times, the other main elements of the Clonard-style Christian Unity Week continued, namely, the address by a visiting Protestant minister to the Monday and Tuesday divisions of the men's Holy Family Confraternity, and the address to the four sessions of the Thursday perpetual novena to Our Lady of Perpetual Help. The one casualty appears to have been the joint ecumenical conference organised in conjunction with the Redemptorist community at St Clement's, Antrim Road. The last recorded conference was held in 1989.[23]

Centrality of the Week of Prayer for Christian Unity

Much space has been given to the ecumenical endeavours of Clonard community and its Protestant friends during the annual Christian Unity Week because, despite the efforts of Bishop Cahal Daly and others to extend inter-church contacts beyond it, Christian unity week remained the most important occasion of the year for ecumenical dialogue. However, contacts at every level were constantly made – at the highest level, as when church leaders united to condemn some atrocity or injustice brought about by 'the troubles', and at the most personal and individual level in the numerous friendships between clergy and laity of all denominations.

Ecumenical visitors to Clonard

The Clonard record from the early 1980s onwards bears ample witness to a wide range of ecumenical contacts outside the annual Christian unity week. One of the earliest and most interesting ecumenical visitors there was Dr

Michael Ryder, an Anglican, described in the domestic record as 'a man of deep religious faith'. He was a brother of Sue Ryder, wife of the famous Group Captain Leonard Cheshire, VC, whose homes for the disabled established after the Second World War did – and continue to do – so much good work throughout Britain. Dr Ryder seems to have been one of those high-minded Englishmen who were affected by what they believed was their country's historic injustice to Ireland. So in 1975 he came to Belfast to offer his medical services, by way of reparation, to the harassed people of the Clonard area. He was given a room and board in the monastery, for which he paid weekly over a period of eight years. Dr Ryder subsequently retired to London, but revisited Clonard from time to time.[24]

From the beginnng of 1984, the Clonard community became host to students from the Irish School of Ecumenics in Dublin. The domestic chronicle notes on 3 January 1984: 'Two students arrived from the Irish School of Ecumenics to do placement with us until January 13th.' One was an Australian Presbyterian minister, Rev Alasdair McCrea, the other an Anglican, Rev Monsell Williams, from Barbados. Occasionally it was the students' supervisor who lodged in Clonard, as in January 1987, when Fr Fergal Brennan, SJ, 'from the Dublin School of Ecumenics,' stayed for ten days: 'He is in charge of a small group of students who are with friends in Belfast.' A few further examples from the monastery chronicle will illustrate the variety of visitors:

'... a Mr David Kirkwood, a married Church of England seminarist ... two years from ordination, ... with us for two weeks; his diocese is in Lincolnshire.' (June 1984)

'We had a visit this evening from 9-10 Methodist students for the ministry – an ecumenical gesture.' (12 December 1989)

'Clergy visit. Canon Matthew O'Hare, PP, and Fr Frank Kearney, CC, of Banbridge, with clergymen of different denominations from Banbridge and the surrounding area, visited us and stayed for lunch. They wanted to see our church and monastery and learn about our apostolate and pastoral problems.' (9 November 1993)

Such visitors, together with others who came under various guises, provided a steady stream during the 1980s and 1990s through the ever-open door of Clonard. They came mostly from England, but also from other parts of Ireland, from North America, Germany, Switzerland, France, India, Nigeria, Madagascar and the West Indies.[25]

Special ecumenical events

Special ecumenical events were arranged from time to time by various agencies within the Clonard-Fitzroy/Cornerstone/Shankill-Falls Fellowship/

Currach Community ambit. They were mostly inspired by the agreed ecumenical desire to offer local people practical opportunities to become
involved in the ecumenical reconciliation ministry. As Shankill-Falls
observed in February 1988: 'Official meetings of the Irish churches have been
going on snce 1972, but there can be no impact locally without the involvement of more local people.'[26]

So, for example, in November 1986, 'A Devotional Day for Peace' was
organised by the Clonard community as part of the 'Christians and Peace'
series to mark the end of the United Nations International Year of Peace,
1986. The venue was the monastery. The invitation claimed, quite modestly:
'Clonard is the home of a community of Redemptorists well-known for their
commitment to reconciliation and inter-church activities.' On Good Friday
1988, at the end of March, one of the most depressing months of the troubles
(the Michael Stone attack on one of the funerals of the 'Gibraltar Three' in
Milltown Cemetery and the attack on two British soldiers at the funeral of
one of Stone's victims: in all, eleven people dead in one week), Cornerstone
Community organised an outdoor Way of the Cross, 'from Mackie's via
Kashmir Road to Bombay St, through the peace wall at Cupar St to
Woodvale Park. A very large crowd walked.' The Shankill-Falls Fellowship
acknowledged at their April meeting that,

> Local people had seemed pleased and relieved at this opportunity to wit-
> ness together, after the terrible events of the previous month. The walkers
> were mostly welcomed by local residents, and the walk had culminated in
> a spirit of celebration and of the victory of the Cross.

In fact, the Fellowship had, since February, been planning their own
'Shankill-Falls witness' for Good Friday. In the event, they were happy to join
with Cornerstone's arrangements. Unknown to them, a similar procession
had taken place from St Agnes's Church, Andersonstown, to the nearby
Casement Park in atonement for the murders of the previous week; they
would have liked to have linked up in some way with it.[27]

Later, in May 1993, Cornerstone Community organised a peace walk
from Springfield Road to Northumberland Street (which links the Shankill
and Falls Roads). At Pentecost 1994 and again the following year, Fr Reynolds
organised a night vigil in Clonard church 'to seek the Holy Spirit's help for
the reconciliation of the churches and the making of political peace ... and
for residents of Clonard area and all involved with them in decisions about
redevelopment'. Each vigil began at 11 pm on the Saturday and after night
watches of one and a half hours each, concluded with Eucharist at 5.00 am.
on the feast. Handbills advertising the occasion carried the invitation,
'Everyone is welcome, Catholic and Protestant, British and Irish'.[28]

'Reminiscences of an ecumenist'

Perhaps there is no better way to conclude an account of the involvement of Clonard community in ecumenism than to quote the personal reminiscence of its effects on a former member of that community. Fr George Wadding was rector of Clonard from September 1978 to September 1984. As he recalled years later, it was, 'the time when the "blanket" and "dirty" protests reached their zenith, culminating in the hunger strikes with their consequent terror and destruction in our part of West Belfast'. Fr Wadding was writing for an ecumenical readership of *Pace*, the journal of Protestant and Catholic Encounter.

In his article he recalls in particular his enrichment through contact with other Christian churches:

My Roman Catholicism is a little more 'Protestant' today – a compliment paid me, in fact, by an extreme right-wing Catholic who, in a letter to the *[Belfast] Telegraph*, spoke disparagingly (as he thought) of the 'Protestant Rector of Clonard'. ... when I look back I am amazed at how much I got involved in, usually dragged in by others, rather than initiating things myself.

For example: the clergy study weeks and other events at Corrymeela, the establishment of the Cornerstone and Columbanus communities, the Mixed Marriage Association, Peace People, Lagan College (still such a *bête noire* to RCs), the Inter-Church Group on Faith and Politics which produced the report: *Breaking Down the Enmities* ... I remember the Ecumenical Services at Clonard when – correct me if I am mistaken – for the first time non-Catholic clergymen spoke from the pulpit of a Roman Catholic church in Northern Ireland. And so on ...[29]

CHAPTER 12

Music in Clonard Church

One of the great disappointments for the historian of Clonard monastery is the serious lack of evidence – written or otherwise – for the first fifty years of one of its great institutions, Clonard choir. There are two possible explanations for this. One is the lack of interest, or expertise, in music of the various scribes who, over the years, kept the domestic chronicle. They wrote precious little and kept virtually no documentation about the choir. The second is the overwhelming attention given to the first organist and choirmaster, Arthur de Meulemeester who, having come to Clonard in 1898, presided over music in the church until his death in 1942. The oral tradition in the monastery is summed up in the following tribute from Fr Patrick O'Donnell:

> a brilliant organist who in later years when Clonard got a first-class organ thrilled many a congregation with his recitals. He was also a distinguished composer who composed several Masses of the highest quality. No less successful was he as a choirmaster. He trained the boys and men who came his way to be one of the best choirs in the North.[1]

It has to be said, however, that, on the basis of evidence presented below, some members of Clonard community in the early 1920s would have taken issue with such a wholehearted endorsement. For several months between late 1924 and early 1925, the organist's position was subjected to a critical attack.

Early days

The first mention of a choir is under the date of 20 May 1897, shortly after the opening of the temporary or 'tin' church. At the last Mass (12 noon) on that occasion, 'a group of men and boys' sang, conducted by a Signor Mora and accompanied by a Mr Kerrigan on the harmonium which was a gift of the rector of the Redemptorist church of St Joseph in Dundalk. Signor Mora was engaged for three months to teach the choir of forty men and boys. A new organist was appointed in December 1897, a Mr John Murray of Limerick. Six months later, he had the joy of presiding at a new organ, London-made at a cost of £150. It was 'considered by those qualified to judge a really excellent [one]'. The occasion was the feast of Our Lady of Perpetual Succour, celebrated with High Mass on Sunday 19 June 1898. The choir was augmented for the occasion and included the celebrated Irish tenor of the time, Joseph O'Mara, a great friend of the Redemptorists. Murray left in

October 1898 and was replaced by the young Belgian Arthur de Meulemeester. He was only twenty-three, but already remarkable as a brilliant organist, a laureate of the Lemmens Institute of Mechelen (Malines) in Belgium.[2]

The Lemmens Institute

This institute had been established in 1879 by the noted organist, teacher and composer Jaak Nikolaas Lemmens (1823-1881) under the auspices of the Belgian bishops. Its formal title was the École de Musique Religieuse and its purpose was to raise the standards of Catholic church music. A parallel development was the encouragement of Gregorian, or plain, chant, later to be given full papal support by Pope St Pius X (1903-14). To this end, Lemmens, with Canon van Demme, founded the Société de St Grégoire. As an organist and teacher, Lemmens had great influence in Belgium; he established a new school of organ playing which also greatly enhanced the art of organ building in Belgium.

Lemmens' own compositions, which include orchestral and sacred vocal works as well as many organ pieces, are seldom performed nowadays. But on the occasion of the blessing and opening of the new Clonard organ, on Pentecost Sunday, 25 May 1912, de Meulemeester included in the special programme a performance of Lemmens' choral work 'Easter Sonata'.[3]

De Meulemeester's talent

The *Irish News*, reporting on the ceremonial laying of the foundation stone of the (new) Clonard church, on Rosary Sunday, 4 October 1908 by Bishop Tohill, had this to say:

> The music of the Mass was rendered in faultless style by the carefully trained choir under the conductorship of Mons De Meulemeester, the well-known organist. All the pieces were sung with taste and beauty, the solemnity and impressiveness of the sacred music being fully expressed.

While such notices tended to be flattering, the use of phrases like 'faultless style', 'carefully trained' and 'rare taste and beauty' may indicate choral work of unusual quality. The musical highlight of the occasion was de Meulemeester's own choral composition, *Ecce Sacerdos Magnus* ('Behold a Great Priest'), a setting of a traditional liturgical salute to a presiding bishop.[4]

The first known de Meulemeester composition, performed in the 'tin' church in 1902, was his *Missa Sanctissimi Redemptoris*, for three male voices and organ. He was ever afterwards reluctant to allow this Mass to be performed again, owing to the difficulty of assembling a male choir of sufficient quality. However, on the occasion of the dedication of the new Clonard church in 1911, he relented. That occasion was also marked by a performance of his motet *Redemisti nos Domine* ('You have redeemed us, O Lord'), composed for four mixed voices.[5]

Of de Meulemeester's musical ability, there can be no doubt. Apart from his training and qualifications, his role in the early organ fund shows clearly his authoritative command of the theory and practice of organ building. We know that he gave a number of recitals on the Ulster Hall organ to raise funds for the Clonard instrument. In May 1911, he edited *The New Redemptorist Hymnal*, based on the penny hymn book of the previous year, 'a wonderful pennyworth', compiled by Fr Thomas Hagan of the Clonard community 'from various directions', adding some new hymns to Irish or Redemptorist saints by Frs Doyle, McNamara, Collier and others:

> Many new airs were printed for the first time, some by the organist and others by other contributors continental or otherwise, notably by Fr McHugh whose setting of Irish music was highly praised and by Fr Cleere who contributed several items.

The chronicler, however, felt that the credit for the new publication should go to Fr Hagan, 'for undertaking the labour of seeing the book through the press. ... the organist and other contributors left to him the burden ...'[6]

The crisis of 1924-5

The de Meulemeester crisis of 1924-5, indicated above, apart from its intrinsic interest as revealing a bitter dispute, is worth examining for the light it throws on the organist's *modus operandi*, his standing in musical circles in the Belfast of the time and in the estimation of various members of Clonard community.

The crisis arose out of the expansion of the men's Holy Family confraternity at the end of October 1924, when a second division was formed. There were difficulties about the most appropriate evening of meeting for the new division, the existing one being Tuesday. After consultation, Monday was agreed upon. De Meulemeester's difficulties began when the confraternity director, Fr Carroll, insisted that the organist attend the new Monday division meetings in person. Despite de Meulemeester's appeal to an arrangement of some thirteen years' standing whereby he was free on Monday and Saturday evenings, the director, supported by the rector and his consultors, insisted that the organist's duty required him to attend. (By coincidence, Fr Carroll was one of the consultors.) For the extra work which the new confraternity meetings would involve, de Meulemeester was to be given an increase of £15, which would bring his salary up to £150 a year.

De Meulemeester insisted that his 'spare' evenings could not be taken away from him. They had been conceded by the then rector, Fr O'Laverty, about the time of the opening of the new church in 1911, in lieu of an increase in salary which could not then be afforded. An additional part of the arrangement was that a local man, Mr Monaghan, would deputise when required on the organist's two free evenings, 'in return for musical training'. The important concern for de Meulemeester was that he had used his free evenings to undertake various professional commitments in order to add to his earnings. Of particular value to him was a series of lectures, variously described by him as 'in musical art' and 'on musical history', which he had been giving in Belfast on Monday evenings for the previous five years. These lectures, with other professional engagements, earned him a total of £200 a year, which was considerably more than his salary from Clonard.[7]

Naturally de Meulemeester was outraged at the prospect of such a loss: 'I am threatened with a crying injustice which may probably involve my ruin as well as that of my wife and family,' he wrote to Fr Patrick Murray in Rome, appealing for his protection against the Clonard administration.[8] He had a very strong case in natural justice. The Redemptorists, it seems, had no contractual documentation about his position. In response to an inquiry from the provincial superior in February 1925, de Meulemeester replied:

> I do not believe that there are any documents in connection with my services as organist or my privilege of two spare evenings weekly. I think you will accept my solemn assertion that this privilege was granted to me ... all rectors and priests of Clonard have accepted it without questioning ...[9]

The rector of Clonard, Fr James Coogan, while initially supporting the confraternity director, was soon convinced that 'the decision must be in the organist's favour ... if extreme measures are to be avoided, then we must be prepared to allow Mr Monaghan to officiate on Monday evening ...' The rector also reported that Fr McHugh, a member of the community and a respected musician, after a long interview with the organist agreed with his point of view. De Meulemeester was convinced that, as always in the past, he had 'the sympathy of all Redemptorists with the exception of two or three' whom he suspected of engineering his trouble. The villain of the piece in his estimation was the confraternity director, Fr Carroll. He regarded the priest as having 'taken up a very ugly attitude to me ...' and as being behind 'a deliberate attempt ... to ruin me'. Even Fr Coogan acknowledged the director's 'inflexible opposition' to the organist's claim to his two free evenings and formally asked the provincial to arbitrate.[10]

What lay behind Fr Carroll's hostility is not clear. It might conceivably have derived from his elation at being at last able to expand the men's confraternity, a development which had been thwarted for so long. Perhaps, having declared the creation of a second men's division, he expected all concerned to mark the occasion with due formality – including the organist, whose duties Fr Carroll seemed to assume included personal attendance at all confraternity meetings. There is no indication that he was in any way moved by the impact his insistence would have on the established financial position of a man with a wife and large family.

It is possible that Fr Carroll (and others) saw de Meulemeester as trying to have the best of all possible worlds. In particular, the organist, in his own words, was 'pressing hard' to have his deputy, Mr Monaghan, installed as official sub-organist. This was a development the opposition was set against. The rector was adamant:

> ... it should not be allowed on any account as it would lead to endless difficulties ... Were there an official sub, Meulemeester would consider himself at liberty to depute him any time he pleased and, furthermore, Mr Monaghan would expect the position of organist later on and, being a Clonard man, he could not be passed over without giving offence. Mr Monaghan, of course, is no musician.[11]

In the eyes of his critics de Meulemeester's record at Clonard was not beyond reproach, so that it is arguable that some members of the community felt he needed to be taught a lesson. Fr Coogan, in revealing to his provincial de Meulemeester's alleged shortcomings, all of which the organist vehemently denied, as 'groundless' and 'untrue', urged him to be difficult:

> ... your rev[erence] should make it clear to Mr de Meulemeester that those best acquainted with Clonard are not at all satisfied with the choir. He makes no attempt to have variety. We are being treated to the same old pieces for years. I pointed out this to him; and previous rectors have done the same, but with no effect, because he has managed with appeals to higher superiors to triumph all along. ... I think, therefore, that the arrangement with Mr de Meulemeester should not be so peaceful as [to] let him go on in security with his present methods.[12]

The provision of greater variety in church music was one of the undertakings de Meulemeester had to give to the provincial in the final arbitration which was worked out, substantially in the organist's favour, by the end of February 1925. He grudgingly acknowledged that the rector had a point, but with a degree of *hauteur* which reminded all concerned of his superiority as a musician. As he wrote to the provincial:

> There is, perhaps, one reason for the lack of greater variety for which I will accept the guilt: it is that I have been too ambitious in supplying too great, too high class music to the services – music which required prodigious efforts and numerous practices to get up. All these efforts resulted in victory – but met with little appreciation. I know now that my ideals are not the ones of my superiors; and, given I am the servant of Clonard I must accept their ideals and bury mine.

He put forward other arguments. Services in Clonard were so numerous that 'a vast repertoire would be required to produce great variety'. Such a repertoire would necessitate 'a vast number of practices and, above all, a first rate choir of competent singers who should know how to read music' – and he claimed that 'not one man in my choir knows a note of music'. (An annotation on the margin of the letter – in another hand – counterclaimed: 'Some had been in the choir who knew music.')[13]

The conclusion of the episode was that de Meulemeester was allowed to retain his two free evenings. Monaghan could deputise on Mondays, being paid by the organist who undertook – and promised to maintain – an extensive programme of more accessible church music. The crisis had been a traumatic experience for him. He had asked that replies to his letters should be addressed to him at Clonard, not at home, because he was anxious that his wife should not know of his difficulty. Towards the end of his final letter to the provincial he wrote poignantly:

> I feel an inexpressively ardent desire for peace; the last four months have blighted my life. ... I am disheartened, I feel sick, my courage is on the brink of complete collapse – my life is no longer worth living for me.[14]

Annual choir banquet
Early accounts of 'the annual banquet given to the choir men' indicate the importance the Clonard community attached to the choir. Not only was the meal lavish – ' ... two courses of meats, sweet portion, dessert fruit and confections, wines, temperance drinks, etc.' (thus an account from 1 January 1910 – the banquet was usually held on the first Sunday of the year) – but so was the accompanying hospitality:

> When the guests have dined they are generally invited to the garden before repairing to the common room for cigars and musical entertainment which verges on [the] time of evening devotions.

Due formalities were observed: an address by the rector to which the organist usually replied, the choirmaster and a member of the choir 'also saying a few words'. At the common-room concert,

> It is customary for senior members of [the] choir or somebody appointed to act as chairman to call out the names of those who contribute to the programme of songs, recitations, etc. and the fathers and brothers attend ... taking their share in the various items of songs or recitations.[15]

While this celebration was essentially for the 'choir men', from the earliest days the church collectors were also invited. With the passage of time, the invitation widened to include, by the 1960s, the church orderlies and secretaries of the men's confraternity (women still being excluded from the monastery 'enclosure').

There was also, from the beginning, a separate annual celebration for the boys of the choir, which they shared with the numerous altar boys attached to the church. It was a great honour for these boys, though many may not have appreciated it, to be admitted to the inner sanctum of the monastery, including the refectory and fathers' common room. By the early 1930s, part of the entertainment was a play of some kind acted by the boys. In 1934, the boys' play was re-enacted in the Cawnpore Street Hall 'for a charitable purpose'.[16]

Death of de Meulemeester

Arthur de Meulemeester died at Lisieux nursing home, Belfast, on 26 June 1942. His health had been failing for some time. In September 1938 he had had an operation for the removal of one eye. The Clonard community accorded him a funeral such as was normally reserved for their own Redemptorist confrères. His remains, removed to Clonard on Saturday 28 June, were met at the church door by the whole community. Then, to the strains of the funeral march from Handel's *Saul,* they were carried to the sanctuary. They rested in the crypt to allow for Sunday services, but were returned on Monday 29, the feast of SS Peter and Paul. Solemn Requiem Mass was sung at 11 am as the final expression of Clonard community's 'thankfulness to the man whose memory will endure long as a high-class musician, as a faithful servant of Clonard and as a most pious Catholic'. In addition to his musical talents, Arthur de Meulemeester looked on his work as 'a special vocation whereby he might offer to Almighty God a tribute of praise in song and melody', in the words of an appreciation in the 1947 Clonard Golden Jubilee publication. He once confided to a friend:

I love to play the invocation 'Heart of Jesus' at the end of Benediction, because it makes me so happy to think of all the glory I can give to God when all these good people join in singing it.[17]

Clonard Boys' Choir

The decade following de Meulemeester's death witnessed a remarkably colourful period in the history of Clonard choir, with the emergence of the boys' section as an ensemble of great distinction. Several factors were at work here. Wartime conditions put an end, for the time being, to the import of continental organists As a result, the Redemptorists had to rely on their own resources. They were fortunate in the musical talents of some of their members. Fr Edward Jones took over choir and organ in the months following de Meulemeester's death. Later that year, he was succeeded by the young Fr John Torney, an outstanding musician. With the help of Fr Frank Burns, who had been 'prefect of the choir' since before de Meulemeester's death, he concentrated on developing the boys' section of the choir. The precise reasons for focusing on the boys' section are not clear. A contemporary report noted that, 'A better quality of voice among the boys and the men has been obtained, with results that make Clonard stand high in the musical world.' At any rate, the boys sang in Clonard church for the first time in January 1943.[18]

It was Fr Burns, a man of considerable managerial and, (dare one say it?), theatrical skills, who proposed the adoption of formal choral dress for the Clonard Boys' Choir, as it quickly came to be known. He saw this as fulfilling two important functions. On the one hand, it would help the church-going public to recognise the importance of church music; on the other, it would at once attract new members to the choir and better secure their fidelity to it. Not only did Fr Burns propose the choral dress, he designed it. And he was undoubtedly responsible for arranging the first public appearance of the choir in their new robes, appropriately on the feast of St Alphonsus, Sunday 1 August 1943.[19]

Attractive choral robes do not make a choir, but Fr Torney's musical talent did. Within a short time, Clonard Boys' Choir was justly regarded as one of the best, if not the best, of its kind in Ireland. It gave its first public performance outside the monastery in November 1943, at the annual Mater Hospital (fund-raising) concert in St Mary's Hall. The *Irish News* noted its 'collective talent and musical understanding that has been nurtured by careful training', and praised the young soloist Jim O'Neill for his outstanding performance. Fr Meighan, the American Redemptorist, in Clonard to launch the perpetual novena in honour of Our Lady of Perpetual Succour, was overwhelmed:

> Their singing has proved an amazing revelation to me and, when the war ends, provided I am granted permission, I will take them on a tour of the USA to let my countrymen see how delightfully little Irish boys can sing.

The choir was in great demand to sing at concerts and on radio during the remainder of the 1940s. In 1946, two of its soloists, Jim O'Neill and Hugh McVeigh, went to sing in America, invited by Fr Flanagan, founder of the famous Boys' Town school for delinquent boys in Nebraska. There they accompanied the Boys' Town choir in a tour of the eastern United States. Nearer home, the choir added colour and formality to some of the early Clonard missions to non-Catholics, as at Christmastide in 1951.

The Don Carl Players

'A naturally beautiful voice is not enough to enable its possessor to sing well ...' Thus ran a memoir written by Fr John Torney early in 1947. 'The Clonard Boys' Choir are not only singers', he continued, 'they are actors as well, belonging to a promising Junior Dramatic Society directed by Miss Betty Torney, LTCL,' hence, 'the clear, easy, natural enunciation of Clonard Boys' Choir receives adequate explanation'. Miss Torney, a well-known elocutionist and drama producer, was a sister of the choirmaster. Under her direction the 'Don Carl Players' (the name an anagram of 'Clonard') won numerous prizes at local drama festivals during the 1940s. Incidentally, Fr Torney noted that, at the time of writing, the strength of the choir was sixty-five members; since January 1943 it had had over two hundred on roll.[20]

Léon Rittweger

By the end of that decade, Clonard had a new organist: another Belgian, another graduate of the Lemmens Institute, M Léon Rittweger. With wartime restrictions ended, the post was advertised in December 1947. It was widely hoped among the community that the organist of Carlow cathedral, 'a Mr [Karl] Seeldrayers', would apply, but he was not to be inveigled northwards.

Léon Rittweger began a twenty-year association with Clonard late in 1948. His great musical talents allied to an incisive wit and an eminently sociable manner (a distinctly 'worldly' man after the pious de Meulemeester!) endeared him to musical circles throughout Northern Ireland. It is arguable that his 'ecumenical' reputation enhanced the musical offerings of the Clonard Choir at each meeting of the mission to non-Catholics in the years that followed. Rittweger's reputation produced a great demand for his musical services in numerous schools and institutions throughout the north. One of the results of this was the appointment of an assistant organist in June 1957 (the first incumbent was Mr Danny Burke, a former choir boy and soloist) and the agreement of the Redemptorists to provide the music for two of the Thursday novena sessions from among their own members. In time, various other musicians helped out at both novena sessions and confraternity meetings. Among them were Margaret McCrisken, Cynthia Mooney, Benedict Wynne and, later, Raymond Lennon.[21]

While there is no doubt that Rittweger maintained the highest standards in the choir and that Clonard as a church and monastic community benefited from his international reputation, his stewardship is particularly remembered for his introduction of female members to the choir. This happened in January 1968, but it was well known that he had been urging the change 'for a long time'. However, new female members were few initially, probably because of an unwillingness to be the first to invade a male preserve of long standing, but some of the first newcomers included former pupils of his own whom he had personally invited to join. But, no sooner had he won the concession for a mixed choir than he accepted, in the same month, a new appointment as organist in St Peter's pro-cathedral.[22]

Rittweger was not due to take up his new post until August 1968. On the Sunday after Easter, he provided a red-letter day for the choir – and Clonard – by inviting his friend and fellow Belgian, the celebrated organist and composer, Flor Peeters, to play for them at the noon Mass. Peeters then proceeded to the pro-cathedral for the 1 pm Mass and, later in the afternoon, gave a recital in the Methodist church, Donegall Square East. Unfortunately, as the Clonard chronicle observed, this recital 'was interrupted by a horrible din caused by Paisleyites gathered outside'.[23]

Rittweger held his last practice with Clonard choir on Saturday 28 August 1968. On the following day, a special dinner was given in his honour. The chronicle notes rather cryptically of this occasion: 'Speeches were brief and prudently worded.' The prudent wording was probably intended to curtail 'Ritty's' often bawdy sense of humour; the brevity may indicate a degree of irritation, not with Rittweger's departure, but with the badly kept secret that he was already '"poaching" members for his new choir from Clonard, despite [his] assurances that he would not ...' In the event, 'quite a number' followed him to St Peter's but, by the end of September, they were 'filtering back'. According to the Clonard chronicle, 'on Rittweger's departure, the member-ship of the choir was very low,' which seems to suggest not only that numbers had been dropping for some time, but that a crisis of sorts had developed.[24]

During September, 'in this difficult time of transition,' Fr Patrick Walsh, home on holiday from India, took temporary charge. The chronicle reported him as 'doing very well' in teaching the Gelineau psalms in four-part harmony to a choir which was 'very balanced', but which would be improved by the addition of some altos. It is interesting that, since the formation of the mixed choir, the boys had been kept 'as a separate choir to help singing at the 10 o'clock Mass' – the Sunday Mass traditionally reserved for children. The value of the children's Mass had waxed and waned over the years, but during 1968, a special effort had been made to make it more meaningful, for exam-ple, by the introduction of new hymns. This was the work, initially, of Fr Colm Kernan, but it was given fresh impetus by Frs Walsh and Martin Cushnan, the latter also recently returned from India. The exclusion of the boys from the main choir was to prove permanent, while the outbreak of the troubles the following year hastened the demise of the boys' choir. The child-ren's Sunday Mass was to remain for several years without permanent musi-cal support – until 1977, when Miss Patricia McGoldrick established a junior or children's choir specifically for it.[25]

Miss Rita McCann
In early October 1968 Miss Rita McCann of Belfast agreed to act as principal organist and choirmistress in an interim arrangement for one year. She was already a member of the choir, having been one of the first ladies to join at the beginning of the year. The youngest of three extremely talented musical sis-ters, Miss McCann was still a student at Queen's University. Her additional qualities – great energy and enthusiasm – were immediately required to the full, because within weeks the choir had to perform at a concert in St Mary's Hall, arranged by Fr Alec Reid before Rittweger's departure in order to raise funds for the Catholic Information Centre. Given the short notice, the pro-gramme was a very demanding one, but the choir members, who had received Miss McCann's appointment 'very enthusiastically', were very supportive.

Organist, choir (and the Clonard community) received a strong endorsement at the high Mass on Christmas Day 1968 – one of the highlights of the
monastery's musical calendar. The head of the Music Department at Queen's
University Belfast, Professor Philip Cranmer, himself a noted organist,
accepted an invitation to accompany the choir. Professor Cranmer was later
complimentary about the choir, commenting in particular on the 'very good
spirit' within it. The chronicler noted, with some pride, that the church was
'tightly packed'.[26]

Orchestral accompaniment

The routine duty of the choir was to sing at the 12 noon Mass every Sunday
(except for the holiday period of July to August). Special occasions were the
great feasts of the church, particularly Holy Week and Easter, Christmas Day,
special Redemptorist feasts and commemorations (for example, the centenary of the Archconfraternity of Our Lady of Perpetual Succour in June 1971
when the choir 'rendered a delightful oratorio'), special ecumenical occasions
and, from the mid-1970s onwards, a special carol, or Christmas-related service on a Sunday in Advent.

A novel element in the Christmas celebrations was the introduction of an
orchestra, made possible by official toleration of liturgical experimentation
following the Second Vatican Council. Thus, under the date of 22 December
1975, the Clonard chronicle recorded:

> Yesterday, Sunday, Clonard Choir and Orchestra presented Bach's
> Christmas Oratorio to an audience which just filled the church. The
> Blessed Sacrament had been removed. The Mass altar also taken away.
> With the help of benches the sanctuary was transformed into a stage to
> accommodate the orchestra.

The chronicler was deeply moved by the beauty of the music and its setting,
especially when placed in the context of strife-torn Belfast:

> What struck the onlooker was that there could be such music and song in
> Belfast of the barricades, of grimfaced military on patrol, of bombings
> and alas – of brutal murders. Against such a sinister background, the
> heavenly atmosphere of the beautiful church, a fine choir and orchestra
> and Bach's Oratorio with Christmas carols must have brought a tear to
> many an eye – of people who had lived and suffered through six years of
> turmoil.[27]

There is no doubt that the appearance of an orchestra in Clonard in 1975 was
a novelty and the occasion was enhanced by the novelty. But there was more
to it than that. The quality of the music needed no verification, but the quality of the playing marked the coming of age of instrumental tuition in
Belfast. While the music department at Queen's University was producing
considerable numbers of well-educated musicians, the City of Belfast School

of Music was producing its first generation of excellent instrumentalists. What is more – and this is intriguing in the context of the troubles – these instrumentalists, who willingly formed ensembles under various auspices, including churches, but always on the basis of personal friendships, were genuinely ecumenical. These friendships were made at Queen's or in the School of Music, based on a shared love of music. The Clonard chronicler, like the vast majority of the audience in the church, was probably unaware of this dimension to 'the heavenly atmosphere' of the occasion. At any rate, in their annual Christmas carol service, the Clonard choir continues to be accompanied by a youthful, but talented, instrumental ensemble drawn from the same sources as in 1975.

'Clonard Choir Sings'

Another first for the choir under Miss McCann was the making of a long-playing record. The recording, made in Clonard Church on 29 August 1979 by a Glengormley-based company, Sine Records, was engineered and produced by Messrs Alan Dickinson and Colin Martin. A very attractive sleeve featured, on the obverse, a splendid colour photograph of Clonard church, monastery and garden bathed in evening sunlight. The title 'Clonard Choir Sings' was set centre foreground of the garden, in Gaelic script. On the reverse of the sleeve, an historical note on the choir by Fr John Niall, the then Clonard chronicler, and an old photograph entitled 'Building Clonard Church 1908-1911' accompanied the list of contents and soloists. The latter were Anne Marie Smith (contralto), Seán Green (tenor) and Bill McKenna (bass).

The release of the record just before Christmas – at £4 – was noted briefly in the local press in Belfast. The *Sunday News*, under the heading 'Choir hits right note', highlighted Miss McCann's work with the choir since 1968.[28]

Vatican II: Liturgical possibilities and stresses

Changes in music provision in Clonard around this time reflected the new possibilities and increasing stresses emanating from the liturgical reforms of the Second Vatican Council. The situation at the beginning of the 1980s is neatly – if not obviously – reflected in the chronicle entry for Christmas Day 1981: 'Our three choirs distinguished themselves – the juniors led by Patricia McGoldrick at 10 [o'clock Mass, the children's Mass], folk group at 11 and "big" choir at 12.' The folk group reflected the new possibilities for liturgical experimentation, as had the introduction by Miss McCann of an accompanying orchestra for the Christmas 'carol' service in 1975.[29]

The Second Vatican Council's Constitution on the Sacred Liturgy, *Sacro Sancto Concilio*, (4 December 1963), while noting the 'high esteem' in which the pipe organ was to be held as 'the traditional instrument' of the Latin

church, admitted to use in divine worship 'other instruments' which were
'suitable, or can be made suitable, for sacred use ...' For better or worse, the
guitar was the most immediately 'suitable' instrument, echoing the worldwide popularity at that time, especially among the young, of 'folk music' and
other forms of music associated with the guitar and with youth. Local
churches, in vast numbers, bowed to the inevitable and the 'folk Mass' was
embraced by many as a breath of fresh air and a welcome change from the
generally stultified state of church music, certainly in Ireland. This is not to
denigrate the intentions and genuine contributions of many young people
throughout the country who, instinctively almost, sensed the need for
change in church music and the wider need to make the liturgy, especially
the central weekly Eucharistic liturgy, more appealing to young people.

It was the 'big' choirs in Clonard and elsewhere – and particularly their
directors – who were subjected to 'increasing stresses' from liturgical reform.
The Vatican Council's Constitution on the Sacred Liturgy placed them in a
difficult position. On the one hand, par. 116 stated:

> The Church acknowledges Gregorian chant as specially suited to the
> Roman liturgy ... But other kinds of sacred music, especially polyphony,
> are by no means excluded from liturgical celebrations.

Yet two paragraphs later it insisted:

> Religious singing by the people is to be skilfully fostered so that in devo-
> tions and sacred exercises, as also during liturgical services, the voices of
> the faithful may ring out according to the norms and requirements of the
> rubrics.[30]

The liturgical reality in Ireland at the very time when the Council was pub-
lishing its constitution (fleshed out, musically, in *Musicam Sacram*, 1967) was
that, apart from some well-endowed cathedral or institutional contexts, the
era of Gregorian chant and, indeed, of polyphony had passed. The choice for
directors of large choirs like Clonard's was whether to maintain the traditional role of the choir as a vocal ensemble performing beautiful music for
the edification of the faithful or to facilitate 'religious singing by the people'
by reducing the role of the choir to mere leadership of congregational
singing. As far as Clonard was concerned, the practical issue was the role of
the choir at the principal Sunday Mass. It is clear that conflicting opinions
were being expressed by members of the community. 'Some confrères would
have [the choir] involve the congregation in the liturgical singing,' noted the
chronicler in August 1982. But he continued: 'This creates a problem. There
is much to be said for this choir continuing to sing in its traditional way; it
does attract quite a number of people to the 12 o'clock Mass.'

These words were penned on the occasion of the second resignation of
organist-choirmistresses within less than a year. Miss McCann had resigned

early in 1982. Mrs May Smyth had agreed to act as caretaker for a year, but resigned in August, when Mr Gerry O'Rawe, Head of Music in the nearby St Dominic's High School, agreed to supply until a permanent appointment could be made. Morale in the choir was so low that the chronicler noted: 'Some members ... are in fear lest the choir be allowed to melt away and disappear. (We refer, of course, to the choir which sings at 12 o'clock Mass on Sunday).' What a sad day for the great Clonard choir to be referred to by one of its loyal supporters as the one 'which sings at 12 o'clock Mass on Sunday'![31]

Dr Peter Downey

The new organist, Peter Downey, faced a difficult situation with great enthusiasm, energy and ability. Like his predecessor, he had only a matter of weeks to prepare for a major occasion. This was the solemn celebration, in the presence of the new bishop of Down and Connor, Dr Cahal Daly, of 250 years of the Redemptorist Congregation. While the first appearance of the new organist is merely recorded, his next major undertaking, the Christmas carol service, is noted as a 'first class' performance.[32]

Peter was maintaining first class work in his own academic life and by the time of the 1983 carol service, he had completed a doctoral dissertation in the history of music, the first Clonard organist so to graduate. Unfortunately, as in the early years of Clonard, the domestic record is very sparse on choir and music matters. The only choral occasion which is recorded with any regularity is the special arrangements for Christmas music – either the annual concert of carols or the music for the midnight Mass of Christmas. The record was usually accompanied by a short complimentary remark, such as 'choir admirable', 'very good job', 'very good'; the compliments were probably genuine considering that they were for private record rather than for publication, where they would, of necessity, have been complimentary.[33]

Fr Clement McManuis

Fr Clement MacManuis was 'prefect of the choir' from 1984 until 1988. The office was a formal Redemptorist appointment by which one of the priests of the community was ultimately responsible for overseeing musical provision for liturgy and devotion in Clonard church. Historically, prefects of the choir were hardly mentioned in the written record. The assumption is that their role was a minimal one of liaison with the organist, who was allowed to get on with the job. Rarely did the prefect assume a high profile. One exception was Fr Frank Burns in the 1940s when he was very actively involved in funding and promoting the boys' choir. Fr MacManuis was also particularly active during his term of office.

In September 1985 he presented a report 'on singing' to a meeting of the Clonard community and shortly afterwards held a seminar 'for the adult choir'. This was followed by a Clonard Festival for Church Folk Groups, which he organised for Sunday 1 December. The festival was intended as a contribution to the International Year of Youth and Music.[34]

In the autumn of the following year, Fr MacManuis helped organise a festival of church music held in Clonard church on the last Sunday in October 1986. The festival was sponsored by the Committee for Church Music of the diocese of Down and Connor whose chairman was Raymond Lennon, organist and choirmaster of St Peter's pro-cathedral.[35] Fr MacManuis seems also to have been heavily involved in the same festival the following year, when the venue was the Good Shepherd Church, Ormeau Road. Meanwhile, a second annual festival of Down and Connor folk groups had been organised in Clonard Hall towards the end of January 1987, with twelve groups participating.[36]

Commissioning of 'Special Ministers of Sacred Music'
The last major event of Fr MacManuis's tenure as 'prefect of the choir' was the formal liturgical recognition of the 'adult choir, organists and leaders of congregational singing'. At the 11.15 am Mass on Sunday 22 November 1987, they were commissioned as 'special ministers of sacred music'. By this commission, according to the order of service, they were 'chosen to serve the people of Clonard monastery church in powerful song to the glory of God'. Each of the forty-one members present was given a certificate of commissioning by the rector of Clonard, Fr John O'Donnell.[37]

Folk group and children's choir
No account of music in Clonard church would be complete without reference to the folk group and the children's choir. First, in order of time, was the children's choir, established in 1977 by Patricia McGoldrick as part of an attempt to revive the special Mass for children at 10 am on Sundays. The provision of suitable hymns, music and drama (as on the great feasts of the church) was seen as a way of engaging and holding the interest of children in eucharistic worship. In 1974, Fr Eamonn Hoey, then director of the women's confraternity, had revived the children's Mass. He had led the children in singing, as did Fr John Hanna for a time. But from 1975 responsibility devolved on one of the senior members of Clonard community, Fr Patrick O'Donnell. He was fully supportive of Miss McGoldrick's work and, after her retirement in 1991, that of her successor, Miss Claire Cassidy.[38]

Patricia McGoldrick brought a strongly pastoral dimension to the children's choir. Aware of the bleakness of children's lives in the Clonard area due to the troubles, she soon began to organise a short annual summer holiday for choir members, with the full support of successive rectors of Clonard. The prospect of such a holiday was, naturally, a strong incentive to children to join the choir, but that was never the primary intention. Moville in county Donegal was the venue of the first recorded holiday (of five days duration) in early July 1984. Subsequently, Ballycastle was visited and then Moville again; in 1987, thirty-one children went to Gormanstown, county Meath and in 1992 'our much depleted junior choir' (following the retirement of Patricia McGoldrick) had an enjoyable holiday in Newcastle, county Down.[39]

Miss McGoldrick founded the Clonard folk choir in 1978 at the request of the rector, Fr George Wadding. One might say that folk groups were 'all the rage' in church at the time, thanks to an amalgam of influences discussed earlier. These included the aspiration towards liturgical music that would attract and hold the teens-to-early-twenties age group, whose attachment to their faith was considered most at risk. The folk group led the singing at the 7 pm. Sunday Mass initially, then the 12.30 pm when Mass times were rearranged in the early 1980s and the church choir switched from the 12 noon Mass to the 11.15 am.

The folk group was disbanded in 1986, apparently on account of the departure to a new job in Poleglass of Sr Claire McKiernan, a member of the Daughters of Charity (Clonard's near neighbours), who had been a leader of the group 'for the last few years'. Following the break-up, some members went to St Paul's parish to sing with the folk group there. Whatever the reason or reasons for the closure, Clonard church remained without a folk-group until early 1994. On 3 March in that year, the church staff decided that a folk group would be allowed once a month at the vigil Mass (that is, on Saturday at 7.30 pm.)[40]

Oblates of the Congregation of the Most Holy Redeemer
A significant decision by the Redemptorists in 1993 provides an appropriate conclusion to this survey of music in Clonard Church. In that year, three senior members of the choir were made oblates of the Congregation of the Most Holy Redeemer, the highest compliment the congregation could pay to non-members. The honour had been conferred only once before on a Clonard 'co-worker', the term increasingly used to refer to lay helpers. That was to Mr Seán Stewart in 1987; he had been a church collector for fifty years. Now Mr Gerry Burke and Mr Harry McNulty, who had joined the choir under de Meulemeester in 1934 and 1936 respectively, were honoured, together with the choir's leading tenor, Mr Seán Green, who had joined in 1943.

The choir committee 'vigorously led by their secretary Kitty O'Donnell' and warmly supported by the Redemptorist community, organised a major event on 2 June to mark the occasion. There was a presentation of diplomas by the rector of Clonard, Fr John O'Donnell, Seán Green replying to the rector's speech. There were many invited guests, a sumptuous banquet, and a presentation booklet for each visitor of a history of Clonard choir, written by yet another O'Donnell, Fr Patrick, archivist and historian of Clonard community.[41]

CHAPTER 13

Clonard and the Troubles, 1969-1994

The profound effect of the recent troubles on Clonard monastery and its community was inevitable. This was due not only to its geographical position close to the heart of the nationalist Falls Road, yet on the frontier with the unionist Shankill, but also to its historic involvement as a focus of reassurance and pride to the Catholic population of the neighbourhood. These were 'the people of Clonard', drawn mainly, but not exclusively, from St Peter's and St Paul's parishes on whose border the monastery sat.

August 1969
The first entry in the domestic chronicle for the month of August 1969 has a grim sense of foreboding about what was unfolding in Northern Ireland:

> 2 Aug. Today began a great and terrible chapter in the history of Belfast and maybe in Irish history. We think, therefore, it is worth recording these events in full because they are very closely connected with the church in the North and with the Redemptorists in Belfast.

The recording of these events 'in full' consisted of a combination of newspaper cuttings (mostly from the Dublin papers, the *Irish Independent* and *Irish Times*), which were pasted into pages of the chronicle, and the chronicler's own account and impressions of happenings in and around the monastery. It hardly needs to be said that, as events widened and trouble deepened in the months and years that followed, the task of 'full' recording had to be abandoned.[1]

The disturbing event of 2 August 1969 was a concerted attack by the Shankill Defence Association on the Catholic enclave of Unity Flats, located on Peter's Hill at the city end of the Shankill Road. The context of this attack was the increasing fears of Protestants/unionists that pressure for reform of the more obvious injustices of Northern Ireland society would weaken their domination of that society. One of the main sources of this pressure was the Northern Ireland Civil Rights Association whose banned march in Derry in October 1968 had exposed the crudities of Northern Ireland's law and order arrangements before the world's television cameras. Derry had, since then, become a focal point of civil rights agitation. It was no surprise to anyone in Northern Ireland that the traditional Apprentice Boys' parade on 12 August 1969 would and did provoke violence. What shocked everyone was the scale and intensity of the violence which, within a couple of hours, degenerated into a running battle between the police, using CS gas, and residents of the Catholic Bogside, flinging large numbers of petrol bombs at the police from the rooftops. This 'battle of the Bogside' continued unabated for fifty hours before an uneasy calm descended, with the arrival of British troops to separate the two sides and the withdrawal of the RUC and 'B' Specials.

On 14 August, the violence spread to Belfast. The first inkling of trouble received in Clonard monastery was a phone call 'just before dinner', that is, just before 1.15 pm, the usual time of the community's main meal of the day. As the chronicler noted, 'The Clonard community has become used over the years to insulting phone calls, but this one seemed more serious in the light of recent events.' As a precaution, two members of the community, Fr Hugh McLaughlin, a former director of the men's confraternity and Fr Paud Egan, the current director, 'got ten men to keep vigil on the house. There were many more ready to come if there was any difficulty.' Whether all, or any, of the ten defenders were armed is unclear, though Maillie and McKitterick (*The Fight for Peace,* (1996) p 66) say two of them were. The popular Falls Road view at the time was that the IRA ('Irish Ran Away,' according to local graffiti) was virtually non-existent. T. P. Coogan, in his *The Troubles* (1995), p 89, provides convincing evidence that the number of weapons in the area, dug up 'by some of the older IRA men from the forties period', barely reached double figures. The anxiety of the Redemptorist community was such that they 'stayed up the whole night keeping vigil and listening to the police radio'. A Redemptorist confrère, Fr Pat Sullivan, who was acting as a temporary chaplain to the Royal Victoria Hospital, reported that there were about forty Catholics among the casualties brought there.[2]

Worse was to come on the following day, 15 August, feast of the Assumption, 'a day that no one in Belfast will easily forget', in the words of the Clonard chronicler. Just after noon, a sniper 'on the old linen mill behind the monastery' began shooting at people in the street. In response, the mill was set on fire and 'by 2 o'c. the air was filled with smoke'. Then,

> We learnt from the people around that there was going to be real trouble. The people were all out of their homes in the streets behind us. Some had time to remove their belongings. They stored them in the monastery and the covered walk [in the garden]. Many men stayed in the monastery to defend it against attack.

At three in the afternoon the older and sick members of the community were evacuated from the monastery to the safety of the homes of Belfast-born Redemptorists, to Frs Harry and Patrick McGowan's family on the Glen Road and to Frs John and Aodh Bennett's in St Meryl Park. At half past three,

The riots in Cupar St began. The Protestants seem to have been well armed. There was a lot of shooting from the Cupar St side, coming past St Gall's school. We tried to phone the police, but found the phone was out of order ... The rector [Fr Hanly] went down to the police station [Springfield Road], but they more or less said they could do nothing. The situation was completely out of hand. The church bells were rung by the men to call more people to defend the monastery.

Round about four o'clock, Fr Egan was one of a number of the community observing the worsening situation from the upstairs windows of the monastery. He 'saw a young man stagger and fall in Waterville street'. He rushed to the community oratory, got the oils for anointing and, followed by Bro Ignatius Blain, ran across the line of fire to attend the young man, later identified as fifteen-year-old Gerard McAuley, a member of the Fianna, the youth wing of the IRA. According to Coogan, Gerard McAuley was helping Catholic families to evacuate their homes; he was still conscious when Fr Egan arrived, but died shortly afterwards on the spot where he had fallen.[3] Meantime, as the chronicle continued,

The houses on Kashmir Road and on the other side of Bombay St were blazing. One assistant fireman got a bullet in the side, was given first-aid in the [monastery] parlour, anointed and rushed to hospital. There was smoke coming from St Gall's school, no one could go over to help to put it out because there were bullets coming from three directions protecting the people throwing petrol bombs. There was also a sniper in the trees at the bottom of the garden.

By 4.30 pm, with fires blazing in Bombay Street, Kashmir Road and Cupar Street – uncontrollably, because the petrol bombers were protected by gun-fire – the community became convinced that the monastery was next: 'It seems certain now,' it is recorded against the time of 4.30 pm, 'that the monastery will be burnt. The Blessed Sacrament has been removed. We are all prepared to move when the worst happens.' However, although over the next couple of hours hopes were raised with the news that troops were being brought in, the verbatim account of the chronicle tells its own bizarre story:

5.30 pm. We get news that the troops are coming.

6 pm. Troops arrive on the Falls Road, but still behind us there are petrol bombs being thrown.

7 pm. Some soldiers [about thirty] came to the monastery and looked over the place, at the fires, at the area where the shooting was coming from. There was a lull in the fighting when we thought we were safe. But not.

8 pm. Mobs came onto Bombay St again protected by guns and began, one by one, to set on fire all that remained of Bombay St and Kashmir

Rd. They even got as far as setting on fire five houses in Clonard Gdns. St Gall's school was ablaze on two sides. The soldiers were useless. They called down Bombay St: 'Come out with your hands up. We won't shoot.' They were answered with a hail of petrol bombs. One soldier was hit by a bullet. They retreated and fired a tear gas bomb and there was silence for a while except for the crackle of sixty or so houses burning. Eventually the shooting stopped and the fire in St Gall's was put out. Most of the houses were left to burn. They were beyond redemption.[4]

Over the next couple of days, with Bombay Street still burning 'and the big mills on the Falls' – the Catholic retaliation for 15 August – the doors of the monastery were opened and, 'with the help of the Sisters of Charity [whose convent stood across Clonard Gardens from the main gates to the church-monastery complex] ... we set up tables in the corridor where people [could] have a meal.' Several of the community – Frs McLaughlin, Egan, Reid and McKenna were named – were 'working hard to house the homeless and get compensaton for lost property'. By 19 August, arrangements were made, under diocesan influence and with the help of 'social welfare' personnel, 'to try and centralise all the efforts to aid the victims'. As a result, St Joseph's Training College, at Trench House on the Stewartstown Road, became the focal point of assistance for the displaced families from the Falls area. Thereafter, the principal material contribution of the Clonard community continued to be the storage of furniture, some of which was still there five years later! One of the earliest offers of help from outside Belfast came, on 16 August, from the Redemptorists' Holy Family Confraternity in Limerick. The mayor of Limerick visited Clonard and was shown around the devastation by Fr Egan. On 21 August, a busload of some fifty-two refugees, escorted by Fr Pat Cunning, went off to accommodation provided in the Redemptorist Retreat House, Limerick.[5]

In the following days and weeks (one might add, months and years) the members of Clonard community played a significant role in identifying with the human pain and hurt of 'the people of Clonard', by their ministry of listening, counselling and absolving; by consoling the dying and injured; by attending the funerals and visiting the families of victims, irrespective of the political status of the deceased; by liaising or intervening between local republicans and the military. A couple of early examples of the latter are significant. The chronicle of 19 August 1969 noted:

> There was a meeting this evening of the men manning the barricades, the Army and the priests. It was agreed, amongst other things, that the Clonard fathers will take it in turn to go round the barricades each night.

Over the following months, as the chronicle recorded in June 1970,

> Meetings to discuss local defence take place frequently in many areas including our own and the Director [of the men's confraternity] is often

invited to attend. British Army officers sometimes meet with 'Republican' leaders to discuss problems of mutual interest. Such meetings have been held in the little hall ... in Waterville St.

As late as November 1972, a British Army major is on record as discussing with the new rector of Clonard, Fr Michael Browne, 'the possibility of organising a civilian police force in the area'. The major said, 'They may be Republicans, but they must be moderates.' What authorisation he had is not known.[6]

Falls Road curfew, 3-5 July 1970

By 1972, of course, the relationship between the Catholics/nationalists and the British Army had become one of open hostility. The 'honeymoon' period, when the Catholics had viewed the army as their saviours from Protestant mobs, was rudely ended by the tactical blunder of the Falls curfew of 3-5 July 1970. The stated objective of the operation was to quell a riot that had developed on a Friday afternoon after the army had uncovered a cache of arms – belonging to the Official IRA – in Balkan Street. But it was also intended as a display of strength to show the natives what could happen to them if they continued to misbehave. Approximately 3,000 troops were sent in, supported by helicopters equipped with loudspeakers which warned the inhabitants of the fifty or so streets to stay indoors. The army invasion was resisted 'by the two IRAs ... with guns, petrol bombs and nail bombs. Civilians used stones or their bare hands.'[7] The Clonard Domestic Chronicle reads:

> July. Two weeks after the Conservatives unexpectedly ousted the Labour Party Government in Britain, the British Army invaded Leeson St area in force. They imposed a 48-hour curfew which they afterwards said was not a curfew! During the operation one man was run down by an Army vehicle and killed. Three [actually four] were shot dead. Afterwards, the British Army claimed they had shot three snipers. It became evident later that none of the dead men was a sniper although there was plenty of sniper fire during this 'rape of the Falls'.

The account continues: 'Aug-Sept: Resentment towards the British Army grows in Catholic areas generally, while support for the IRA increases.' At the same time, noted the chronicler, 'A move began to get the British Army off our tower and out of our monastery. After a long haul, this move succeeded and the "observation" post was abandoned.' There is no doubt that this change of attitude to British forces was quickened by the Falls Road curfew. According to Coogan, many, if not most, of the early leadership of the Provisional IRA 'gave the Falls Road curfew as their reason for joining'.[8]

Internment, 9 August 1971

If the Falls curfew of July 1970 rudely ended the 'honeymoon' between the 'security forces' and the Catholic/nationalist community, the introduction of internment without trial in August 1971 created a chasm between the two which remains to this day. The Clonard archival record echoes accurately the bitter feelings of the minority community:

> 9 Aug. A black day in the history of our northern Catholic community. Without warning, internment without charge or trial was begun in the early hours of the morning. A massive invasion by the British army and RUC of Catholic homes. Men and boys (fathers, husbands, brothers) were dragged from their beds and, in the presence of weeping and terrified wives and children, were taken off under the iniquitous 'Special Powers Act' to unknown destinations. Often they weren't allowed to dress or bring sufficient clothes. As was afterwards verified, several hundreds were thus arrested, brought to Palace Barracks, Holywood, county Down, to Ballykinlar, to Crumlin Road jail, subjected to many barbaric forms of torture and ill treatment, even drugged in order to elicit information regarding the IRA. Around 800 Catholic men with literally no more than one or other Protestant were thus interned without trial at 'Long Kesh' near Lisburn and Magilligan in county Derry. This barbarity, carried out by Brian Faulkner, Stormont PM and Ted Heath, British Conservative PM, was afterwards to be a major issue and obstacle to peace at home and before the world.[9]

For some unknown reason, this entry of 9 August 1971 is the only one for that year to refer to the continuing 'troubles'. Not until March of the following year does the subject reappear, when an episode was recorded as 'a very tragic affair', the premature explosion of a bomb in a house in Clonard Street,

> ... around 10 am, killing four young men who belong to the area and were known personally to many of us at the monastery. Fathers Egan, Reid and Cunning did heroic work among the rescue workers ... and succeeded in anointing the victims. Eternal rest grant to them, O Lord.[10]

A hostile, indeed, a neutral reader of this passage might well deplore the ministry of these Redemptorist priests to four men evidently preparing a bomb for a mission of destruction, might even accuse them of some form of collusion or, at least, resent the short prayer with which the entry ends. Such an interpretation would seriously misunderstand the Redemptorists' attitude.

The principles guiding the Clonard Redemptorist community throughout the troubles were stated from time to time in the domestic chronicle. These statements were recorded for the community itself, not for the benefit of any third party or for issue to the media outside, so they can be taken as honest and unadorned. One such is found in a wide-ranging review of the

Clonard apostolate in February 1978. Under the heading 'The Northern "Situation" ... since 1969', is the following observation:

> ... During the early years, when assassinations were frequent, it was community policy to be represented at the funerals of the victims and to make known to the relations our sympathy. To this day, a constant liaison is maintained with the security forces, with Republican elements, with local people, with the relations of Republican prisoners, with Protestants on the peace line, with interested groups – with a view to settling differences, mitigating hardship, redressing grievances, preventing violence if possible or at least to bring about peace. ... From the beginning of the trouble, the Community here in Clonard has tried to show its feeling for the sufferer, without taking any political stand. Excellent work has been and is being done, but of its nature it is quiet and, often, very confidential.[11]

Searches of monastery and grounds

From time to time the Clonard community had to endure the embarrassment and inconvenience of searches of either the monastery or grounds for weapons or explosives. The first recorded search, in early November 1972, was probably the most distasteful because of its timing (two o'clock in the morning) and the fact that it came shortly after a quite unpleasant visit from an ill-informed army major, which suggests possible malice. The major insisted, at a few minutes' notice, on a search of the church and monastery vaults. Nothing was found. A few weeks later, the army raided Clonard Hall in the course of a dance, during which, 'Men and women were very roughly treated and some arrests were made.' Fr Browne the rector, accompanied by Fr Bennett 'went to the army post to complain'. At the end of December 1972, the army raided the monastery grounds. This time they found 'about 500-1,000 rounds of ammunition hidden under a wooden shed'. Presumably connected to this find was another raid on Clonard Hall during a New Year's Eve function, the second raid in four weeks, in which the hall was searched and five men arrested. In another episode at the end of January 1973, a few of the community were in the television room on the top corridor of the monastery when they heard shooting and bullets hitting the bell tower of the church. The priests lay on the floor until the shooting stopped. Then,

> The army were at the door and said that two of their patrols had seen flashes from the bell tower. Their claim that shooting had come from the tower was so ridiculous that it was not taken seriously and the army was not let in. [Sunday, 28 January]
>
> Mon 29. Next day they returned and Fr Bennett brought an officer up to inspect the tower. The officer agreed that the shooting could not have been from there.[12]

In July 1978, after a 'painstaking search' by the military of the monastery garden and back premises (towards Waterville Street), a large quantity of 'sweating' dynamite was found in a manhole, together with detonators and, under concrete slabs, 'A rather rusty gun and several incendiaries ... altogether, the findings were impressive and, indeed, alarming ...' The chronicler expressed his compassion for a number of families in Waterville Street who had to be moved from their homes and for the soldiers engaged in the search – 'Not a very attractive job on this bleak, wet evening, more typical of November than July'. He concluded:

> It is very disturbing to think that people would use the monastery for dumping dangerous explosives, but it does bring home to us that we have a vicious little war on our hands.

This was not the last such episode. The following year, one of the community was digging in the garden around a rhododendron when he 'struck something hard', found a bomb wrapped in a bag and, 'against all the rules of prudence' carried it to the end of the garden. There it was later dealt with by a bomb disposal team.[13]

At a much later date, in mid-January 1992, the monastery complex was again searched. The details are given in a cutting from the *Belfast Newsletter* inserted in the monastery chronicle, which carried the headline, *Bomb find at church*. The find consisted of 'twelve bags of fertiliser used for making PIRA bombs' which were found 'under the floorboards of a parochial [sic] hall attached to Clonard monastery', the search, by a joint police-army team, being approved by 'the Roman Catholic church authorities'. The report continued:

> ... The Clonard find has shocked monastery clergy. ... Fr John O'Donnell, rector of the Redemptorist order, said that they were 'grateful that the material cannot now be used to destroy life and property'. He explained: 'Just over a year ago Clonard monastic community assigned the church hall for use by a youth club in the area and we are deeply disturbed that young people's lives have been put at risk by those who placed explosive material under the floorboards of the hall. No member of Clonard monastic community has any knowledge of how, when and by whom the materials were placed in the hall.'

The reporter went on to explain that Clonard monastery was 'intensively used', the priests conducting counselling duties on a twenty-four hour basis. According to the chronicler, the material found in the hall 'was in a handcart formerly used in our garden. It disappeared a long time ago, perhaps a year.'[14]

Tensions between Redemptorists and republicans
Such episodes are a reminder of the paramilitaries' disregard from time to time of the traditional respect for the monastery as a holy place and a polit-

ically neutral one. Furthermore, there were occasional attempts to browbeat the Clonard community when it acted in ways the Provisional IRA disapproved of. For example, there were objections from 'extreme Republican elements' to the ringing of the Clonard church bell on Saturday 20 November 1976 in support of the burgeoning peace movement: 'It was even threatened to send "streakers" into the church in retaliation. But the bells were rung and the streakers did not arrive.' On the following day, the preacher at all the Sunday Masses, giving the formal community response,

> made it very clear that Clonard church is not the church of any particular brand of political opinion – it is for all, of every shade of opinion.[15]

The community seem to have been informed subsequently that the 'streakers' were meant to emphasise the 'blanket' protest, that is, the refusal of some republican prisoners to wear prison clothes and to do prison work in reply to the withdrawal from them of political status. Since 1 March 1976, they had been wearing blankets only; in the meantime, some of the republican women prisoners in Armagh jail had joined the protest. If Clonard church was spared the embarrassment of 'streakers' on this occasion, it was not exempt from the 'blanket' protest the following year. At the midnight Mass of Christmas 1977, two 'blanket ladies' appeared in the church, continuing the pattern of 'blanket' demonstrations in various places in support of the agitation by their menfolk for the restoration of political status. Fortunately, both for Clonard and for the two protesters, 'to the eye, the girls were modestly clad and well behaved'. As a result, 'officially at least, no remarks were passed, though most people must have felt that they should not have used the church for propaganda purposes'.[16]

There were numerous other occasions when the Clonard domestic chronicle privately recorded strong disapproval of certain republican activity, whether of major 'headline-grabbing' episodes or relatively minor local ones. For example, the bombing of the Bayardo Bar on the Shankill Road on 13 August 1975 was condemned as 'savagery of the worst sort'. Two days later, a retaliatory loyalist car bomb at the end of Dunlewey Street caused extensive damage to nearby houses, shops and the Bon Secours convent nursing home. Members of the Clonard community were quickly on the scene to help. So was a repair team from emergency services, whose van driver was a Protestant. As the chronicle recorded:

> Later in the evening the Protestant driver for the emergency services who was making his third run with hardboard for patching houses was brutally murdered by Republican gunmen. His name was Samuel Llewelyn.

Having given a detailed account of the funeral, at which Protestant mourners handed over on the Donegall Road to Catholic mourners led by several senior Catholic clergy who escorted the cortege to the City Cemetery, the

chronicle concluded: 'While a good Protestant was assassinated while helping Catholics fix their houses, Catholic thugs looted shops and houses.'[17]

As another example, the death of Mary Travers, the 'young Andersonstown
schoolteacher', killed alongside her father, a magistrate and the PIRA gunmen's principal target, as they left midday Mass at St Brigid's, Belfast, on a
Sunday early in April 1984, was described as 'another of the horrific murders
that have brought shame on the perpetrators and their Republican cause …'[18]

While the monastery chronicle tended to be severe on the IRA as the
main paramilitary group claiming to defend and act for 'our' side, it unre-
servedly condemned loyalist atrocities as well. Neither was it slow to censure
the misdeeds and misbehaviour of British soldiers. A clear example of this is
recorded during the Christmas period of 1976. Indeed, on Christmas Day
itself, the chronicle reads:

> A tense situation built up outside the church grounds this morning. A
> detachment of paratroopers stationed themselves … near the convent and
> held up a number of people for questioning and frisking. … A small
> crowd gathered and, by the time a member of the community arrived,
> tempers were frayed and voices were at a high pitch. Fortunately, a clash
> was avoided and the soldiers moved on … Local people regarded the exer-
> cise as provocative and it did seem out of place to hold up people going
> to Mass on Christmas morning.

Weeks later the situation was unchanged. Complaints kept coming to the
monastery of 'the agressive over-activity of the paratroopers' who were still
holding up and searching young men on their way to Mass, which people
found 'particularly odious'. The chronicler concluded: 'We should be very
happy to wave "goodbye" to the "paras" when their span of duty gets over.'

When the chronicle looked broadly at the local situation, from time to
time it acknowledged that the IRA were not the sole perpetrators of injustice.
Thus the entry for 6 August 1986 which, while severe on the IRA, concluded:

> … to blame the IRA for all our divisions would be a travesty of the truth.
> There is the tragic sectarian conflict between Catholic and Protestant
> which periodically has erupted into community rioting for the last 150
> years. There is also the intolerance and bigotry of the unionist majority;
> and there is the partition of the country by the British.[19]

Reflections on a decade of strife
It was natural that the Clonard chronicler should reflect in some way on the
state of things after ten years of civil strife. This is how he began his epilogue:

> And 1979 dies ever so quietly, or so it seems in the monastery. The world
> outside is indeed troubled. Almost daily there is news of a killing, sectar-
> ian or non-sectarian, the maiming or assassination, ambush or land-mine
> casualty, which come under the category of 'war' objectives.

He touched on the particularly acute difficulties experienced by people in nationalist areas when he drew attention to the display on the monastery notice board of a lengthy letter from Fr Denis Faul of Dungannon,

> giving instructions about what people are to do when 'brought in' for interrogation by the RUC, when held up or questioned by army or UDR ... the point of it all is to protect people, especially the young, from being brutalised and forced to make incriminating statements – also to collect material on the violation of human rights for the Vatican and other international bodies.

He paid tribute to the members of Clonard community 'who literally risked life and limb to be with the people all through the worst phases of these years', which formed '... the most momentous decade of Clonard's history since the early founding years. Bloody civil war has raged round about us ... Ten years later and 2,000 dead, apart from the maimed and broken, the troubles are still with us ...'

There follows a poignant, if somewhat self-indulgent, lament for the Clonard faithful of earlier days:

> ... The Falls Road area is, by and large, a shambles; between bombings and demolition [for redevelopment] ... the area in places looks like a blitzed city with series of houses bricked up or falling down, open spaces where once little brick houses built during the industrial revolution jostled one another in a labyrinth of streets which fed their human content into the great linen factories ...
>
> The 'Clonard-going' population has fallen in numbers and emotional attachment. So many old friends have died or moved away ... who knew Clonard in the days of its glory in the first half of the century, the years of the great confraternities; when you had to come half an hour before time to find a seat for the Advent and Lent course of sermons; ... men and women worked from six in the morning to six in the evening, Monday to Saturday, to eke out a meagre living and looked to and loved Clonard, with its lights and choir and music and prayer and preaching and confessional, as a spot of heaven in their dull lives.[20]

Spiritual ministry at Long Kesh

From a very early stage in the troubles, members of the Clonard community were called upon to assist in ministering to the spiritual needs of the hundreds of republican prisoners held in Long Kesh. (The domestic chronicle of Easter Sunday, 14 April 1974 gives a figure of 600 prisoners.) On most Sundays, by way of assisting the diocesan chaplains, priests from Clonard went to hear confessions and say Mass in one of the 'cages'. From time to time, they took part, sometimes in considerable numbers, in missions or retreats to the prisoners. Likewise, they were regularly called upon, often in the company of Passionist fathers from Ardoyne, to hear large numbers of confessions in preparation for Christmas and Easter.

A disastrous mission

In general, the spiritual ministry of the Redemptorists was well received and appreciated by the prisoners. The priests, in turn, acknowledged the good spiritual dispositions of the prisoners. There was one exception to this, an apparently disastrous retreat reported at great length in the chronicle of 23 January 1978. The writer had taken part in a previous mission in June 1973, when he had found quite different attitudes among the prisoners:

> God be with the older generation of OCs we met on the last mission about 4 years ago! ... Most of them have been released by now. They had the old IRA tradition – devoted to the Mass, to the Rosary, deep respect for the priest, etc. Times have changed – even in Long Kesh.

Limiting his remarks to those republican prisoners still accorded political – 'POW' – status, of whom ninety per cent belonged to the Provisional IRA, the missioner was at first inclined to blame the failure on '... the lack of inspiration, example and leadership religion-wise of the OCs. A man who does not come to Mass or lectures himself can scarcely influence others.'

However, he also acknowledged serious shortcomings on the part of the retreat team who were guilty of 'bad planning, or rather no planning. We walked into a compound to find a large section of the "boys" making for the games enclosure,' or, on some afternoons, the weekly movie. Five days for the retreat was too long; two or three days would have sufficed, as in 1973.

There were other factors influencing religious attitudes: the general apathy which can settle on men after years of confinement; 'the "anti-religion, anti-church" pose which is the "in thing" among many young Irish people today,' together with 'a grudge against "the Church" as represented by the hierarchy, for condemning their acts of violence ...' Yet another element was, 'the current craze for socialism in different shades'. This was 'meat and drink' to the IRSP who were good at propaganda; the Officials had it 'to a degree' and it was 'gaining ground' among the Provisionals. Finally, there were

> brainwashing and human respect ... individuals swept along by the crowd, the crowd itself influenced by individuals who have education, the gift of persuasion, glib tongue, strong personality, deep convictions, etc.[21]

Whatever the mixture of circumstances that brought about the negative attitudes of the prisoners, this retreat seems to have marked a low point in the Redemptorist ministry to Long Kesh. Happily, the next recorded exercise of that ministry, pre-Christmas confessions later in the year, found a markedly different atmosphere: 'At least nine priests, seven of them C.Ss.R., "invaded" ... the H-blocks in the Maze prison. ... we were well received and 90% went to confession ...' Except for Block 4 that is, where the prisoners were 'in very

bad humour because they had been forcibly shaved, had their hair cut, etc.'
But after an hour these men relented 'and declared themselves ready to co-
operate ...'[22]

The 'dirty' protest

Among the seven Redemptorists was the chronicler. He was assigned to H-
Block 3 which, together with 4 and 5, housed the men 'on the blanket'. The
blanket protest, designed by republicans to pressurise the Thatcher government into restoring political status, had begun on 1 March 1978. By the summer of that year it had become also a 'dirty' protest in which the prisoners
refused to 'slop out' or clean their cells. The priest's account of his experience
ran as follows:

> I had four warders with me as I was conducted from cell to cell. One
> opened the steel door – in some cases the slot meant for observation from
> outside had been blocked by – God knows what! 'Anyone for confession?
> Both of you? Right, one step out, please.' One man emerges covered
> around the legs and waist with a blue bath towel to stand outside while I
> step gingerly over a fringe of discarded food (maybe) possibly placed there
> to prevent the draught from blowing underneath. There is normally
> water, too; is it from the overflowing chamber-pot by the wall, with bits
> of bread, half-potatoes, etc., heaped in the corner? The smell of excrement
> is all-pervading, though it did not affect me much. Hours afterwards I
> still seemed to smell it and found the use of some Vick's inhalant helpful.
> ... Once the confession is over, they shrink down into the corner on their
> respective mattresses to escape the icy blast that comes through the win-
> dows. Some of them ask for news, a cigarette, a message to be brought to
> someone outside, a pencil. Here the priest is embarrassed for the rules for-
> bid such things ...[23]

Hunger strikes, 1980-81

The final stage in the Republican pressure campaign was the addition of a
hunger strike to the 'dirty' protest. The hunger strikes of 1980-81 presented
nationalist Ireland, north and south, with an emotionally charged situation
– a dilemma for many – in which a rational opinion on one side or the other
was difficult. The Clonard community was particularly aware of the dilemma
and the pressures it brought. The chronicler, in a lengthy reflection in
November 1980, noted:

> For the armchair politician/patriot, the situation presents endless scope
> for arguing the pros and cons, but Clonard is at the heart of things; we
> have to meet flesh and blood people who have relations in the H-blocks
> or Armagh jail.

By this date the H-block hunger strike (by seven men, commemorating the seven signatories of the proclamation of the Irish Republic in 1916) had been under way for just three weeks. But already the Clonard chronicle was recording, 'rising tension in connection with H-block "Fast unto Death" strike' and the whipping up of political and sectarian tensions on both sides, with killings or attempted killings. The direct pressure on Clonard was explained as follows:

> In our West Belfast area, protest processions, public Rosaries, etc., are increasing in number. The community of Clonard is placed in a difficult situation, owing to the pressure exercised to allow the use of Clonard Hall for public meetings and committee meetings of the protest organisers. We are asked to lead the Rosary in processions through the streets. The inmates of the political status section of the Maze (Long Kesh) prison who all but ignored us when we preached a mission to them a few years ago, have come round to writing a letter asking this community to help, etc., the cause of the hunger strikers. What stand do we take? Or do we take a stand at all, i.e. as a community?[24]

The letter took the form of a general 'Appeal to the Clergy and those in Orders by Republican POWs (with status)' to 'raise your voices, the voice of humanitarian concern at the inhuman and callous intransigence of the British Government on the H-block issue ...' and to support a restoration of political status to those from whom it had been removed. Together with other local matters, such as requests for use of the hall for meetings and for priests to lead the Rosary in street processions, the letter was discussed by the community in early November. The chronicler noted that the discussion, 'highlighted the anxiety of the community and the difficulty of arriving at a statement of policy acceptable within the community'.[25]

This episode was particularly painful for the Redemptorists who were anxious to keep faith with their ministry 'to all men', including the hunger-strikers and their families. At the same time, they were equally determined, as the chronicler remarked, 'to preserve the image of Clonard as non-political, non-sectarian, open to all, compassionate and ready to help, but without committing ourselves to any political platform'. That they succeeded in the long run is borne out by the continuing role of Clonard monastery, particularly through the mediation of some members of its community, in assisting the long and tortuous stumblings towards peace and reconciliation in Northern Ireland's divided society.[26]

A brief interlude

In confused circumstances, the hunger strike was called off on 18 December, tension was diffused and 'people felt they could get on with the Christmas celebrations'. Certainly the end – for the time being only, as it turned out – of the 1980 hunger strikes led to, 'The quietest Christmas we have had for years,' as the chronicler expressed it. He was one of a team of seven Redemptorists and three Passionists who, on the Monday before Christmas, 'worked our way through the Maze Prison (Long Kesh) hearing confessions'.[27]

The easing of tension about the hunger strikes ('situation improved, but ... not completely resolved') enabled the chronicler, early in 1981, to reflect on matters other than the immediate political situation. He directed his attention to what he regarded as the beneficial effects of two television series then being broadcast, the Robert Kee programmes on Irish History on BBC and the ITV series 'The Troubles':

> ...These are surprisingly objective and must come as a shock to many an Englishman ... whose only idea about Ireland is that it is a troublesome corner of the UK – for the most part under the domination of the RC church; populated largely by a factious people who unite a weakness for the bottle with an incurable sense of ingratitude towards Big Sister Britannia for all she had done for them over the centuries ... .

On a domestic note, he continued, with reference to that part of the ITV series which covered the aftermath of 1969:

> We were thrilled and delighted to see our own community confrère Fr Frankie Burns standing between angry baton-wielding British troops and a crowd of distracted people (mostly women) driven hysterical by the arrests of their dear ones and rough usage from the security forces. We are reminded of those confrères who ... did so much (and often at risk to themselves) to calm and reassure a distracted people.

(On Fr Burns' sudden death in August 1983, at the age of 77, the chronicler noted: 'He allowed himself to get emotionally involved in the troubles of the 1969-plus years and fell foul more than once of the British soldiers.')[28]

Hunger strikes resumed

At the end of January 1981, with resentment still smouldering over the manner in which the 1980 hunger strikes ended, republican prisoners in the Maze wrecked their cells, claiming the authorities had broken their word. A new wave of hunger strikes began on 1 March 1981, the date chosen because it marked the fifth anniversary of the withdrawal of political status. Having visited the prison in mid-April for Easter confessions, the chronicler noted the end of the 'dirty' protest, but the continuation of the 'blanket' protest. He remarked that some men were still recovering from the earlier hunger strike, but 'a number' were on again. 'None of us met Bobby Sands MP whose condition has entered a critical stage after six weeks hunger strike.'

The chronicler was away from the monastery during the month of May. On resuming his task he recorded:

> History has been made during that month; alas, a history of civil disturbance, violence and vandalism. The four hunger strikers Sands, Hughes,

McCreesh and O'Hara died at intervals and each death was marked by outbreaks of violence, confrontation with military and police, etc.

It fell to a new chronicler to record, on 3 October, the end of the hunger strikes, 'which', he observed, 'have claimed the lives, not only of ten prisoners, but of sixty-four people outside the prison walls'. He then listed the ten dead hunger strikers, with their dates of death, paramilitary affiliation, age and home district.[29]

Gibraltar and its aftermath

It would have been surprising if any chronicler of Clonard monastery had not recorded in some fashion one of the most bizarre periods of our troubles, namely, the two weeks from 6-19 March 1988. These two weeks began with the controversial shooting of three IRA volunteers 'on active service' in Gibraltar by an SAS unit on Saturday 6 March. They ended with the tragic killings of two British soldiers who drove into an IRA funeral which had just left St Agnes' Church, Andersonstown, for Milltown cemetery on Friday 19 March. In between was the single-handed attack by UFF man Michael Stone on mourners at the funeral of the 'Gibraltar Three', on Tuesday 16 March, at which, using guns and hand grenades, he killed three men. It was the funeral of one of these men, Caoimhín Mac Brádaigh, an IRA member, into which the two soldiers stumbled on 19 March. And it was the poignant photograph, broadcast around the world, of Fr Alec Reid, the Clonard Redemptorist, ministering to one of the dead soldiers, which is possibly the best remembered image – throughout the world – of this gruesome period and which links its events indelibly with Clonard.

What is not widely known is that two of the 'Gibraltar Three' had close Clonard connections. Seán Savage, aged 23, had been an altar boy in Clonard. The other man, Danny McCann, aged 30, belonged to a well-known Falls Road family which, from early in the century, had a butcher's shop on the Falls Road, just around the corner from Clonard St. He had lived with his wife and two children in nearby Cavendish St.

The domestic chronicle account of the events ran as follows:

Sun. 7 March. Three IRA (two men and a woman) shot dead in Gibraltar. Some of the community have visited the homes of the dead men, one of whom, Seán Savage, was for a while an altar boy in Clonard.

Wed. 16 March. The burial of the IRA three took place to Milltown about 12 noon. Fr Reid accompanied the bodies from Dublin to Belfast and carried each of two coffins part of its last journey up the Falls ...

19 March. Two British soldiers strayed into an IRA funeral opposite Casement Park. Dragged out of their car beyond St Agnes', savagely beaten and then shot dead. A horrible act which has caused a widespread reaction

of horror. Fr A. Reid administered to the murdered men. During this week eleven people have been killed in the North.

Inserted in the chronicle is a newspaper cutting of a photograph showing Fr Reid praying over the body of one of the dead soldiers. The chronicler comments:

... Because of his part in this tragedy, Fr Reid has become famous throughout the world. The press of the world is pursuing him. Members of the community have been invited to take part in radio and TV interviews and programmes. The phone for a few days has been ringing endlessly.[30]

Mediation

Fr Reid had been much involved as a mediator for many years. More than a decade previously he had worked with Fr Desmond Wilson ('the Ballymurphy priest'), helped by fellow Redemptorist Fr Paud Egan and other priests, to broker a truce between provisional and official IRA. That was in October-November 1975. In 1986-7, with his confrère Fr Gerry Reynolds, he was 'working day and night' to reconcile factions engaged in a 'vicious feud' which had 'split the INLA and led to 9-10 killings in the last few months'. The feud was brought close to Clonard with the killing of Gerard Steenson, a near neighbour. Mediation helped end the killing, but a new faction calling itself the Irish People's Liberation Army emerged.[31]

The two Redemptorists were also called on to mediate between republicans and the RUC in the matter of IRA funerals. Government policy at the time was to ensure a heavy police presence at paramilitary funerals in order to minimise militaristic display. The almost inevitable result was violence. Thus, for example, following the UVF shooting of IRA man Laurence Marley in Ardoyne on 3 April 1987, there was a stand-off lasting several days between republicans and police over the manner of the man's funeral from his home. 'Violence again erupts with burning of buses, etc.,' noted the Clonard record; 'Fr Gerry Reynolds has been much involved in trying to have a peaceful funeral from the dead man's home.' On that occasion Bishop Cahal Daly called on the RUC to rethink its policy on paramilitary funerals. A few weeks later, on 2 May, IRA man Finbarr McKenna of Colinward St – another neighbour of Clonard – 'accidentally blew himself up' when a blast bomb he was throwing at the rear of the Springfield Road RUC station exploded prematurely. On 7 May, the day of the funeral, the Clonard chronicle recorded:

Quite a bit of rioting in West Belfast this evening following the funeral ... The heavy police presence at the funeral caused a lot of tension before, during and after it. Fr Alec Reid was much involved in trying to defuse the situation.[32]

The Shankill Road bomb, October 1993

A tragic event which particularly shocked the Clonard community was the Shankill bomb of Saturday 23 October 1993. The chronicler caught something of the poignancy of the human tragedy when he noted that it happened, 'on a lovely autumn day ... ten dead including two little girls aged seven and thirteen years'. Clonard was deeply affected because of the strong ecumenical links forged in the Shankill-Falls Fellowship.

Loyalist reprisals followed quickly. On Tuesday 26 October, 'Two Catholic council workers murdered in Kennedy Way and four to five wounded. (4 Catholics dead since Saturday, making a total of 14 dead since Saturday.)' In expectation of further loyalist violence, the chronicler noted, 'Belfast is a city of fear.' That this fear was real is shown by the fact that, for the first time since 1969, a Clonard function was cancelled, namely, the choir practice for the evening of Wednesday 27 October. On Saturday 30 came the main loyalist retaliation, the UDA/UFF gun attack on the 'Rising Sun' bar in the quiet, mainly Catholic village of Greysteel, near Derry. Seven people were killed, one of them a Protestant (a former member of the UDR) and eleven people wounded. Another Protestant, a man in his late seventies, died later of his wounds. In Belfast, the annual 'Cemetery Sunday' at Milltown on the Falls Road, 'was cancelled due to fear of a "loyalist" attack' and was postponed until the spring. Many sources confirm that the aftermath of the Shankill bombing created a climate of fear in Catholic areas which had not been experienced since 1969.[33]

Towards peace

The domestic chroniclers of Clonard were always happy to record peace initiatives. Numerous intercessions for peace, whether in Clonard itself or ecumenically elsewhere, were noted, both religious services in churches and public processions. For example, the 'torchlight ecumenical procession to the City Hall', on the evening of 4 December 1988, 'which attracted over 6,000 marchers [and] was attended by several confrères'; or the 'peace march of 3,000 school pupils in Belfast' on 31 March 1992; or the 'peace meeting in Fitzroy church' on the Sunday week after the Shankill bomb, which several members of Clonard community attended.[34]

In 1988, under the date of Monday 11 January, the chronicler noted baldly in two short sentences:

> John Hume, the leader of the SDLP and Gerry Adams, leader of Sinn Féin, are having secret talks in Clonard. Fr A. Reid seems to have brought them together.

Nearly five years later, the 'Downing street Declaration,' signed on 15 December 1993 by Prime Minister John Major and Taoiseach Albert Reynolds, was recorded in the monastery under the headline: ' ... *An historic declaration*

concerning Ireland north and south.' The declaration 'promised that the people of Northern Ireland would decide their own future, but that everything
could be "on the table" for discussion'. The view from Clonard was:

> It is a very important peace initiative. The discussions between Hume and
> Adams that led up to the ... declaration took place in Clonard monastery.
> Fr Al Reid had a lot to do with these.

This was a very simplistic view of the 'discussions'. But the Clonard chronicler was as much in the dark about what had been going on as was the man
in the street. Living under the same roof as Fr Reid gave no access to his
secret shuttle diplomacy. True, from time to time Fr Reid spoke to his community about his work, typically on study days or retreat days. He also wrote
occasionally for the 'in-house' bulletin of the Irish Redemptorists, *Search*. But
he always dealt with principles and general issues, as he did in a rare public
statement, 'a long, closely reasoned article' for the *Irish Times* in 1990. Details
of his involvement in what came to be called 'the peace process' have to be
gleaned from the comments of other participants for, apart from a natural
preference to keep in the background, Fr Reid has never given an interview
to anyone.[35]

Intensive and protracted background negotiations finally led, it seemed,
to the objective that Hume, Adams, Albert Reynolds and Fr Reid had set
themselves. The Clonard record was brief:

> 31 August [1994]. The war of 25 years is over (1969-1994). An IRA state-
> ment from Dublin said there would be 'a complete cessation of its mili-
> tary operations from midnight'.

Subsequent events were to dash the optimism generated by this ceasefire. The
British government and the Ulster unionists immediately raised doubts
about its permanence. John Major, the British Prime Minister, insisted the
IRA should 'decommission' its arms before Sinn Féin should join all-party
talks. Broadly, nationalist feeling in the North blamed Major for frittering
away the possibilities raised by the ceasefire. Eventually, the IRA lost patience
and, in its own words, 'with reluctance', called off the cessation by detonat-
ing a huge bomb in the prestigious Canary Wharf district of London's dock-
land on 9 February 1996. It was May the following year before a change of
government in Britain helped shift the Northern situation again, opening
possibilities for renewed progress towards peace.

But in August 1994, all that lay in the future. In the optimism of the IRA's
'complete cessation of military operations', the Clonard chronicle carried the
following entry:

> In a letter to our rector [Fr Kevin Browne], Gerry Adams, President of
> Sinn Féin, expressed his 'thanks to you and the entire Clonard commu-
> nity for all your help over the last years of the peace process'. He added,

'a special commendation from me for Fr Alec Reid. Without him we would not be opening up this potentially historic opportunity.' He concluded, 'Na Reds abú. Fr Alec for Pope.'[36]

An early photograph of the altar of Our Lady of Perpetual Succour. Like the original high altar, it was designed by Henry Berghman, C.Ss.R.

The icon of Our Lady of Perpetual Help, entrusted to the Redemptorists by Pope Pius IX in 1866 with the injunction: 'Make her known to the world.'

The novena drew huge attendances on 'Clonard Thursday' during the 1940s.

The revival of the annual solemn novena in the early 1980s turned these nine days in June into a 'spiritual fiesta'. Photograph taken in 1994.

Dr Magean, bishop of Down and Connor (1929-62), on one of his numerous visits to Clonard, this time for the celebration, in November 1946, of the Redemptorists' fifty years in Clonard.

Front row, L to R: Mgr A. H. Ryan, Canon John O'Neill, Dr Magean, Canon McAuley, Gerard Reynolds, C.Ss.R. (Rector).

Back row, L to R: A. McHugh, C.Ss.R., P. Whelan, C.Ss.R., V Rev John McMullan, President, St Malachy's College, Belfast, J. Whelan, C.Ss.R., J. Mangan, C.Ss.R. Mgr Ryan preached at the Solemn High Mass.

Mount St Clement's Retreat House, Ardglass, Co Down, was under the administration of Clonard Monastery from its inception early in 1946 until October 1947. This Clonard confraternity group was photographed in December 1956.

Brother Bernard McKenna, (d. 1981) 'prince of sacristans'.
A photograph taken in 1977.

Brother Michael Bradley (1897-1991).

Brother Tommy Walsh.

Brother Hugh Murray.

Seán Stewart, the first Clonard co-worker to be declared an Oblate of the C.Ss.R, in 1987. This photograph was taken in 1982.

Leon Rittweger, KOCB, was
organist from 1948-68.

Arthur de Meulemeester, KOL, KOCB,
(1875-1942). He was organist from 1898 until
his death. In addition to his two knighthoods
(of the Order of Leopold and of the Crown
of Belgium), he received the papal honour
Pro Pontifice et Ecclesia.

Interior showing the 1912 organ
and the rose window.

John Torney, C.Ss.R. and Frank Burns, C.Ss.R., founders of the
Clonard Boys' Choir in 1943. Both men were Falls Road born.

Messrs Gerry Burke, Seán Greene, and Harry McNulty, honoured in 1993
as Oblates of the C.Ss.R. for long service to music in Clonard Church.

Daniel Cummings, C.Ss.R, (1907-77) and Christopher McCarthy, C.Ss.R, (1910-83),
two great Clonard ecumenists.
(Fr Cummings' photograph courtesy of his niece, Mrs Colette McEvoy.)

Canon John Baker signing the visitors' book at the City Hall, Belfast, January 1981.
With him is the High Sheriff and, back, L to R: Mrs Baker, Fr McCarthy, the High
Sheriff's secretary and Mr Leslie Fox. Canon Baker became (Anglican) bishop of Salisbury
the following year.

An ecumenical trio. L to R: Rev Ken Newell, Fitzroy Presbyterian Church;
Gerry Reynolds C.Ss.R., Clonard; Rev Sam Burch, Methodist and founder
member of Cornerstone Community, Springfield Road, Belfast.

Alec Reid, C.Ss.R, right, and Gerry Reynolds, C.Ss.R, leaders of Clonard's work for peace and reconciliation.

Redemptorist acknowledgement of co-workers: Superior General Phab meets apostolic workers on a visit to Clonard in February, 1983. Front row, L to R: Molly Howard, Kathleen McMahon, Fr General, Peggy Brady, Bridie Sharpe. Back row, L to R: Mrs McClean, Margaret Duffy, Hugh Arthurs, C.Ss.R, Monica McAleese, Mrs Moyna, Rose McKevitt.

The refurbished sanctuary, 1992.

Patrick O'Donnell, C.Ss.R., chronicler, archivist and historian of
Clonard monastery and community, whose skill and dedicated work
over many years have created a superb archive. Floreat!

Lisbreen
73 Somerton Road
BELFAST BT15 4DE
Tel: (01232) 776185
Fax: (01232) 779377

From the Bishop of Down and Connor

28th February, 1996.

The Very Reverend Kevin Browne, C.Ss.R.,
Rector,
Clonard Monastery,
Clonard Gardens,
Belfast.
BT13 2RL.

It gives me great pleasure to congratulate the Redemptorist Congregation on the Centenary of the founding of their Monastery and the opening of their first Church - the 'Tin-Church' - at Clonard.

The Redemptorists were invited to establish themselves permanently in Belfast by Bishop Henry Henry in order to work with the diocesan priests in ministering to the rapidly growing Catholic population of that part of Belfast. They have continued to do that unstintingly for the past one hundred years very often, indeed all too often, in very difficult and trying circumstances.

The people of Belfast responded with enthusiasm to the presence of the Redemptorists and that enthusiasm is still evident today in the huge number of people - not only from Belfast but from further afield - who attend the Special Novenas.

For their contribution to the spiritual life of the Diocese over the past one hundred years, I thank the Redemptorist Congregation most warmly and I pray God's blessing on them as they face the challenges of the next century.

Yours sincerely,

+ Patrick Walsh

59. Letter of congratulations from Bishop Patrick Walsh (left) on the occasion of Clonard's centenary.

CHAPTER 14

Change, 1960s-1990s

There is but one idea which jumps from the pages of the Clonard community's journal from the 1960s to the 1990s. The word 'change' rarely, if ever, occurs. Yet 'change' is the theme of those decades, reflecting the pace of reform in the Catholic Church as a whole which led to and, especially, flowed from the Second Vatican Council (1962-5). While change in liturgical practice in Clonard church is reflected extensively, the great change is in the Redemptorist Congregation itself and this is the primary preoccupation of the monastery chronicle of these decades. As a measure of the extent of change affecting the Redemptorists themselves, a new set of constitutions was promulgated in 1969, only to be replaced by yet another in 1980. Within the Irish province, the period from the mid-1970s to the late 1980s is characterised by a series of critical examinations of current apostolates and a search for new approaches. Much of the focus of these examinations was on Clonard itself.[1]

Liturgical changes

The Clonard Domestic Chronicle is an excellent guide to the numerous liturgical changes of this dramatic period in the history of the Church at large. The first of these occurred in 1961 with the introduction of evening Mass, which was seen generally in Clonard as helpful because it enabled greater numbers of the faithful to attend. By the end of 1964, new-style 'biblical devotions' replaced the traditional Sunday evening format.[2] In Lent 1965, the use of the vernacular in the Mass was introduced and the celebrant faced the people from a temporary altar on the sanctuary. The changes in the Mass were generally welcomed by the people, although there were some dissentient voices, especially among the elderly.[3]

New Penitential Rite

Changes in the sacramental rite of penance did not occur until the mid-1970s. While the new rite was officially inaugurated on Ash Wednesday 1976, a full year later the Clonard record noted that, 'the confrères have been trying to indoctrinate the people in the [new rite] with different degrees of success or failure'. It has to be said that the new rite of penance was the least successful of the liturgical reforms of this period. An additional complication was the decline in the use of the sacrament among Catholics generally. This decline was commented on by the Clonard chronicler in the days before Christmas 1978, 'Christmas confessions' being traditionally a major event in the church year:

> ... speaking generally ... we are very conscious of the fact that confessions of men and young people of both sexes are not numerically in proportion to the large population we have around us. ... Perhaps we are on the way to striking a balance between the Jansenism which undoubtedly prevailed up to and after the decree of [Pope] St Pius X on frequent communion [1905] and the present softness and spiritual indifference which 'can't be bothered with religion'.[4]

Despite such negative impressions, the Clonard community in 1979 pressed ahead with another facet of the new thinking on penance as 'reconciliation'. This took the form of the expansion of 'the confessional near St Alphonsus' altar' into a 'reconciliation room'. It was an attempt to break the traditional view of the sacrament as extremely formal, even severe, as represented by the confinement and rigidity of the 'confession box'. The 'reconciliation room' gave the penitent the choice, in agreeable surroundings, of continuing to speak to the priest through a grille or, less formally, of sitting and meeting him face to face.[5]

Vigil Mass of Sunday

The final change of significance was the introduction, early in 1984, of the vigil Mass of Sunday, to be celebrated on Saturday evening. The practical objective here was to ease pressure on Sunday morning Mass schedules which were frequently so tightly packed that, in many parishes, outgoing and incoming congregations produced serious congestion both of people and of cars.[6]

Changes in the Redemptorist congregation

Changes affecting the Redemptorists as a religious congregation and Clonard community as part of that congregation were even more pronounced. The first indication of change – coincidentally just a matter of weeks after the announcement of the Second Vatican Council, which was made on 2 February 1962 – was the arrival of a 'new book of common prayers' for Redemptorists.[7]

In January 1965, a Redemptorist Mission Council held in Limerick issued directives for the adaptation of missions 'to present-day conditions'. As a result, in November of that year, Fr Seán O'Riordan gave the Clonard community a four-day course in theology, 'to keep the fathers abreast of modern developments'. The following year Fr Gerard Crotty, another of the Irish

Redemptorists' leading theologians, contributed a series of talks on 'updating retreats for religious'.[8]

New thinking on how the Redemptorists were governed is clear from the Clonard preparation for their provincial chapter in the autumn of 1966, where it was emphasised that, 'All members of C.Ss.R. have the right and obligation to participate in the work of preparation.'[9]

Changes in science and technology

It is hard not to associate the changes in the Church and in religious orders with the wider winds of change blowing through the human community at large. Changes, particularly in science and technology, had been observed and recorded with great interest for some time by the writers of the Clonard domestic record. For example, the first manned space flight, 'a flight into outer space round the earth' by 'The Russian Communist Gagarin', was noted on 12 April 1961, followed by 'an historic day' on 1 May when the American navy commander, Alan Shepard, did the same. The launch of the satellite 'Telstar' and its first transmission of television pictures from the US to Europe in July 1962 was described as, 'A truly wonderful tribute to our advances in science ... Yet perhaps more wonderful things to come.'[10]

It was late in 1962 before the Redemptorists' general administration allowed a television set within the monastery. Prior to that, members of Clonard community had to depend on invitations from neighbouring communities of sisters (Bon Secours and Sisters of Charity) and brothers (de la Salle) to view major ecclesiastical ceremonies such as the funeral of Pope Pius XII or the splendid coronation of his successor John XXIII. Permission was finally given to enable the Clonard community to follow the Second Vatican Council, the 'glory and splendour' of whose opening they witnessed on 11 October 1962.[11]

Continuing change in the Redemptorist world

In the late 1960s and early 1970s, the 'modernisation' of the Redemptorist congregation continued apace. During November 1968, the Clonard community was subjected to a two-week blitz from the finest minds in the Irish province. Frs Crotty and O'Riordan held a four-day seminar on 'The Apostolic Life Today', while the leading canon lawyer, Fr Thomas Larkin, led four days of community discussions on 'Apostolic Life in the Redemptorist Congregation'. Sandwiched between these sessions was a three-day seminar in which Fr Peter Ward introduced his confrères to the most recent psychological and theological thinking on 'Maturity, Human and Spiritual'. Such programmes were part of an intensive process of re-learning theology which followed the Second Vatican Council. Seminars, community meetings, discussions and, later, workshops were the order of the day.[12]

Change difficult for older Redemptorists

It became clear about this time that new thinking and proposed new structures within the Redemptorist way of life were taking their toll on older members of the community. A practical illustration of the problem of change for them was the decision, implemented in Clonard in December 1971, to introduce into the refectory, 'Small tables to seat four, [to] replace old style large tables, etc.' While to the outside world such a change might seem trivial, for older Redemptorists it symbolised a dramatic break from a practice that had obtained for over two hundred years. It was the abandonment of the simple, ascetic practice of sitting 'in community' in a place determined by the seniority assigned to each Redemptorist according to the date of his first profession and which he carried with him throughout the Redemptorist world until his death. It was also symbolic of the deeper debate about the very nature of 'community' in the religious sense which was taking place in the early 1970s. The Clonard community at this time was, by normal religious standards, quite large, with sixteen priests and seven brothers. While quite large, it was not so large that any member might seek to avoid the stresses of change by taking refuge in anonymity. It was also an ageing community ('rather elderly' is the phrase in the record) with the average age of the priests 58 years and of the brothers 61 years.

Difficulty with change had been foreseen at the highest level at the very beginning of the process. On a visit to Clonard in October 1970, Fr General Amaral had,

> ... held a special community meeting on Sunday 18th afternoon. Chief matter: the new constitutions and statutes – in general, our new form of life. ... With his excellent command of English, he reassured several of the more senior confrères of the security, on theological grounds, of the new structures.[13]

However, while much anxiety remained among Redemptorists about their changing way of life, not to mention the even greater anxieties pressing on them from the political 'troubles' around them, life in Clonard went on:

> ... we get on with the business of living religious life amid sick-calls, supplies, parlour duty, telephone calls, group apostolates, church work, missions as they come and all that goes to make Clonard as busy and sometimes as noisy as a railway station.[14]

The apostolate of Clonard

Next to changes in the community's way of life, the other great preoccupation of the Clonard Redemptorists in these decades was the apostolate of Clonard itself. This matter was first formally raised in June 1974 by the provincial superior, Fr James McGrath. While visiting the three Belfast communities – Clonard, St Clement's and St Gerard's – he drew attention to a document, *Focus for Action*, which the Irish Conference of Major Religious Superiors was preparing for the Irish bishops. The subject of the document was the pastoral work of religious men and women. Fr McGrath announced that the Redemptorists were to prepare a pilot scheme for Belfast. So members of the Belfast communities, together with a number of lay people and other Redemptorists of the Irish province, were invited to form a working group. Four members of the group belonged to the Clonard community.[15]

1974: 'Towards a new Redemptorist Apostolate in Belfast'
This group suggested guidelines under the general title, 'Towards a new Redemptorist Apostolate in Belfast'. While the intention of the exercise was to advise on a new apostolate for all three Belfast communities, in practice the emphasis was on Clonard's situation. Clonard, caught in the midst of political and sectarian strife, was the one with the obvious problems.[16]

The group considered that future developments were likely to require retraining of members for their involvement in small-group apostolates. Within the latter, a priority should be the education of adults in human and Christian development, this to be 'on a large scale'. Other priorities were the provision of a marriage counselling service and the opening of discussions with other clergy in Belfast 'with a view to broadening pastoral strategy'. Extra manpower would be needed for new initiatives, so that Clonard community would need its maximum staff complement. They would also 'engage the co-operation of a group of lay advisers and associates in the work', and there was the possible need of 'fully employed lay apostles'.

Eventually, the working group proposed a radical solution which was to be based on a core group of Clonard Redemptorists and 'collaborators' who would include lay people and, possibly, other religious. Having prepared themselves by study and pastoral experimentation, members of the basic community would 'go out and form other basic communities'. These would 'take the gospel and live by it', by praying and living together and by taking 'practical action to raise the level of human living within the group and among others'.[17]

Given the circumstances of the Clonard area, the scheme was visionary and unrealistic. In the event, it never got off the ground. Strongly influenced by ideas about basic Christian communities emanating from Brazil, where the Irish Redemptorists had been working since 1961-2, it came from the top and was never 'owned' by the Clonard community. However, one issue to which much attention was given in the group's discussions was whether or not Clonard ought to have a parish.[18]

A parish for Clonard?

It is surprising, given the repeated discussions in the community about the need for a parish or an 'assigned pastoral area' for Clonard, that the matter is barely mentioned in one important document from these years and quite ignored in another. The first is a report of a general visitation of the monastery conducted in mid-January 1975 by Fr Ignatius Dekkers, the Vicar General of the Redemptorists. It contains but two short sentences which simply record community opinion: 'Some thought it would be useful if we had a parish here. Some consider this important as such, others as inevitable.' The second document is a report on the Clonard apostolate, covering the period from September 1972 until May 1975, prepared for presentation to the forthcoming provincial chapter. It makes no mention at all even of discussions about a possible parish or pastoral area. Perhaps the report saw the matter as still too much in the early stages of discussion to merit serious attention. It may also be – and this is difficult to tell from the written record – that the question was being raised only by a small minority within the community.[19] However, there is an interesting entry in the Clonard Domestic Chronicle towards the end of 1977, which throws some light on the recurrent anxieties among some – possibly older – members of the community about the future and on their desire to take action of some kind. The chronicler is reporting on topics raised during a visitation of the monastery by the provincial superior:

> The future of Clonard was another matter to pass under review and the annual soul-searching exercise took place with regard to 'what are we doing for the people round about us?' Some think we are not doing enough and are genuinely worried by the fact that we walk past the doors of people living in the shadow of the monastery and not 'going to church or kirk', without stepping inside or doing anything for them. The reason of course is – fear of offending the clergy. We are 'cabin'd, cribbed, confined' but should we remain so? ... What should we suggest – a parish, an area of pastoral care, just [the bishop's] approval to visit and administer the sacraments? Fr Provincial was sympathetic and suggested that we brief ourselves well on the pastoral situation and prepare to risk (if risk there be) an encounter with bishop and clergy.[20]

The encounter with bishop and clergy never took place. While speculation continued sporadically, a substantial offer of help (three men to work four days a week or more for a year) was made a short time later to the parish priest of St Paul's, Archdeacon Montague, by the then Clonard rector, Fr George Wadding. This was at the beginning of 1979. The offer was declined. When the archdeacon retired in 1987 and was replaced by Canon Michael Dallat, the monastery chronicle noted:

> ... it is being freely mooted that Bishop Daly may ask for a Clonard priest

as CC of a district in St Paul's parish. Also he may ask for us to take on some special task in the apostolate of West Belfast.
All of which was little more than gossip.[21]

1978: 'Operation Overman' – A complex planning process
The Irish provincial chapter of 1978 approved what the Clonard chronicler described as 'a rather complex and extended planning process'. Rather unusually, the process was given a codename, 'Operation Overman,' like some military operation, and it seems to have proceeded like one. 'Overman' actually referred to the author of the 'system' on which the process was based. The first priority was the production, in conjunction with each community, of an agreed mission statement for the Irish Redemptorists. The following statement was finally arrived at:

> The mission of the Irish Redemptorists is to create a gospel brotherhood devoted to the renewal of Christian life in contemporary society through full preaching of the good news, especially to those who need it most.[22]

Agreed goals dealt with internal issues, such as recruitment and fostering vocations; ongoing formation and professionalism; poverty and lifestyle; community prayers and worship. Other preoccupations were involvement of the laity; youth; missionary message; justice in society; reaching the alienated. When each community reported back, it was given the final task of proposing objectives for each goal, that is, how each could be practically achieved. Unfortunately, there is little clear evidence of the outcome of this, the most important phase of the operation.[23]

We know that the Clonard community subsequently agreed a number of resolutions relating to involvement of the laity in their work. Unfortunately, as a later report observed, 'these resolutions were implemented only partially, if at all'. However, there seems to be one goal which was followed up by the Belfast communities, namely, 'Recruitment and fostering vocations,' for a series of 'open days' for boys interested in the Redemptorists was inaugurated at Clonard in February 1980 (when seventeen attended).[24]

1986: 'Facing the Future'
Yet another major effort to press forward with change was made by the Irish provincial administration in Advent 1986. In an aptly-named document, *Facing the Future*, a review was announced of the apostolates and viability of all the communities in the province. The document envisaged 'one major centre in each region as a framework for the future of the province'; each such centre was seen as 'a stable base for new initiatives, fresh beginnings'. Clonard was identified as 'our main centre in the north'. This document was discussed at the provincial chapter of early June 1987. As a result, the provincial admin

istration appointed, on 5 February 1988, a 'Committee for the Review of the Redemptorist Apostolate in the North of Ireland (RANI)'.[25]

1987: The Redemptorist apostolic ministry in Northern Ireland
Meantime, some members of the Clonard and St Clement's communities had drawn up yet another document, *The Redemptorist Apostolic Ministry in Northern Ireland*, for submission to the 1987 chapter. It was too late for inclusion in the chapter agenda, but its ideas helped influence the gathering 'to recognise the North as an area of pastoral priority for the province'. The main points of the document were, first, that whatever strategy it proposed must be 'worked out in dialogue with the local bishops and clergy'. Without such dialogue no development of ministry would be possible. Secondly, there should be 'an active role for laity in our Redemptorist ministry'. Thirdly, both Clonard and St Clement's should develop as centres of reconciliation, adult religious education, spiritual direction and counselling. For Clonard, the document envisaged, 'a dynamic apostolate through novena, the confraternities and the ministry of the sacraments' and it urged negotiation with bishops and priests,

> for Clonard community to have pastoral responsibility for specific needs, e.g., converts, travellers, people living in a defined area. (Taking a parish in Clonard is not envisaged.)

Other priorities identified were the youth apostolate and a mission team in Clonard, 'which will have a deep understanding of the Northern Ireland situation'.[26]

1989: Report of the Committee for the Review of the Redemptorist Apostolate in the North of Ireland (RANI)
There is no doubt that the Clonard-St Clement's document considerably influenced the review committee established by the Irish provincial administration in February 1988. This committee undertook its task with thoroughness and, in May 1989, presented a major report of over 30,000 words. It offered a brief historical overview of the Redemptorist presence since the foundation of Clonard in 1896. It attempted an honest examination of the deep divisions in Northern Ireland society. It reviewed the actual apostolates in all three Belfast houses. It surveyed previous inquiries into the Redemptorist apostolate in Northern Ireland since 1974. Finally, it offered a series of recommendations.[27]

These recommendations were presented as 'responses' to five 'areas of need' which the committee had identified. They were, briefly, as follows:

> *Area of Need*: Faith and church affiliation (referring to decline in religious practice, alienation from Church, etc.).

Response: The provision of high quality liturgy and preaching ...

Area of Need: Divisions in society and church.

Response: Cross-community dialogue, ecumenism, Clonard as a centre of reconciliation.

Area of Need: Youth and faith.

Response: Commitment to Clonard and St Gerard's youth clubs.

Area of Need: Consequences for individuals of secularism and violence in society.

Response: Counselling, spiritual direction, pre- and post-marriage courses.

Area of Need: Popular religiosity.

Response: Novena in honour of Our Lady of Perpetual Help in both Clonard and St Gerard's, subject to a review of its theological and liturgical dimensions.

But, first, the committee insisted that all the 'responses' they recommended should fulfil four major criteria. They must be:

    a. In harmony with our Redemptorist charism;

    b. Realistic and feasible;

    c. Challenging and inspiring;

    d. Have community support and commitment.

These criteria were intended to avoid the 'radical' proposals of previous reviews of the Redemptorist apostolate which had had little practical value. But what is most striking is the emphasis on the 'Redemptorist Charism', the realisation that the Redemptorists should be true to and have confidence in their own tradition – which the 'mission statement' of 1978 had identified as, 'full preaching of the good news'.[28]

Comment

What these various reviews of the Redemptorist apostolate, from 1979-1989, had in common was, first of all, the re-discovery of the 'Redemptorist charism' of 'full preaching of the good news.' It seems almost as if the nerve of the Redemptorists in the North, and especially in Clonard, had been shaken by the relentless pressure of the early years of the troubles which devastated their confraternities and novenas and left the Clonard district in turmoil. That nerve was now restored by a clear realisation of who they were and what their *raison d'être* was.

Next, the reviews show a great preoccupation with the Redemptorists' 'missionary message'. Further, there was agreement on the imperative to involve the laity in the Redemptorist apostolate. The apparent drift of young people was another matter requiring urgent attention, as was the widespread need for programmes of adult education in the faith. It was also acknowledged that the state of society in Northern Ireland cried out for serious efforts in reconciliation and ecumenism. Finally – and this seems another aspect of the Redemptorist charism – the 1987 and 1989 documents called for the re-instatement of 'Popular religiosity', particularly through the novena in honour of Our Lady of Perpetual Help, but also through the confraternities and ministry of the sacraments.

Clonard Hall

Several of the issues of great concern raised in the above-mentioned reviews have been considered in separate chapters. Another aspect of the monastery apostolate which was a constant worry to the community in the 1970s and 80s was Clonard Hall.

The first mention of 'a new hall for Clonard' is made in the monastery chronicle in September 1968. Plans had been under discussion for a new building 'to replace the present structure, for long quite inadequate for the crowds and already leaking very badly in many areas'. The 'present structure' was the old 'poor hall' attached to the monastery at the Waterville Street side. Designed to seat 400 at a total cost of just under £34,000, the new hall was completed in November 1970.

A short time before its completion, there was a wide-ranging community discussion 'as to the purpose and style of the new "Clonard Hall"', which concluded with the appointment of a management committee of three community members, Frs Egan (Vicar), P. Cunning and Bro Ignatius Blain (hall manager). The formal opening of the hall took place on 18 November 1973. Star attraction for the occasion was 'Dana, the winner of the Eurovision song contest who certainly was well up to expectation'. On the Redemptorist side, the distinguished guest was the Kerry-born Bishop of Miracema do Norte, Brazil, Most Rev James Collins, C.Ss.R., accompanied by the provincial superior, Very Rev James McGrath.

All the activities of the old hall in Waterville Street, except for the youth club, were transferred to the new hall and many more added. By the mid-1970s, the new premises were being used for school meals, choir practice, bowling club, céilíthe, chess club, library, Irish dancing classes, charismatic prayer sessions, yoga, art club, art classes, bridge club, indoor bowling, pensioners' activities, sewing club, ladies 'keep fit', adult dances on Wednesday evenings and discos for the 15-20 year olds on Saturday evenings. Occasional activities included concerts, guest teas, bazaars, art exhibitions, feiseanna, boxing contests, annual general meetings of a variety of organisations, etc. In the beginning, a bar was available in the hall. Always a matter of great anxiety to some members of the community, it eventually closed in the late 1970s.[29]

Missionary message

Given the long and vigorous tradition of the Clonard Redemptorists in the preaching of missions throughout Ireland, it is surprising that something of a crisis developed in this area of their apostolate in the 1970s and 80s. But crisis there was, as indicated by the recurrence of anxiety about their 'missionary message' during those decades.

Furthermore, a sense of crisis seems to pervade the monastery record, making it extremely difficult to give an accurate account of the Clonard missionary apostolate in these years. Normally the domestic chronicle logged with considerable accuracy the comings and goings of community members on mission and retreat work. But during the years 1969-73, for example, not a single mission is recorded. The continuation of violence after 1969 undoubtedly preoccupied the keepers of the chronicle. What is certain is that the first mission to be recorded in the 1970s was a big mission in St Peter's parish, Belfast, in January 1974. Of the team of twelve Redemptorists who gave this four-week exercise, six were from Clonard. Several other missions are noted later in 1974: 'This autumn time is a busy time for missions and retreats ...' Greencastle, Kircubbin, Magheralin and Ligoniel are mentioned. Yet, 'because of the disruption caused by the Troubles,' Clonard lost its mission team in 1975 and missions in the north were entrusted to Redemptorists from St Joseph's, Dundalk. In the meantime, the Clonard chronicle of 23 April 1976 claimed the equivalent of ninety weeks' parish missions and retreats ('in the traditional style') since May the previous year, while the RANI report was 'certain' that the Dundalk team gave very few missions (no more than five) in the large diocese of Down and Connor.[30]

A possible reason for this limited activity is that the 'new' type of mission being promoted by the Dundalk missioners created serious difficulties in particular areas of the north. The principal feature of the new style of mission was the introduction of group meetings of parishioners in selected houses, particularly during the first week which was set aside for house to house visitation, before the preaching began. As an example, under the date of St Patrick's Day 1976, the Clonard record had this to say, with reference to two missions then going on in Belfast:

> ... house meetings are not being held, as in St Paul's, or not consistently, as in H[oly] Family parish. It is a sign of the times. In some areas, a house meeting may bring the two opposing factions in the IRA into dangerous proximity or, in other areas, people are afraid to leave their homes at night time and the movement of people into one house for a meeting might attract hostile attention. This latter is particularly true of the H[oly] Family (Newington) parish ...[31]

Despite the great difficulties posed by the troubles, parochial missions and retreats continued, even though the total for the calendar year 1976 dropped dramatically to thirty-two weeks. This was still 'gratifying' to the chronicler, 'considering that we had only three members committed to the mission staff'. The lack of manpower for missions was due in part to the requirements of Clonard church which was 'run on the lines of a mission church and a high standard of service [was] maintained throughout the year'. Indeed, in early 1980 the mission team was reduced to two senior members of the community, Fr James Gormley and Fr John Niall.[32]

Lack of missionary activity from a house like Clonard could be attributable to lack of manpower. But other factors played their part. On the one hand, the traditional annual (or biennial) parish mission or retreat was yet another devotional practice to suffer in the post-Vatican II environment. It was certainly not seen, generally, as important as it had been before; and, in any case, the Redemptorists, like other missionary bodies, had always to wait to be invited into parishes. On the other hand, a by-product of the troubles, especially in the early years, was the reluctance of some parish priests to call for missions in areas where paramilitary, military or police activity was intense. Hence, it seems that mission activity from Clonard virtually ceased in the late 1970s.

Experimental mission group
Late in 1984, a small mission team, nominated by the new provincial superior, Fr Stephen Mahony, was restored to Clonard. Under the leadership of Fr John Doherty, it was asked to undertake experimental work, for example, with parish priests who wanted 'something different, something beyond mere maintenance' in their parishes. The team, which included Frs Brendan Keane and Bill Keeney, assisted by Bro Adrian Egan, undertook two missions in 1985, at Hilltown, county Down and St Anne's parish, Derriaghy, Belfast. These included elements of 'parishioner empowerment'. The group was particularly busy in 1986 and 1987, especially in the dioceses of Down and Connor and Derry and, to a lesser extent, Dromore. But it ceased to function after two missions in 1988, one in Poleglass, Belfast, and one in Lifford, county Donegal. Details of its activity can be found in the notes.[33]

New Clonard mission team
Only one mission is recorded in the north in 1989, and that by a six-strong team from Dundalk, in Holy Trinity parish, Turf Lodge, Belfast. The next two years seem to have been lean years, but 1992 was busier and was marked by the appointment of a new Clonard mission team made up of Frs S. Moore, J. Hanna, S. Keeney, and M. Durkin, Ms Trish Rockett and, later, Fr M. Kelleher. 1994 was the best year of the early 90s; a four-week Newry mission in February was important for the fact that it was the first mission in which members of the Redemptorist Youth Movement were involved.[34]

In general, during the 1980s and early 90s, while there were energetic efforts to establish a capable mission team attached to Clonard, and while much good work was done, momentum was not sustained. The results appear to be quite disappointing. No clear explanation seems available, apart from a serious shortage of staff, given that Clonard church requirements came first. There was also the fact that some members of the community were committed to other virtually full-time apostolates. Nor should the important point be overlooked that, in common with all religious communities, shortage of new vocations rendered Clonard an ageing community. Perhaps the very unevenness of results during these two decades made it all the more imperative that the Redemptorist missionary message from Clonard should be constantly worked at.

Religious education for adults

Historically, the Clonard pulpit was used for 'evangelical and prophetic ... proclamation of the good news of Jesus Christ'. But it was also used as a platform to bring adult education to the confraternity members, especially of the men's Holy Family. Essentially, such addresses were intended to enable members to give to the world at large an account of the faith that was in them.

Unfortunately, the Clonard Domestic Chronicle for the period under review is erratic in its record of educational initiatives. The first clear indication of adult education in the faith occurs in the Advent season of 1977, when 'A Series of Talks and Discussions' was announced for four Wednesday evenings, ending on 14 December. The title of the series was 'Knowing God'. It was promised that, 'each meeting will include a talk, discussion and the answering of questions'. Six members of the Clonard community contributed, led by Fr Christopher McCarthy. In the following February, Fr McCarthy introduced 'Growth – *Fás*' (an 'enrichment programme, an invitation to growth at personal and communal level, within a parish context, open to adults and teenagers of any educational background'). The first programme was a six-session treatment of the sacraments.[35]

Certainly from 1986 onwards an annual Lenten series of talks/discussions was being offered on topics such as: The Bible and Life Today; A New Look at Our Faith; A New Look at the Sacraments; Looking again at the Commandments; Prayer; Scripture; Liturgy; The New Catechism; Building Bridges, etc. In 1990, the novel device was used of charging £2 per evening or £10 for the series, 'as a means of committing people to attend'. (Pensioners and unwaged were exempt from payment.) Attendances were generally very satisfactory, usually in the range of sixty to one hundred adults. In 1992, the decision was made to duplicate the series. The talks continued in Clonard on the six Lenten Sunday evenings,while St Clement's hosted them on Friday evenings.[36]

There is no doubt, then, that the Clonard community made a serious commitment to the apostolate of adult education, following the views on the subject shared, in the late 1980s, with the St Gerard's community and strongly recommended by the report of the review body in 1989. In one sense it can be said that the community was, at last, affirming the earlier pioneering efforts of two of its own members, Frs Hugh Arthurs and Alec Reid, in the late 1950s and early 60s.

Provision for youth

Anxiety about provision for youth was as old as the Clonard confraternities, so it is not surprising that it featured yet again in the reviews of apostolate. The Clonard Redemptorists' response to their agreed demand for a strengthening of their 'youth apostolate' had four facets. These were, the work of the Clonard Youth Club, the Scala initiative for the young unemployed, the development of school retreats and the Redemptorist Youth Movement.

Clonard Youth Club

Clonard Youth Club was formed in 1971, 'under direction of members of the community and a committee of laymen'. Its formation was 'against a background of civil disturbance' and an appalling lack of recreational facilities in the area. Registered with the Department of Education for Northern Ireland, it was grant aided.

From the beginning, the club's activities were centred in the small hall in Waterville Street. The hall was so small and dilapidated that the Department of Education was unwilling to give money for its development. But when the committee and friends 'tackled the job themselves,' providing a new kitchen, showers and a corridor to link with the adjoining St Gall's school, the department was impressed and awarded a 75 per cent grant. The club achieved full-time status in 1978, with the appointment of its first professional youth worker. The department also paid ninety per cent of the wages of five youth leaders including the Redemptorist manager. By 1987, the full-time youth leader was assisted by fourteen part-time workers. Initially for boys only, the club soon welcomed girls.[37]

The activities provided by the club were typical of similar clubs – football, swimming, boxing, table tennis, darts, snooker, volleyball, netball, basketball, discos on Thursdays and Sundays. On Saturdays, three soccer teams participated in competitions. There was an annual trip to Butlin's holiday camp at Mosney, county Meath. Problems, too, were those common to most clubs: lack of interest, lack of attendance, so that for instance, while there were around 400 registered members, the largest active membership at any time was 150. There were complaints, too, especially from parents, about the way the club was run, but there were also compliments – from parents and, a matter of particular pleasure to the Redemptorists, from Archdeacon Montague, the parish priest of St Paul's, who 'indicated that he appreciated what the Clonard community [was] doing for the youth of the area'.[38]

It must be admitted that the Clonard community was ambivalent in its commitment to the youth club. For instance, there was at least a hint of disagreement on the subject as reported in the 1978 'Summary'. Concluding on a cautious note in regard to the youth club, it observed: 'The whole youth club effort will become more fruitful if and when it becomes more a part of the whole apostolic effort of the community.' Then, in the summer of 1989, when Bro Michael Gileece, the 'founding father' of the youth club in 1971, was transferred to St Gerard's community on the Antrim Road, it was the clear intention of provincial management not to replace him, hardly proof of serious commitment.[39]

The reality was that, despite their genuine commitment to a youth apostolate in principle, the Redemptorists never really regarded themselves as youth club leaders, even apart from their chronic lack of manpower.

The dilemma of the Clonard community was resolved in June 1990 when it 'generally accepted' the dual proposal that the youth club should transfer from the Waterville Street hall to Clonard Hall and effectively undertake the management of the latter. To survive, the club needed new premises because it was in no position to undertake the expense of an extension to the old hall required by the Department of Education, Northern Ireland, if funding were to continue. If the club had new premises and had control of its management, the department would support the new venture generously.[40]

In November 1990, the community 'not reluctantly' agreed to the new arrangement, whereby the hall was 'leased indefinitely' to the youth club. Clonard Hall, like the youth club, had always been a difficult part of the community's apostolate. By 1990, it was not being used to its full potential and, from the Redemptorist point of view, there had always been 'chronic difficulty in obtaining from the community a manager to run [it]'. Now these burdens were lifted and placed squarely on the new sixteen-member youth club management committee. The rector of Clonard, as representing the owners of the hall, was entitled to nominate eight committee members; the youth club nominated the other eight. So, in one move, the anxieties the community had endured for nearly two decades over youth club and hall were resolved.[41]

Scala

In 1979, the Clonard Redemptorists decided to join an initiative whose object was to provide practical training for the young, mostly male, unemployed. The scheme, the Youth Training Programme, was funded by the Department of Economic Development and appears to have been administered through the Northern Ireland Association of Community Workshops of which Scala became a member.

Scala, located at 329, Springfiel Road, offered classes in joinery, bricklaying, gardening, computers, hairdressing, plumbing/heating, mechanics, dressmaking, photography and painting. Throughout its sixteen-year existence (it finally closed in March 1995), it was managed by Mr Joe McCann ('its dedicated boss to the end,' as the Clonard chronicler remarked). In 1985, on the occasion of a visit by Bishop Walsh of Down and Connor, Mr McCann had estimated that, since its inception, Scala had seen 700 trainees take its courses. He observed: '... the scheme offers young people a 50:50 chance of employment and in the present economic climate that is excellent, especially in West Belfast.'[42]

School retreats

The practice of giving school retreats of a half or full day's duration in Clonard monastery began in November 1983. What was new in 1983 was that the retreats were held in the monastery. The new situation appears to have come about because of a number of requests from schools in the vicinity whose heads of Religious Education thought that secondary pupils might respond well to a short retreat held within the monastery.[43]

The community response to these requests was unanimous. The retreats were seen as providing a form of 'corporate apostolate' which would 'draw us together as a community' and, at the same time, would offer the opportunity of a 'positive approach' to the underprivileged. Some of the community saw this outreach as extending beyond schools to include 'unemployed youths and adults' as well as 'underprivileged children and youths'. Two schools which had already asked for day retreats, St Peter's Secondary, Whiterock, and Little Flower Secondary, Somerton Road, were noted as drawing their pupils mainly from the Divis and New Lodge areas respectively, each of which could be regarded as underprivileged.

Retreats tended to be held in the autumn term, though occasionally during Lent. They also tended to be confined to girls' schools from West Belfast, such as St Rose's, St Louise's, St Genevieve's, St Dominic's (but also Little Flower); some boys' schools also participated, like St Peter's, St Patrick's, Knock, and Christian Brothers' Secondary, Glen Road. In 1989 some retreats were held in schools as far apart as St Colman's, Violet Hill, Newry, and St Monica's Girls', Ravenhill Road, but such in-school exercises seem to have been very much the exception.[44]

As a general rule, the retreats were conducted by younger members of the

Clonard community, like Frs John Hanna, Gerry Cassidy and Willie McGettrick in the beginning. There was actually a radical proposal put to the community in 1985 by Fr John Doherty that a Clonard school mission team be established, 'consisting of a husband and wife and a nun but no Redemptorist priest'; the suggestion was simply recorded as 'discussed'. However, the proposal helped to emphasise the importance of the right combination of retreat personnel to capture and focus the attention of young people on matters spiritual. As a result, by the early 1990s, young women were being asked to help the Redemptorists with retreats for girls. The first such helper recorded in the chronicle was a Ms Anne O'Brien from Dundalk, who worked with Fr Durkin during a busy week in March 1991, when retreats were given daily, Monday to Friday, to classes of girls, 'most of them from St Dominic's'. Thereafter, the school retreats for girls invariably included at least one female assistant in the team. In the autumn of 1994, when retreats addressed drug and alcohol addiction, speakers were invited from Cornerstone community and 'Panda', the latter an acronym for a club, 'People's Alternative to Narcotics, Drugs and Alcohol', which had been set up in Donegall Pass, Belfast, in 1991.[45]

It should be noted that, while these retreats in the monastery were the main thrust of the youth apostolate for schools, much other good work was being done quietly. For example, Fr Patrick O'Donnell, one of the most senior members of the community, was directing an on-going programme of half-day retreats every other Wednesday throughout the year in Rathmore Grammar School, Dunmurry. At the same time, Frs John Hanna and Michael Kelleher undertook chaplaincy work in St Louise's Comprehensive College, Belfast.[46]

Redemptorist Youth Movement
One of the principal outcomes of Redemptorist youth policy formulated in the 1980s was the Redemptorist Youth Movement. It was established in 1989 with strong support from the general government of the congregation. Indeed, its most ardent supporter was the Superior General, the Spaniard Fr Lasso Vega.

The Clonard RYM group consists of second- and third-level students, ranging from sixteen to twenty years of age. By early 1992 there were about twenty members, of whom about fifteen regularly attended meetings. The meetings consisted mainly of group discussions on questions of personal and faith development. There was a continuing association with a Protestant youth group with whom the members participated in discussions, ecumenical prayer and social outings.

The Clonard group, accompanied by Frs John Hanna and Michael

Durkin, attended the first Irish Redemptorist Youth Congress in Galway in August 1990. In the following year sixteen members travelled to the third European Redemptorist Youth Congress at Eggenburg in Austria. Those who participated in these congresses prepared and facilitated liturgies and also led discussion groups. Some expressed a desire to become more involved in Peer Ministry and, by early 1991, were assisting with school retreats in the monastery.

In September 1992, RYM was reconstituted. Fr Michael Kelleher was appointed national co-ordinator for Ireland. The Redemptorist provincial government undertook 'to make funds available for the work of the [RYM] council' and each community was to put rooms and resources at its disposal. In 1994, the status of the council was reinforced with the establishment of an executive and the confirmation of Fr Kelleher as national director. By that time, the movement was producing its own lively newsletter, *Cara*, edited by Fr Gerry Maloney, (later editor of *Reality*, the Irish Redemptorist monthly magazine).[47]

Two important points should be made about members of the Redemptorist Youth Movement. The first affirms their youth and their lay status. On this account, their social life is considered important. So, for example, the twenty-strong Clonard group had their first formal dinner-dance in an hotel near Belfast in November 1992.[48]

The second point emphasises the continuing role of RYM in the Clonard apostolate, in particular their significant involvement in parish missions for youth, or youth-to-youth missions as they are now called. When Redemptorists are invited for a youth-to-youth mission, they ask the parish to provide between twenty and twenty-five young people aged in the mid- to late teens. These young people are then trained, in a series of weekend meetings, in dance, mime and drama. They are also encouraged to share ideas on how best to present certain themes to their peers. For the participants, sharing the work of evangelising is an enriching experience. For those to whom they present the mission, the experience is usually a joyful one, underlining the fact that religion can speak to us in a powerful way and, far from being 'a crashing bore', can be enjoyable and relevant to our daily lives.[49]

Involvement of laity

From its very foundation, Clonard monastery and, particularly, Clonard church has been heavily dependent on lay help. One has only to think of the veritable army of church orderlies policing sometimes vast crowds at the apparently endless services – Masses, novenas, confraternities, jubilees – of a busy church; collectors, confraternity prefects and sub-prefects, secretaries, altar boys and, in more recent times, ministers of the Eucharist, of the Word, of Sacred Music and so on, to appreciate the importance of the involvement of the laity in the Redemptorist apostolates. But the involvement of the laity which was being urged in the reviews of the 1970s and 80s was of quite a different kind. While it had its roots in what the Vatican Council had to say about the vocation of the laity in the church, its development had been stifled by the instability of society in Northern Ireland during the troubles.

From the mid-1980s onwards, the domestic chronicle begins to refer to (traditional) lay helpers as 'co-workers'. At its September 1985 meetings, the community asked two of its members, Frs Doherty and Reynolds, to prepare a position paper, 'on ways of promoting the active participation of the laity in our apostolic life'. Having listed the laity, from 'our voluntary co-workers', to worshippers in Clonard church, neighbbours, employees, personal friends and families of community members, the paper suggested that, 'in 1986 we take a step towards facilitating "feed-back" from all of these groups'. The following year, a seminar, conducted by Fr Enda Lyons of the Archdiocese of Tuam, was held in Clonard Hall for 'members of the various groups who help us in our church apostolate'. Such initiatives established a pattern of action in relation to the 'Clonard laity' which has been followed with considerable success in subsequent years, supported by periodic meetings for discussion, planning, prayer and reflection.[50]

In the midst of these new concerns of the closing decades of the twentieth century, the various facets of the Redemptorist apostolate at Clonard monastery continued without interruption, now ever conscious of the support of co-workers – the daily and weekly sacramental ministry of Eucharist and Reconciliation; the faithful observance of the Liturgical Year of the church, with its seasonal celebration and sacred music; the confraternities, novenas, support for the poor and the marginalised; the constant round of counselling in the monastery parlours; the apparently ceaseless activity of the reception area; continuing help to the local parishes and religious communities; the work of ecumenism and community reconciliation. All of which contributed, as the chronicler had noted in the late 1970s, 'to make Clonard as busy and sometimes as noisy as a railway station'.[51]

EPILOGUE

Towards century's end:
Change among Clonard's neighbours

Throughout its hundred-year history, the most important neighbours to the Clonard community were the people of the immediate area, 'the people of Clonard'. These people were the first congregations at Masses and devotions, the first confraternity members, the first contributors to the material needs of the community, the first defenders of the monastery in times of danger, the people who decorated their streets and homes, often lavishly, as their contribution to the numerous Redemptorist celebratory occasions over the years.

It is not surprising then that the chronicler of the monastery should record, with affection and sadness, the passing of the Clonard area as it had survived for nearly four generations. The combination of 'bloody civil war [raging] round about us' and the need for housing redevelopment, which left parts of the area looking like 'a blitzed city', were first reflected on in the chronicle at the end of 1979, after ten years of 'troubles'. In the summer of 1983 came the turn of Clonard Street for demolition. Milford Linen Mill (later Carrington's 'Silk and Rayon'), which had fronted Clonard Street opposite Ross's mill since about 1860, was 'razed for [the] erection of a small housing estate'. The first ten houses were ready for occupation a week before Christmas 1984.[1]

Ten years later the domestic chronicle carried a full report on the redevelopment proposals, including a map of the precise area to be affected: 'On 25 September 1993, Clonard was formally declared a redevelopment area by the Board of Directors of the Housing Executive.' Vesting of property in the Housing Executive would occur in the period from October to December 1994. The building of a projected 260-270 houses replacing the existing 600 would begin early in 1995. The chronicler, naturally, saw serious implications for the monastery: 'The new Clonard will have a very much smaller population than the old. This will have some effect on our church attendances.'[2]

Close upon the 'people of Clonard' came the good neighbourly religious institutes of the immediate area: the Bon Secours sisters, whose nursing home had tended the occasional Redemptorist patient. They were well established before the Redemptorists came. It will be recalled that Bishop Henry tried to get them to surrender their convent to the Redemptorists. Then there were the Daughters of Charity of St Vincent de Paul and the de la Salle brothers, both of whom came to the area about the same time, being invited by Bishop Henry for the express purpose of establishing schools for the 'half-timers', the mill children. The Daughters of Charity occupied Clonard House on 1 May 1900, the day the Redemptorists left it to move into their new monastery. On the same day the sisters opened their school, St Vincent's, in Dunlewey Street. It remained a school for 'half-timers' (female) until about 1920, then widened its enrolment. Later the same year (1900), the de la Salle brothers opened St Gall's school in Waterville Street for 'half-timer' boys, and in August 1901, they opened St Finnian's school for boys to cope with the overflow from St Gall's.

In 1989, due to educational reorganisation, itself consequent on a falling population in the area, both St Vincent's and St Finnian's schools closed. The closure of the schools was a matter of genuine regret, particularly to those older members of Clonard community who remembered that the boys of St Finnian's provided numerous altar boys, choir boys and members of the boys' confraternity and that the pupils of St Vincent's '[had] been faithful worshippers at Clonard all through their lives'.

Just at this time, the Redemptorists received a reminder of change as a positive force. They acquired new neighbours in the Adoration Sisters who had taken over the old Bon Secours convent (on the Falls Road, opposite Leeson Street) and, on 30 April 1989, opened their oratory to the public, with an invitation to join with them in their ministry of adoration. According to the Clonard record, over one thousand people had volunteered to participate in their perpetual prayer.[3]

However, the cycle of closures in the Clonard neighbourhood had not quite finished. For the Redemptorist community, the most significant closure of these years was that of the convent of the Daughters of Charity of St Vincent de Paul, Clonard House, the first home in Belfast of the Redemptorists themselves. The sisters had decided to move to two smaller houses, one in Cavendish St (still within the ambit of Clonard) and one on the Glen Road. The chronicler reflected:

> During their years here, the sisters did visitation of the poor and sick, ran St Vincent's school, had charge of St Vincent's Hostel [for working girls] in Clonard St and taught in St Louise's College. And the sisters were always 'prominent in their attendance' at devotions in Clonard church.

The last of the sisters left Clonard House on 10 August, 1990.

After the departure of the sisters, the property was under a series of temporary caretakers. In 1955 it was taken over by the Oaklee Housing Association which provides sheltered accommodation for the elderly. Oaklee refurbished Clonard House and provided extensive accommodation at the rear. Unwittingly, Oaklee has presented the Clonard Redemptorists with a magnificent centenary gift, the splendid restoration of their first home.[4]

CENTENARY: THE CLONARD REDEMPTORIST LEGACY

So, what have the Redemptorists to show for one hundred years in Clonard monastery?

A reputation for rigorous monastic living

There is no doubt that the early Redemptorists of Clonard had an enviable reputation among the faithful for disciplined and rigorous monastic living which befitted missionary priests committed to the most abandoned souls, and brothers who had chosen the vocation of largely hidden and silent service. The rigour may have mellowed somewhat in the decades since the Second Vatican Council, but the discipline remains. The perception has always been that the Redemptorists were committed men of God who could be trusted, hence their extensive, compassionate service of counselling which remains one of their most laborious, if hidden, apostolates.

A vibrant church ministry

The Redemptorists have sustained throughout the century a vibrant church ministry of Eucharist, Reconciliation and the Word. Their especial charism, 'rediscovered' in their searching reviews of their work in the 1970s and 80s, they describe as 'full preaching of the Good News'. Or, as the Clonard faithful would have said, 'You always get a good sermon in Clonard.' In addition, the various seasons of the liturgical year of the church have always been observed with great solemnity and, where appropriate, celebration, with music and colour and lights. Pre-Vatican II generations will remember the splendid decoration of the high altar of Clonard church with a profusion of flowers and hundreds of lighted candles on joyous occasions. This church apostolate was sustained, in the words of Bishop Patrick Walsh, 'unstintingly ... often, indeed, all too often, in very difficult and trying circumstances'.[5]

A beautiful church

The church building itself must be acknowledged as part of the Clonard legacy. It stands as a fine example of the neo-Gothic style which was widely adopted in Ireland in the latter half of the nineteenth century. As a much used church enjoying a vibrant ministry throughout the century, it has been well maintained so that, while a disappointment to the modern liturgical purist, it is widely acknowledged as a beautiful church, a haven of peace in a bustling city and, above all, a place of prayer.

Confraternity tradition

The Clonard Redemptorists can be proud of their confraternity tradition.

From the beginnings in 1897, the women's (under the patronage of Our Lady and St Alphonsus) and the men's and boys' (Holy Family) flourished for more than two generations and became a part of the fabric of Catholicism in West Belfast and further afield. Associated with the confraternities – the only 'congregation' of Clonard church, since the Redemptorists had no parish – were the public celebrations of important jubilees and anniversaries of the church at large, of the Redemptorist Congregation and of the confraternities themselves. These were invariably carried out with great pomp, style, precision and enthusiasm but without loss of spirituality.

Perpetual novena
Another institution of which the Clonard Redemptorists can be justly proud is the Perpetual Novena in honour of Our Lady of Perpetual Help. Devotion to the Mother of God under this title had been observed in Clonard church since its foundation. Its mutation into the form of a perpetual novena was a product of the Second World War years, indeed, an import from the United States of America. The Redemptorists have always viewed the novena – and, particularly, its later off-shoot, the solemn novena – as, unashamedly, a manifestation of 'popular religiosity'. While the populist approach to the novena and its religious enthusiasm did not appeal to all tastes, 'Clonard Thursday' became, from the 1940s to the 1960s, a very important part of Belfast Catholicism. Indeed, the very success of the novena encouraged its widespread adoption in parishes throughout the diocese of Down and Connor and beyond.

The 'Bill Gerard' era
There is one black mark against the Irish Redemptorists which must be acknowledged. This was the propagation in the late 1940s and into the early 1960s, of extremely negative views on the whole subject of 'company keeping' and preparation for marriage, by which 'long engagements' were anathematised. At least some of the Clonard community in these years supported such narrowness, both in pulpit and confessional. Their views are epitomised in the popular memory by the 'Bill Gerard' contributions to the *Redemptorist Record*, and in pamphlets such as *The Devil at Dances, May I keep company?*, etc. These views were taken very seriously by young people attending Clonard, among whom they caused considerable distress. They also gave the Clonard community as a whole an undeserved reputation for moral narrowness.

The Diocese of Down and Connor
The Clonard community over the century could claim to have been fully supportive of the bishops and priests of Down and Connor diocese, a disposition which was, in general, warmly reciprocated. There were frictions from

time to time, of course, but a part of Redemptorist thinking from their own beginnings was that they should work in harmony with bishops and their priests; this they broadly succeeded in doing. The custom whereby the priests of Down and Connor made their annual retreat with the Redemptorists was at once a clear indication of goodwill and a source of continuing good relations.

Post-1969: Mediation and reconciliation

The Clonard apostolates of confraternity and novena suffered grievously from the outbreak of sectarian violence in 1969 and subsequent years. In the course of these years, church and monastery became a bulwark against extremism and political violence from whatever quarter. The years of the hunger strikes were particularly painful, when the community came under severe pressure, as they saw it, to take sides politically. This they resisted with a determination to keep faith with their ministry 'to all men', including the hunger strikers and their families, yet preserving the image of Clonard as, 'non-political, non-sectarian, open to all, compassionate and ready to help but without committing [themselves] to any political platform'. In fact, some members of the community became deeply involved with other clergy, Catholic and Protestant, in the search for reconciliation. Much of the early involvement of Clonard personnel took the form of mediation within republican paramilitary groups. Later, contacts were made with both republican and loyalist paramilitaries, the major political parties and the British and Irish governments. The contribution of the Redemptorists, particularly of Fr Alec Reid, to what ultimately came to be called 'the peace process' was substantial.[6]

A centre for ecumenism

It was undoubtedly this 'open to all' attitude which enabled Clonard to offer, and have accepted, sincere and imaginative ecumenical gestures from the early 1980s onwards. It might be argued, too, that the seeds of this ecumenism had been sown a generation earlier in, as it was then called, the 'Mission to non-Catholics' of the post-war years and its successor, the Catholic Information Centre. More immediately, ecumenism at Clonard derived from the new thinking of the Second Vatican Council on relations with the other Christian churches. At the end of its first century, Clonard stands as an important centre for ecumenism and reconciliation.

What of the future?

There is no doubt that attendances at all the services of Clonard church were on the wane from the mid-1960s as the old certainties of a faith sustained by a multiplicity of popular religious devotions gave way to the fresh theological, biblical and liturgical thinking of the Second Vatican Council. There is equally no doubt that, in normal circumstances, the changes wrought by the council would, in course of time, have transformed all the apostolates operating within and around Clonard monastery and church. How far this transformation would have gone we can never know, because the sectarian riots of 1969 ravaged those apostolates. Clonard's geographical location ensured that it would suffer much in the upheavals that followed. What we do know is that, by the early 1970s, attendances at Clonard church were decimated and the very existence of its novena and confraternities was threatened.

However, confraternities and novena have survived. Indeed, in its annual solemn form, the perpetual novena blossomed from the decade of the 1980s, as did ecumenical undertakings. In their numerous reviews of their work in the 1970s and 1980s, the Redemptorists committed themselves to 'popular religiosity' through novena and confraternity. Likewise they committed themselves to a strong presence in the north of Ireland, with Clonard as its centre.

As their centenary project, at a time when so many religious communities were seriously 'downsizing', the Irish Redemptorists undertook, at great expense and over a period of nearly two years, a complete refurbishment of their four-storey monastery which had remained substantially unchanged since its completion in 1900. This act of faith can mean only one thing: the Redemptorists intend to stay in Clonard for (at least) another hundred years.

Men's Confraternity: Holy Thursday Night Vigil

One of the most impressive of the Holy Family Confraternity's devotional practices – not surprising, given St Alphonsus' great devotion to the Eucharist – was the annual 'nocturnal adoration' of the Blessed Sacrament throughout Holy Thursday night. As the confraternity chronicle for 1926 explained:

> There was exposition of the Most Blessed Sacrament in this church all day and all night until Good Friday morning. From 11 o'clock onwards until [4 am on] Good Friday morning, seven sections from each division of the men's Confraternity kept vigil every hour. During each hour the rosary was recited by the spiritual director Fr Carroll. After each decade a hymn was sung. Then the director gave a short lecture on the life of Our Lord and exhorted the members present to meditate on his sufferings.[1]

The special esteem in which this practice was held is attested by the fact that it was recorded virtually every year in some detail by each director in turn. So it is possible to note accurately variations in practice from time to time, such as the night hours being shared by a number of priests taking their turn in the pulpit or, as in 1929, '... Mr Monaghan played the organ for the first two hours (11 pm-1 am) and Fr McHugh the remainder (1 am-4 am).' – presumably not continuously! In 1930 there was some misunderstanding with the new bishop, Dr Mageean, about night adoration, as a result of which the Clonard community thought he might withdraw 'the permission given by Cardinal MacRory when he was bishop' (1915-28). But when the matter was raised with him in 1931, Dr Mageean 'sent a most gracious reply by return' in which he suggested, 'If the Limerick men can carry it through, I think the Belfast Confraternity should be able to do it equally.' As if to celebrate the bishop's approval and to respond to the implied challenge to 'the Limerick men', in 1931 the adoration was extended by an hour, lasting from 11 pm on Holy Thursday until 5 am on Good Friday. The estimated attendance was 3,500, which was surpassed by a 'new record' of 4,000 the next year. In 1940, another record was established for the first hour, 11 pm to midnight. This was traditionally the best attended hour – for obvious reasons – which, however, led to appeals from the director from time to time asking the men to come at their allocated hour. At any rate, on Holy Thursday 1940 was witnessed 'the largest [attendance] ever seen in Clonard. Men were standing in two rows up the side aisles.'[2]

The war put an end to night adoration. As the chronicle tersely recorded under 1941 (10 April): 'No night adoration. Danger of air raid.' There is reference in 1944 to a 'Holy hour for men', without any indication of which hour. However, there was some drama: 'The sirens were sounded just as the men were going into the church. Some returned home, but the majority went in. All clear went during Rosary.' A 'holy hour for the men' the following year produced a 'splendid congregation', but in 1946, the all-night vigil was resumed. The *Irish News* proclaimed the event with an eloquent compliment:

> After a lapse of six years during the war period the beautiful custom of spending the night in adoration before the altar of repose was resumed by the members of Clonard Holy Family Confraternity. The night was divided into six holy hours, beginning at 11 pm and ending at 5 am. At each of these hours, fourteen sections, drawn in lots from the Confraternity, were invited to attend. It is calculated that 5,500 men responded. Average attendance at each holy hour was 900. Fr Russell conducted the six holy hours ...'

Fr Russell, director since October 1945, was quoted as saying that 'it was only on a night such as this that he realised what a high honour and privilege it was to be the spiritual director of such a magnificent confraternity.'[3]

The practice of drawing sections by lots for the adoration had raised complaints from time to time from some men who felt that their sections tended to be drawn frequently for the later hours. So, in 1949, Fr David Harris abandoned random selection in favour of 'a more equitable' rotation of sections. Such hardship on the men was hardly comparable to the hardship on the director conducting six holy hours during the night. Fr Harris was one director who commented on this (1947): 'Though it is hard on the director, the men appreciate [it] if he can be with them every hour.' Fr Michael Connolly made similar observations: 'Six hours in the pulpit is unquestionably very difficult but if it can be managed it is worth the effort. It makes a great impression on the men and they appreciate it.'[4]

The men had evidently made a great impression on Fr Connolly on this, the occasion of his first encounter with the all-night vigil. He noted: 'Most inspiring. I could not but notice many men who stayed the whole night through – especially some young men.' Another observant director was Fr Seán O'Loughlin (January 1949-October 1952). He recorded watching 'one young fellow, about 20, who remained in his position under the pulpit for four hours'. In fact, in each of his years as director, he made the same observation: '... Some stayed the whole night – and many for three or four hours adoration.' And he related a particularly edifying story, 'a touching example of sacrifice', as he called it, of a man (whose name and address he recorded):

His section was on 4-5 am. [He] had a very bad leg owing to an accident. He left home [in the Markets area] at 3 am – took a full hour to crawl up to Clonard – and another hour to get back. Such episodes make up for many disappointments.

The picture of this disabled man, struggling to Clonard in the middle of the night, is a reminder that, according to Fr O'Loughlin, Holy Thursday night was, 'known to Protestants as "The night the Catholics spend walking about the city".'[5]

The 'beautiful custom' which certainly edified so many directors of the confraternity and Catholic Belfast at large and, apparently, numbers of non-Catholics as well, came to an abrupt end in 1956. The end was due not to any lapse of fervour or war or civil commotion, but to liturgical changes within the Church. As part of the desire for reform which was moving within the church in the 1950s and which Pope John XXIII channelled into the Second Vatican Council (1962-5), night adoration, with its focus on the Blessed Sacrament, was seen as emphasising Holy Thursday, with its last supper and institution of the Eucharist, to the neglect of the suffering Christ who, during that night, was being cruelly shuffled from one authority to the next on his inexorable way to crucifixion and death. The liturgical effect on Holy Thursday was stated concisely in the Confraternity Chronicle: 'Due to the return to the old Holy Week ceremonies ... Holy Thursday adoration was limited to the two hours before midnight.'[6]

APPENDIX 2

The Eucharistic Congress 1932[7]

The director of the Holy Family Confraternity at the time, Fr Cornelius Mangan, went to extraordinary lengths to involve its members (men and boys) in the celebration of the 1932 Eucharistic Congress in Dublin. For those who participated, it seems to have been a truly unforgettable experience, possibly surpassing the impact on a later generation of Pope John Paul II's visit to Ireland in 1979.

The first announcements about the forthcoming Congress were made in June 1931, when a collection was taken up 'towards the expenses [of the Congress]'. In December, members intending to travel to Dublin for the celebrations were asked to give their names to their section prefects. At the beginning of January 1932 a special prayer for the success of the Congress was introduced, to be recited at every meeting until the Congress should be over. By the end of January, 2,300 names had been submitted of those wishing to travel.

The organisation of the confraternity participation caused the director, Fr Con Mangan, 'a lot of worry and trouble', despite the support of a strong Congress Committee made up of six confraternity secretaries, Messrs Clarke, Greene, McGowan, Kennedy, Smyth and Rice. The first difficulty was with the Congress organising committee in Dublin who declined to allocate a special place in the Phoenix Park for the confraternity. However, a place was finally allocated 'to Most Holy Redeemer Church, Belfast' and it turned out to be a good one, near the high altar. The next, and major difficulty, was transport for so many travellers. Applications to the Great Northern Railway in January for trains were 'entirely refused. The manager of the GNR said only six trains would leave Belfast on Sunday June 26th.' Fr Mangan then explored with Thomas Cook & Son the possibility of transporting the men by boat, but without success. Finally, he entered into negotiations with the Belfast Omnibus Company who, 'after much difficulty over the border question', agreed to provide sixty-two buses which could accommodate 2,000 men. Return tickets were to cost nine shillings each. During the month of February, the Down and Connor Eucharistic Congress Committee, whose secretary was Fr McCarthy of St Malachy's College, succeeded in persuading the GNR to provide a further eight trains, on which the Clonard men were eventually allocated 300 seats.

Meantime, the boys' confraternity had been organised to travel to the Congress, by train, on Saturday 25 June. There were over 1,300 boys, with fifty adults as stewards:

> Trams conveyed them from Oranmore Street to [the] station. At the Hippodrome they got off and marched in processional order to the trains. Twelve Christian Brothers met the trains in Dublin and remained with the contingent the whole day. The Belfast Omnibus Company had buses to convey the boys from Amiens Street to the Phoenix monument ... After Mass the boys got lunch in a marquee [at] 1s. a head, following which they all marched back through the city to Amiens Street. The homeward journey passed uneventfully, thus ending 'the greatest day the boys' confraternity ever experienced'.

Sunday was the big day for the men. There were special Masses in the church at midnight (which was 'overcrowded') and 4 am:

> At five o'clock the 62 buses entered Clonard Street by Kashmir Road. Two rows of the buses filled the street. In less than ¾ hour all were filled and at 5.55 [they] started with an interval of about half a minute between each ...

Owing to a delay in Newry 'purposely caused, it would seem, by the NI Customs Officials', the buses did not keep to their schedule. The three hundred men who had travelled by train were in their places in the Phoenix Park long before the 2,020 who came in the buses. According to Fr Mangan's record, the Clonard men were 'the subject of many laudatory remarks', particularly when, after the ceremonies, they returned to central Dublin:

> Almost every man wore a ribbon and medal as well as a E[ucharistic] C[ongress] badge that cost a shilling. They formed a magnificent body as they marched from their allotted section, near the High Altar in the Park to O'Connell's bridge ... The director heard one [Garda] officer say to another ... 'They are the finest body of men who have passed out this gate today!'

The return journey began in Mountjoy Square from 9 pm onwards and the convoy returned unhindered to Belfast, unlike many other pilgrims who were attacked at various places between Newry and Belfast. With a flourish of rather misplaced bravado, Fr Mangan noted: '... not as much as a stone was thrown at the Clonard buses. Of course, the fact that over 2,000 men travelled in these buses prevented the hooligans of Northern Ireland from making an attack.'

The contributions of confraternity members, supported by individual offerings to 'Congress expenses' was sufficient to cover 'all the expenses incurred by the boys', except their tickets. Fifty tickets were given free to poor boys, some of whom were also provided with clothes. 'Messrs Hughes and Kennedy, bakers, supplied a nice luncheon for the boys to be eaten on the way. The director supplemented this with fruit costing £10. The boys' tea in Dublin cost £62.10s.' – about 1s. per head. A number of poor members of the men's confraternity were also provided for. Thirty-five railway tickets at 7s.6d. each and about thirty bus tickets at 9s. each were given free.

Finally, complimentary letters were exchanged between Fr Mangan and the managing director of the Belfast Omnibus Company, Mr J. McCrea. The latter said it was 'a privilege to be entrusted with a huge business of this nature, particularly for a gentleman of your standing with a flock of the best-behaved persons we have ever transported'. And he went on to claim that 'the order we carried out on your behalf was the largest ever undertaken by any road transport company in Britain'. Interestingly, the Belfast Omnibus Company was also active in Dublin in ferrying people between Amiens Street and the Phoenix Park, and at the keenest prices. The boys who travelled by train on Saturday 25 June were met by BOC buses and carried to the Phoenix monument 'at 3d. a head, although the Dublin buses fixed their price at 6d. first, then 4d'.

Fr Mangan concluded, in relief: 'The enterprise was a big one, but infinite thanks to Jesus, Mary and Joseph, all was carried through, in spite of many obstacles, with great success.'[7]

APPENDIX 3

The Loire Mosaics [8]

The Loire mosaics decorate the central elevation of the nave, both the 'vee' spaces above the pillars and the clerestory. The theme of the mosaics is, 'The Story of the Redemption from the Old and New Testaments'. The artist set out an account of the mosaics in six plates (planches), three on each side of the church. They are described here, beginning on the left-hand side of the church (as one faces the altar), reading from front (altar) to back (porch):

PLATE 1
Clerestory windows:
1 Hand of God creating heaven, earth, man.
2 Denial of Judas – purse, coins, rope.
3 The Burning Bush.
4 The Paschal Lamb – sign of Redemption.
5 Denial of Peter – cock crowing.

Above pillars:
1 The Fall of Man.
2 Passage through the Red Sea – God saves his people.

PLATE 2
Clerestory windows:
1 Tables of the Law – appeal of God and man's response.
2 Fire of Sacrifice.
3 Reeds of the Passion.
4 King David – harp, crown, parchment.
5 Joshua's trumpet – felling walls of Jericho.

Above pillars
1 Empty sepulchre and Star of Glory.
2 The Temple (alliance between the old and new testaments).

PLATE 3
Clerestory windows:
1 Crown of Thorns.
2 The Messiah, King and Priest, come to save his people.
3 The Seed of New Life.
4 Tunic of Christ and the dice.
5 Star of Bethlehem.
6 Expectation of Mary in hope.

Above pillars
1 Broken chain – Return from exile.
2 Restoration (dispersal and reunion).

Continuing on the right-hand side of the church, reading from back (porch) to front (altar):

PLATE 4
Clerestory windows:
1 Virgin and Infant – the Son of God is born.
2 Public life and preaching of Jesus.
3 The Nails of the Passion.
4 The Chalice of the Passion.
5 The Lance and the Sponge.

Above pillars:
1 The Coming of Christ - the chi-rho symbol.
2 He has died on the Cross to save us.

PLATE 5
Clerestory windows:
1 Jesus united to his Father by his Ascension.
2 Flame of Pentecost.
3 Eucharist – bread and grapes.
4 Unity of the Church – Communion of Saints.

Above pillars:
1 The Resurrection of Christ.
2 The Church – Rome guided by the Holy Spirit continues the work of Redemption.

PLATE 6
Clerestory windows:
1 Keys of Peter – Authority of the Papacy.
2, 3 Alpha and Omega – the Beginning and the End.
4 Last Judgment – scales of justice.
5 Light of the heavenly Jerusalem.

Above pillars:
1 The Parousia – its great fulfilment in his glory.
2 The Lamb of Redemption of the Apocalypse – the heavenly Jerusalem.

Office holders, 1896-1996

BISHOPS OF THE DIOCESE OF DOWN AND CONNOR

1895-1908 Henry Henry
1908-1914 John Tohill
1914-1928 Joseph MacRory (to Armagh 1928; Cardinal 1929; d. 1945)
1929-1962 Daniel Mageean
1962-1982 William Philbin (retired 1982; d. 1991)
1982-1990 Cahal B Daly (to Armagh 1990; Cardinal 1991; retired 1996)
1991- Patrick Walsh (Auxiliary 1983)
    Anthony Farquhar (Auxiliary 1983)
    Michael Dallat (Auxiliary1994; d. 2000)

RECTORS OF CLONARD MONASTERY

1896-1904	Patrick Griffith	1950-1953	Gerard McDonnell
1904-1907	Patrick Murray	1953-1956	Peter Byrne
1907-1909	Augustine O'Flynn	1956-1959	Charles McNiffe
1909-1912	Edward O'Laverty	1959-1962	Thomas Loughnane
1913-1918	Denis Turner	1962-1964	Peter Byrne
1918-1920	Patrick Crotty (died in office)	1964-1967	Thomas McKinley
1920-1921	John Kelly	1967-1969	William Hanly
1921-1924	Timothy O'Twomey	1969-1972	Gerard Crotty
1924-1927	James Coogan	1972-1975	Michael Browne
1927-1930	William Treacy	1975-1978	Brian McGrath
1930-1936	John Brady	1978-1984	George Wadding
1936-1939	James Coogan	1984-1987	Seamus Enright
1939-1942	James Deeney	1987-1993	John O'Donnell
1942-1945	Thomas J. Regan	1993-1996	Kevin Browne
1945-1950	Gerard Reynolds		

DIRECTORS OF CLONARD HOLY FAMILY CONFRATERNITY

1897-98	Vincent Bourke	1941-42	Peter Byrne
1898-99	Patrick Leo	1942-45	John Ryan
1899-1902	J. P. Lowham	1945-47	Frank Russell
1902-6	P. S. Cussen	1947-49	David Harris

1906-11	Patrick Crotty	1949-52	Seán O'Loughlin
1911-14	Timothy O'Twomey	1952-55	Michael Connolly
1914-15	T. O'Connor	1955-61	Christopher McCarthy
1915 (July-Sept)	P. Hannigan	1961-63	Frank Mullaghy
1915-18	J. Walsh	1963-68	Hugh McLaughlin
1918-19	V. MacManus	1968-69	Seán Mullin
1919-23	Peter Paul Carthy	1969-72	Patrick Egan
1924-27	Patrick Carroll	1972-75	Aodh Bennett
1927-30	James Deeney	1975-76	Hugh McLaughlin
1930-32	Cornelius Mangan	1976-78	Peter Burns
1932-36	James Reynolds	1978-81	Patrick O'Keefe
1936-37	James Deeney	1981-84	Seán Keeney
1937-40	James Murray	1984-90	Edward Lynch
1940-41	J. Walsh	1990-97	Gerry Reynolds

APPENDIX 5

The Church fabric – interior and exterior

The development of the interior of Clonard church was, in the tradition of most large churches, a gradual business. Rarely are initial funds so large as to allow furnishings and decoration to be complete from the day of opening. However, we know that the altars of Our Lady of Perpetual Succour and the Sacred Heart were, together with the communion rail, contracted for with Davis of Cork at the same time as the high altar, as noted in the chapter on the building of the church. Fr Patrick O'Donnell, in his *Clonard Church and Monastery, 1896-1995,* has shown the otherwise piecemeal commissioning of even the largest furnishings, like the side altars: those of St Alphonsus and St Gerard were blessed in 1917; that of St Joseph in September 1923. The famous – and beautiful – pulpit was not installed until April 1913, the marble statue of Our Lady Immaculate in the sanctuary not until August 1917.[9]

An early commentator on the church furnishings was the anonymous author of the 1922 manuscript, *Foundation of the Redemptorist Monastery, Clonard, Belfast.* He dismissed the altar of Our Lady of Perpetual Succour designed, as was the high altar, by Fr Berghman, a member of the Clonard community: while 'in itself ... very beautiful [it] does not fit in with the architecture of the church and so has been adversely criticised by many'. He allowed the other altars (Sacred Heart, St Joseph, St Alphonsus and St Gerard) to pass without comment, but was withering about the Sacred Heart statue:

> There are two white marble statues inside the altar rails, one of Our Blessed Lady, which is very beautiful, another of the Sacred Heart which is very ugly. These were gifts [of the Caffrey brewing family of Glen Road] and cost nearly £300 each. The Sacred Heart is an eyesore.

Fortunately, the Stations of the Cross passed muster; they were 'very fine' and 'the marble pulpit is a work of art'. The pulpit cost £465 and was the gift of the Misses Hamill of Trench House, Belfast. Entrusted to Earley & Co. of Dublin, preparations for its erection were made in late April 1913.[10]

Details of St Joseph's altar
Earley & Co were also responsible for St Joseph's altar, for which the specific-ation, prepared in June 1910, might give the modern reader an insight into the lavish detail invested in a major item of church furnishing at that time:

... the altar candle bench and reredos panels ... to be very white Sicilian marble specially [selected] to be of a good bright ground, superior to the ordinary Sicilian. The first plinth above the predella to be Irish red marble or granite, as selected. The columns (supporting altar table) to be Siena, the background of tracery panels in altar front to be Galway green marble ... The altar group representing the death of St Joseph to be in white Carrara ... the columns supporting the [tabenacle] arch to be onyx. The statue of St Joseph to be in white Carrara marble, 5 feet high ... The coloured marble panels of reredos to be alabaster (same as used for Maynooth altar), to be selected of a lightest pink colour, all highly polished ...[11]

As with furnishings, so with the decoration of the church. A chronicle entry of 17 July 1909 shows the strong desire of the Redemptorists to do things well. It records the visit of three continental confrères, 'to see the new Clonard with a view to suggest designs for decoration and painting'. The account which follows, based on the monastery's written records, is of necessity incomplete because not every improvement or alteration in the church is recorded. Likewise, the necessary work of maintenance and refurbishment is noted only occasionally, but sufficiently often to provide reminders of the ravages of time and the demands of changing needs and fashions on the fabric of a building.[12]

Church mosaics

The one aspect of church decoration which can be followed most satisfactorily from the written records is the mosaicing of the interior surfaces, though the exact progress is difficult to tie down. The high altar seems (naturally) to have been done first, then the side chapels on the sanctuary, then the lower walls around the church and, finally, the central elevation of the nave. Most of the work was done in three phases, the 1930s, the mid-to-late 1950s and, finally, the early 1960s.

The domestic chronicle has one curious entry in February 1912 – just four months after the dedication of the church. Unfortunately, the account is not specific about the precise time of the event it describes:

The mosaic panel on [the] gospel side of the altar, part of which had fallen away, was repaired and finished. It began to peel off one Sunday during the sermon at the last Mass to the amazement of the people, the choir and the celebrant, who felt it difficult to look unconcerned and listen to the preacher as the images were seen one after another to lose their heads and members which dropped in wee particles to the pavement.

The problem appears to have been with one of the mosaics on the altar reredos: on the 'gospel side' is the mosaic of the Ascension of Christ; the mosaic on the epistle side is of the Birth of Christ.[13]

Sanctuary and major side altars

The most striking of all the mosaics in the church is the huge apse mosaic of Christ the Redeemer, set against a gold background. This was executed by the firm of Ludwig Oppenheimer of Manchester in 1931-2. Among the Clonard papers are two letters, with design sketches, from these years which seem to suggest that Oppenheimer had been asked for a wider range of proposals, including the central elevation of the nave, now occupied by the Gabriel Loire mosaics (see below). Oppenheimer won another contract in the mid-1930s for further work on the sanctuary, including the important side altars of Our Lady and St Joseph. His tender of just under £4,500 was by far the lowest, the highest, at £13,850, coming from Messrs Mayer of Munich. That was in April 1935, but it was October of the following year before the first materials were delivered and late November before work on the sanctuary was resumed. Just before Christmas the chronicler noted that, 'work of decoration with mosaics progressed at Our Lady's altar'. Work on St Joseph's altar began on St Patrick's Day 1937 and was completed in late June, with the reservation that 'some parts had to be refitted and all have to be washed – before the rest of the church is painted', which it was, beginning in mid-August, by 'Morrow, the painter and decorator'.[14]

It was 1956 before the next phase of mosaicing began. On 29 July, 'In the church all around the walls nothing can be seen but scaffolding – and dust. ... the mosaics are going to cover all of the walls.' Then the Sacred Heart altar would be done; by early December 1959, it was just nearing completion. Meantime, the rest of the interior of the church was painted.[15]

Clerestory: The Gabriel Loire mosaics

The provincial administration under V Rev Michael Curran gave its approval in February 1961, 'to have the clerestory in Clonard mosaiced'. After months of negotiations with the French firm of Gabriel Loire of Chartres, M Loire came to Belfast and signed a contract on 4 February. The rector, Fr Loughnane, 'went to France by plane' in early November to inspect work in progress and came back a week later 'highly pleased'. The first consignment of mosaics arrived in Clonard on 5 December; two days later, the French workmen began their task and by early March 1962 the work was completed. The theme of the mosaics is, 'The Story of the Redemption from the Old and New Testaments'. Unfortunately, as Fr Patrick O'Donnell points out, these beautiful mosaics are 'little appreciated or understood'.[16] (See Appendix 3.)

Lighting

Given their location high in the nave of the church, the Loire mosaics required special illumination. The practical decision was taken to redesign the whole lighting system for the nave and aisles of the church. To this end, a special appeal was made in the autumn of 1961, 'at the close of each Holy Family retreat,' for funds. The appeal had 'a very gratifying result' of nearly £1,200, with more money expected. By mid-February 1962, the last of the chandeliers, which had hung from the nave arches since the church was opened in 1911, were removed. While this electrical work was going on, the opportunity was taken to replace the 1930s sound amplification system in the church, new 'oblong' speakers being placed 'just over the windows'. The system would be replaced yet again in the interior renovations of 1989.[17]

Interior changes

Apart from mosaicing, lighting and amplification, numerous alterations, big and small, decorative and functional, have been made to the interior of the church, particularly in the last fifty years.

The development of Our Lady's altar as a shrine has already been described in chapter nine. Possibly under the influence of the new St Gerard's Church on the Antrim Road, consecrated the previous December, the recently-appointed (September 1957) rector of Clonard, Charles McNiffe, decided it was time to do something for St Gerard's altar in Clonard. The decision was made to renovate the chapel in marble at an estimated cost of £3,900, the money to be 'donated by the confraternity'. Fr McNiffe got his approval from the provincial administration on condition that he should wait 'until collection was well under way and a substantial part of the money [was] well in hand'. By the end of January 1958, Fr McNiffe indicated that 'money [was] coming in', so permission was given for the work to go ahead.[18]

External renovations

There are numerous reminders in the Clonard record of the maintenance demands of the exterior of a large church. Thus, on 26 November 1962, the monastery chronicle recorded:

> Work has begun on [the] complete external renovation of the church. There has been so much deterioration and corrosion that this work was a necessity. Some stones are so dilapidated that they must be removed and other stones put in their places ... Finally, three coats of silicone will be applied to ensure against water infiltration.

From this period of the early 1960s there are also reminders of the kind of anti-social activities which added to the burden of maintenance. On a Monday morning in March 1963, the community awoke to find the doors of the church painted with offensive slogans. There was no particular evidence of malicious intent, though the domestic chronicle had noted at least three episodes of monastery windows being broken by stone throwers from the Cupar Street side in the previous six to twelve months. Another paint daubing episode was nipped in the bud in July 1966. There was no doubt then that the intention was malicious: ' ... a group of men were surprised by the police in an attempt to paint the doors of our church. They escaped, leaving behind them tins of paint and brushes.'[19]

Re-roofing the monastery

The next large scale maintenance operation to be recorded was the complete re-roofing of the monastery in February-March 1982. Described as 'a £50,000 job', the work was initially paid for by the provincial administration. But before March was out, two of the Clonard community were documented as busy raising the Clonard contribution:

> During these times, Frs John Bennett and Frank Burns have a daily chore of getting covenants to help pay for [the] re-roofing of [the] monastery. Their work has been singularly successful. In a few weeks, they have raised £25,000.[20]

Church facade

In the summer of 1985 it was the turn of the church facade. During July and August, the front of the church was cleaned and 'the rose window restored. In the window a lot of small glass had been broken or was disintegrating.' The work was carried out by the local firm, Caldermac, at a cost of over £9,000. Further works followed, including the construction of a new inner porch (which was to be further improved in 1989) and adjustments to the heating in the church. In the monastery, the community oratory was painted and, outside, the garden wall had to be rebuilt. All these works became the subject of yet another appeal for funds, made by the rector, Fr Enright, at all the Sunday Masses on 26 January 1986. Later that year, the Department of the Environment (Northern Ireland) declared Clonard ('monastery, church, gates and railings') a listed building, as of special architectural and historic interest.[21]

Church interior 1989

At the end of the 1980s, it was decided that the interior of the church needed renovation yet again. Local contractor Peter Woods was given the task, under the community's architect, J. J. Brennan,

> ... in ten weeks to paint the church ceiling, to clean the mosaics, rewire the church, improve the doors inside the porch, put down a non-slip ramp, install [a] new sound system, varnish all seats.

Work began in late March 1989 and was completed by 8 June, just one week before the solemn novena in honour of Our Lady of Perpetual Help. Weekday Masses were held in the monastery common room and confraternity meetings in Clonard Hall. The total cost was £180,000 of which Clonard had to meet one third.[22]

Lower tribune: crying room or chapel?

The tribunes, upper and lower, of Clonard church were originally designed as annexes to provide, on the one hand, quiet areas for private prayer and, on the other, overflow space at times of pressure on church accommodation. In 1973, it was decided to transform the lower tribune into a crying room. Depending on one's point of view, crying rooms were a questionable post-Vatican II fashion or a serious attempt to cope with the problem of noisy infants in church, particularly at Sunday Masses.

The crying room was to be put to another use in the mid-1980s. In the week of 11-19 February 1985, in an experiment 'motivated by a desire to save heating oil', the early morning weekday Masses, 6.30 am, 7.30 am and 8.30 am, were transferred from the church to the sacristy. At the same time, the chronicle carried the warning that the 'crying chamber' would be the next place of experiment and '[might] well become a normal early morning chapel [on] weekdays'. The church staff indeed decided that this should be so and on 26 March 'the first step' was taken with the laying of carpet.

The use of the 'crying chamber' appears to have continued for several years. The subject was not mentioned again until June 1988, when a poll was taken among those attending each of the early Masses, asking them to choose between the tribune and the church. Each group voted in favour of a return to the church, none more decisively than those attending the 6.30 am Mass; they voted forty-eight for the church, none for the tribune and seven had no strong preference.[23]

While in retrospect the whole matter may appear as a storm in a teacup, it does bring out very clearly the lack of a proper or adequate chapel within Clonard church. On the one hand, it was never foreseen that numbers attending even daily Mass in Clonard would fall so low as to require such an arrangement as was employed between 1985 and 1988. On the other, the absence of a chapel provided proof that Clonard was neither a basilica nor a cathedral.

Remodelling of the sanctuary

By far the biggest and certainly the most controversial of the alterations to the interior of Clonard church was the remodelling of the sanctuary, undertaken in 1992 during the rectorship of Fr John O'Donnell. Changes to the sanctuary date back to 1965, when a 'temporary altar on [the] sanctuary at which [the] celebrant said Mass facing the people' was installed, replaced in March 1978 by a more permanent altar, ambo and lectern, designed by the Belfast firm of McLean and Forte.[24]

In 1985 an extremely forceful document was prepared, presumably within Clonard community, which set forth various analyses of life in community and church. Something of the style of the document can be illustrated by its listing of furnishings in the church which, by its cumulative effect, made a devastating criticism of what had been allowed to happen:

> There are six shrines, six pictures of devotion, one relic, fifteen collection boxes, five devotional candle stands, a Way of the Cross, a petition/thanksgiving box. ... There are two prominent images to the B[lessed] V[irgin] M[ary]. The church is strong in golden colours and brass, objects that glitter. The strongest object of attraction is the Lady chapel, dominant in colour and light. The pulpit is dominant in the body of the church.

Putting it very bluntly, the widely regarded beautiful church of Clonard was in profound disagreement with what a church ought to be. The main points of the current view, shaped by church 'directives and instructions for renewal' were:

> 1. The location for the celebration of the Eucharist should be visually an expression of community gathered – communion, not division, positioning according to role of service as distinct from position of superiority.
>
> 2 The lectern/ambo should have equal expression of importance with the table of the Eucharist and ... all adornment should be to the centralising of attention to the sacrament of the Word and the Eucharist.
>
> 3 ... That the consecrated host or Blessed Sacrament should not be in reservation during the Eucharistic celebration ...[25]

For some of those within the community who were steeped in the Clonard tradition by early family association or by the fact of having spent much of their lives as Redemptorists in the monastery, this document was deeply shocking. Likewise, for those lay devotees of the monastery who, as the document acknowledged, still found in Clonard 'the old ways that have not changed', the implementation would be similarly disturbing. Fortunately for posterity, one of the community so offended by the suggestions of the document was the chronicler of these years, whose account of proceedings provides what we might call a traditionalist's riposte to the majority modernisers in the controversial restructuring of Clonard sanctuary.

A foretaste of the controversy to come was given in early September 1986. On the initiative of the church group of the community, that is, the group responsible for overseeing all matters related to Clonard church, the community agreed to the establishment of a liturgical committee which would include laymen. It also decided that 'the statue of the Infant Jesus will be removed from the altar-rails and the statue of St John Neumann and the picture of [Blessed] Peter Donders from the back of the church'. (The last two named were Redemptorists, Czech-American and Dutch respectively.) The chronicler penned his bitter commentary on the decision to remove the statue of the Infant Jesus:

> In the darkness of this day a statue was removed from the church which

many people loved. It was the statue of the Boy Jesus which was in a recess at the end of the altar rails facing St Joseph's altar. It had been given to us by the La Salle brothers. The statue was removed on 'liturgical grounds' by a majority vote of the church group, approved by a majority of the community. Fr X (named) spearheaded this act. Some members regretted very much this act. What harm was the Boy Jesus doing in his remote corner far from the activity that surrounded the altar? Where the lovely statue has gone we don't know. We highlight this removal of one small statue as it may be a pointer to what is to come, e.g., the removal of all statues from the sanctuary and of the altar rails. This is our idea of helping people come closer to God. Go dtugadh Dia ciall dúinn! (May God give us sense!)[26]

How right the chronicler was in seeing the removal of one small statue as a pointer 'to what is to come'! However, the plans for the sanctuary were slow in maturing and it was January 1992 before reconstruction finally began.[27] The chronicler kept a watching brief.

The altar rails were removed on 27 and 28 January. On 29 January, 'Pulpit partially demolished: nearly completely by 4 February.' This news was accompanied by a brief history of the pulpit, including the preachers of the first and last sermons from it (Fr Denis Turner, rector, on July 20th [1913] and Fr Peter Ward at the 9 pm Thursday novena on 30 January 1992), and the regret, 'It was a gem of a marble pulpit, none like it in Ireland.' By 26 February, the 'wooden base platform' of the extended sanctuary was completed and two days later, a new altar of Mourne granite put in place, which was first used for Mass on 8 March. Meantime, the altar, ambo and lectern erected in 1978 were 'removed, some say demolished'. Some three weeks before Easter 'the tapestry on the High Altar reredos was put in place', this tapestry covering the 'throne niche' over the tabernacle which had caused so much controversy when the church was being built. In the same week the carpeting of the sanctuary was completed. On Easter Tuesday, 21 April, the ambo was put in place; it is of brass, with the dove representing the Holy Spirit on front; its base is of Mourne granite. The celebrant's chair is of white American oak, as is the evangelarium.[28]

Finally, on 23 May 1992, a screen carrying four tapestry panels prefiguring the Eucharist, was put in place 'before the old high altar'. The panels represent respectively: Manna from Heaven (Exodus 16:14-15); Water from the Rock (Numbers 20:11); Marriage at Cana (John 2:6-9) and The Loaves and Fishes (Matthew 15:34-37). The chronicler gives a valuable commentary on the large central tapestry on the high altar reredos:

[It] is a symbol of the mysterious presence of God. You can see it as the burning bush or the descent of the Holy Spirit or the Resurrection of

Christ as the rising sun, or even a monstrance radiating the presence of God. We never actually see God, but we have a sense of his mysterious presence. The tapestry is meant to draw the eye towards the sacramental presence of Christ in the tabernacle just below.

All the tapestries were made of wool and designed and crafted by Erica Ryan. She dyed the wool herself in order to pick out the colours already in the church. Every single stitch she did by hand.[29]

It was a major programme indeed – and a costly one. First estimates were £36,000-£40,000. Actual final cost was £70,000. There is no record of a subsequent appeal to the Clonard faithful for funds.[30]

Other refurbishments

The early years of the 1990s were a busy period of refurbishment for both monastery and church grounds. An important break with the tradition of the monastic 'cell' was the provision of several rooms for elderly members of the community, each with en suite bathroom facilities. Outside, the perimeter wall of the Clonard campus on the Clonard Street side, which had been the boundary of the car park (created in the mid-1960s) and was in a sorry state, was rebuilt in time for the centenary. The impetus for this work came from the vicar, Fr Peter Burns who, as house manager, was responsible for the maintenance of church and monastery. The new wall was of Mourne granite and the considerable funding for the project was met largely by the Department of the Environment (the perimeter wall and gates being formally listed as part of the monastic complex) and by the 'Making Belfast Work' scheme.

Clonard and its donors

The remarkable generosity of those people attending the solemn novena in June 1989 serves as an appropriate reminder of the enduring loyalty and open-handedness of 'the people of Clonard' throughout the century. The first contributors in the 1890s were the mill-working women with their small contributions of hard-earned pennies and sixpences. Then there were the generous landed and business people who furnished the church – the Hamills, the Caffreys, the McGowans, the Kennedys, people like Miss Hodgson or those émigré 'Clonardites' who (themselves or their families) marked their attachment by generous gifts. Most important of all, perhaps, were the men and women of the confraternities, the novena-goers and the 'regulars' at Sunday and daily Masses and devotions. These were the people on whom the Clonard Redemptorists knew they could rely for both spiritual and material support.

Clonard church today

Controversy surrounded the changes to the interior of Clonard church which were intended to bring it more into harmony with recent theological and liturgical ideas on what a church building should be. Opinions will continue to differ not only on such fundamentals, but also on the success or otherwise of the changes in harmonising with what was already there. What is there is a beautiful neo-Gothic building, a product of its time and of the fine architectural gifts of J. J. McDonnell, MRIA. But above all, Clonard church is a place of prayer, a holy place, as numerous visitors have attested. Writing in the centenary booklet, the rector, Fr Kevin Browne, had this to say:

> ... over the past hundred years ... generations of people from Belfast and the surrounding area have come to Clonard to worship God through Christ, to pray through good times and bad, to make the novena to Our Lady of Perpetual Help, and to receive the Sacrament of Reconciliation. They have made this a holy place.[31]

BIBLIOGRAPHY

MANUSCRIPT SOURCES

The numerous documents in the manuscript sources are annotated in the references.

a) In Clonard Monastery
Clonard Domestic Archives
Clonard Domestic Chronicle
Clonard Monastery External Apostolate, 1896-1924 (Vol 1 Missionary Works)
Chronicle of the Holy Family Confraternity (1924 onwards)

b) In Liguori House, Dublin
Archives Dublin Province

PRINTED SOURCES

Works which were of particular help in the writing of this history are indicated in bold type.
Primary
a) Redemptorist
Clonard Monastery 1896-1996 100 Years of Service (1996), official centenary booklet.
Cummings, Daniel, C.Ss.R., 'A Mission in Ireland for Non-Catholics,' in *Irish Ecclesiastical Record,* 1948, pp 481-494
— 'Missions for Non-Catholics in Ireland,' in *Irish Ecclesiastical Record,* 1951, pp 3-24
Directory of the Apostolic Labours in the Irish Province of the Congregation of the Most Holy Redeemer (Limerick, 1927)
Mangan, C., C.Ss.R., *Clonard Confraternity of Our Lady of Perpetual Succour and St Alphonsus: A Short history of 30 Years* (Belfast, 1927)
Murphy, T. A., C.Ss.R., 'Mary's Perpetual Novena,' in *Irish Ecclesiastical Record,* 1947, pp 822-831
O'Donnell, Patrick, C.Ss.R., *Clonard Church and Monastery, 1896-1995* (Typescript, Clonard, 1996)
— *The Story of Clonard Choir* (Typescript, Clonard, 1987)
— *Clonard Church and Monastery* (n.d., but probably mid-1980s)
Report of the Committee for the Review of the Redemptorist Apostolate in the North of Ireland* (1989)
The Mission Book, Eleventh Revised Edition (Dublin, 1913)

b) Other
Cathechism of the Catholic Church (Dublin, 1994)

Gonzalez, J.L., C.S.P. and the Daughters of St Paul (Compilers), *The Sixteen Documents of Vatican II, with Commentaries by the Council Fathers* (Boston, 1967)

Official Report of Debates, Parliament of Northern Ireland (Commons), Vol. XXIII, 19 December 1939-18 February 1941

Violence and Civil Disturbances in Northern Ireland in 1969 – Report of Tribunal of Inquiry, Cmd. 566, HMSO, Belfast, (2 Vols), 1972. (Scarman Tribunal.)

Secondary

Bardon, Jonathan, *Belfast: An Illustrated History* (Belfast, 1982)

Bell, J. Bowyer, *The Secret Army: The IRA 1916-1979* (Dublin, 1979; pbk edition 1989)

Buckley, D. J., C.Ss.R., *The Miraculous Picture of the Mother of Perpetual Succour* (Cork, 1948)

Collins, Peter, *The Making of Irish Linen: Historic Photographs of an Ulster Industry* (Belfast, 1994)

Coogan, T. P., *The Troubles* (Dublin, 1995)

Corish, P. J., *The Irish Catholic Experience* (Dublin, 1985)

Gilbert, M., *Second World War* (Revised edition, pbk, London, 1990)

Gray, John, *City in Revolt: James Larkin and the Belfast Dock Strike of 1907* (Belfast, 1985)

Harkness, David, *Northern Ireland since 1922* (Dublin, 1983)

Harris, Mary, *The Catholic Church and the Foundation of the Northern Irish State* (Cork, 1993)

Hepburn, A.C., *A Past Apart: Studies in the History of Catholic Belfast 1850-1950* (Belfast, 1996)

Jones, Frederick M., C.Ss.R., *Alphonsus de Liguori, The Saint of Bourbon Naples, 1696-1787* (Dublin, 1992)

Lee, J. J., *Ireland 1912-1985: Politics and Society* (Cambridge, 1989)

Macaulay, Ambrose, *Patrick Dorrian, Bishop of Down and Connor, 1865-1885* (Dublin, 1987)

— *Dr Russell of Maynooth* (London, 1983)

McGrogan, T. J., *Sevastopol Street: A Local Study* (unpublished, 1996)

McKittrick, D., Kelters, S., Feeney, B., and Thornton, C., *Lost Lives: The stories of the men, women and children who died as a result of the Northern Ireland troubles* (Edinburgh, 1999)

Maillie, E. and McKittrick, D., *The Fight for Peace: The Inside Story of the Irish Peace Process* (London, 1996; paperback edition, 1997)

Phoenix, E., *Northern Nationalism: Nationalist Politics, Partition and the Catholic Minority in Northern Ireland, 1890-1940* (Belfast, 1994)

Sadie, Stanley (ed.), *The New Grove Dictionary of Music and Musicians,* (London, 1980), Vols 4, 10.

Sharp, John, *Reapers of the Harvest: The Redemptorists in Great Britain and Ireland, 1843-1898* (Dublin, 1989)

Two Hundred Years with the Redemptorists (Dublin, 1933)

Williams, N., *Chronology of the Modern World 1763-1965* (London, 1966, Penguin pbk, 1975)

REFERENCES

CHAPTER I: BEFORE CLONARD

1. Jones, Frederick M., C.Ss.R., *Alphonsus de Liguori, The Saint of Bourbon Naples, 1696-1787* (Dublin, 1992), p 8.
2. Ibid., pp 11-14, 62.
3. Ibid., pp 11, 13, 19-21.
4. Ibid., pp 35-37.
5. Ibid., pp 41-44.
6. Ibid., pp 25, 49-50, 62-65.
7. Ibid., pp 75-6, 78-88, 92-110.
8. Ibid., pp 214-223.
9. Ibid., pp 449-454, 463-4, 469 ff.
10. Ibid., pp 471-2.
11. Kerr, Hugo, C.Ss.R., 'Two Hundred Years with the Redemptorists,' in *Two Hundred Years with the Redemptorists* (Dublin, 1933), pp 11-12.
12. Sharp, John, *Reapers of the Harvest: The Redemptorists in Great Britain and Ireland, 1843-1898* (Dublin, 1989), pp 3-4.
13. Ibid., pp 5-8; Kerr, loc. cit., p 14.
14. Sharp (1989), pp 10-11.
15. Ibid., pp 20-22, 25, 241.
16. Ibid., pp 34, 245.
17. Ibid., pp 34-5, 42, 50-52.
18. Ibid., p 43; Kerr, loc.cit., p. 17.
19. Ibid., pp 51-58; Clonard Domestic Chronicle 1897, 1-5 November.
20. Corish, P. J., *The Irish Catholic Experience* (Dublin,1985), p 195.
21. Ibid., p 194.
22. Ibid., pp 193-4; Macaulay, Ambrose, *Dr Russell of Maynooth* (London, 1983), p 112.
23. Ibid., pp 194-7, 211-213.
24. Ibid., pp 214-5.
25. Ibid., pp 215-7. For a more measured view, see Macaulay, Ambrose, *Patrick Dorrian Bishop of Down and Connor 1865-1885* (Dublin, 1987), especially pp 113-130.
26. Ibid., pp 219-222.
27. Bardon, Jonathan, *Belfast: An Illustrated History* (Belfast, 1982), pp 128-30, 141-2, 175-6.
28. Ibid., pp 132-3.
29. Ibid., pp 123, 157.
30. Ibid., p 124; Collins, Peter, *The Making of Irish Linen: Historic Photographs of an Ulster Industry* (Belfast, 1994), p 21; O'Donnell, Patrick, C.Ss.R., *Clonard Church and Monastery, 1896-1995* (Typescript, Clonard 1996), p 10.
31. Ibid., pp 119-121; Collins (1994), p 20.
32. Ibid., pp 124-6, 139-141; O'Donnell (1996), p 10.
33. Ibid., p 126.

34. Hepburn, A.C., *A Past Apart: Studies in the History of Catholic Belfast 1850-1950* (Belfast, 1996), p 74-76.

35. Ibid., pp 76-77.

36..Bardon (1982), pp 157-8.

37. Harris, Mary, *The Catholic Church and the Foundation of the Northern Irish State* (Cork, 1993), pp 16-17.

38. Ibid., p 16; Hepburn (1996), pp 52-53.

39. Hepburn (1996), pp 9, 151-2.

40. Ibid., pp 58-61.

41. McGrogan, T. J., *Sevastopol Street: A Local Study* (unpublished, 1996).

CHAPTER 2: THE FOUNDATION OF CLONARD

1. O'Donnell, (1996), pp 8, 39.1. Patrick Griffith (1844-1926), born Mountmellick, county Laois; ordained priest of the diocese of Kildare and Leighlin and worked there as a curate until he entered the Redemptorists in 1881-2; master of novices at Bishop Eton, 1890-4; rector of Mt St Alphonsus, Limerick, 1894-97.

2. Macaulay, (1987), p 139; Archives Dublin Province (C1), Magnier to Griffith, 23 November 1896.

3. O'Donnell, (1996), p 8; Clonard Domestic Chronicle 1896; Archives Dublin Province (C3), 'Foundation of Redemptorist Monastery, Clonard, Belfast,' (1922), p 1.

4. O'Donnell, (1996), p 9; Sharp, (1989), p 57; O'Donnell, (1996), pp 9-10.

5. Clonard Domestic Chronicle, Vol I, pp 30-40, 'The History of the Enclosing of our Grounds from 1896 to 1899.' The account itself, which is signed, 'P. Griffith, Rector,' specifies that it carried the history up to February 1900. See Clonard Domestic Chronicle, 1904, August.

6. O'Donnell, (1996), p 11; Archives Dublin Province (C3), 'Foundation ...' (1922), p 1; Clonard Domestic Chronicle 1896.

7. O'Donnell, (1996), p 11.

8. Ibid., pp 17(a), 17(b).

9. Ibid; Clonard Domestic Chronicle 1896; Clonard Domestic Archives (A), under heading 'Received 1896-1911': Book of Receipts of the house of the Most Holy Redeemer, Belfast, opened 1 November 1896.

10. Quoted in O'Donnell, (1996), p 9.

11. O'Donnell, (1996), p 12.

12. Archives Dublin Province (C1), 'Copy of Contract between Dr Henry, bishop of Down and Connor and Most Rev Fr General regarding Foundation in Belfast, 21 November 1896'; Ibid. (C3), 'Foundation ... (1922),' p 5.

13. O'Donnell, (1996), pp 17(a), 17(b).

14. Ibid., p 21. Copy of bishop's letter in Clonard Domestic Archives (A). Mrs Ann Colgan has kindly supplied notes on J. J. McDonnell's father: he had studied architecture at Lisieux in France and had also been a pupil of Pugin (1812-52), the main champion of the Gothic revival. The McDonnell family home was named 'Lisieux'.

15. Clonard Domestic Chronicle 1897, April.
16. Ibid., May; O'Donnell, (1996), p 21.
17. Clonard Domestic Chronicle 1897, June, 29 July; 1898, 11 May, 19 June; O'Donnell, (1996), p 21.
18. Clonard Domestic Chronicle 1897, 2 August.
19. Ibid., 1898, 20 March.
20. Ibid., 27 May, 9 June, 15 August; cuttings from *Irish Catholic*, 4 June 1898 and *Irish News*, 16 August 1898.
21. *Irish Catholic*, 4 June 1898.
22. O'Donnell, (1996), pp 18-19.
23. Ibid., p 19.
24. Clonard Domestic Chronicle 1898, 2 May, July.
25. Ibid. 1903, January, March, including undated newspaper cutting, probably from the *Irish News*. Bishop's letter dated 23 January 1903.
26. Clonard Domestic Chronicle 1900, 17 August, 2 September.
27. Ibid. 1901, 29 December; 1902, September; 1903, September, 20 December; 1904, 1 January, 4, 8, 11 September, 27 December; 1905, 14 July.
28. Ibid. 1905, 14 July.

CHAPTER 3: FROM 'CATHOLIC DISSENSION' TO REDEMPTORIST REJOICING, 1904-1909
1. Clonard Domestic Chronicle 1908, 8 March.
2. Macaulay, (1987), p 122. Macaulay notes that Hughes employed 150 in his bakery and Ross 600 in his mill; Hepburn, A.C., *A Past Apart: Studies in the History of Catholic Belfast 1850-1950* (Belfast, 1996), pp 9, 131-4, 150-3, 158-160, 210-214; Phoenix, E., *Northern Nationalism: Nationalist Politics, Partition and the Catholic Minority in Northern Ireland, 1890-1940* (Belfast 1994), pp 3-4; Harris, Mary, *The Catholic Church and the Foundation of the Northern Irish State* (Cork, 1993), pp 19-20. It is Phoenix who asserts the close personal friendship between O'Donnell and Devlin. He further describes the bishop as, 'the chief episcopal protector' of the AOH.
3. Clonard Domestic Chronicle 1906, 15 July.
4. Ibid., 16, 18 January.
5. Ibid. 1905, 1-21 October. The account of the 'odious subject' takes up five closely written pages of the chronicle.
6. Macaulay, (1987), p 178; Clonard Domestic Chronicle 1906, 15 July.
7. Clonard Domestic Chronicle 1908, 8 March. The bracketed phrase is unclear in the chronicle, but seems to read, 'just qualities'.
8. Ibid., 11 March. The chronicle further notes here that Dr Laverty, the new vicar, 'at the instance of V Rev Fr Rector ... restored to our fathers the faculty of hearing confessions of the sick which the deceased Prelate had, without any sufficiently reasonable cause, restricted to cases of extreme necessity ...' This speedy restoration of faculties seems to support the suggestion that the matter of clerical supplies had been more than just a 'routine disciplinary adjustment' by Bishop Henry.
9. Ibid., 8 April.

10. Ibid., 20 September.

11. Ibid. 1909, 3 May. Fr Murray had been a Raphoe diocesan student at Maynooth before joining the Redemptorists.

12. Ibid., 19-20 September.

CHAPTER 4: BUILDING THE CHURCH

1. Clonard Domestic Chronicle 1906, 13 July.

2. Ibid., December.

3. Ibid., 1907, 5 August.

4. Ibid., 13 August.

5. Gray, John, *City in Revolt: James Larkin and the Belfast Dock Strike of 1907* (Belfast, 1985), pp 154 ff.

6. Clonard Domestic Chronicle 1907, 13 August.

7. Ibid., 5 August, 29 November.

8. Ibid. 1908, 4 October.

9. Ibid.

10. Ibid. 1909, 18 July.

11. O'Donnell (1996), p 27; Archives Dublin Province (C3), 'Foundation ...,' (1922), p 6; Clonard Domestic Chronicle 1910, 21 May.

12. Clonard Domestic Chronicle 1910, 11 July.

13. Archives Dublin Province, Folder entitled, 'Clonard Building, miscellaneous,' J. J. McDonnell to V Rev Fr Provincial, 7 October 1910.

14. Ibid., P. Murray, Rector Major, to P. Griffith, Provincial, 3 November 1910.

15. Ibid., Berghman to Provincial, 9 November 1910; McDonnell to Provincial, 21 November 1910; Davis to Provincial, 23 and 25 November 1910; Provincial to Davis, 24 and 27 November 1910.

16. Clonard Domestic Chronicle 1909, 25 January.

17. Archives Dublin Province (C3), 'Foundation ...' (1922). 'The church is designed in early French Gothic. It consists of nave and aisles with shallow transepts and semi-circular apse and side chapels. The nave is 151 feet long and 70 feet wide. The height from nave floor to the apex of the roof is 60 feet. ...Octagonal turrets rising to a height of 100 feet flank the entrance.' The rose window is 22 feet in diameter. See O'Donnell (1996), p 31.1.

18. Ibid., Folder entitled, 'Clonard Building, miscellaneous,' O'Laverty to Provincial, 24 August 1911.

19. Clonard Domestic Chronicle 1911, 27 August.

20. Archives Dublin Province, Folder entitled, 'Clonard Building, miscellaneous,' O'Laverty to Provincial, 24 August 1911.

21. Clonard Domestic Chronicle 1911, 6 September.

22. Ibid., April-May.

23. Ibid., 11 October.

24. Ibid. 1912, 12 March.

25. Archives Dublin Province, O'Byrne to Griffith, 23 August 1909.

26. Ibid., O'Byrne to Griffith, 23 October 1909.

27. O'Donnell (1996), p 30.

28. Clonard Domestic Chronicle 1911, 1 October.

29. Ibid. 1937, June-August.

30. Ibid. 1911, November.

31. Ibid.

32. Louis Paul-Dubois, *Contemporary Ireland* (Dublin, 1908), quoted in Corish (1985), p 237.

33 Archives Dublin Province, folder entitled, 'Clonard Organ,' J. Cleere to V Rev Fr Provincial, 31 Decamber 1909.

34. Ibid., H. Evans to de Meulemeester, 20 September 1910.

35. Ibid., De Meulemeester to Provincial, 6 September 1910.

36. Ibid., Murray to Griffith, no date.

37. Clonard Domestic Chronicle 1909, 25 November.

38. Archives Dublin Province, folder entitled, 'Clonard Organ,' Cleere to Provincial, 1 January 1910; P. Crotty to Provincial, 10 January 1910.

39. Ibid., Cleere to Provincial, 1 and 14 January 1910.

40. Ibid., Cleere to Provincial, 9 January 1910; Crotty to Provincial 10 January 1910.

41. Ibid., J. J. McGarry (6 McAlinden Terrace, Falls Road) to Provincial, 23 May 1911, enclosing a resolution of the organ committee; John McGinley to Fr Collins, 14 June 1912; *The New Grove Dictionary of Music and Musicians*, ed. Stanley Sadie (London 1980), Vol. 4, p. 800; Carnegie Trust Internet Website. 'Carnegie Organ Grants' were the first scheme under the Carnegie United Kingdom Trust (1913) by which organs were installed in about 3,500 churches and chapels in Great Britain. In June 1912, the Clonard committee enlisted the help of Joe Devlin, the local MP. As the then secretary, John McGinley, wrote, 'Mr Devlin is a great admirer of the Redemptorist order and I know it will not be his fault if he fails in extracting a substantial cheque from the multi-millionaire.'

42. Clonard Domestic Chronicle 1911, 12-13 July.

43. Archives Dublin Province, folder entitled, 'Clonard Organ,' John McGinley to Fr M. Collins, 18 January, 26 April, 14 June 1912.

44. *Irish News*, 26 May 1912; Clonard Domestic Chronicle 1912, 19 May.

CHAPTER 5: EARLY EXTERNAL APOSTOLIC LABOURS FROM CLONARD

1. Clonard Domestic Archives (H), *Directory of the Apostolic Labours in the Irish Province of the Congregation of the Most Holy Redeemer* (Limerick, 1927); see especially p 26. There is also in the Clonard archive a 1959 edition; between them, they record the history of the *Directory*. The practice whereby the chronicler wrote up the mission reports continued until the late 1950s, when his duties were reduced to indexing and filing the report forms, since according to the 1959 edition of the *Directory*, 'they, and not the Chronicle-book which has hitherto been in use, will in future form the permanent Chronicle of Missions and Retreats'.

2 Ibid., 'Clonard Monastery External Apostolate, 1896-1924 (Vol I Missionary Works).'

3 For ease of reference, the early missions from Clonard and others referred to in the text are listed here by alphabetical order of parishes in which conducted; they

are recorded chronologically in 'Clonard Monastery External Apostolate, 1896-1924 (Vol. I Missionary Works)'. All parishes were in Down and Connor diocese, unless otherwise stated (in brackets):

Ahoghill/Cullybackey: 1905, 16-30 July; renewal 1906, 24 June-1 July; 1920, 16-23 May.

Ballygalget: 1897, 10-17 October; 1899, May.

Ballymena: 1901, 9-16 January; 1902, 25 May-1 June (both retreats).

Bellaghy/Ballyscullion (Derry): 1901, 20 October-3 November.

Beragh (Armagh): 1901, June; renewal 1902, 22-29 June.

Buncrana (Raphoe): 1920, 13 June-4 July.

Carnlough: 1900, 20-27 May; renewal 1901, 19-26 May.

Carrickfergus: 1897, October.

Clogher (Clogher): 1900, 13-29 May.

Coleraine: 1897, 20 November-12 December.

Crossgar: 1899, 17-30 September; renewal 1900, (no date).

Culfeightrin: 1897, 15-29 August; renewal 1898, 2-16 October.

Downpatrick: 1901, 28 April-12 May.

Drumquin (Derry): 1902, 1-15 June; renewal 1903, (no date).

Dungiven/Drumsurn (Derry): 1900, 1-22 July; 1905, 30 July-20 August.

Glenarm: 1903, 3-17 May.

Glenravel: 1900, 20-27 May; renewal 1901, 6-13 May.

Glenties (Raphoe): 1902, (no date).

Killyleagh: 1899, 29 October-2 November; renewal 1900, (no date).

Larne: 1898, 8-22 May; 1901, 19 May-2 June.

Ligoniel: 1898, (no date); renewal 1899, (no date, but April or May).

Moneymore (Armagh): 1898, 23 October-6 November.

Newcastle: 1902, 25 May-8 June.

Newry (Dromore): 1901, 17 February-10 March.

Portaferry: 1899, 15 June-2 July; renewal 1899, 10-17 December; 1901 April retreat.

Portglenone: 1898, 22 May-5 June.

Portrush/Bushmills: 1898, 6-16 March; 1901, 3-13 March.

Randalstown: 1900, 25 February-4 March (retreat).

Rasharkin: 1900, 27 May-10 June; renewal 1901, 2-9 June.

Strabane (Derry): 1899, 1-22 October; renewal 1900, 3-10 June.

Termon (Raphoe): 1903, (no date, but July or August).

Toomebridge: 1905, 8-22 October.

Tullylish/Gilford (Dromore): 1903, 14-28 June.

Whitehouse: 1898, 22 May-5 June.

Belfast city parishes:

Holy Family: 1899, 28 May-4 June (retreat).

St Mary's, Chapel Lane: 1897, 11-17 October; 1898, 15-21 August, for St Vincent de Paul Society (both retreats).

St Patrick's: 1897, 3-10 October; 1901, (no date, March?); 1902, 7-12 May (retreats).

St Paul's: 1899, 1-22 October (mission held in Clonard church).

St Peter's: 1897, 18-24 October; 1901, 10-17 March (retreats).

4. The Redemptorist view of annual retreats was expressed even more strongly on a later occasion, at the Waterside in Derry in 1940, where, they believed, 'annual retreats have become a kind of superstition'.
5 After the Second Vatican Council II, the tone of the 'Mission Remembrance' changed quite dramatically from the strongly didactic, black or white, heaven or hell choices of the traditional format to a more inclusive and humane style.
6. Occasionally the 'Mission Remembrance' appeared as a six-page leaflet, of a slightly smaller page size. The six-page format may have been used exclusively for a bilingual version of the 'Remembrance' which certainly appeared during the 1910s and 1920s. There are two surviving examples in the Clonard archives, one dated October 1917 and commemorating a mission given in Clonard itself, the other dated 1925 and recalling a Redemptorist mission in St Malachy's parish, Coleraine. In these examples, some of the prayers are given in both English and Irish, which would reflect the considerable interest shown by the Clonard community at that time in the Irish language and its revival.
7. By 1891, *The Mission Book* had run to a fourth revised edition in Ireland and, by 1913, to an eleventh revised edition and had become a very substantial volume of over 700 pages. Details from copy of 1913 edition in Clonard Domestic Archives.
8. Sharp (1989), p 149.

CHAPTER 6: 1920S TO 1940S

1. Clonard Domestic Chronicle 1921, 9-12 July, July.
2. See Phoenix (1994), pp 391-3.
3. Harris (1993), pp 260-1; Lee, J. J., *Ireland 1912-1985: Politics and Society* (Cambridge, 1989), p 12.
4. Phoenix (1994), pp 87-88; Clonard Domestic Chronicle 1921, July (giving retrospective view of the summer of 1920); 1920, 22 July; Harris (1993), p 84.
5. Phoenix (1994), pp 88-89; Clonard Domestic Chronicle 1920, 24 September.
6. Clonard Domestic Chronicle 1921, 25 May, June, 9-12 July; Phoenix (1994), p 190. John Duffin, a prominent supporter of Michael Collins, subsequently organised the northern teachers' 'non-recognition' of the northern government when their salaries were paid by the provisional government in Dublin.
7. Ibid., 9-12 July.
8. Ibid., 17 July.
9. Ibid., August. Harris (1993), pp 259-60. Bishop Joseph MacRory, (bishop of Down and Connor 1915-28; archbishop of Armagh 1928-45; cardinal 1929), was, like his predecessor John Tohill, a deeply compassionate pastoral bishop, quick to the defence of his flock when they were the victims of sectarian attacks. During the worst years 1920-22, MacRory's pastoral concern, personal courage and financial generosity were unquestionable. His statements gained widespread publicity and brought him so many death threats that he had to abandon his residence, Trench House, Andersonstown, for the comparative safety of St Malachy's College on the Antrim Road. Trench House was, in the early 1920s, quite remote from Belfast and in 'hostile territory'.

10. Clonard Domestic Chronicle 1922, 10 July.

11. Ibid; Harris (1993), pp 132-3.

12. Phoenix (1994), p 399.

13. Clonard Domestic Chronicle 1935, 12 July. This sole reference to the 1935 riots reads (the hospital referred to was clearly the Mater Infirmorum): 'Fr G. Reynolds, while giving the Retreat to the sisters of Mercy at Crumlin Road, assisted between fifteen and twenty victims of the riots on 12 July. Between 8 and 9 pm he was the only priest available and there were only five medical attendants. No priests or doctors could approach the hospital from abroad. One woman, Mrs Broderick, shot through the lung died before two hours a most edifying death – 28 years of age.'

14. Clonard Domestic Chronicle 1939, 29 August; Gilbert, M., *Second World War* (Revised edition, pbk. London 1990), p 1.

15. Ibid., 2, 6, 10 September.

16. Bell, J. Bowyer, *The Secret Army: The IRA 1916-1979* (Dublin 1979; pbk edition 1989), p 169; Clonard Domestic Chronicle 1939, 4 September.

17. Gilbert (1990), p 101; Harkness, David, *Northern Ireland since 1922* (Dublin 1983), p 85.

18. Clonard Domestic Chronicle 1940, 16 September, 25, 26 October, 14 December.

19. Ibid. 1941, 8, 10 April; Harkness (1983), p 86.

20. Ibid., 15 April; Chronicle of the Holy Family Confraternity 1941, Easter: 'A terrible blitz on Easter Tuesday night from 11 pm to 4 am ...'; Harkness (1983), p 86.

21. Harkness (1983), p 87; Clonard Domestic Chronicle 1941, 5, 7, 8, 9 May, 23 July.

22. 'Clonard Monastery External Apostolate, 1896-1924 (Vol I Missionary Works)', 1941, 22-24 April, 4-11 May.

23. Chronicle of the Holy Family Confraternity 1939, September; 1940, 2 September.

24. Ibid. 1941, May, 30 June-1 July, 8 September.

25. Ibid. 1940, 15 September; 1941, 7-8 July; 1942, 16 February; 1945, May.

26. Ibid. 1942, 12 October; 1943, 4-5 January; 1944, Holy Thursday night.

27. Ibid. 1943, 13, 20 September; 1944, 23, 27 August, 11-18 September; Williams, N., *Chronology of the Modern World 1763-1965* (London 1966, Penguin pbk. 1975), p 592; Gilbert (1990), p 580. Florence was liberated on 19 August, Paris on 25-26 August.

28. Archives Dublin Province (C 11), a four-page printed notice of 'A Service of Remembering in Clonard Church, Belfast, April 15/16 1991 of those killed, those bereaved and those who risked their lives in the blitz of 1941.'

29. Ibid., Folder entitled, 'Clonard building, miscellaneous, 1910-60,' Murray, Curia Generalizia, Roma, to Kerr, Limerick, 20 January, 1945. About the original plans for the church, Murray commented, 'there were two insuperable difficulties, the pond (see Chapter 2) and the bishop' (see Chapter 4). He also revealed that he had himself made plans to extend the church, 'by another arch and pillar,' as in the original, but he had had, 'little hope that any bishop would ever allow it'.

30. Chronicle of the Holy Family Confraternity 1945, 26, 27 March, 16, 17 April (first church extension collection); 1946, 28, 29 January; 1949, 31 January, 1, 2, February.

31. O'Donnell, P., C.Ss.R., 'The Life of Father Hugo Kerr, C.Ss.R., 1895-1986,' in *Search*, vol 3, no 2, December 1986, p 12: Fr Kerr had hoped to start enclosed retreats in the south, but finally asked Fr G. Reynolds to approach Dr Mageean for permission to begin in his diocese; Clonard Domestic Archives (G), 'House Consultations 1916-1950,' 1946, 1947, various dates monthly from 24 April to 18 December 1946 and March 1947; Clonard Domestic Chronicle 1946, 16 October. Dr George Rice of Ardglass has kindly supplied notes on the Beauclerk Estate. The erection of the hut 'as allowed by the Ministry' at a cost of around £400 was agreed in March (1947).
32. Clonard Domestic Chronicle 1947, 18 May. The chronicler noted that the young men kept the silence 'very well'.
33. Ibid., 6 July, 31 August.
34. Ibid., 2 October.
35. Ibid. 1948, date uncertain, but probably late summer; entry precedes 25 September.
36. Ibid. 1951, 21 June; 1953, 22 February.
37. Ibid. 1954, 21-22 August.
38. Ibid. 1960, 23 August; 1961, 5 February.
39. Ibid. 1961, 12 February.

CHAPTER 7: CONFRATERNITIES I
1. Archives Dublin Province (C 1), Magnier to Griffith, 23 November 1896.
2. (Mangan, C., C.Ss.R.), *Clonard Confraternity of Our Lady of Perpetual Succour and St Alphonsus: A Short history of 30 Years* (Belfast, 1927), p 5; Chronicle of the Holy Family Confraternity 1950, October. (On the title page of his *Short History*, Fr Mangan identifies himself by his initials in Irish: 'C.Ó M., C.Ss.R., do scríobh.'
3. Chronicle of the Holy Family Confraternity 1924, 27, 28 October; 1925, January.
4. Ibid. 1932, November (the director was Fr James Reynolds); 1949, March.
5. Clonard Domestic Chronicle 1909, 13 February; Chronicle of the Holy Family Confraternity 1936, 20, 21 July; 1947, July.
6. Chronicle of the Holy Family Confraternity 1925, May, June; 1949, 23-25 May (the director in 1949 was Fr Seán O'Loughlin.)
7. Ibid. 1937, 27 September.
8. Ibid. 1933, April; 1935, June.
9. Ibid. 1936, 12 January, 29 June, October, November; 1955, 11 January (when Fr Michael Connolly wrote, 'I have been unable to discover whether this is the tradition or not.' That is, whether the usual high Mass was for the intentions of the confraternity men); 1956, January.
10. Ibid. 1956, 24 January; 1957, 27 January; 1958, 29-31 December; 1959, 23-25 February.
11. Ibid. 1949, 1 April; 1957, 20-22 May; 1958, January; 1952, 7-9 January. The Young Christian Workers movement (known in continental Europe as Jocists) was founded in Belgium after the First World War by Fr Joseph Cardijn (1882-1967) and was given formal approval by Pope Pius XI in 1925. (See website of Irish YCW: www.iol.ie/~ycw).

12. Ibid. 1931, August, including undated cutting from the *Irish News*.
13. Ibid. 1965, 25 January.
14. Ibid. 1931, February.
15. Ibid. 1933, July.
16. Clonard Domestic Chronicle 1926, May, June; Chronicle of the Holy Family Confraternity 1926, May, June, July.
17. Ibid.
18. Mangan (1927), pp 19-22; Chronicle of the Holy Family Confraternity 1926, May, June, July.
19. Chronicle of the Holy Family Confraternity 1951, 10 June. The 'pace-maker' for the procession was Mr Frank McCrory who 'had done this job very well on several occasions'.

CHAPTER 8: CONFRATERNITIES 2: GROWTH AND DECLINE

1. Mangan (1927), pp 8-9.
2. Ibid., pp 9-10.
3. Ibid., p 12.
4. Ibid., pp 13-14.
5. Ibid., pp 16-19.
6. Ibid., pp 22-26.
7. Chronicle of the Holy Family Confraternity 1924, Introductory.
8. Ibid. and 26 October.
9. Ibid., 1930, 11, 18 May (number on roll, 1930, was 4,327); 1933, October (boys' general communion 1933: 1,751); 1936, April, May (boys' general communion 1936: 1,129).
10. Ibid., 1936, April, May, 15-16 December; 1938, September.
11. Ibid., 1940, 15 September, with undated cutting from *Irish News*. The matter was certainly raised at Stormont by T. J. Campbell, KC, the Nationalist MP for Cromac, on 19 November 1940. Campbell was acting on information supplied to him by the Society of St Vincent de Paul, whose funds were being drawn upon by the families of such men. The Minister of Labour, John F. Gordon, disputed Campbell's claims. The regulations governing payments to such men were so complicated as to make political rebuttal of any claim easy. See *Official Report of Debates, Parliament of Northern Ireland (Commons)*, Vol XXIII, 19 December 1939-18 February 1941, cols 2603-4.
12. Ibid., 1944, 11-18 September; 1945, 15, 29, 30 October; 1946, 14 February, 18 April.
13. Ibid., 1946, 18 April, 8, 13, 14, 15 May.
14. Ibid., 1947, 14 April, 18-20, 31 August, with six pages of cuttings from newspapers, mainly *Irish News* and *Irish Weekly and Ulster Examiner*; many photographs and accounts of speeches.
15. Ibid., 1950, October; 1951, March, June.
16. Ibid., 1960, 29 February; 1964, early in year. Unfortunately, there is no further reference to this division.
17. Ibid., 1957, 17-19, 24-26 June.

18. Ibid., 10-12 June; commemorative booklets: *Diamond Jubilee 1897-1957 Clonard Holy Family Confraternity* and *Diamond Jubilee Archconfraternity of Our Lady of Perpetual Succour and St Alphonsus Clonard.*

19. Ibid., 1950, 1 January.

20. Ibid., 1963, October; 1950, November; 1964, beginning of year.

21. Ibid., 1964, Holy Thursday, December; 1966, January; 1968, 27 October; Clonard Domestic Chronicle 1968, December.

22. Clonard Domestic Chronicle 1969, 15, 21, 27 August.

23. Chronicle of the Holy Family Confraternity 1970, May.

24. Clonard Domestic Chronicle 1972, September, October.

25. Ibid., 10, 17 October; Archives Dublin Province (C 18), 'Report for Provincial Chapter: Clonard September 1972-May 1975'.

26. Clonard Domestic Chronicle 1973, 31 August, October; 1977, 31 December; 1978, 27 October; 1979, 4 October.

27. Ibid., 1981, 5-11 October; 1982, March, 16 May.

28. Ibid., 1982, 4-10 October; 1990, 1-7 October; 1994, September; 1988, 18 September.

29. Ibid., 1983, 28 April-1 May, 5-8 May, 5-18 September; 1985, 5 November; 1988, 5-11 September.

30. Clonard Domestic Archives (L). This booklet is found among miscellaneous documents relating to the Holy Family Confraternity. The men's director at the time of its publication was Fr Gerry Reynolds.

CHAPTER 9: THE PERPETUAL NOVENA
IN HONOUR OF OUR LADY OF PERPETUAL SUCCOUR

1. See *Cathechism of the Catholic Church* (Dublin, 1994), paragraphs 954-9, 962, 963, 971, pp 218-222.

2. Murphy, T. A., C.Ss.R., 'Mary's Perpetual Novena,' in *Irish Ecclesiastical Record* 1947, p 826.

3. Buckley, D. J., C.Ss.R., *The Miraculous Picture of the Mother of Perpetual Succour* (Cork 1948), pp 28-9. When the words 'miraculous' or 'miracle' are used in relation to images, the words imply an appeal only to human evidence. There is no suggestion of formal investigation or approval by the church.

4. See Buckley (1948), pp 71-77 for details.

5. Ibid., p 77.

6. Ibid., pp 29-30.

7. Clonard Domestic Chronicle 1943, 15 October.

8. Ibid., 17 October; Clonard Domestic Archives (K 2), manuscript account by Fr T. J. Regan, C.Ss.R., rector; O'Donnell. Patrick, C.Ss.R., article in the Irish Redemptorist journal *Reality*, June 1993, marking fifty years of the perpetual novena.

9. Ibid., 29 November.

10. Ibid., 9 December; Murphy, T. A., C.Ss.R., loc. cit., pp 822-831.

11. Ibid., 9 December; 1944, 20 January, 3 February, 17, 20, 23 April, 4 May; Murphy, loc. cit., p. 830; O'Donnell, Patrick, C.Ss.R., Ms. notes in Clonard Domestic Archives (K 2).

12. Clonard Domestic Chronicle 1947, 13 October.
13. Ibid., 1948, 28 January, 20 June; 1947, 22 June.
14. Magee, Malachy, 'A Miracle of Modern Belfast,' in *Clonard's New Shrine, Souvenir Booklet,* 1949, see Clonard Domestic Archives (K 2).
15. Clonard Domestic Chronicle 1949, 25 August, 5, 8, 9 September.
16. Ibid., 1950, August, 1 November (cuttings from *Irish News,* no date, but late August 1950) and 2 November. No details are given about the other bishops, apart from the fact that one was from South Africa and the other from Bangalore in India.
17. Clonard Domestic Chronicle 1954, 7 October; 1947, 4 November.
18. Ibid., 1956, 10 June, 29 November; 1957, 29 November; 1958, 2 February; 1963, 30 November.
19. Ibid., 1965, 18 June.
20. Ibid., 1973, 6 December; 1976, 4 July, 15 October; 1977, 27 June.
21. Clonard Domestic Archives (K 9), 'Solemn Novena 1971-1983, A Report on the Solemn Novena Apostolate prepared for Father General by Members of the Novena Team, Mount St Alphonsus, Limerick, January 1983'; Clonard Domestic Chronicle 1979, 17 July.
22. Clonard Domestic Chronicle 1979, 17 July.
23. Ibid., 1980, 1 June, 1 July.
24. Ibid., 1981, 3 June; 1978, 1 January.
25. Ibid., 1983, 18-26 June; 1981, June.
26. Clonard Domestic Chronicle. See entries for month of June in years 1984, 1982, 1985, 1988, 1989, 1990-2, 1994 and 1996. Note: In 1984 the solemn novena was rescheduled from a Saturday-to-Sunday week to a Wednesday-to-Thursday week. The earlier arrangement, encompassing two Sundays, had long been an irritant to many city parish priests as diminishing their congregations – and collections.
27. Ibid., 1984, June, 16, 20 October; 1996, June.
28. Ibid., 1984, June.
29. Ibid. See entries for month of June in years 1993-6 inclusive.
30. Ibid., 1985, 18 June; 1993, June.
31. Ibid., 1989, June.
32. Ibid., 1973, 6 December; 1984, 4, 5 February; 1993, 21 January.

CHAPTER 10: MISSION TO NON-CATHOLICS

1. The contents of this chapter rely heavily on two articles by Fr Daniel Cummings, C.Ss.R., published in the *Irish Ecclesiastical Record* as follows: i) 'A Mission in Ireland for Non-Catholics,' (5th Series, Vol xxx), June 1948, pp 481-494, which gave an account of the first such mission held during Lent 1948; ii) 'Missions for Non-Catholics in Ireland,' 1951, pp 3-24, which traced the course of the second to fifth missions, inclusive.
2. *Irish Ecclesiastical Record* 1948, p 482.
3. Ibid., pp 482-3.
4. Ibid., p 483.

5. Ibid., pp 483-4.
6. Ibid., p 484.
7. Ibid., p 486.
8. Ibid., p 487.
9. Ibid., p 488.
10. Ibid., p 490.
11. Ibid., p 492.
12. Ibid.
13. Ibid., p 494.
14. *Irish Ecclesiastical Record*, 1951, p 5.
15. Ibid., pp 4-5.
16. *Irish Ecclesiastical Record*, 1948, p 488.
17. *Irish Ecclesiastical Record*, 1951, pp 6-7.
18. Ibid., p 8.
19. Ibid., p 9.
20. Ibid., pp 9-10.
21. Ibid., p 10.
22. Ibid., p 11. The Redemptorist communication with the National Union of Protestants is treated in some detail in pp 11-16.
23. Ibid., pp 11-12.
24. Ibid., p 15.
25. Ibid., pp 13-14.
26. Ibid., pp 14-15.
27. Ibid., p 15.
28. Ibid., pp 17-18.
29. Ibid., p 22.
30. Ibid.
31. Ibid., pp 23-4.
32. Clonard Domestic Chronicle 1950, 12 November; 1952, 2 November.
33. Ibid., 1966, November.
34. Ibid., 1967, November. Participating choirs were: Belfast Gaelic and St Malachy's Old Boys'. November 1968 was the last occasion on which the new-style lectures for non-Catholics were held.
35. See ibid., 1952, 2 November; 1956, 25 November.
36. Ibid., 1956, 8 September.
37. Ibid., 1965, April, 31 October.
38. Ibid., 1966, 2 June, 15 July.
39. Ibid., 1977, 31 December.

CHAPTER II: ECUMENISM AT CLONARD

1. Clonard Domestic Chronicle 1961, late February, 5 May. (February entries include cuttings from three newspapers, the *Irish Independent*, the *Irish Press* and the *Irish News*.)
2. Ibid., 1962, 16 January.
3. Ibid., 1980, 25 January.

4. Clonard Domestic Archives (K): 'An Account of the Ecumenical Efforts being made by the Redemptorist community at Clonard Monastery,' a ten-page type-script dated March 15th 1981, bearing the name of Jim Lynn, 'Chairman, Thursday Evening Clonard Bible Group' and signed by Christopher McCarthy, C.Ss.R.

5. Ibid., 'Clonard Apostolate for Unity': A densely-written five-page manuscript, an undated letter of Fr Christopher McCarthy to his confrère Fr John Casey in Mount St Alphonsus, Limerick. It deals with the beginnings of the Clonard Bible Group, contacts with All Saints, Dulwich and significant individuals. It carries a personal note: 'The meeting together of Cath[olic] and Prot[estant] is very essential for progress of unity. We find this is so in daily life up here.'

6. Ibid., 'An Account ...' (1981).

7. Clonard Domestic Chronicle 1980, 22 April.

8. Ibid., 1981, 24 January; Clonard Domestic Archives (K): 'An Account ...' (1981). The account mentions the singing at the ecumenical service and vigil, by Mrs Pearl Page, of hymns composed by her late father, Rev William Hendron, who founded the Church of Christ in Berlin Street, Shankill Road.

9. Ibid., 1982, 19 November.

10. Ibid., 1 February; 1983, 18-25 January, 28 July (which contains a cutting from the *Irish News* of 16 August, an obituary notice of Fr McCarthy.)

11. Ibid., 1983, 28 July.

12. Ibid., 22 May.

13. Ibid., 1984, 8-12 October; 1983, 18 January (which includes a copy of the letter of invitation, dated 1 December 1982 and signed, 'George Wadding, Rector; Christopher McCarthy, Reconciliation Director'); 1985, 11-12 November; 1986, January; 1987, 18-25 January.

14. Ibid., see January entries for 1984-88 inclusive.

15. Clonard Domestic Archives (K): Miscellaneous documents relating to Shankill-Falls Fellowship.

16. Clonard Domestic Chronicle 1990, 2 December; 1992, 11 September.

17. Ibid., 1985, 11-13 February.

18. Clonard Domestic Archives (K): Report from Fr Gerry Reynolds.

19. Ibid., Miscellaneous documents relating to Shankill-Falls Fellowship, including minutes of meetings held in 1988.

20. Clonard Domestic Chronicle 1988, 27 October; 1989, 18 January.

21. Ibid., 1986, 6 August, 3 September; see January entries for 1988-95 inclusive.

22. Clonard Domestic Chronicle, see January entries for 1990-91.

23. Ibid., see January entries for relevant years.

24. Ibid., 1983, 31 August.

25. Ibid., 1984, 3 January, June; 1987, January; 1989, 12 December; 1993, 9 November.

26. Clonard Domestic Archives (K): Minutes of Shankill-Falls Fellowship meeting, February, 1988.

27. Clonard Domestic Chronicle 1986, 18 November; 1988, Good Friday.

28. Ibid., 1993, 23 May; 1994, 19 May.

29. Wadding, George, C.Ss.R., 'Looking Back – A few personal reflections on my years in Belfast' in *Pace*, Vol. 17, No. 3, 1985-6, pp 6-8. Fr Wadding had written to Bishop Daly in 1983 to ask his approval of 'some help' from Clonard to Lagan College. (See Clonard Domestic Archives (P 14), 23 October 1983.)

CHAPTER 12: MUSIC IN CLONARD CHURCH

1. O'Donnell (1996), p 46.
2. O'Donnell, Patrick, C.Ss.R., *The Story of Clonard Choir* (Typescript, Clonard, 1987), pp 1-2.
3. *The New Grove Dictionary of Music and Musicians*, ed. Stanley Sadie (London 1980), Vol 10, p 654; Clonard Domestic Chronicle 1912, 26 May. Lemmens' influence spread into France through the success of several of his pupils, the most famous of whom was Charles-Marie Widor (1844-1937), whose compositions for organ still attract a wide audience.
4. Quoted in O'Donnell (1987), pp 2-3.
5. Ibid., p 3.
6. Clonard Domestic Chronicle 1910, 21 May; 1911, 25 May; 1912, 14 February.
7. Chronicle of Clonard Holy Family Confraternity 1924, 26 October; Clonard Domestic Archives (M 5-6), De Meulemeester to Murray, 28 November 1924. All the letters in the dispute are substantial pieces, the last one, from de Meulemeester to the provincial, running to nearly 2,000 words.
8. Clonard Domestic Archives (M 5-6), De Meulemeester to Murray, 28 November 1924.
9. Ibid., De Meulemeester to Provincial (Hartigan), February 1925.
10. Ibid., Coogan to Provincial, 15 December 1924; De Meulemeester to Murray, 28 November 1924; De Meulemeester to Provincial, February 1925.
11. Ibid., De Meulemeester to Murray, 28 November 1924; Coogan to Provincial, 16 February 1925.
12. Ibid., De Meulemeester to Provincial, February 1925; Coogan to Provincial, 15 December 1924. De Meulemeester manifested a clear view of his own worth: 'It must be remembered that my reputation as a musician is unassailable, and my record as a man of duty stands equally firm.' Coogan had complained that, in contrast to Clonard, 'Every effort is made in Ardoyne to secure attractive church music and singing.'
13. Ibid., De Meulemeester to Provincial, February 1925.
14. Ibid.
15. Clonard Domestic Chronicle 1910, 1 January.
16. Ibid., 1934, 2 January.
17. Ibid., 1938, 21 September; 1942, 26 June; O'Donnell (1987), p 6. De Meulemeester's last residence was 9 Mount Charles, in St Brigid's parish.
18. Ibid., 1942, 19 July, 1 January; 1943, 1 January; Clonard Domestic Archives (C 11), Photocopy of a manuscript account of Clonard Boys' Choir (in Fr Torney's hand?), early 1947. The contemporary account is in Archives Dublin Province, miscellaneous (1939-43), 'A summary of events in Clonard for 1943,' which further remarks: 'While the death of M. de Meulemeester was an irreparable loss, still it meant that the choir in Clonard has taken a new and a decidedly better change ...'

19. Ibid., 1943, 1 August.
20. Clonard Domestic Archives (C 11); see also (CA 3). The November 1943 concert was organised by the Christian Brothers Past Pupils Union. In his memoir Fr Torney further noted: 'Present soloists are D. Burke, George ? and Gerard O'Neill. George will be soloist in a recital May 17th. Gerard O'Neill bids fair to rival his brother Jim of the American tour, while Danny Burke's lovely voice is well known and appreciated in Belfast and beyond its confines.' These notes help to date the memoir to some time before 17 May 1947. Mr Danny Burke has tried unsuccessfully to identify the surname of the soloist George.
21. Clonard Domestic Chronicle 1947, 20 December; 1957, 2 June; Clonard Domestic Archives (G 5), 'House Consultations 1916-1950,' 6 October 1948.
22. Ibid., 1968, January.
23. Ibid., 21 April.
24. Ibid., 29 August, September.
25. Ibid., September, 28 September, 20 June; O'Donnell (1987), p 20.
26. Ibid., 29 October, 25 December.
27. Ibid., 1971, 27 June; 1975, 22 December.
28. Ibid., 1979, 26 December. The sleeve was designed by Mr Andy Johnstone; the photograph was taken by Mr Paul Kavanagh.
29. Ibid., 1981, 25 December.
30. Gonzalez, J. L., CSP and the Daughters of St Paul (Compilers), *The Sixteen Documents of Vatican II, with Commentaries by the Council Fathers* (Boston, 1967), pp 50-51.
31. Clonard Domestic Chronicle 1982, 14 August; O'Donnell (1987), p 17. Mr Raymond Lennon has kindly helped with conciliar documentation.
32. Ibid., 21 November, 19 December.
33. Ibid., 1983, 18 December; 1984, Third Sunday in Advent; 1985, 15 December; 1987, 13 December.
34. Ibid., 1985, 11 September. Archives Dublin Province (C 21), 'Analysis of devotional life in Clonard,' May 1985. Clonard Domestic Chronicle 1985, 17 November, 1 December.
35. Clonard Domestic Chronicle 1986, 26 October. Raymond Lennon, having succeeded Léon Rittweger at the pro-Cathedral, went on to become Director of Sacred Music for Down and Connor (1996-2000). He helped to develop courses at Clonard for the provision of lay cantors who led the singing at novenas and confraternities. In 2001 he became a full-time pastoral worker in Clonard with responsibility for liturgy and music.
36. Ibid., 1987, 18 October, 25 January.
37. Ibid., 22 November; 1988, 5 February.
38. O'Donnell (1987), p 20.
39. Clonard Domestic Chronicle 1984, 2 July; 1985, 12-16 August; 1986, 17-27 July; 1987, 17-21 August; 1992, 12-14 June.
40. Ibid., 1986, 25 December; 1994, 3 March.
41. Ibid., 1987, 20 December; 1993, 2 June. Of Seán Stewart, the chronicler said, 'Clonard is his life.'

CHAPTER 13: CLONARD AND THE TROUBLES, 1969-1994

1. Clonard Domestic Chronicle 1969, 2 August.

2. Ibid., 14 August; Maillie, E. and McKittrick, D., *The Fight for Peace: The Inside Story of the Irish Peace Process* (London,1996; paperback edition, 1997), p 66; Coogan, T. P., *The Troubles* (Dublin, 1995), p 89. The chronicle further states, presumably quoting Fr Sullivan, that 'Many of the RUC who were brought to the hospital were Catholics.'

3. Coogan (1995), p 89.

4. Clonard Domestic Chronicle 1969, 15 August. For a clearer account of activity in and around the monastery, see the evidence of Frs Hugh McLaughlin and Paud Egan to the Scarman Tribunal: *Violence and Civil Disturbances in Northern Ireland in 1969 - Report of Tribunal of Inquiry*, Cmd. 566, HMSO, Belfast, 1972, Vol I, Chapter 25, pp 195-209.

5. Ibid., 16-21 August; 1974, 9-16 September. The chronicle notes, under the date of 19 August 1969, that thirty soldiers 'who will guard the monastery night and day' slept on the lower corridor.

6. Ibid., 19 August; 1970, June; 1972, November.

7. Coogan (1995), pp 108-9.

8. Clonard Domestic Chronicle 1970, July, August-September; Coogan (1995), p 109.

9. Ibid., 1971, 9 August.

10. Ibid., 1972, 9 March.

11. Ibid., 1978, February: the precise date is uncertain, but the review was inserted in the chronicle after 7 February.

12. Ibid., 1972, November and 29, 30, 31 December; 1973, 1 January.

13. Ibid., 1978, 25 July; 1979, 28 August. The 'vicious little war' was witnessed in Clonard Street that very day: 'About 12.30 p.m. ... a booby trap set in a lamp standard ... opposite the old people's "hostel" seriously injured a young lieu-tenant.' (28 July 1979).

14. Ibid., 1992, 13 January; extract from *Belfast Newsletter* of same date.

15. Ibid., 1976, 20, 21 November.

16. Ibid., 1977, 31 December.

17. Ibid., 1975, 14, 15, 19 August. The chronicler added: 'The people of bomb-shattered Dunlewey St. bought a wreath, had Mass said and gave a donation of over £30 for Mr Llewelyn, father of the deceased. At the Holy Family confraternity, two Masses were offered for Samuel Llewelyn and in reparation for the ungrateful murder.'

18. Ibid., 1984, 8 April.

19. Ibid., 1976, 25 December; 1977, 23 January; 1986, 6 August.

20. Ibid., 1979, 31 December.

21. Ibid., 1978, 23 January.

22. Ibid., 21 December.

23. Ibid.

24. Ibid., 1980, 16 November.

25. Ibid., and see Appendix 3 of the Domestic Chronicle.

26. Ibid., 10 December. 'In Clonard, Frs McGettrick and Keane conducted an all-night vigil for peace on the eve of the feast of the Immaculate Conception, 8 December.'
27. Ibid., 1980, 30 December.
28. Ibid., 1981, 28 January; 1983, 27 August.
29. Ibid., 1981, March, 26 May, 3 October.
30. Ibid., 1988, 7, 16, 19 March.
31. Ibid., 1975, 14 November; 1987, 11 March. The context in which the mediators worked in 1975 was: '... a fortnight's bombings and shootings in which eleven people died and more than fifty were injured.' – Chronicle 1975, 14 November.
32. Ibid., 1987, 7 April, 7 May.
33. Ibid., 1993, 23, 26, 30 October; McKittrick, D., Kelters, S., Feeney, B., and Thornton, C., *Lost Lives: The stories of the men, women and children who died as a result of the Northern Ireland troubles* (Edinburgh,1999), pp 1337, 1353.
34 Clonard Domestic Chronicle 1988, 4 December; 1992, 2 April; 1993, 7 November.
35 Ibid., 1988, 11 January; 1993, 15 December; *Lost Lives* (1999), p 1307; Maillie and McKittrick (pbk. 1997), p 109. By far the best account of the peace process, and of Fr Reid's part in it, is Maillie, E. and McKittrick, D., (1996, pbk. 1997).
36. Clonard Domestic Chronicle 1994, 31 August. 'Na Reds abú,' means, 'The Red[emptorist]s forever', an exuberant salutation.

CHAPTER 14: CHANGE, 1960S-1990S

1. Clonard Domestic Chronicle 1979, 29 November. This entry refers to new constitutions nearing completion. 'Meantime, 1969 constiutions remain in force.'
2. Ibid., 1961, 1, 5 May, 24 January; 1964, December.
3. Ibid., 1965, Lent.
4. Ibid., 1975, 3 December; 1977, 27 February; 1978, 2 December.
5. Ibid., 1979, 26 December; 1989, 8 December; 1990, 5 February. For those readers who are confused about the terminology of this sacrament, it might be helpful to refer to the *Catechism of the Catholic Church* (Veritas, Dublin, 1994). Paragraphs 1423-4 summarise the various titles of the sacrament: of conversion, of penance, of confession, of forgiveness, of reconciliation. A second reconciliation room, near St Gerard's altar, was not completed until February 1990.
6. Ibid., 1984, 16, 27, 29 January. This change had several repercussions in Clonard. The first casualty was the Saturday evening devotions which had begun in the old 'tin' church on 6 June 1897 and had continued uninterrupted since. In order to allow greater spacing of Sunday Masses, the 7.00 a.m. and 7.00 p.m. on Sunday were dropped.
7. Ibid., 1962, 11 March. The changes were 'in the main ... towards the liturgical forms of prayer'.
8. Ibid., 1965, Lent, 22-26 November; 1966, 28 November.
9. Ibid., 1966, mid-September.
10. Ibid., 1961, 12 April, 5 May; 1962, 20 July.
11. Ibid., 1958, 4 November; 1962, 12 March, 11 October.

12. Ibid., 1968, 11-14, 19-21, 22-25 November.

13. Ibid., 1971, 16 December; 1978, 1 January; 1970, 17-18 October.

14. Ibid., 1979, 4 October.

15. Report of the Committee for the Review of the Redemptorist Apostolate in the North of Ireland (1989), p 39. (Hereafter abbreviated RANI (1989) for convenience of reference.)

16. Clonard Domestic Chronicle 1974, June, 30 August.

17. RANI (1989), pp 58, 59.

18. Ibid., p. 39.

19. Archives Dublin Province (C 17), Report on Visitation of Clonard, 16-20 February 1975, signed by Frs Dekkers and d'Sousa; (C 18) 'Report for Provincial Chapter: Clonard September 1972-May 1975'.

20. Clonard Domestic Chronicle 1977, 9 December. Fr Tom McKinley was rector of Clonard from 1964-67; he had approached Dr Philbin, bishop of Down and Connor, offering pastoral visitation of either Ballymurphy or Turf Lodge – the chronicler was unsure of the district proposed. The offer was declined.

21. Clonard Domestic Archives (P), 'House Apostolate,' letters from G. Wadding to Archdeacon Montague, 24 January, 7 February and 6 March 1979, and undated report of the offer by Fr Wadding to his provincial superior. The offer was for 'areas of special need' in the parish, 'visiting houses, stirring up faith, trying to create some sense of Christian community, etc.' See also Clonard Domestic Chronicle 1987, 18 August.

22. Clonard Domestic Chronicle 1978, 17-18 October, 12 December.

23. Ibid., 1979, 18 February, 11 May; RANI (1989), p 40.

24. Clonard Domestic Chronicle 1980, 17 February. This first 'open day' was organised by Fr Michael Browne, Vocations Director. See RANI (1989), p 40.

25. RANI (1989), pp 2, 41.

26. Ibid., pp 42-3.

27. Ibid., pp 7-43, 44-53. The membership of the review committee was as follows: John O'Donnell, C.Ss.R., chairman, Peter Burns, C.Ss.R., Brendan McConvery, C.Ss.R., and Matt Salters, the noted educationalist, who, like Brendan McConvery, was born and reared within the ambit of Clonard.

28. Ibid., pp 47-53; Clonard Domestic Chronicle 1978, 12 December.

29. Clonard Domestic Chronicle 1968, 9 September, 28 November; 1970, 21 September, 18 November; 1973, 26-27 June; 1975, January; 1978, February ('A Summary ofApostolic Activities in Clonard Community, apart from the activities which are common to C.Ss.R. foundations, e.g., Church work, missions and retreats, confraternities, etc.' – hereafter 'Summary').

30. Ibid., 1978, 12 December; 1974, 29 January, 16 September; 1977, 31 December; 1976, 23 April; RANI (1989), p. 28, notes: 'For most of the time between 1975 and 1988, the Dundalk mission team have had responsibility for missions in Northern Ireland. Records for these missions are incomplete.'

31. Ibid., 1976, 17 March.

32. Ibid., 1977, 1 January; 1976, 28 September; 1977, 31 December; 1979, 18 February; 1980, 1 March; 1984, March, April, May.

33. Ibid., 1986, 23 February (Poleglass), 5 April (Hilltown), 3 May (Carnhill, Derry), November (St Anne's, Derriaghy); 1987, 30 March (Isle of Bute – Frs Enright and Turley; Poleglass – preaching of Solemn Novena), after Easter, (Derry City, Holy Rosary, Belfast, Desertmartin), 13 September (Twinbrook), 28 November (Dungannon); 1988, 29 May (Lifford, Raphoe diocese). The help of Fr Brendan Keane, C.Ss.R., in clarifying this difficult period is warmly acknowledged.

34. Ibid., 1989, 26 February (Turf Lodge, Belfast – 3 weeks); 1990, March-April (Newcastle/Bryansford – 3 weeks), December (St Michael's, Belfast – no duration given); 1991, early January (St Bernadette's, Belfast – 2 weeks), 13 April (Glengormley – 1 week); 1992, early (Holy Rosary – 10 days, St Anne's – 3 weeks, Ardoyne – 3 weeks), 2 May (Coleraine – no duration given), September (Mourne parish, Derry diocese – 3 weeks); 1993, no missions recorded; 1994, 5 February (Newry – 4 weeks), Lent (Newcastle – 3 weeks), 16 April (Bellaghy – 2 weeks), 18 September (St Oliver Plunkett's, Belfast – 4 weeks, Larne – 3 weeks), 22 October (Fintona – 1 week), 13 November (St Gerard's, Belfast – 2 weeks).

35. Ibid., 1977, December, detailed typescript inserted in chronicle; 1978, 8 February.

36. Ibid., 1990, 4 March; 1991, 17 February; Clonard Domestic Archives (P), 'House Apostolate,' folder containing brochures advertising Lenten talks from 1986 onwards. Clonard Domestic Chronicle 1992, 8 March; 1993, 28 February, 7 March; See also 1994, 13 February.

37. Ibid., 1978, 'Summary' inserted in chronicle after 8 February; Clonard Domestic Archives (P), 'House Apostolate', Youth Club (P2), Copy of Inspector's Report, November 1987.

38. Clonard Domestic Chronicle, 1978, 'Summary' inserted in chronicle after 8 February.

39. Ibid; see also 1989, 31 May, 12 September. Under the latter date, the chronicle also observes of Bro Michael: '... he was the soul of the Clonard prayer group founded by Fr C. McCarthy in 1973. Only for his interest it would likely not have survived.' See also Clonard Domestic Chronicle, 1973, 20-27 October; 1987, 20 July-7 August, for generous praise of 'dedicated helpers' like Messrs Tommy Johnston in the 1970s and Crawford Fitzsimon in the 1980s and 90s.

40. Ibid., 1990, 7 June.

41. Ibid., 1984, October; 1990, November.

42. Clonard Domestic Archives, House Apostolate (P), Miscellaneous items. This initiative was named for the birthplace of the Redemptorist congregation in the Kingdom of Naples.

43. Clonard Domestic Chronicle 1983, 16 September, 2 November; 1979, 13 March.

44. Ibid., 1983, 16 September; 1989, 21-22 October.

45. Ibid., 1985, 11-13 February; 1991, 18-22 March; 1994, 24 October; see *Lost Lives* (1999), p 1352.

46. Ibid., 1994, 24 October.

47. Ibid., 1989, 23 February; 1990, 22-29 August; 1992, January (where a substantial typescript is inserted in the chronicle, giving information on the Redemptorist Youth Movement), 9 May, insert at 11 June.

48. Ibid., 1992, 28 November; see also 1993, 2-4 January, 4 December.

49. Down and Connor Diocesan newspaper, *Herald*, November 1995. (Article by Jim Gargan, CSsR.) Copy in Clonard Domestic Archives (P), 'House Apostolate.'

50. Clonard Domestic Archives, 'House Apostolate' (P), Miscellaneous Papers; Clonard Domestic Chronicle 1987, 12 April: see also 1987, 27 June; 1988, 24 March.

51. Clonard Domestic Chronicle 1979, 4 October.

EPILOGUE

1. Clonard Domestic Chronicle 1979, 31 December; 1983, July-August; 1984, 18 December.

2. Ibid., 1994, August. The rapid reconstruction of the houses in Bombay Sreet had been undertaken by the Bombay Street Housing Association of which the most active members were Rita Canavan, Séan Mackle, Séan and Séamus MacSéain, Agnes McPeake, Séamus Napier and Ciaran O'Kane. Financial adviser to the Association was Harry Connolly of the Society of St Vincent de Paul. The first person to resume residence – in a new house – was Mrs Dinnen, in June 1970.

3. Ibid., 1989, 10 March, Easter, 30 April.

4. Ibid., 1990, June. This chronicle entry also contains material of a later date.

5. *Clonard Monastery 1896-1996: 100 Years of Service* (1996), p 2. Bishop Walsh's congratulatory letter is dated 28 February 1996.

6. See Clonard Domestic Chronicle 1980, 10 December.

APPENDICES

1. Chronicle of the Holy Family Confraternity 1926, 1 April.

2. Ibid., 1929, 28 March; 1931, 18 January, Holy Thursday Night; 1932, Holy Thursday Night; 1940, Holy Thursday Night.

3. Ibid., 1941, 10 April; 1944, Holy Thursday Night; 1946, 18 April.

4. Ibid., 1949, 14 April; 1947, 3 April; 1953, Holy Thursday Night.

5. Ibid., 1949, 14 April; 1951, Holy Thursday Night; 1952, 10 April.

6. Ibid., 1956, 19-21 March.

7. The account given by Fr Mangan is to be found in the Chronicle of the Holy Family Confraternity 1931, 16, 22 June; 1932, January, February, June. See also Clonard Domestic Chronicle 1932, 26 June.

8. This account of the Loire Mosaics is adapted from O'Donnell, Patrick, C.Ss.R., *Clonard Church and Monastery* (n.d., but probably mid 1980s). Fr O'Donnell has translated the artist's notes from the French.

9. O'Donnell (1996), pp 28-29.

10. Archives Dublin Province (C3), 'Foundation ...' (1922), p 15; O'Donnell (1996), pp 28-29.

11. Ibid., Folder entitled, 'Clonard Church, 1909-10'.

12. Clonard Domestic Chronicle 1909, 19 July. The visitors were Frs Schmerz and Peeters and Bro Maximilian Schmalzl.

13. Ibid., 1912, 4 February.

14. O'Donnell (1996), p 31; Clonard Domestic Chronicle 1936, 29 October, 25

November, 22 December. There was one tender from the local firm of Purdy and Millard at £6,676. Ibid., 1937, 17 March, 25 June, 16, 19 August.

15. Clonard Domestic Chronicle 1956, 29 July; 1959, 3 December.

16. Archives Dublin Province (W3), 'Provincial consultations, 1953-64', February 1961; Clonard Domestic Chronicle 1961, 3 February, 4, 11 November, 5, 7 December; 1962, 10 March; O'Donnell (1996), p 28.

17. Clonard Domestic Chronicle 1961, 24 November; 1962, 14 February, 8 April.

18. Archives Dublin Province (W3), 'Provincial consultations, 1953-64', 1957, 7 December; 1958, 24 January, 25 March.

19. Clonard Domestic Chronicle 1933, 15, 16 February, 3 April; 1962, 26 November; 1963, 11 March; 1964, January; 1966, July.

20. Ibid., 1982, March, 29 March.

21. Ibid., 1985, August; 1986, 26 January, 22 September. The listing was dated 8 September 1986.

22. Ibid., 1989, 26 March, 8, 14-22 June.

23. Ibid., 1973, March; 1985, 11-19 February, 26 March; 1988, 9 June.

24. Ibid., 1965, Lent; O'Donnell (1996), p 28.

25. Archives Dublin Province (C21), 'Analysis of devotional life in Clonard church, 1985.'

26. Clonard Domestic Chronicle 1986, 1-3 September.

27. Ibid., 1990, 5 October; 1992, January.

28. Ibid., 1992, 27, 29 January and various dates until the end of April.

29. Ibid., 1992, 23 May, June.

30. Ibid., 1992, January.

31. *Clonard Monastery 1896-1996: 100 Years of Service* (1996), p 1.(Introduction to the official Centenary booklet.)